Contracting Human Rights

ELGAR STUDIES IN HUMAN RIGHTS

Discourse on human rights has grown ever more visible and essential, with human rights principles being discussed and scrutinized on both the international and national stage. This series brings together high-quality works of scholarship in the field of human rights, primarily in law, but particularly those with a critical or analytical edge, or those taking innovative and interdisciplinary approaches. Books in the series also address concerns at the intersection of human rights and other fields such as trade, the environment, international investment and religion, thus contributing to the depth and breadth of scholarship so vital to understanding the complicated matters at stake.

Titles in the series include:

Refugees, Regionalism and Responsibility
Penelope Mathew and Tristan Harley

Expanding Human Rights
21st Century Norms and Governance
Edited by Alison Brysk and Michael Stohl

The Legal Protection of Refugees with Disabilities
Forgotten and Invisible?
Mary Crock, Laura Smith-Khan, Ron McCallum and Ben Saul

Contracting Human Rights
Crisis, Accountability, and Opportunity
Edited by Alison Brysk and Michael Stohl

Contracting Human Rights

Crisis, Accountability, and Opportunity

Edited by

Alison Brysk

Chair, Global Studies Department, Mellichamp Chair of Global Governance, University of California, Santa Barbara, USA

Michael Stohl

Director, Orfalea Center for Global and International Studies, Professor of Communication, Political Science and Global Studies, University of California, Santa Barbara, USA

ELGAR STUDIES IN HUMAN RIGHTS

Edward Elgar PUBLISHING

Cheltenham, UK • Northampton, MA, USA

Published by
Edward Elgar Publishing Limited
The Lypiatts
15 Lansdown Road
Cheltenham
Glos GL50 2JA
UK

Edward Elgar Publishing, Inc.
William Pratt House
9 Dewey Court
Northampton
Massachusetts 01060
USA

A catalogue record for this book
is available from the British Library

Library of Congress Control Number: 2017950482

This book is available electronically in the **Elgar**online
Social and Political Science subject collection
DOI 10.4337/9781788112338

MIX
Paper from responsible sources
FSC® C013056
FSC www.fsc.org

ISBN 978 1 78811 232 1 (cased)
ISBN 978 1 78811 233 8 (eBook)

Typeset by Servis Filmsetting Ltd, Stockport, Cheshire
Printed and bound in Great Britain by TJ International Ltd, Padstow

Contents

Figures

Tables

Contributors

Kirsten Ainley is Assistant Professor in the Department of International Relations and Director of the Centre for International Studies at the London School of Economics.

George Andreopoulos is Professor of Political Science and Criminal Justice at the City University of New York (CUNY) and Founding Director of the Center for International Human Rights at John Jay College of Criminal Justice, CUNY.

Clair Apodaca is an Associate Professor in the Department of Political Science at Virginia Tech.

Phillip M. Ayoub is Assistant Professor of Politics at Drexel University.

Yining Bei is a BA student in the School of International Relations at the University of Southern California.

Natasha Bennett is a PhD candidate in political science, with a focus on human rights and an interdisciplinary emphasis in global studies at the University of California, Santa Barbara.

Alison Brysk is the Mellichamp Professor of Global Governance and Department Chair in the Global Studies Department at the University of California, Santa Barbara.

Kayla Caldwell is a recent graduate of the School of International Relations at the University of Southern California.

Feryal M. Cherif is Associate Professor of Political Science at Loyola Marymount University.

Michael Etter is Marie Curie Research Fellow at the ETHOS Centre for Responsible Enterprise at City, University of London, United Kingdom.

Jesilyn Faust is a second year PhD student in the Department of Global Studies at the University of California, Santa Barbara.

Shiv Ganesh is Professor in Communication, School of Communication, Journalism and Marketing at Massey University, New Zealand.

Felipe Gómez Isa is Professor of Public International Law and researcher at the Pedro Arrupe Institute of Human Rights of the University of Deusto, in Bilbao, Spain.

Arturo Jimenez-Bacardi is Assistant Professor of International Relations in the History and Politics Department at the University of South Florida, St. Petersburg.

Nora Katona is Legal Researcher at the Ludwig Boltzmann Institute of Human Rights in Vienna.

Barbara Linder is Senior Researcher at the Ludwig Boltzmann Institute of Human Rights in Vienna, with a research focus on corporate responsibility.

Karin Lukas is head of the team 'Social Justice' at the Ludwig Boltzmann Institute of Human Rights in Vienna and Vice-President of the European Committee of Social Rights (Council of Europe).

Julia Planitzer is Senior Researcher at the Ludwig Boltzmann Institute of Human Rights in Vienna, with a research focus on trafficking in human beings and business and human rights.

Wayne Sandholtz is the John A. McCone Professor of International Relations at the University of Southern California.

Gershon Shafir is Professor in the Department of Sociology at the University of California, San Diego.

Cynthia Stohl is Distinguished Professor of Communication and Director of the Center for Information Technology and Society at the University of California, Santa Barbara.

Michael Stohl is Professor of Communication and Director of the Orfalea Center for Global and International Studies at the University of California, Santa Barbara.

Anne Vestergaard is Associate Professor of CSR and Organizational Communication at the Center for Corporate Social Responsibility, Copenhagen Business School, Denmark.

Claire Wright is Lecturer in Social Sciences at the Universidad de Monterrey, Mexico.

Acknowledgements

We would like to thank all of the participants for their contributions to the discussion that shaped our thinking, including the contributors to this volume as well as Anthony Chase-Tirado, Kirk Boyd, Keith Watenpaugh and the Orfalea Center for Global and International Studies at the University of California Santa Barbara. We also extend our appreciation to our careful and insightful peer reviewers: Claire Apodaca, Philip Ayoub, Raymond Clemencon, and Wayne Sandholtz. We are grateful for the research assistance of Mellichamp Graduate Fellows Natasha Bennett and Yunuen Gomez Ocampo and the logistical support of Orfalea Center graduate assistant Melissa Bator. Thanks to the Edward Elgar Studies in Human Rights Series for hosting this continuing conversation on the fate of human rights in the 21st century, beginning with our previous volume *Expanding Human Rights* (2017). We are grateful for the opportunity to contribute our collective deliberation to the public sphere in these critical times, and dedicate this volume to preserving the power of voice and academic freedom for our colleagues worldwide.

1. Introduction: contracting human rights

Alison Brysk

Human rights at 70 is both expanding and contracting. On the one hand, the human rights regime is expanding through introducing new actors, claims, mechanisms, and proposed responsibilities (Brysk and Stohl 2017). These expansions may contest dehumanization, introduce new frames, foster rights interdependence, build new transnational networks and processes, construct global governance beyond law and state-based institutions, and transform practice through disseminating new norms, models, and benchmarks. Yet our survey of that expansion concluded that responsibilities to protect remain tragically inadequate to current conditions, new problems continue to arise that transcend the current system, new actors seeking to transform the system may instead be suppressed, and promising new human rights claims too often encounter resistance and counter-mobilization.

In this volume, we assess the historic status of these contractions, in the global context of worldwide increases in economic inequality and security threats that have added new costs to chronic gaps that affect the legitimacy and leverage of the international human rights regime. Are contemporary shortfalls in the rights regime the reflection of continuities or a reemergence of long-standing trends? Or do they represent a regression from the hard-won gains of generations of global governance, in response to fundamental shifts in underlying conditions or understandings?

We find that the current contraction of human rights reflects a reconfiguration of global governance in a post-cosmopolitan era, marked by a simultaneous resilience of sovereignty in some domains contrasting with a relocation of authority above and below the state in other areas. Just as international relations theorist Susan Strange concluded at the dawn of the era of globalization that the state is at the same time "widening, wavering, and withering," a generation later states and publics meet the expanding demands of the human rights regime with an uneasy blend of compliance, resistance, evasion, and undermining. We know from a generation of human rights research that the general drivers of rights reform include norm change, social mobilization, institutionalization, state capacity, coalition-building and shifting interests of authorities (Risse et al. 2013). Our task will be to map some of the determinants and parameters of rights regression: from citizenship gaps to declining state capacity, legal zones of permanent exception, disempowerment of challengers, and contradictions between national and global citizenship.

MAPPING CONTRACTIONS

Human rights are contracting in the sense of growing smaller, but also in the sense of becoming more contractual. Rights are often impeded by various shortfalls in the social contract at all levels: citizenship gaps that block the standing of new actors, accountability gaps that undermine the potential of new mechanisms, and increasingly legalized backlash by sovereign states who thrive on the breakdown of solidarity. Increasingly, it appears that the key variable in the gap between commitment and compliance is an emerging contraction of accountability for some domains of authority, alongside the long-standing dilemmas of contracting accountability for the full range of national, international, and transnational actors. At the same time, we propose that the most innovative and helpful strategies for human rights promotion and expansion will be precisely those that address these contractions.

We will focus on these global and local challenges to human rights in the areas of gaps, backlash, accountability—and new opportunities that point the way forward. We examine these problems in a global perspective, including rights problems in Europe, the Middle East, Latin America, and the U.S. We will analyze trends across multiple issue-areas of international institutions, development struggles, humanitarian action, censorship and communications, discrimination, democracy promotion, human trafficking, counter-terrorism, corporate social responsibility, and civil society and social movements. Our contributors represent a wide range of international scholarship from the U.S., Mexico, Spain, Austria, the UK, and Denmark, with backgrounds in law, political science, sociology, history, and communications.

First, we review the widening citizenship gaps in human rights coverage for refugees, socioeconomic rights, women's rights in patriarchal societies, and civil liberties in chronic conflict, first outlined in Brysk and Shafir (2004). These are cases where the rights regime is incomplete or permits unsustainable exception, and current security and development crises are intensifying these contradictions. For several of these issues—refugees, Latin American states of emergency, and Israeli occupation—there is a systematic contradiction between popular democracy and international rights norms.

Alison Brysk begins with the long-standing gap between universal rights and sovereign citizenship enforcement noted by Hannah Arendt, tragically illustrated generations later by the 21st century refugee crisis (Arendt 1958). In a different register, Gershon Shafir documents how Israel's securitization of citizenship inspired by the occupation's unsustainable exceptionalism to international law blows back to undermine civil liberties even of the dominant population. For Claire Wright, the gaps built into the international regime are exceptionalist legacies of states of emergency in Latin America, now abused by democratic governments to subvert popular participation in decision-making over natural resource extraction. In another illustration of how unequal development undermines rights in developing democracies, Natasha Bennett shows how lack of state capacity and political will leaves slum areas ungoverned and states unaccountable for contracting social and economic rights such as housing.

Then, we move to consider a new layer of unexpected problems for rights promotion following a generation of expansion: backlash. In these cases, the successful development of new rights norms and policies triggers counter-mobilization and state suppression. States may ban, attack, or condition international and local human rights monitors and defenders and the international regime offers little recourse against violence, censorship, harassment, or defunding. Beyond behavioral non-compliance, both states and local civil societies may regress and reject hard-won international norms even on first-generation war crimes and anti-discrimination, especially in areas of high perceived threat, such as national insecurity and struggles over sexuality and gender identity.

Clair Apodaca shows how well-intentioned universalist campaigns by NGOs may founder on state retribution against local partners, while Philip M. Ayoub depicts a parallel state manipulation of nationalist and religious counter-norms to discredit transnational campaigns for LGBT rights in the new Europe. At the interstate level, Felipe Gómez Isa analyzes Egypt's resistance to EU democracy and human rights initiatives, as a dependent authoritarian state that still has the power to evade leverage by one of the strongest regional promotion regimes. Finally, deep in the heart of the state, Arturo Jimenez-Bacardi documents the rise and fall of legalized bureaucratic politics as a mechanism for human rights accountability in U.S. foreign policy on torture and targeted assassination.

We go on to examine how, in the face of these continuing and emerging challenges, the international regime's legal mechanisms of accountability often struggle for traction (Brysk 2013). In the second and third generation of legalization, George Andreopoulos and Wayne Sandholtz et al. show

how global governance institutions like the UN Security Council and regional courts often still fail to overcome the constraints of state sovereignty to uphold rights. As Kirsten Ainley discusses, resistant states may even come to contest the foundations of universalism, as in withdrawal from the International Criminal Court. Meanwhile, accountability for non-state perpetrators of labor abuse expand in theory but contract in practice in the absence of compulsory enforcement, as seen in the chapter by Julia Planitzer et al. Even as regional regimes and civil litigation advance potential mechanisms of accountability for "private wrongs" (Brysk 2005), the private sector actors at the table or in the courtroom are less relevant for the harms of trafficking and exploitation than lower-level perpetrators in weakly governed zones.

However, despite these growing gaps, the globalization of human rights continues to present new opportunities as well as challenges (Brysk 2002). Our analysis suggests increased attention to expanding mobilizations, norms, and mechanisms that address the patterns identified above. Thus, we consider new grassroots mechanisms to address the accountability gap in corporate social responsibility (Vestergaard and Etter), new uses of communication to deepen citizen participation and inclusion for recognition of sexual minorities (Stohl et al.), and new movements and transnational coalitions that bridge rival norms and identities of feminism and Islam (Faust). Moreover, Feryal M. Cherif demonstrates the forward linkages and positive interdependence of promotion of women's social and economic rights to increase women's legal rights, ameliorating one of the most widespread and chronic global inequities.

CONCLUSION

Taken together, these chapters suggest we may need to rethink some of the assumptions of a generation of human rights scholarship concerning the evolution of norms, the nature of law, and the relationship between the national and global order. Why do new rights norms and claims inspire backlash despite diffusion of rights talk and changes in world culture? When does legalization unwittingly undermine rights or permit evasion rather than compliance? As we move from the state as target of protest to intermittent enforcer of rights, how can we cope with contradictions between the state's multiple interests in maximizing its own authority, supporting world order, and reflecting citizen preferences—which in each case may be liberal or nationalist?

Beyond academic analysis to policy and practice, *Contracting Human Rights* aims to contribute to building understanding of the 21st century maturation of human rights, from a dissident doctrine to a dynamic parameter of global governance and civil society. We chronicle the continuing contest over the reach, range, and regime of rights in order to analyze the way forward, in an era of great challenge. In that process, we will see that even though some dimensions of rights are now unexpectedly contracting, the contract for the next generation of rights is still being written—and that we are all potential participants in rewriting rights with the knowledge we gain.

REFERENCES

Arendt, Hannah. *The Human Condition*. University of Chicago Press, 1958.

Brysk, Alison (ed.). *Globalization and Human Rights*. Berkeley, CA: University of California Press, 2002.

Brysk, Alison. *Human Rights and Private Wrongs*. Routledge Press, 2005.

Brysk, Alison (ed.). *The Politics of the Globalization of Law*. Routledge Press, 2013.

Brysk, Alison and Gershon Shafir (eds). *People Out of Place: Globalization and the Citizenship Gap*. Routledge Press, 2004.

Brysk, Alison and Michael Stohl (eds). *Expanding Rights: 21st Century Norms and Governance*. Edward Elgar, 2017.

Risse, Thomas, Stephen Ropp, and Kathryn Sikkink (eds). *The Persistent Power of Human Rights*. Cambridge University Press, 2013.

PART I

Gaps

2. Contracting the refugee regime: the global citizenship gap

Alison Brysk

The refugee regime represents an extension of one of the first global social contracts into the post-war human rights regime: the right to asylum. But from the beginnings of the rights regime, refugee scholar Hannah Arendt, herself a former refugee, worried that universal rights could never meet the needs of people displaced from citizenship (Arendt 1958). With the highest number of refugees in world history, despite decades of the development of global governance, the fate of persons forcibly displaced *across* states remains the vast unfinished business of the human rights regime.

All rights regimes may face a citizenship gap of inclusion of rights-bearing subjects (Brysk and Shafir 2004), an enforcement gap to gain compliance from sovereign states, or a governance gap in which global institutions lack leverage over non-state perpetrators. The refugee regime faces all three problems, layering new dimensions on chronic deficits: asylum-seekers are non-citizens, seeking protection from states that may be unable or unwilling to comply with their obligations, and the interstate regime increasingly lacks leverage. The current refugee crisis represents more than a gap in institutions or statelessness—it is a multi-level collapse of citizenship contracts in a human condition of widespread mobility across multiple governance environments; a veritable run on the bank of authority and accountability. The problem is not just refugee rights, as William Maley concludes: "Refugees are symptoms of a system of states that has failed to live up to its responsibilities" (Maley 2016).

In the 21st century, citizenship is not an absolute condition that is the opposite of statelessness, but a spectrum of social contracts that confer different levels of ability to claim rights in different environments: states of origin, host states, globally-governed spaces such as refugee camps, and ungoverned zones like borderlands and lawless enclaves. The global citizenship contract of asylum is meant to serve as a safety net for forced migrants to reclaim rights and reconstruct membership in a responsible political community. The security and freedom of refugees depends on the quality of the citizenship they carry and the drawing rights of that citizenship contract as they move through distinct governance environments. Even weak citizens stripped of state membership may become secure in strong states with universal citizenship regimes, while even strong citizens who are internally displaced without losing state status, ineligible for asylum, or trapped in collapsing ungoverned zones may suffer catastrophic rights deflation. In conflict conditions, those civilians with documents, resources, and networks are more likely to become rights-claiming asylum seekers in a developed country or to qualify as United Nations High Commission on Refugees (UNHC) mandate refugees in a camp than ambiguous internally displaced persons (IDPs). Now we have added a global citizenship gap in which liberal regime-maker host states evade and undermine the global social contract of asylum.

Contemporary refugees are the bearers of deflated, dysfunctional, or inconvertible rights claims that call into question the structure of global responsibility. Refugees face three kinds of rights problems, which we can describe as originating oppression, transitional statelessness, and asylum access. Vulnerability to these genres of violation typically corresponds to displacement in the sending state; statelessness in camps, borderlands, and transit zones; and access to justice in the receiving state. But one of the unforeseen gaps in the refugee regime is the instability of these zones and dislocation of conditions. Sovereignty may contract in a sending country through state failure or secession; receiving states may extend or withdraw authority from transit zones and borderlands; camps may be administered by international, receiving state, or private authority; and host nations may displace asylum determination beyond their borders. These governance gaps interact with the quality of citizenship. The withdrawal of historic host states from accepting a significant proportion of refugees, funding caretaking and resettlement programs, and fostering rights standards in front-line and first-refuge states is the final blow to the global social contract.

REFUGEES: BEYOND BORDERS, BEYOND RIGHTS?

Refugees are defined by the United Nations Refugee Convention as persons who have fled and cannot return to their country of origin due to a "well-founded fear of persecution" on the basis of race, religion, nationality, political opinion, or "membership in a particular social group" (sometimes interpreted to include gender roles). A 1969 Organization of African Unity Convention further broadens the definition of a refugee from individual persecution to displacement driven by generalized insecurity due to war, civil conflict, breakdown of public order, or "massive violations of human rights"—a standard echoed in Latin America's regional 1984

Cartagena Declaration. While refugees petition for admission to a new state from outside its borders via global institutions, asylum-seekers arrive in the new state and seek admission directly through the national process of the host state (theoretically governed by the same global standards).

The refugee regime has contracted as its governing assumptions have been overcome by (1) spillovers of the drivers and locations of forced migration to wider areas, (2) an unforeseen surge in refugee numbers and scale, (3) securitization of migration flows by most states, and (4) the construction of threat perception by nationalist political entrepreneurs. The 20th-century system assumes that most qualified refugees will be received in capable, democratic states overseas, whereas currently about two-thirds of forced migration is internal within troubled nations that are weakened by war or crisis. Most of the remainder seek refuge in neighboring states that are generally poorer, less democratic, and less stable than the Northern pillars of global governance. The increasing phenomenon of serial displacement also blurs the assessment of the numbers and status of refugees. Often the same person who originally migrates for forced or voluntary labor, within or beyond borders, is subsequently vulnerable to forcible displacement by political persecution or conflict—especially if they belong to an ethnic or religious minority. Another driver of serial displacement has been waves of conflict, post-conflict ethnic purges, or the interaction of natural disaster with civil war—all prominent patterns in Central Africa and South Asia.

Currently, an estimated 65 million people are forcibly displaced worldwide, the highest level ever recorded (UN News Centre, "Unprecedented 65 million", 2016). This includes over 20 million cross-border refugees. About 10 million are stateless, around half are under 18 years of age, and a significant proportion are women (UNHCR, "Figures at a Glance" 2016). Over 5 million are Palestinians—who are the longest-standing refugee population, and the subjects of an exceptional global institution separate from the main refugee regime: the United Nations Relief Works Agency for Palestine Refugees in the Near East (UNRWA). Over half of refugees come from the three source states of Syria (almost 5 million), Afghanistan, and Somalia—and around two-thirds of each of these major flows are hosted in neighboring countries such as Turkey, Jordan, Lebanon, Pakistan, and Ethiopia (UNHCR, "Figures at a Glance", 2016). It is also important to recognize slightly less massive but quite significant, long-standing and extremely abusive displacements in central and southern Africa following the wars in Congo, Sudan, and Rwanda. As one marker of the gap between supply and demand for asylum and resettlement, in 2015 the UNHCR recorded 1.15 million refugees in need of resettlement but only 73,331 departures (Maley 2016: 96).

The Syrian war and aftermath of neighboring conflicts in Iraq has played a leading role in the current crisis. There are at least 4 million Syrian refugees in the neighboring countries of Turkey, Jordan, Lebanon, and Iraq—over two million in Turkey alone—and around half a million Iraqis had sought refuge in Syria, with most of this group now doubly displaced to surrounding states such as Lebanon. On top of this, Jordan's long-standing population of Palestinian refugees now numbers around 2 million and Lebanon hosts almost half a million Palestinians, putting additional pressures on humanitarian protection, labor markets, law enforcement, and community resettlement in those countries for the newly arriving Syrian refugees (ICMPD 2015). According to European Union (EU) and UNHCR figures, almost one million migrants arrived in Europe in 2015, about half fleeing the Syrian civil war via Turkey, with most arriving in Greece. That year the UN estimated that 40 percent were women and children, but by late 2015 the proportion of single women (including war widows), unaccompanied minors, and pregnant women seemed to be increasing. More than 55 percent of those traveling in 2016 were women and children (UNHCR, "Refugees/ Migrants Response" n.d.).

Displaced persons experience extreme levels of war crimes and rights abuses, including assassination, torture, discrimination and ethnic persecution, physical and sexual abuse by armed actors, state authorities, and smugglers, lack of food, health care, housing, and education—and of course, abuses and casualties of flight. At least 5,000 refugees died in transit to Europe crossing the Mediterranean in 2015, and almost an equal number are reported to have perished in 2016 (Townsend and McVeigh 2016). Police in transit countries of Hungary and Greece have assaulted and imprisoned refugees. On another continent, tens of thousands of Central Americans fleeing epidemic levels of gang violence and state terror to Mexico and the U.S. form another significant vector of refugees' rights abuse. It is estimated that over 2,000 migrants have died in the deserts of U.S. border areas since 2001—typically several hundred perish each year (Smith-Spark 2014). Mexican police have also been linked to assaults and even killing of Central American migrants (Suarez Enriquez et al. 2016). As the U.S. pressed Mexico to outsource migration enforcement, by March 2016, Human Rights Watch reported there were at least 35,000 asylum-seeking children detained in Mexico vulnerable to abuse (Human Rights Watch, 2016).

The current wave of migration worldwide presents marked levels of gender violence, from front-line refugee camps plagued by sexual assault and peacekeeper exploitation in Africa to violations in transit during the Mediterranean and American migrations. A joint UN study documents multiple and linked vulnerabilities to gender-based violence for the Syrian refugees, that includes wartime sexual violence in Syria; assaults, forced marriage, and trafficking in refugee camps in neighboring countries such as Turkey and Lebanon; exploitation by smugglers en route; and attacks on women in detention centers and open-air encampments in European host countries (UN Refugee Agency et al. "Initial Assessment" 2016). In the Americas, trafficking and femicide are rampant at the U.S.-Mexico border. While a 2010 Amnesty International report had previously estimated that 60 percent of migrant women were raped by smugglers and officials en route to the U.S., a new journalistic investigation based on interviews with migrant shelters suggests that as many as 80 percent of women now suffer sexual assault in transit (McIntyre and Bonello 2014).

RIGHTS, RESPONSIBILITIES AND RESOURCES

Have refugees actually lost "the right to have rights" as non-citizens? Or are asylum-seekers' rights in theory denied, deflated, or diverted in practice? And does this make a difference? If there is theoretical accountability for refugees' rights that is simply unenforced, what is the barrier to fulfillment? Are the contractions in the rights of displaced persons rooted in the generic limits of the human rights regime, specific features of displacement, statelessness, the nature or quality of citizenship, or some combination?

The Universal Declaration of Human Rights that lays the foundation for the global regime states that "Everyone has the right to seek and to enjoy in other countries asylum from persecution" (Universal Declaration of Human Rights, Article 14(1)). The 1951 UN Convention on the Status of Refugees is the standard-setting document, but it is also important to note that all of the other key widely subscribed human rights and war crimes conventions with binding status in international law also apply—regardless of residency or citizenship status. The 1951 Refugee Convention is a binding document in international law, ratified by 147 countries including almost all host nations. This treaty defines refugees' human rights, including life, physical integrity, fundamental freedoms, the right to work, the right to freedom of movement, the right to housing, education, justice, and more. This standard was followed by an even more broadly subscribed but less binding 1967 UN General Assembly Declaration on Asylum and follow-up 1967 Protocol to the Refugee Convention, and paralleled by 1954 and 1961 Conventions on Statelessness. States adhering to these treaties are obliged to cooperate with the UN High Commission on Refugees, and to grant protection and status to refugees independent of their status in their home state (Jastram and Achiron 2011). In addition, a growing corpus of parallel norms addresses internal displacement.

One of the most important features of the Refugee Convention is the principle of non-refoulement, meaning no return to danger, which states: "No Contracting State shall expel or return ('refouler') a refugee in any manner whatsoever to the frontiers of territories where his life or freedom would be threatened on account of his race, religion, nationality, membership of a particular social group or political opinion" (Article 33(1)). The key right to protection against forcible return to danger is also guaranteed in even stronger terms by:

- the Convention against Torture and other Cruel, Inhuman or Degrading Treatment or Punishment (Article 3);
- the Fourth Geneva Convention of 1949 (Article 45, para. 4);
- the International Covenant on Civil and Political Rights (Article 7);
- the Declaration on the Protection of All Persons from Enforced Disappearance (Article 8);
- the Principles on the Effective Prevention and Investigation of Extra-Legal, Arbitrary and Summary Executions (Principle 5);
- the European Convention for the Protection of Human Rights and Fundamental Freedoms (Article 3);
- the American Convention on Human Rights (Article 22), the OAU Refugee Convention (Article II);
- the Cairo Declaration on the Protection of Refugees and Displaced Persons in the Arab World (Article 2).

It is thus one of the best delineated norms in international human rights law.

Beyond these specified protections linked to the vulnerable condition of displacement, all residents of all territories retain their universal human rights and "complementary protection" under human rights and international humanitarian law during conflict. Displaced persons possess universal rights to life, liberty, physical integrity, food, health, and housing regardless of citizenship, statelessness, or venue under the ICCPR, ICECSR, Convention Against Torture, CEDAW, Convention on the Elimination of Racial Discrimination, and Convention on the Rights of the Child. If they are displaced within their countries, their home government is theoretically responsible, and even cross-border refugees who circulate within a region are covered by the additional regional standards of the European Convention and Inter-American Conventions on Human Rights. Noncombatants displaced by war are protected by the 1949 Geneva Convention.

The ensemble of institutions that comprise the international refugee regime includes the global institutions already discussed—UNHCR, UNRWA, the UN High Commissioner for Human Rights (UNOHCHR), the UN Office for the Coordination of Humanitarian Affairs (OCHA), as well as regional bodies such as the EU, African Union, and OAS. The International Organization for Migration that bridges 162 states and NGOs facilitates repatriation and resettlement. Service provider NGOs like the International Committee of the Red Cross, the International Rescue Committee, Caritas, and Oxfam, and a vast array of local NGOs serve quasi-governmental functions running refugee camps, resettlement programs, and providing basic services in ungoverned or contested areas (one report on internal displacement lists 500) (UNHCR, "Handbook for the Protection of Internally Displaced Persons" n.d.).

In theory, the only critical constraining role of states for refugee rights that differentiates them from any other kind of rights claim is the state's exclusive power to determine asylum—although this is a hugely important filter. The "UNHCR estimates that, over the past decade, 1.1 million refugees around the world became citizens in their country of asylum" [out of approximately 20 million recognized refugees]. Many states do navigate between the non-refoulement obligation and reluctance to grant asylum in the absence of demonstrable individual persecution by offering a variety of "temporary" protected humanitarian status which are often multi-year and renewable, including both chronic conflicts and natural disasters (UNHCR, "Local Integration"), which may be accessible to some resettled but unrecognized asylum-seekers. But a substantial number of refugees are neither repatriated nor resettled; they are warehoused for indefinite periods in refugee camps, detention centers, and informal settlements in neighboring countries.

RESPONSES TO REFUGEES: THE GOVERNANCE GAP

The first problem refugees face in fulfilling their rights is the generic human rights problem of sovereign monopoly of authority and force by both sending and host states. Both originating and receiving states can block refugees' freedom of movement, deny them legal status or recognition, detain them, and prevent their access to essential supplies and services. In this sense, refugees possess rights they cannot enjoy simply because might trumps right, regardless of their citizenship status. On the sending side, by definition, states generating refugee flows are usually either human rights pariahs or failing states that do not meet their obligations to any of their citizens and are not accountable to global governance. On the receiving side, front-line, transit, and resettlement host states are usually subscribers to the international regime, but increasingly resist, ignore, or undermine it.

Within the sovereign right to determine asylum, even willing states use discriminatory and inconsistent standards. From the Central American wars of the 1980's onwards, the U.S. infamously privileged similarly situated refugees from enemy socialist dictatorships in Nicaragua and Cuba over equally threatened migrants from allied dictatorships in El Salvador and Guatemala. Currently, many European states grant nearly automatic status to fleeing Syrians and variable protection to equally conflict-affected Afghans. In 2016, the EU reached an agreement to return tens of thousands to Afghanistan, despite various European governments declaring Afghanistan unsafe in other venues such as human rights institutions. Almost all developed countries grant fewer asylum petitions for individual dissidents from semi-democratic states than pariah dictatorships, even when the individual can document political imprisonment, torture, or ethnic persecution by an elected government. As a journalist observing asylum hearings in Italy concludes, "For the moment, a hierarchy of misery prevails: People fleeing well-defined conflicts, like the civil war in Syria, or oppressive states, like Eritrea, have a far higher chance of success, while the fate of many others can hinge on their individual stories" (Yardley 2016).

Apart from the question of asylum, receiving and transit states abuse their sovereign authority as they police borders or detain asylum seekers. Even internationally recognized Syrian war refugees transiting Europe have been beaten, detained, and denied basic services in Hungary and Greece. Migrants to the U.S. including asylum-seekers have been shot at the border, summarily deported without due process, physically abused in transit, and detained in private prisons that violate international standards (Morrison 2015).

Finally, and perhaps most significantly in the current crisis, refugee rights are contracting because democratic host states have developed systematic strategies to evade the regime they helped to construct. It is an ironic testimony to the status of refugee norms as a global social contract, and a correction to the human rights fulfillment literature, that capable democratic states committed to international law now regularly seek extra-legal and extraterritorial means to deflate the currency of refugees' rights claims—precisely because they are democratic, and their own citizens demand a withdrawal of the rights of strangers. The refugee regime was designed as a rights-based exception to the rule of sovereign determination of migration that complements and reinforces democracy at home, but in this regard, it appears that national and global citizenship are in tension.

Even in the most rights-respecting democracies, citizen solidarity stops at the water's edge. Limiting or refusing admission to refugees has been a successful election strategy in the United States, UK, Hungary, France,

Greece, and Australia, among others—and on this issue, political parties are faithfully reflecting popular views. An MP from democratic Denmark's second-largest party suggested that EU-bound migrants should be fired upon when they entered territorial waters (Associated Press 2016). Solid majorities of public opinion in Poland, Hungary, Greece, Italy, and the UK see refugees from Syria and Iraq as a threat (Poushter 2016). Americans have shifted from receptiveness to opposition to refugees (McElevin 2016).

STRATEGIES OF RIGHTS DEFLATION

Caught between overall public humanitarianism and the requisites of global good citizenship on the one side and mobilized anti-refugee constituencies, resource constraints, and security challenges on the other, democratic states split the difference by continuing to adhere to the refugee regime in theory but constructing increasingly elaborate detours. Refugee-receiving nations evade their acknowledged obligation to offer asylum by a combination of interdiction, deflection, outsourcing, offshoring, forced or induced repatriation, and deflation of asylum access.

Long-standing and widespread filtering mechanisms include requiring visas from the most refugee-originating countries (now coupled with "carrier sanctions" holding transportation companies responsible), bilateral readmission treaties, "safe third country" policies that demand refuge in the first safe country refugees reach, and the creation of artificial international zones including borders and airports that block territorial admission (Hathaway and Neve 1997). Each of these filtering mechanisms has been expanded and extended over the past generation, and are now joined by various forms of displacement or suppression of asylum access.

Interdiction involves the extension of state authority to migrants' transit areas, where they are physically intercepted before reaching the border where they retain the right to apply for asylum. This has been applied by the U.S. to Haitians in the Caribbean, Australia to North African and South Asians off its coasts, and British naval forces in the Mediterranean off the coast of Libya to migrants from throughout the African continent. Upon apprehension, these migrants are either returned to their point of origin or detained—often in offshore facilities—and subsequently deported.

Deflection is centered on "safe third country" policies that limit or return asylum seekers to a previous point of arrival. EU member states have designated Eastern European states safe for migrants from the Middle East, even when the designated states do not offer asylum. The U.S. and Canada have an official agreement that prevents an asylum applicant who landed in or was refused asylum in the U.S. from seeking refuge in Canada, even though the U.S. process falls considerably short of the international standard and Canada has agreed to accept higher numbers of Syrians. Under the Dublin Regulation, EU member states can refuse or return asylum seekers to any non-conflict country deemed secure. This has been prominently applied by Norway to return refugees to Russia and throughout the EU to deflect Mideast refugees who had transited Turkey—in both cases, returning asylum seekers to countries with structurally limited asylum regimes that may not even be safe for certain populations.

In a March 2016 accord, Turkey agreed to accept the return of asylum seekers from Greece in exchange for EU processing of a limited number of Syrians directly from Turkey, along with billions of Euros of aid, and improved visas for Turks in the EU. However, this arrangement deflates refugee rights since Turkey grants Syrians (like all non-Europeans) only temporary protection and not full-fledged asylum. Meanwhile, over 600 Greek arrivals have been forcibly returned to Turkey without an opportunity to request asylum. Moreover, the EU has lagged tremendously in accepting refugees who did qualify in Turkey under the new arrangement; about 1,600 in 2016, a fraction of the roughly 15,000 migrants detained in Greece and estimated 60,000 encamped irregularly. Disturbingly, this "model" has now been cited to displace and deport even more vulnerable refugee populations elsewhere, especially with lower-resourced and less democratic host nations in Kenya and Pakistan (Amnesty International, "Q&A: The EU-Turkey Migration Deal is No Blueprint", 2016).

Outsourcing is the delegation of interdiction or refugee processing to a neighboring transit country in order to prevent arrival and potential asylum claims in the unwilling host; it may overlap with deflection but involves a more active role, agreements, and resource transfers to the third-party nation. Prominent current cases are the U.S. arrangement with Mexico to apprehend Central American migrants, and Australia's delegation of indefinite detention of asylum seekers to former colonies in Papua New Guinea.

Australia houses more than 2,000 asylum seekers in Manus and Nauru. Detention conditions are so oppressive that in the past year alone, an Iranian asylum seeker immolated himself, an Iranian Kurd was beaten to death by a local mob, and an Iraqi young man perished from a treatable infection when his evacuation to a mainland hospital was delayed for days. The accounts of Sudanese and Afghan migrants in these facilities clearly reflect flight from persecution and conflict that meet the international refugee standards Australia has signed, but are never assessed. Australia has given its former colony Papua New Guinea hundreds of millions of dollars in development projects, but has housed hundreds of refugees in horrific conditions for over three years. In response to a Papua Supreme Court ruling ordering an end to the illegal detention, Australia refused to modify its lifetime ban on resettlement of Nauru detainees, instead concluding a one-time agreement with the U.S. to resettle a handful of women, children, and injured refugees (Cohen 2016). Maley points out the underlying perversity of Australian aid policy in this regard: in exchange for running an Australian detention center Nauru receives over $21 million in aid for its 10,000 residents, while needy source country Afghanistan receives $78.5 million for its nearly 30 million conflict-affected and desperately poor citizens (Maley 2016: 139).

On another continent, at the behest of the U.S., in July 2014 Mexico moved to secure its Southern Border to stem the flow of Central American migrants. The U.S. has pledged over $75 million to bolster migration enforcement in Mexico (Reuters in Mexico City 2015; Ribando Seelke and Finklea 2016). Between mid-2014 and July 2016, Mexico detained over 425,000 Central Americans. Migrants from El Salvador, Honduras, and Guatemala are fleeing conditions of profound social disorder that make El Salvador the murder capital of the world, and often cite personal threats and abuses by corrupt officials, narco-traffickers, and paramilitary gangs. Many would qualify for asylum under U.S. standards, including many women and children who suffer gender-based violence and human trafficking. With inadequate opportunities and information to apply for asylum and strong pressures for deportation back to Central America, less than 1 percent apply for asylum in Mexico, and less than a third of applicants receive it (Suarez et al. 2016).

A related strategy that also overlaps but may extend beyond deflection and outsourcing is offshoring: the creation of permanent zones of exception for the detention of asylum seekers that are not subject to national law and corresponding treaty obligations. The U.S. has long offshore-processed Caribbean migrants at Guantanamo (Rabinovitch 2014). France declares certain arrival areas exempt from its own laws, including some airports and port areas. Detainees in France and Belgium have complained to the European Court of Human Rights about prolonged irregular detention in exceptional transit zones with inadequate conditions, sometimes followed by illicit deportation of a migrant such as a minor seeking family reunification (European Court of Human Rights 2016).

Forced or induced repatriation may involve a collaboration with international agencies to declare a safe zone in a conflict country, to negotiate unsustainable or abusive resettlement programs for a vulnerable population, or to offer financial incentives and one-way transportation to return to an abusive or failing state. International declaration of safe zones for ethnic minorities during the Bosnian war of the 1990s and Iraq War of the 2000s limited refugee flows but rendered targeted populations vulnerable to war crimes. Turkey was allowed to close its border to unwanted

Iraqi Kurds because the UN coalition declared a safe zone that kept them in place. Recently, Israel has induced repatriation of a number of its estimated 50,000 African migrants fleeing humanitarian crises and failing states. Eritrean, Ethiopian, and Sudanese migrants seeking asylum have instead been shipped to Rwanda or Uganda, where they are often subject to trafficking (Zonszein 2015; Harcombe 2016).

Finally, host states contracted to the refugee regime that cannot deflect or outsource asylum seekers undermine their own asylum determination process to deflate access and drive down acceptance rates. Historic asylum hosts like the Netherlands deflate access when they create 48-hour rapid assessment routines that systematically disadvantage women, children, less educated applicants, and those displaced by complex conflicts rather than individual documented persecution (Asylum Information Database n.d.). Host nations like the U.S. limit or eliminate legal representation and even translation services for asylum seekers, or relegate representation to underfunded and overcrowded NGOs (Kerwin 2011). Almost all the Northern countries now do not assist with the investigation or documentation of persecution claims or sending state conditions, forcing asylum seekers to gather their own evidence and expert assessments that demonstrate protected conditions, usually provided by a patchwork of pro bono lawyers, NGOs, and volunteer academic experts. All of these limitations on asylum assessment structurally discriminate against precisely the most vulnerable asylum seekers: ethnic minorities with limited language skills, women who require expert assistance and witness protection to report gender violence or trafficking, children forced or tricked into conflict or smuggling, poorer and less educated victims of abuse who have been forced to travel over land through multiple transit zones, undocumented persons who have been multiple displaced or born in transit zones, unregistered youth of unrecognized nationality or family status, and anyone fleeing a failed state.

These patterns play out visibly in Europe's leading site of landfall for Mediterranean migrants. Italy has played an exemplary humanitarian role in rescuing migrants, and attempts to shelter them in relatively humane conditions. But about two-thirds of asylum seekers in Italy are denied—with over 83,000 requests last year. Italy has been forced to shift asylum commission board hearings to single-member interviews, and migrants receive preparation for asylum screening only if they happen to be living in a shelter run by an NGO with available and trained staff. Italy accepts around 90 percent of Syrians, but only 2 percent of Nigerians—yet many Nigerians were contract laborers in Libya who are now fleeing a conflict and collapsing state. One asylum seeker from Bangladesh responded to an interviewer in Italy hoping to determine his fit with a legitimated category of persecution, "I'm an orphan. . .I don't know my ethnic group" (Yardley 2016).

REMEDIES?

As we have seen, refugee rights are contracting through a combination of unprecedented demand on a deeply flawed regime—but also devolution of the regime in unforeseen directions. The generic human rights limitation of sovereignty is layered on top of the citizenship gap of statelessness, but there are additional distortions of host states' global citizenship that generate additional vulnerabilities and insecurities. The problem now lies less in delineating rights, only somewhat in enforcing them, and primarily in access to a well-defined but collapsing regime.

Refugees' ability to access their rights depends on the quality of their citizenship in the sending state, the quality of democracy and global citizenship of the receiving state, and the quality of governance in transit and arrival zones. Although sovereign control of asylum always complicates enforcement of refugee rights, the higher quality citizenship they carry and the higher level of receiving state participation in the international regime, the greater chance refugees have to access that filter. The hazard of arrival in a lawless internal conflict zone, borderland, or ungoverned transit area such as the high seas has always diminished further access to the regime. What has changed is a conscious strategy by receiving states to deflate refugee claims by pushing migrants away from formal governed access points.

This means that remedies must now address multiple dimensions of accountability for citizenship and responsibility. The refugee regime must expand the definition and basis for recognition, due process for asylum seekers, and rights standards for border enforcement, detention, and deportation. Front-line states must be pressed to formalize refugee reception and processing, and all states to improve access to asylum determination for the most vulnerable second-class citizens who lack documents, resources, education, and status. Beyond this, the democratic developed states best equipped to welcome refugees, most committed to the regime in theory, and increasingly targeted by migrants desperately seeking security must be prevented from undermining their own global citizenship.

REFERENCES

Amnesty International. "Q&A: Why the Eu-Turkey Migration Deal Is No Blueprint." https://www.hrw.org/news/2016/11/14/qa-why-eu-turkey-migration-deal-no-blueprint, n.d.

Arendt, Hannah. *The Human Condition*. University of Chicago Press, 1958.

Associated Press. "'Warning Shots' Should Be Fired to Deter Eu-Bound Migrants, Says Danish MP." *The Guardian* (2016). Published electronically 8 December. https://www.theguardian.com/world/2016/dec/09/warning-shots-should-be-fired-to-deter-eu-bound-migrants-says-danish-mp.
Asylum Information Database. "Regular Procedure: Netherlands." Asylum Information Database, n.d. http://www.asylumineurope.org/reports/country/Netherlands/asylum-procedure/procedures/regular-procedure.
Brysk, Alison, and Gershon Shafir. *People out of Place: Globalization, Human Rights, and the Citizenship Gap* (in English). New York: Routledge, 2004.
Cohen, Roger. "Broken Men in Paradise." *The New York Times* (2016). Published electronically 9 December. http://www.nytimes.com/2016/12/09/opinion/sunday/australia-refugee-prisons-manus-island.html.
European Court of Human Rights. "Migrants in Detention." European Court of Human Rights, 2016.
Harcombe, Kathy. "Israel's Unwanted African Migrants." *BBC News* (2016). Published electronically 3 February. http://www.bbc.com/news/magazine-35475403.
Hathaway, James C., and Alexander Neve, R. "Making International Refugee Law Relevant Again: A Proposal for Collectivized Solution Oriented Protection." *Harvard Human Rights Journal* 10 (1997): 115–213.
Human Rights Watch. "Closed Doors: Mexico's Failure to Protect Central American Refugee and Migrant Children," 2016, https://www.hrw.org/report/2016/03/31/closed-doors/mexicos-failure-protect-central-american-refugee-and-migrant-children.
International Centre for Migration Policy Development. "Targeting Vulnerabilities: The Impact of the Syrian War and Refugee Situation on Trafficking in Persons a Study of Syria, Turkey, Lebanon, Jordan and Iraq," December 2015.
Jastram, Kate, and Marilyn Achiron. "Refugee Protection: A Guide to International Refugee Law," edited by Erika Feller, Irene Khan, Stephane Jaquemet and Philippe Leclerc: UNHCR, 2001.
Kerwin, Donald M. "The Faltering U.S. Refugee Protection System: Legal and Policy Responses to Refugees, Asylum Seekers, and Others in Need of Protection." *Migration Policy Institute* (2011). Published electronically May 2011. http://www.migrationpolicy.org/research/faltering-us-refugee-protection-system.
Maley, William. *What is a Refugee?* Oxford University Press, 2016.
McElvein, Elizabeth. "What Do Americans Really Think About Syrian Refugees." *Brookings* (2016). Published electronically 4 March. https://www.brookings.edu/blog/markaz/2016/03/04/what-do-americans-really-think-about-syrian-refugees/.
McIntyre, Erin Siegal, and Deborah Bonello. "Is Rape the Price to Pay for Migrant Women Chasing the American Dream?", 2014, http://fusion.net/story/17321/is-rape-the-price-to-pay-for-migrant-women-chasing-the-american-dream.
Morrison, Aaron. "Illegal Immigration 2015: 40% of Mexican Migrants Abused, Separated in Deportation by Us Border Patrol, Report Sas." *International Business Times* (2015). Published electronically 22 September, http://www.ibtimes.com/illegal-immigration-2015-40-mexican-migrants-abused-separated-deportation-us-border-2108256.
Poushter, Jacob. "European Onions of the Refugee Crisis in 5 Charts." (2016). Published electronically 16 September, http://www.pewresearch.org/fact-tank/2016/09/16/european-opinions-of-the-refugee-crisis-in-5-charts/.
Rabinovitch, Zara. "Pushing out the Boundaries of Humanitarian Screening with in-Country and Offshore Processing." *Migration Policy Institute* (2014).

Published electronically 16 October, http://www.migrationpolicy.org/article/pushing-out-boundaries-humanitarian-screening-country-and-offshore-processing.
Reuters in Mexico City. "War Zone at the Border: Abuse of Migrants in Mexico Rises." *The Guardian* (2015). Published electronically 16 October. https://www.theguardian.com/world/2015/oct/16/abuse-central-american-migrants-mexico-border-rises.
Ribando Seelke, Clare, and Kristin Finklea. "U.S.-Mexican Security Cooperation: The Merida Initiative and Beyond." Congressional Research Service, 2016.
Risse, Thomas, Steve C. Ropp, and Kathryn Sikkink, eds. *The Persistent Power of Human Rights: From Commitment to Compliance*. New York: Cambridge University Press, 2013.
Smith-Spark, Laura. "Report: 40,000 Migrant Deaths Worldwide since 2000." *CNN* (2014). Published electronically 30 September, http://www.cnn.com/2014/09/30/world/migrant-deaths/.
Suarez Enriquez, Ximena, Jose Knippen, and Maureen Meyer. "A Trail of Impunity: Thousands of Migrants in Transit Face Abuses Amid Mexico's Crackdown." Washington Office on Latin America, 2016.
Townsend, Mark, and Tracy McVeigh. "Migrant Death Toll Expected to Exceed 10,000 in 2016." *The Guardian* (2016). Published electronically 17 September, https://www.theguardian.com/world/2016/sep/17/migrant-death-toll-2016-syria-united-nations.
UN News Centre. "Unprecedented 65 Million People Displaced by War and Persecution in 2015." UN News Centre, (2016). http://www.un.org/apps/news/story.asp?NewsID=54269#.WKTzqxIrJE4.
UNHCR. "Figures at a Glance." http://www.unhcr.org/en-us/figures-at-a-glance.html.
UNHCR. "Handbook for the Protection of Internally Displaced Persons."
UNHCR. "Local Integration." http://www.unhcr.org/en-us/local-integration-49c3646c101.html.
UNHCR. "Refugees/ Migrants Response." http://data.unhcr.org/mediterranean/regional.php.
Yardley, Jim. "One Man in Italy Begs for Asylum, and Another Decides His Fate." *The New York Times* (2016). Published electronically 10 December, https://www.nytimes.com/2016/12/10/world/europe/italy-asylum-refugees.html?mcubz=1.
Zonszein, Mairav. "Israel to Deport Eritrean and Sudanese Asylum Seeks to Third Countries." *The Guardian* (2015). Published electronically 31 March. https://www.theguardian.com/world/2015/mar/31/israel-to-deport-eritrean-and-sudanese-asylum-seekers-to-third-countries.

3. Has the occupation occupied Israel?

Gershon Shafir

In 1984, in the concluding paragraph of the very first academic article I published about the Israeli occupation of the West Bank, I suggested that in addition to seeking to understand the dynamic of Israeli settlement, we need to ask what the likely impact will be on Israel's democracy. I asked: "Can the Israeli personality, institutions and forms of domination created in the West Bank be prevented from filtering through into the mainstream of Israeli society and subverting the spirit, even if not necessarily the formal expressions of its democracy?" (Shafir 1984: 824). A half-century into the occupation the question rings with greater urgency. Just how far and how deeply has the occupation occupied Israel itself?

Israeli circumstances are unique since military occupation is a rare phenomenon in today's world. Ongoing, decades-long occupation is ever rarer. The controlling legal authority in the Occupied Palestinian Territories (OPT) is international humanitarian law (IHL), also referred to as the law of armed conflict, and in particular its sub-category of the law of belligerent occupation. But in this chapter, I am examining the effects of violations of IHL in the OPT in Israel within the Green Lines—and therefore, the impact on contracting human rights and citizenship as well.

Though the Israeli legal situation is uncommon, the intrusion of the occupation into Israel falls into more general and familiar categories. These can be charted along a spectrum of potential threats: the contraction of human rights, through dilution of citizenship, to the undermining of democracy, itself running the range from populism and authoritarianism to fascism. In each case, threats to and loss of human rights are a gateway to ever greater perils. In this case there is another, early, way station that needs to be added to the spectrum of threats: the undermining of those who speak for international humanitarian law, parallel to other cases of backlash against international law.

The rise of authoritarian tendencies in Israel with a clear intention to suppress dissent and criticism of the occupation, colonization, and their manifold practices is a terrifying peril. The direction in which Israeli politics and culture are being driven is clear, but just how far has it gone? I will seek to address this question in Section A by focusing first on a single incident and its wide-ranging reverberations that became something of an Israeli "Dreyfus Affair." I will then broaden the horizon of my analysis in Section B to examine the concerted assaults on the customary bastions of pluralist and liberal thinking: the schools, the free press, and cultural institutions in general. Finally, I will seek to take the temperature of Israeli democracy and the human rights regime in light of these ominous developments.

I will argue that the unusual role played by the Israeli military as defender of humanitarian protections under IHL serves as a powerful indicator of the diminished status of other institutions and casts sharp light on the topsy-turvy status of rights in the country. The goal of right-wing extra-parliamentary groups and the Knesset's own legal steamroller is to construct a legal and mental separation wall between an artificial entity that lumps the State of Israel together with the West Bank and the rest of the world. Should it succeed in bludgeoning the Israeli public into a homogenized mass, any alternative view can be denounced as foreign or foreign-influenced and its adherents as enemies within and hence as anti-Israeli. With such a mental wall in place, it would be easier to suppress the practices, institutions, and the very value of democracy should the reigning colonization lobby find itself besieged in the future.

AN ISRAELI "DREYFUS AFFAIR"

On March 24, 2016, two Palestinian civilians attacked IDF soldiers in the Tel Rumeida neighborhood of Hebron, wounding one lightly. The soldiers opened fire, killing one and wounding the other, Abdelfattah al-Sharif who fell on the ground incapacitated. We know what happened subsequently because a Palestinian activist of B'Tselem, the Israeli Information Center for Human Rights in the Occupied Territories, surreptitiously filmed the rest of the incident. This practice is encouraged and assisted by Israeli human rights organizations that hand out cameras to Palestinians to help them document IHL violations. A soldier on active duty, Sgt. Elor Azaria, a medic from the Kfir Division that serves in the West Bank, approached the wounded Palestinian and shot him at close range without an order from his superiors, as much as six minutes later. Azaria was investigated, charged with manslaughter, and in his trial justified his action by arguing that he was fearful that the incapacitated Palestinian might be wearing a suicide belt under his coat. His commander at his trial testified that Azaria told him immediately after the incident that he shot the terrorist "because he deserved to die"— in short, that he acted out of revenge (Blum 2017; "Ex-defense" 2016; Fischer 2017).

Soon after the video was made public and before the relevant facts became public, a poll found that the majority of Israelis supported the soldier's action and were opposed to his arrest. It was at this point that the shooting incident turned into the "Elor Azaria Affair." Support for the shooter spread to the social networks and was expressed through petitions and demonstrations. Prime Minister Netanyahu called the soldier's father, and other politicians arrived at his first court hearing to express their support. Against them stood the Minister of Defense Moshe Ya'alon and the Chief of the Staff Lt. General Gadi Eizenkot, who described the shooting following the preliminary hearing as a "severe incident," since the soldier appeared to have violated the IDF's rules of engagement and ethical code, which requires soldiers to open fire only when the triple criteria of necessity, distinction, and proportionality—the IHL standards that set legitimate fighting and war crimes apart—have been met. Ya'alon also encouraged military commanders to speak their mind on issues of morality.

Shortly thereafter, Netanyahu replaced the veteran Minister of Defense with Avigdor Lieberman who was one of the politicians in attendance at the Azaria trial, and while additional political considerations played a role in the shuffle this move was seen as a direct repudiation of Ya'alon's defense of the military. Sgt. Azaria, taking his cue from the political upheaval, adopted the most uncompromising position in his trial, testifying that he lost his trust in his commanders all the way up to the military's higher echelon, including the Minister of Defense, and felt betrayed by them. This extreme stance presented Israel's battle-hardened commanders as soft-hearted lefties who care more for the lives of Palestinians than of their own soldiers, raised an anonymous soldier into a hero while belittling the military brass, legitimated political assaults against the military—until now the most prestigious and trusted Israeli institution—and transformed the trial into a political showcase.

Key aspects of the Azaria Affair bear resemblance to the Dreyfus Affair, as a struggle between universal and particularistic sets of values and visions of society focused on the legal case concerning an individual's potential guilt. In France, the anti-Dreyfusards deemed the "honor" of the military more important than the potential innocence of the suspect, whereas the Dreyfusards, in contrast, held that no individual's rights can be trampled by reasons of state. Dreyfus's Jewishness further deepened the division, and coincidentally the anti-Semitic outbursts accompanying the trial led Theodor Herzl, a Jewish-Austrian correspondent at the trial, to conceive his Zionist vision.

In Israel, in a reverse image, for Azaria's supporters, the superiority of the Jewish values that undergird the occupation and colonization of the

West Bank mattered more than whether Sgt. Azaria was guilty of violating the laws of war. The question of guilt and innocence also took back seat to the religious identity of the accused. Being Jewish, however, also played the reverse role in the two cases. While Dreyfus was suspect because of his Jewish religion and anti-Semitism played an important role in his public condemnation, Azaria was deemed innocent for the same reason. Several religious-Zionist and Likud leaders share the widespread sentiment that anyone who wishes to murder a Jew under any circumstances should not be allowed to survive (Caspit 2016). Jewish values, in short, should not be secondary to IHL and Jews could not be guilty in any confrontation with Palestinians.

The unprecedented public criticism of the military and its doctrines is part and parcel of the foundational struggle in Israeli society between democratic and so-called "Jewish values;" in this case between IHL and ancient or halachic Jewish military ethics. In the context of *al-habbah al-sha'biyya* (the youth outburst) of the near daily individual Palestinian knife attacks which started in September 2015, the reaction of religious-Zionist rabbis associated with the colonization movement has taken on an extremely harsh tone. Particularly notable was a speech by Rabbi Yigal Levinstein, a co-director of the most distinguished preparatory school in the Eli settlement which serves as a feeder of religious-Zionist soldiers to the very military he severely sought to castigate. Levinstein denounced what he described as a dramatic shift in Israel's identity and the values of the IDF. He singled out education for tolerance towards gays whom he described as "perverts," but his ire was directed broadly at the support for pluralism that is offered in the education courses for IDF officers. His criticism, amplified by others, charged the military with having lost its ability to define victory. In his opinion, the IDF replaced the desire to win with self-restraint and allegedly holds that it is better for its soldiers to be killed so that the IDF will not be perceived as an amoral military and negatively influence international public opinion on Israel. In contrast, the religious-Zionist demand is to strengthen the IDF by eliminating the liberal values that managed to infiltrate the military and have the military be based on a Jewish military ethos and a willingness to use all available military tools and all necessary force (Cohen and Lis 2016).

Another difference is notable. Though the Israeli military commanders protest against attempts to subjugate their institution's standards and professional judgement to extraneous—either religious or political considerations—their attempt to present the military as adhering to IHL at times rings hollow. Since the start of the Second Intifada, over fifteen years ago, the Israeli NGO Breaking the Silence has been gathering, investigating, and publicizing anonymous testimonies of human rights abuses by Israeli mandatory and reserve combat soldiers, a quarter of them officers, who had served in the OPT and participated in the Gaza Wars. The soldiers testify to collective punishment, takeover of private homes as temporary posts or for purposes of surveillance on neighborhoods, and confrontations with local residents to provoke violent reactions. Particularly damning are testimonies of soldiers from the July–August 2014 Protective Edge Operation in Gaza, in which lax rules of engagement called for indiscriminate targeting of civilian areas at the beginning of the operation and use of weapons incapable of precise fire. They also testified that every person in what was defined as a combat zone was viewed as a legitimate target, and orders were given to fire at ill-defined suspicious points and at any suspected threat. These rules of engagement during the operation hardly respected the IHL or the IDF's own moral code requirements since their guiding principle was "minimum risk to our forces even at the cost of harming innocent civilians" which, in Breaking the Silence's summation "led to massive and unprecedented harm to the population and the civilian infrastructure in Gaza" (2014: 16).

According to the UN Office for the Coordination of Humanitarian Affairs (OCHA), 2,200 Palestinians, among them 1,473 civilian and of these 501 children were killed; according to Israel, 66 of its soldiers and five civilians were killed and during the operation; and according to Palestinian officials 18,000 homes and many factories were severely damaged, 220 schools and 62 hospitals and clinics were damaged, and the main power plants and two sewage pumping stations were damaged (UN-OCHAOPT 2015).

Israeli military investigation of human rights violations during Gaza wars have not shown the thoroughness the IDF's ethics code seems to demand. Following the December 2007–January 2008 Operation Cast Lead, 50 investigations of the military police led to only 3 convictions. Accountability for human rights violations is so scarce that after many years of submitting complaints to the Israeli military on behalf of affected Palestinians, B'Tselem announced in May 2016, namely during Lt. General Eizenkot's command, that "there is no longer any point in pursuing justice and defending human rights by working with a system whose real function is measured by its ability to successfully cover up unlawful acts and protect perpetrators," and consequently ceased submitting further complaints ("B'Tselem" 2016). In fact, the Elor Azaria investigation was the result of its unique circumstances: the execution style shooting of the prostrate Palestinian attacker was filmed and made public. Most other cases in which terror suspects are killed do not lead to indictments.

The military's professional ethics, in particular its rules of engagement, are the key to its professional autonomy—much as the Hippocratic Oath is used to justify why we should not mistrust physicians' autonomous judgement. Furthermore, the Israeli brass is concerned that boldfaced and unapologetic violations of IHL are likely to land it in the docket of the International Criminal Court in The Hague under the principles of universal jurisdiction, should they be charged while traveling outside Israel. In fact, there were already several close calls of retired Israeli generals being spirited out of countries or kept waiting on airplanes while warrants were pending against them (Lipman 2011).

When a flawed institution such as the military, which is after all the very institution in charge of wielding the tools of war and administering the occupation as required by IHL, finds itself standing in defense of the values of democracy and of international law shows just how far the influence of other institutions, including human rights NGOs, schools, and cultural elites have diminished. In addition to the desire to maintain its professional autonomy, and deep-seated opposition to reckless and provocative policies, the security establishment, having reached the conclusion that the tide against democracy is turning, is trying to step into the breech. Religious-Zionist rabbis and leaders singled out the IDF's Chief Educational Officer, Brigadier General Avner Paz-Tzuk, for the publication of a pamphlet titled "An Evaluation of the Social and Educational Aspects and the Values the IDF in 2016," clearly on behalf of Eizenkot, which observed that "as the democratic consciousness of Israeli society is eroded and sectarianism and racism are growing, there is a growing need for education for democratic values in the IDF" (Dahan 2016).

During Israel's Holocaust Remembrance Day in May 2016, Yair Golan, the Deputy Chief of Staff and the second in command of the IDF, in a bombshell of a speech stated that what frightens him about contemporary Israeli society is the rise of the revolting trends that characterized Europe, and in particular Germany during the 1930s. As the legacy of the Holocaust, he suggested both personal and national soul-searching are called forth, since "There is nothing easier and simpler than to become thuggish, morally bankrupt, and self-righteous" ("IDF General" 2015). A few days later, former Prime Minister Ehud Barak, in response to the Elor Azar Affair which culminated with Ya'alon's replacement, denounced the current Israeli government in the most unusual terms by suggesting that it is "exhibiting signs of fascism." A student of European fascism can point to the burgeoning in Israel of the movement's central characteristics: hatred of the stranger, the repression of individual rights and sanctification of the collective and national unity, anti-intellectualism, constant use of nationalist symbols and paraphernalia, obsession with perceived slights and a desire to restore past historical greatness, singling out of domestic dissenters and peaceniks as collaborators and traitors, centralized control over mass media, aggressive foreign policy, militarism and normalization of endless warfare.

In February 2017, the military court found Sgt. Azaria guilty of manslaughter, since he acted with the intent to kill rather than from feeling threatened. At the same time, it meted out the minimum allowable sentence of a year and half in jail, (Cohen 2017) raising the suspicion that it buckled to the pressures of Azaria's powerful supporters.

SHUTTING THE EYES THAT SEE

Israel is a sovereign state and recognized member of the United Nations, while the West Bank and East Jerusalem under the international law of armed conflict remain occupied territories. With the methodical precision of a dumb machine, the Knesset has passed each month for the past two years a new law or amendment not so much to do away with this distinction but to make it harder to talk about it openly. Many of these have been in response to demands by right-wing extra-parliamentary groups that far from being autonomous are indirectly supported by politicians associated with the settler lobby. The most draconian among these is the amendment to the Entry to Israel Law, which authorizes the prohibition of entry of foreign nationals, not excluding Jews, if they call for a boycott even of settlements alone.

The Likud and the Jewish Home Parties, the champions of the continued occupation regime and settlement enterprise, target the customary bastions of pluralist and liberal thinking: the schools, the free press, and cultural institutions in general. The silencing of those who criticize the continued occupation operates through three main channels: assaults by vigilante organizations and denunciations by ultra-nationalist NGOs, the adoption and implementation of their demands by members of the Israeli government through restrictive regulation and budgetary cuts, and a feverish outbidding among religious-Zionist and Likud Members of the Knesset (MK) to submit punitive laws.

Though the silencing legislation is commonly toned down by the government, the earlier, punitive versions of bills, suggest that adopted law may eventually be tightened and thus continue exerting a chilling effect that goes beyond the purview of the legislation. They also mark institutions such as universities, liberal media outlets, plays, movies, exhibitions etc., and their academics, journalists, and artists as enemies within whose lives and employment are subsequently threatened in social and public media. What the new legislation and administrative and budgetary practices have in common is an attempt to rein in the freedom of speech, press, religion, and academic expression when these are aimed at debating, highlighting, exposing, and critiquing the Israeli occupation. In particular, the laws and denunciations intend to name and shame human rights and liberal NGOs whose documentation of the violations of Palestinian human rights and tracking of further colonization are viewed as undermining Israel's international reputation. In short, they deride dissent and are willing to undermine the civil and legislative protections available under democracy to dissenters and minorities (Susser 2016).

While Netanyahu has served continuously as the Prime Minister of right-wing governments since March 2009, his newest government formed in 2015 made a sharp turn towards soft authoritarianism. As we shall see below, particularly virulent initiatives to enforce conformity with government policies are proposed and enacted by the newly appointed Ministers of Education and Justice from the religious-Zionist Jewish Home Party that is closely allied with the settlement project. Israel's human rights NGOs sense of loss is bolstered by the fact that until the end of the 1990s. Israel enjoyed a growing process of liberalization—including the legislation of a mini bill of rights—in its public life that extended new protections to Jewish and Arab citizens alike.

In Israel assaults on human rights NGOs take place in the context of the country's legal self-definition as "a Jewish and democratic state." But Israel is a Jewish state for its Palestinian Arab citizens and a democratic state for its Jewish citizens in many respects. Adalah, the Legal Center for Arab Minority Rights in Israel, lists some fifty laws that effectively discriminate against or single out for special treatment the country's Palestinian Arab citizens. Many of these laws concern equal access to land, planning authorities, choice of residence, social services, but more recently they also target cultural and political rights. For example, the 2011 "Naqba Law" authorizes the Finance Minister to reduce state funding for institutions that commemorate Israel's Independence Day as a day of mourning, as Palestinians do in observance of their defeat, flight, and expulsion in the 1948 War. The law restricts citizen-Palestinians' freedom of expression as well as singles out their educational institutions and, overall, seeks to render their history invisible (Adalah n.d.).

By far more radical is the "Expulsion Law" which allows a majority of 90 out of 120 MKs, including 10 opposition members, to dismiss another sitting MK accused of incitement for racism or support for armed struggle against Israel from the Knesset. In effect, this law authorizes the government to punish parts of the opposition by bypassing the judicial authority which until now was the only branch of government with the power to charge and convict elected officials. It was adopted with the case in mind of Haneen Zoabi, a Palestinian Arab MK who is outspoken in defense of

Palestinian rights and challenged the Jewish establishment by participating in the Turkish Mavi Marmara flotilla that sought to break the embargo on Gaza by delivering supplies. While it has a clear chilling effect on the freedom of expression and activities of Arab MKs and brought together a group of Jewish parties much larger than the ruling coalition to adopt it, thus far it has not been put into effect even against her. This law undermines the principle of representation that is a foundational aspect of a democratic regime (Beaumont 2016).

What is new in the concentrated assault during Netanyahu's fourth government, is that some of the restrictions and exclusions that were imposed on Israel's 2.1 million Palestinian citizens are now directed, in yet weakened forms, against some of its Jewish citizens as well. Among the long list of anti-democratic legislation recently adopted, the most typical one is the "Transparency Law"—chillingly similar to laws adopted in authoritarian regimes worldwide. It requires Israelis NGOs that receive more than half of their funding from "foreign government entities," to make a public disclosure in their publications and in contacts with elected officials. It is based on the premise that these NGOs operate as foreign agents. An earlier requirement that staffers of the effected NGOs wear a special tag that would signal this fact was scrapped. The law was carefully crafted to target only left-wing NGOs since those that support settlements and other right-wing institutions receive their foreign donations from like-minded individuals abroad or are funded by the government. It is even more ironical that many of the foreign governments that provide funding for the human rights NGOs—the US, Germany, France, as well as the EU—are among Israel's closest Western supporters, which protested the law but did not translate their disagreement to policy. Though the law serves to intimidate and incite the Israeli public against the targeted anti-occupation activists, it has not stopped or reduced their level of activity.

Side by side with legislative restrictions, the free press is being brought under closer governmental supervision. Israel's largest circulation daily, *Yisrael Hayom*, is financed by one of Prime Minister Netanyahu's American Jewish political allies, Las Vegas casino billionaire Sheldon Adelson, and consequently is freely distributed. It is a government mouthpiece, frequently compared with *Pravda*, and according to the *Economist* its major headlines are approved by the Prime Minister's Office ("A Tough" 2015). Adelson, who views Palestinians as a made-up nation, argued that "the Bible . . . didn't talk about Israel remaining as a democratic state . . . Israel isn't going to be a democratic state—so what?" It is the importance of this media organ for Netanyahu that apparently led him to break up his coalition government and call new elections for March 2015 to forestall a bill prohibiting the free distribution of daily newspapers. Following the elections, Netanyahu kept, in addition to the post of Prime Minister, the portfolio of the Minister of Communications. In his new position, he facilitated the appointment of Rami Sadan, his former communications advisor, as the director of the commercial Channel 10 that in the past had investigated the financing of the Netanyahu family foreign trips. Most recently, he halted the replacement of the older Israel Broadcasting Authority with a new streamlined independent Broadcasting Corporation, since, as his new Minister of Culture Miri Regev explained, "Why set up a new Broadcasting Corporation if we don't control it?" (Ravid 2016). In March 2017, Netanyahu again threatened to dissolve the Knesset if his demand to increase governmental control over the new Broadcasting Corporation and, in particular, over news broadcasts were not heeded by Moshe Kahalon, the Minister of Finance. Though Netanyahu failed to gain complete control over the new body, he will be able to exercise considerable authority over its composition (Niv 2017).

These laws and the greater political control over the public sphere are not exceptional but examples of a broader stratagem to curtail the workings of mass media. There is an abundance of practices that seek to ensure loyalty to the state and root out dissent, starting with official requests to foreign artists, including Elton John, to sign a loyalty oath to Israel as a precondition for receiving a labor permit (Arad 2016), through the preventive arrest of individuals by the police ahead of demonstrations they planned, refusal of the Ministry of the Interior to license or renew licenses of at least 62 new newspapers in the past decade, request by the Military Censor to bloggers who cover security related subjects to submit Facebook postings prior to their posting, adoption of a law to increase the punishment for the desecration of the flag to three years, to yet another law that permits the police to search individuals even if they carry no weapons or were engaged in suspicious behavior as long as the police declared a risk of terror attacks.

A particularly fiercely contested sphere are Israel's schools through the close collaboration of ultra-nationalist NGOs and the government. In December 2015, a video issued by the *Im Tirzu* (If You Will It) ultranationalist group displayed the photos of the leaders of four human rights NGOs—Breaking the Silence, *B'Tselem*, the Public Committee Against Torture, and *Hamoked*—and accused them of being "moles," who defend Palestinian terrorists, and slander Israel in the world (Sucharov 2015). Soon thereafter, the Minister of Education, Naftali Bennett from the Jewish Home religious-Zionist Party, forbade representatives of Breaking the Silence, that collects testimonies of combat soldiers on the violation of Palestinian human rights during their service in the OPT, from speaking in public schools and the Minister of Defense barred them from appearing in front of soldiers.

As part of effecting long-term change, the Minister of Education is engaged in revising civics education. The 2016 edition of the high school textbook *Being Citizens in Israel* revised the understanding of the state. It endorses majority rule while sidelining minorities; the text no longer views the individual as the source of governmental authority but rather promotes the view that the government alone determines the public good. The value of pluralism is abated and the standing of the Arab minority is diminished. The new textbook clearly places the state's Jewish identity and prominent place in the public sphere above civil identity and invests Jewishness with a more prominent religious character. The Education Ministry also banned the teaching in high schools of the contemporary novel *Borderlife* by Israeli author Dorit Rabinyan, about a love story between an Israeli woman and Palestinian man for fear that it will lead to assimilation ("Novel" 2015), the religious terminology for justifying the prevention of Jewish-Arab mixing. The Ministry expanded the list of books not to be included in its extra-curricular reading list for religious schools, though it includes other books that encourage Israel's transformation into a halachic state and suggest that "Jews have no desire to have Arabs living in their midst." Finally, Bennet dismissed the Ministry's expert in charge of developing an index to measure the level of racism among Israeli Jews and halted the project.

WHITHER ISRAELI DEMOCRACY?

It is easy to place Israel within the wide retreat of the wave of democratization of the past half-decade or so. A new wave of 21st century regimes, from Russia's Putin through Poland to Hungary, have perfected a new form of *authoritarianism*. The new regimes monopolize control over the media, are centered on anti-foreigner sentiments, complain of slights to the nation and accusations of penetration of or even conspiracies by foreign powers, and weaken the authority of autonomous bodies, in particular the free press and educational system. Nor are the liberal democracies of the West, their media and political life, immune to these processes. Israel's turn toward soft authoritarianism is riding on the back of its half century long occupation and without it might not exist or pack a lesser punch.

Israel's growing authoritarianism is best compared to McCarthyism, a politically-inspired practice of whipping up a moral panic against human rights and left-center NGOs for alleged subversion and treason. In addition, government funds are withheld from media and arts that are critical of the occupation. Israel's 1998 Freedom of Information Law is still in use, there exist a wide range of critical print and online publications, and cultural institutions and events critical of the occupation and colonization. And yet, the anti-democratic campaigns that seek to hobble human rights NGOs as well as the limited reliance of the IDF and the HCJ on IHL, pose a grave danger to the future of Israeli democracy, its human rights and limited application of IHL. Signaling out enemies within marks them for future clampdown.

The current McCarthyist accusations and legislation to limit access to public resources and institutions, as well as to legal succor, aim to curtail human rights organization combine with ever-spreading and harsher incitement by both government ministers and extra-parliamentary and in some cases vigilante groups against proponents of democracy and human rights. The continued expansion and popularity of such reckless incitement mobilizes public support for and readiness for a transition from curtailing on to the abolition of such NGOs and the punishment of their activists. In the year of the 50th anniversary of the occupation, Israeli democracy is in grave and growing danger.

In the past half-century, the fate of Israeli democracy has been contingent on the character of the occupation. Particularly notable are the effects of two turning points. In the 1990s, roughly corresponding to the Oslo process, the Knesset passed two basic laws, Human Dignity and Freedom of Employment, which are commonly viewed as a small-scale "constitutional revolution" in a country without a written constitution. These laws designate Israel as "a Jewish and democratic state" without ever specifying what its Jewish values are, but under Chief Justice Aharon Barak they became coterminous with liberalism. Oslo was good for Israeli democracy.

Since the end of the Israeli-Palestinian negotiations in April 2014, without even the pretense of their resumptions, Jewish values have taken on an ethnocentric character towering over democracy in both the public sphere and governmental approach, but not necessarily in court rulings. Israeli authoritarianism is gaining force but is still softer, in particular for Jewish citizens, than in other contemporary authoritarian regimes, and takes the character of McCarthyism and increased control over the media. The infiltration of the imperious occupation has reduced and continues to endanger Israeli democracy, but its formal aspects stand and many of its liberal protections remain in force. Israeli democracy has lost its stature and confidence but the opposition to the occupation remains vibrant and resilient. The debate over the future of the OPT is not over, and the supporters of territorial partition have not been driven underground.

At the same time, the construction of a legal and mental separation wall between an artificial entity that lumps the State of Israel together with the

West Bank on one side and the rest of the world on the other continues apace. Mobilized through a permanent moral panic which views Arabs as unalterable enemies and homogenized behind this mental wall, the Israeli public will find it harder to resist further erosion. The occupation of Israeli democracy will in turn make it easier for the champions of continued colonization to rupture the fabric of Israeli democracy and its rights regime.

REFERENCES

A Tough Deal to Swallow. *The Economist* (2015). Published electronically 8 April. http://www.economist.com/news/middle-east-and-africa/21647937-first-political-ramifications-agreement-iran-may-be-felt-israel-tough-deal.

Adalah. Discriminatory Laws in Israel. http://www.adalah.org/en/law/index.

Arad, Dafna. Elton John Was Asked to Declare Loyalty to Israel Ahead of Tel Aviv Show, Producer Claims. *Ha'aretz* (2016). Published electronically 29 May. http://www.haaretz.com/israel-news/1.711432.

Beaumont, Peter. Israeli Parliament Passes Controversial Legislation Allowing MP Expulsion. *The Guardian* (2016). Published electronically 20 July. https://www.theguardian.com/world/2016/jul/20/israeli-parliament-passes-controversial-legislation-allowing-mp-expulsion.

Blum, Ruthie. A Testament to Israeli Engagement: The Elor Azaria Story. *The New York Times* (2017). Published electronically 6 January. https://www.algemeiner.com/2017/01/06/a-testament-to-israeli-engagement-the-elor-azaria-story/.

Breaking the Silence. *This is How We Fought in Gaza. Soldiers' testimonies and photographs from Operation "Protective Edge"*. (2014). http://www.breakingthesilence.org.il/pdf/ProtectiveEdge.pdf.

B'Tselem to Stop Referring Complaints to the Military Law Enforcement System. *B'Tselem* (2016). Published electronically 25 May. http://www.btselem.org/press_releases/20160525_occupations_fig_leaf.

Caspit, Ben. Why Israelis are Defending IDF Soldier Who Shot Palestinian Attacker. *Al Monitor* (2016). Published electronically 6 March. http://www.al-monitor.com/pulse/originals/2016/03/israel-public-idf-soldier-new-hero-hebron-palestinian-shot.html.

Cohen, Gili. Hebron Shooter Elor Azaria Sentenced to 1.5 Years for Shooting Wounded Palestinian Attacker. *Ha'aretz* (2017). Published electronically 21 February. http://www.haaretz.com/israel-news/1.767137.

Cohen, Gili and Lis, Jonathan. Anti-gay Rabbi Who Heads pre-IDF Academy Blasts Attempts to Prevent Civilian Deaths. *Ha'aretz* (2016). Published electronically 17 July. http://www.haaretz.com/misc/haaretzcomsmartphoneapp/.premium-1.731650.

Dahan, Yossi. The Struggle Has Just Begun. *Yediot Achronot* (2016). 7 July. https://www.yediot.co.il/articles/0,7340,L-4830713,00.html (in Hebrew).

Ex-defense minister slams Netanyahu over Azaria trial. *The Times of Israel* (2016). Published electronically 29 December. http://www.timesofisrael.com/ex-defense-minister-slams-netanyahu-over-azaria-trial/.

Fischer, Ian. Elor Azaria, Israeli Soldier Who Killed Wounded Assailant, Gets 18 Months in Prison. *The New York Times* (2017). Published electronically

21 February https://www.nytimes.com/2017/02/21/world/middleeast/elor-azaria-israel-sentence.html?_r=0.

IDF General in Bombshell Speech: Israel Today Shows Signs of 1930 Germany. *Jerusalem Post* (2015). Published electronically 4 May. http://www.jpost.com/Israel-News/Politics-And-Diplomacy/IDF-general-in-bombshell-speech-Israel-today-shows-signs-of-1930s-Germany-453142.

Lipman, Jennifer. Almog to Test Universal Jurisdiction Reform. *The Jewish Chronicle* (2011). Published electronically 4 October. https://www.thejc.com/news/israel/israeli-general-to-test-universal-jurisdiction-reform-1.28086.

Niv, Shay. Netanyahu, Kahlon reach coalition-saving deal on broadcasting. *Globe's. Israel Business Arena* (2017). Published electronically 30 March. http://www.globes.co.il/en/article-netanyahu-kahlon-reach-coalition-saving-deal-on-broadcasting-1001183412.

Novel about Jewish-Palestinian Love Affair is Barred from Israeli Curriculum. *The Guardian* (2015). Published electronically 31 December. https://www.theguardian.com/world/2016/jan/01/novel-about-jewish-palestinian-love-affair-is-barred-from-israeli-curriculum.

Ravid, Barak. Miri Regev: Why Set Up New Broadcasting Corporation if We Don't Control It? *Ha'aretz* (2016). Published electronically 31 July. http://www.haaretz.com/israel-news/1.734527.

Shafir, Gershon. Changing Nationalism and Israel's "Open Frontier". In the West Bank, *Theory and Society*, vol. 13, no. 6, November 1984.

Sucharov, Mira. Im Tirzu's Pernicious Video Equates Human Rights with Treason. *Ha'aretz* (2015). Published electronically 16 December. http://www.haaretz.com/opinion/.premium-1.692139.

Susser, Leslie. Israeli Democracy under threat. *The Jerusalem Post* (2016). Published electronically 11 February. http://www.jpost.com/printarticle.aspx?id=442264.

UN-OCHAOPT (United Nations Office for the Coordination of Humanitarian Affairs occupied Palestinian territory). *Fragmented Lives: Humanitarian Overview* (2014). Published electronically March, 2015. http://www.ochaopt.org/documents/annual_humanitarian_overview_2014_english_final.pdf.

4. Expanding extractive industries, contracting indigenous rights? Gains, setbacks, and missed opportunities in Latin America

Claire Wright

The conflict over the Dakota Access Pipeline is a global wake-up call to the extent to which extractive projects can affect the cultural and environmental rights of indigenous peoples and, indeed, the lengths to which governments will go in order to fulfil their commitments to big business. The project, which transports gas from North Dakota to Illinois, crosses four States and runs for nearly 2,000 kilometers, threatening the upper Missouri River, affecting water supplies and cutting through sacred sites on the Standing Rock Reservation. The resistance offered by the Sioux earned the solidarity of other Native Americans and created a dense network of national and international support both in person (at the sacred camps established along the river) and online (through social media, intense campaigns,[1] and an array of news articles that fiercely criticized the project). The use of dogs and pepper spray by private security firms to forcefully remove activists who had chained themselves to bulldozers, as well as a series of high-profile arrests, mobilized public support for the plight of the Sioux. Although the project was halted in December 2016 on environmental grounds, the recent go-ahead given, unilaterally, by President Trump has created further protests and indignation. A series of petitions against the Pipe Line have received hundreds of thousands of signatures. Never before has an extractive project created such an overwhelming, negative response both at home and abroad.

Although it does not regularly make the international news headlines in the same way, indigenous people throughout the world are currently embroiled in conflicts over the use of their land and the natural resources found therein. Latin America, which is home to at least 40 million members of almost 600 Indigenous Peoples,[2] is the scenario of multiple conflicts over highly lucrative projects to extract natural resources (Martí i Puig,

Wright, Aylwin and Yáñez, 2013). In a context of historical grievances, the situation has become critical in many countries in the last decade, given the explosion of extractive industries that accompanied the boom in commodity prices. Although by no means the first of its type, the conflict of Bagua, Peru, came to represent in Latin America what Standing Rock currently represents in the United States. The source of the conflict was widespread opposition to two emergency decrees issued in 2008 by President García that would effectively open up indigenous territories to foreign investment and extractive projects. In the face of intense opposition, the President infamously claimed that Peru's indigenous peoples were like "a dog in a manger," opposing a sure route to economic development and job creation for the majority. After several months of protests by native Peruvians and the declaration of a state of emergency, tension grew in the area known as the *Curva del Diablo*, where members of the Awajun and Wampis peoples were camping. On the day of a police operation to evict the protesters, a conflict ensued and over 30 people died. The government's immediate reaction was to declare a curfew and extend the state of emergency, but in the face of an international and national outcry, roundtable talks were established, leading to Latin America's first Prior Consultation Law, which was finally promulgated in 2011.

While the extraction of natural resources has been promoted and prioritized by national governments as a fast-track route to the economic development of the majority, its negative impact on minority groups, particularly indigenous people, has been a cause of concern with regard to the protection of their individual and collective rights. In this sense, Latin American governments face considerable pressure from the international human rights regime to protect the rights of indigenous peoples in the context of extractive industries, particularly the right to consultation and free prior and informed consent (López Bárcenas, 2013). At the same time, however, domestic mechanisms of emergency continue to facilitate the use of special powers to subvert due participation over natural resource extraction, with national development serving as a 21st century interpretation of the "exceptional threat," as the case of Bagua mentioned above demonstrates.

With evidence from Latin America, the aim of this study is to analyze this clear contradiction between compliance with an emerging *social contract* on the one hand and, on the other, deference to lucrative *business contracts*. The following pages will chart gains, setbacks and, indeed, missed opportunities for the protection of indigenous rights in the context of a renewed wave of extractivism in Latin America.

EXPANDING EXTRACTIVE INDUSTRIES

Latin America has had a centuries-old love affair with the extraction of natural resources. From 19th century Independence to the present day, prized materials have been sought after and fought over throughout the region. Indeed, Latin America is home to a whole wealth of natural resources (petrol, gas, oil, copper, silver, gold, zinc etc.), found in varying quantities from the North of Mexico all the way down to the Tierra del Fuego (Perreault, 2012). Recent years have seen an explosion of extractive industries in the region—particularly although not exclusively in the Andean countries—due to the discovery of new reserves and the global commodities boom, as of 2004 (United Nations Development Programme, 2013). The profile of natural resource extraction varies from country to country. For instance, in Bolivia and Brazil hydrocarbons are the primary extractive sector; in Ecuador, the focus is on oil; mining is the main extractive activity in Chile; and in Argentina, Colombia, Mexico, and Peru extractive activity revolves around both mining and oil (ECLAC, 2013).

It is important to note that both right- and left-wing governments in Latin America continue to base their national economic development on extractive industries (Acosta, 2011). However, the role of the State and global firms varies considerably. On one hand, right-leaning governments prioritize the participation of foreign companies in a classic extractivist model (Portillo, 2014). For example, in Colombia and Peru Foreign Direct Investment (FDI) in extractive industries has reached a high in recent years, and considerable areas of national territories have been concessioned off for mining activity.[3] For its part, Mexico famously opened up the State Petrol Company—PEMEX—to foreign investment following a controversial constitutional reform in 2013. On the other hand, left-leaning governments have emphasized state control of and participation in the extraction of natural resources, in what has become known as a new extractivist model (Portillo Riascos, 2014). As of 2000, a wave of processes to nationalize extractive industries made its way through the ALBA countries—Venezuela in 2001, Bolivia in 2006, Ecuador in 2010 and Argentina in 2012. It is important to note, however, that the readjustment of contracts (particularly with regard to higher tax burdens) and increased state participation in extractive industries have not been a hindrance to FDI in these countries (Altomonte and Sánchez, 2016).

The appeal of extracting minerals and other natural resources as a fast-track route to development is rather self-evident. For its part, the United Nations Development Programme notes several highly developed economies with significant revenues from extractive industries, including Norway, Canada and Australia.[4] It also notes that in resource-dependent countries, average scores on the Human Development Index (HDI) have risen over the past thirty years, from 0.47 in 1980, to 0.61 in 2011.[5] Monge (2015) notes positive development trends in mineral-rich Latin American countries, together with a reduction in poverty and inequality in the case of Ecuador, which has captured significant revenues and increased expenditure on social programs. Likewise, Ceppi (2006) observes a considerable increase in the Bolivian State's petrol rents between 2005 (US$ 673 million) and 2012 (US$ 4292 million), together with significant reductions in levels of both poverty and inequality during the same period as a result of social spending.[6]

Nevertheless, as Altomonte and Sánchez (2016) point out, the evidence to support the potential for extractive industries to promote sustainable growth and reduce poverty is, at best, inconclusive. Indeed, there is plenty of evidence pointing to what could be considered "perverse" effects of natural resource wealth. The notion of the "Resource Curse" said to affect natural resource-rich states comprises three pillars: the persistence of authoritarian regimes, a lack of economic development, and civil war (Ross, 2001). Despite its economic potential and isolated cases of poverty reduction, Latin America offers a regional variation on this general theme, given that extractivism occurs in a context of weakly consolidated democracies, has—generally speaking—not done much to reduce social equality, and has caused a wave of conflicts concerning decision-making regarding extractive industries (McNeish, 2010). For their part, Latin America's indigenous peoples—who make up roughly 10 percent of the total population—are particularly vulnerable to the negative social, cultural, and environmental effects of resource extraction, given the abundance of natural resources within their territories (CIDH, 2016).

The governments of resource-dependent states find themselves in a difficult situation: how to harness the potential of extractive industries to promote national development and—crucially—respect the rights of vulnerable groups, particularly indigenous peoples. As UNDP (2017) and CIDH (2016) note, the degree to which extractivism can follow a human-rights based path of sustainable development depends on the adherence of States to international obligations and standards, together with the strength of democratic institutions.

PROTECTING INDIGENOUS RIGHTS?

Although indigenous peoples have been involved in a struggle for cultural and territorial resistance for over 500 years, over the past decades they have systematically organized to achieve recognition of their status as peoples as well as protection for their territories and cultures (Cunningham Kain, 2014). After decades of mobilizing, indigenous movements have made their voices heard in important international (Brysk, 2000) and national fora, particularly in Latin America (Martínez Espinoza, 2015). As a result of this process, there has been an emerging *social contract* written into international and national law regarding indigenous peoples' collective rights. This is a crucial step forward in the path towards more inclusive models of the State and democracy in the region. More specifically, substantial progress has been made at the international level to protect indigenous peoples specifically from the negative impacts of natural resource exploitation on their lands by establishing their right to participation, particularly the right to consultation and the principle of free, prior and informed consent (FPIC), through the game-changing ILO Convention 169 (ILO C169) that was adopted in 1989.

The Convention emphasizes the importance of indigenous peoples' participation in decision-making processes (Rea Granados, 2015) and in its article 6 establishes the obligation of governmental authorities to carry out a consultation process every time they take legislative or administrative measures that could affect indigenous peoples' rights. This right to consultation is given special emphasis in relation to the use of natural resources (Article 15). ILO C169 has now been ratified by 22 countries, 15 of which are in Latin America, making it a legally-binding international norm in most of the region. For its part, and although it is non-binding, the United Nations Declaration on the Rights of Indigenous Peoples (UNDRIP) adopted in 2007 strengthens collective rights to self-governance, ownership and control of lands, territories and natural resources, as well as indigenous participation in decision-making. In its Article 19 it reiterates States' obligations to carry out consultations and, most importantly, it expands the principle of FPIC, particularly in relation to projects that could affect indigenous territories or resources (Article 32). While consultation requires participation, consent is a more powerful principle as it refers to informed agreement (Sieder, 2012). For its part, the Inter-American Court of Human Rights (IACHR)—in the face of intense mobilization of indigenous peoples and their allies—has handed down sentences to various Latin American governments relating to indigenous rights in extractive contexts. Key sentences that further interpretations of consultation and consent in these contexts are *Awas Tingni vs. Nicaragua* (2001); *Saramaka vs. Surinam* (2007); *Sarayaku vs. Ecuador* (2012); and *Garífuna Punta Piedra y sus Miembros vs. Honduras* (2015).

Thanks to national ratifications of ILO C169, the sentences of the IACHR, and the continuing mobilization of indigenous organizations throughout the region, consultation and consent have become key items on national agendas. Indeed, as of 1990 there has been a wave of constitutional reforms throughout the region acknowledging indigenous peoples as subjects of rights, including the key right to self-determination. Some of the most significant reforms relate to consultation rights, although very few States have passed secondary norms to regulate their commitments in ratifying ILO C169 (Sieder, 2012). In this sense, Peru's Law of Prior Consultation of 2011 has become a key reference point in the region and to date Panama (2016) is the only other Latin American State to have issued a national consultation law.

While Latin American legislators have been relatively slow to act, the judiciary of several countries has taken a more proactive stance regarding indigenous consultation and consent in the context of extractive industries. In the case of Colombia, the Constitutional Court has assumed a crucial role, dictating over 100 sentences on prior consultation, which have established a series of parameters and standards that have become a reference point throughout Latin America (PNUD/FIIAPP, 2016). For their part, the Guatemalan courts have produced considerable jurisprudence on mining and consultation rights (Sieder, 2012) and likewise in Mexico, with several emblematic cases reaching the courts in recent years (CNDH, 2016). As well as reflecting the judiciary's protective stance on indigenous people and consultation rights, resorting to the courts reflects a strategy of litigation on the part of indigenous organizations, with international standards offering considerable leverage at the national level.

In terms of consultation in practice, Colombia is a truly exceptional case, with thousands of processes carried out in different sectors, mainly hydrocarbons. For its part, as of June 2016 Peru had carried out 24 processes in relation to extractive industries. In Bolivia, a series of consultations regarding the hydro-carbon sector have been implemented (Schilling-Vacaflor, 2012). In Panama, several consultations have taken place regarding hydroelectric projects and in Honduras a consultation process was organized over petrol exploitation in the Misquito territory (PNUD/FIIAPP, 2016). As for Mexico, several consultation processes have been carried out over extractive projects, including gas ducts, wind farms, the use of water, and hydro-electric dams (CNDH, 2016).

Despite these breakthroughs, consultation and consent are generally underachievers at local level, reflecting the implementation gap identified by scholars in relation to indigenous rights in practice. Part of the explanation is technical: although both international and domestic laws have established a series of criteria, there is no specific format or formula for consultation processes in practice (PNUD/FIIAPP, 2016). Another part of the explanation is strategic: States continue to prioritize their *business contracts* over their emerging *social contract* with (and responsibility to protect) indigenous peoples (McGee, 2009). Often, pseudo-consultations are carried out, bearing little or no resemblance to the criteria of international or national laws (CNDH, 2016; PNUD/FIIAPP, 2016; Stavenhagen, 2014) and in several Latin American countries consultation is systematically avoided (Stavenhagen, 2014). Finally, it is not clear how consultation processes relate to the incidence of conflict over natural resources: rather than unlocking the potential of extractive industries for sustainable development, consultation and consent have been both highly contested by indigenous organizations and employed as a means to gain leverage for their human rights claims.

CONTRACTING INDIGENOUS RIGHTS?

At this stage, it has become clear that there is a trade-off between national governments' *social contracts* with indigenous peoples—expressed in respect for consultation and consent—and their interests in guaranteeing their lucrative *business contracts* for natural resource extraction. As we have already seen, despite legal victories, there are many ways in which governments can reduce the participation of indigenous organizations in decision-making processes—by reducing consultation to a mere formality or avoiding it all together. However, on occasions governments have resorted directly to practices more akin to authoritarian regimes in order to guarantee investments and protect extractive industries (Acosta, 2011). In line with Ross' revision of the resource curse (2015), rather than a rentier effect (by which autocrats buy off potential opponents thanks to resource wealth), this phenomenon ties in with the possibility of governments aiming to block democratic opposition by the use of force, although—rather than authoritarian regimes—these are fledgling democracies with authoritarian pasts. This was certainly the case with the violent reaction of the Bolivian police in the conflict of TIPNIS or with the application of anti-terror laws against the Mapuche People of Chile. Furthermore, in recent years, Latin American executives have resorted directly to emergency powers to limit participation in decisions regarding natural resources, declaring lucrative projects to be a matter of national interest and, even, security.[7]

Emergency powers are an old concern of political theorists and have been revised and debated by influential thinkers over the centuries.[8] Whilst emergency powers are by no means a stranger to democratic regimes, they are implicitly linked to authoritarian forms of government, due to changes in procedure and temporary removal of checks and balances in the name of "the exception." Recognizing the prevalence of states of emergency throughout the world, in the 1980s the United Nations established a special rapporteur on the question of states of emergency to monitor their use and establish a series of minimum standards, including the key principles of proportionality and temporality (Despouy, 1999). In the post 9/11 context, however, international concern and vigilance over states of emergency has been set aside; as of 2005 the UN no longer produces annual reports and the special rapporteur no longer exists (Wright, 2015). The veil of the exception and securitization dominates political life in the context of the War on Terror, the aftermath of the Arab Spring, and the Israel–Palestine conflict, to the extent that significant items of public interest are depoliticized and removed from public discretion, with the justification of the "exceptional" circumstances that all-to-easily become permanent (Taureck, 2006).

In the case of Latin America, the historical use of emergency powers in contexts of social conflict and political crisis is one of the clearest manifestations of the weakness of the State and the concentration of power in the executive. During the 20th century there was a clear link between military regimes, the national security doctrine and the application of emergency measures as a means of government (Loveman, 1994). For Brian Loveman and Thomas M. Davies (1997), the major legacy of these military regimes are precisely the emergency provisions established in the constitutions that survived the transitions to democracy that began at the end of the 1970s. Until the present day, regimes are far from consolidated in the region and there is a clear tendency for presidents to resort to old tools to concentrate power in the executive, including emergency powers (Wright, 2015). According to the literature, the most prominent models of emergency power in Latin America are: on the one hand, decree powers (what I call *proactive exceptionalism*); and on the other, the suspension of civil liberties and deployment of the Armed Forces (what I call *reactive exceptionalism*). The two powers may be included as separate figures in national constitutions, or indeed combined within the framework of a "regime of exception" (state of emergency, state of exception etc.).

Although the role of emergency law-making powers in the governance of natural resources has not been studied systematically, scholars have duly noted their use in specific cases[9] as well as the link between extractivism and the persistence of authoritarian practices in the region (Acosta, 2011). The two case studies below demonstrate how both *proactive* and *reactive* emergency powers undermine indigenous consultation rights in both *new* and *classic extractivist* models.

Venezuela: Arco Minero Orinoco (2016)[10]

In the context of an inflation crisis caused by falling petrol prices, in January 2016 President Maduro issued decree number 2184 by which an economic state of emergency was declared for a period of 60 days. Venezuela's Constitution of 1999 includes different types of regimes of exception to be declared by the executive in circumstances of a social, economic, political, or ecological nature that seriously affect the security of the nation, institutions or citizens. Any extension of the state of emergency depends on the approval of the National Assembly and within eight days of the declaration of the state of exception the decree is to be sent to the Supreme Court of Justice to decide on its constitutionality.

One of the most controversial measures taken in the framework of the economic state of emergency of January 2016 was the "Decree to Create the Orinoco Mining Arc as a Strategic Area of Development" (Decree 2248), issued on 24 February the same year. The Mining Arc is a polygon in the basin of the Orinoco river which contains deposits of natural resources including iron, bauxite, gold and coltan. The area is particularly large, making up 12 percent of Venezuela's total territory. Decree 2248 refers to the use of natural resources as "a key opportunity to contribute to the economic, productive and social development of the Nation." Reference is also made to the importance of moving from rent-seeking from petrol to more sustainable models of development, including—rather surprisingly—mining. The decree establishes several important aspects of the extractive project that need to be defined as soon as possible, including the geographical limits of the Arc, a plan of action for mining operations, tax incentives for mining firms, and the role of the Armed Forces.

The measure provoked a wave of criticism and protests by different sectors of civil society, due to the environmental impact of mining operations, the agreements signed with foreign companies behind closed doors, and—above all—the lack of prior consultation of indigenous peoples whose territories are found within the proposed arc. A legal action to declare the nullity of the decree was studied by the relevant court,[11] however it came to no avail and operations in the area began as of August. In May 2016, President Maduro extended the economic state of emergency, including an executive resolution which established that 60 percent of the income from the resources extracted from the Orinoco Mining Arc should be spent on social projects. The measure reflects a *new extractivist* approach to mining which, nevertheless, was taken unilaterally.

The case of the Orinoco Mining Arc offers a clear example of how the emergency prism is used in a *proactive way* to prioritize *business contracts* over the *social contract* with indigenous peoples clearly affected by the project. With no prior consultation or environmental impact assessment, and no response from the National Assembly or Judiciary, the executive assumed special powers for itself and the military in an area that is of great economic interest to the Venezuelan state. Nevertheless, in the face of considerable social opposition, the case was brought before the Inter-American Human Rights Commission in December 2016. The final outcome of the hearing is as of yet unclear, but the fact that the government has acknowledged the lack of an environmental impact assessment as well as its omission of prior consultation holds a degree of symbolic importance for those affected.

Peru: Las Bambas (2015)[12]

Las Bambas, located in the Department of Apurímac and developed by the Chinese firm MMG, is the biggest mining operation in Peru, with an estimated investment of 10 billion dollars. There has been considerable opposition to the project among indigenous organizations in the area since it began in 2014, particularly due to the modification of an environmental impact study in 2015 without the necessary consultation of local people. Furthermore, there have been concerns over the possibility of pollution in the Challhuahuacho River due to the company's decision not to build an underground duct to transport extracted materials. In this context, indigenous organizations carried out a significant protest, which led to clashes between police and protesters on 28 September 2015. Three people died and over 20 were wounded as a result.

After this incident, and with pressure from MMG to protect investments in the area, a state of emergency was declared in several provinces in Apurímac and Cusco for a period of 30 days via Supreme Decree 068-2015 PCM. Article 137 of Peru's Constitution of 1993 establishes the figure of a state of emergency, which is to be declared by the President with the agreement of the Council of Ministers for a period of no longer than 60 days, although this can be extended via decree without seeking the approval of the Congress or Constitutional Court. The state of emergency facilitates the suspension of several civil rights (personal liberty and security, the inviolability of the home and freedom of reunion and movement). Likewise, the President has the power to hand over control of internal order to the Armed Forces.

Supreme Decree 068-2015-PCM offers a vague justification for the declaration: "considering . . . that there are acts against internal order that affect normal activities in the aforementioned provinces, it is necessary to adopt the measures included in the constitution to restore internal order and defend citizen's rights . . .." During the state of emergency, the rights established in Article 137 of the constitution were suspended, the Armed Forces were deployed, a curfew was imposed to stop local people moving between towns and villages, and police were sent to the area to protect the mine. A month after the state of emergency was declared, the measures were lifted and a series of discussions between local leaders and authorities took place. In April 2016, round table talks were established to discuss the violation of human rights during the state of emergency, with the conclusion that the widows of the men who died would receive a small pension on humanitarian grounds. The representatives of indigenous organizations fiercely criticized the amount of the compensation and the conflict over the project continues to this day, with the latest state of emergency being declared in August 2017.

The case of Las Bambas is an example of the use of the emergency prism in a *reactive* way to put a halt to protests created by a disregard for the *social contract* of consultation rights. Particularly interesting in this case is the pressure from the *business contract*, given that the declaration of the state of emergency was due in a large part to pressure from the mining company. Furthermore, the military and police were deployed in order to protect the mining operations, rather than citizens. Again, the lack of action on the part of the legislative and the judiciary left the executive plenty of room to maneuver. Only the resistance and persistence on the part of local communities provided the necessary pressure for the measure to be lifted, although calm in the region would prove to be short-lived.

FINAL REMARKS

The purpose of this chapter has been to chart the clear contradiction between an emerging *social contract* surrounding indigenous consultation rights and the continuing protection of lucrative *business contracts* with extractive industries. Although significant progress has been made at the legal level to protect indigenous *minorities* in the face of incursions that could seriously affect their cultural, political and environmental rights, in practice the balance is still tipped towards guaranteeing the exploitation of natural resources, which is presented as a fast-track route to development for the benefit of the *majority*. In this process, not only have consultation rights been misinterpreted and circumvented, but old authoritarian practices—including emergency powers—have been invoked with both symbolic and physical violence to guarantee extractive operations. The cases described here show how Latin American executives, on very different ends of the ideological spectrum, have called upon the Armed Forces to securitize operations and guarantee investments both *proactively* and *reactively*, with no counterweight role for the courts or legislature. The study sheds light on a clear duality of encouraging, democratic breakthroughs on the one hand and disheartening, authoritarian setbacks on the other. This duality lies at the heart of present-day political regimes in the region and is resulting in missed opportunities for the protection of Latin America's indigenous peoples.

Going forward, the role of international and national courts together with the organization of indigenous peoples and their sympathizers, will be key in shifting the balance from deference to *business contracts* to respect for the *social contract*. The gains achieved in terms of rights to consultation and consent at the international level should be matched with a diagnosis of the different routes offered by national legal frameworks to subvert due participation in practice. Given their devastating effect of securitizing natural resource extraction, emergency powers—an old foe of democracy in the region—might be a sensible place to start.

NOTES

1. See www.rezpectourwater.com and www.standingwithstandingrock.net.
2. http://www.iwgia.org/regions/latin-america/indigenous-peoples-in-latin-america.
3. Information from Parques Nacionales Naturales de Colombia website: http://goo.gl/yaf8f4; Grupo Propuesta Ciudadana, *Concesiones Mineras en el Perú Análisis y Propuestas de Política* (Lima, Grupo Propuesta Ciudadana, September 2014), available from: http://goo.gl/Mufdaa and Sociedad Nacional de Minería, Petróleo y Energía, *Hidrocarburos en Cifras* (Lima, SNMPE, January 2013), available from: http://goo.gl/cgCFtm.
4. http://www.undp.org/content/undp/en/home/presscenter/speeches/2015/09/27/helen-clark-speech-at-the-event-extractive-industries-and-the-sustainable-development-goals-enhancing-collaboration-for-sustainability-.html.
5. UNDP "Extractive Industries for Sustainable Development," Policy Briefing.
6. Between 2005 and 2011, poverty levels fell from 60.6% to 45% and inequality from 0.6 to 0.46 on the GINI Index (Ceppi, 2016).
7. Examples include (but are not limited to): Executive Decrees 001-2011 y 002-2011 in Peru; Executive Decree 1979 in Colombia; Executive Decree 2248 in Venezuela; Executive Decree 349/2016 in Argentina; Executive Decree 1-2012 in Guatemala; Executive Decree 068-2015-PCM in Peru; and Executive Decree DS-040-2015-PCM in Peru.
8. Niccolo Machiavelli (2000), Jean-Jacques Rousseau (1999), Benjamin Constant (1988), Carl Schmitt (2013), Clinton Rossiter (2002) and Karl Friedrich (1950).
9. See for instance Assies, 2003; García Gallegos, 2008, Le Calvez, 2008; Narváez Q, 2009; Rousseau, 2008; Wright, 2013.
10. See Agencia EFE, 2016; Alonso, 2016; Maduro, 2016; Servindi, 2016c.
11. Juzgado de Sustanciación de la Sala Político Administrativa.
12. See "Conflicto," 2015; "Declaran," 2015a; "Declaran," 2015b; Fowks, 2015; Pérez, 2015; Servindi 2016a; Servindi 2016b.

REFERENCES

Acosta, A. *Extractivismo y neoextractivismo: dos caras de la misma maldición. Más allá del desarrollo* (1a Ed.), (2011). Grupo permanente de trabajo sobre alternativas al desarrollo, Fundación Rosa Luxemburg, Abya Yala, Quito, pp. 83–118.

Agencia EFE. "Declaran 'constitucional' estado de excepción en Venezuela." *El Universal*, 2016. Published electronically May 19 http://www.eluniversal.com.mx/articulo/mundo/2016/05/19/declaran-constitucional-estado-de-excepcion-en-venezuela.

Alonso, Juan Francisco. "TSJ estudiará la decisión presidencial de permitir explotar el Arco Minero." *El Universal*, 2016. Published electronically June 22 http://www.eluniversal.com/noticias/politica/tsj-estudiara-decision-presidencial-permitir-explotar-arco-minero_315989.

Altomonte, H. and Sánchez, R.J. *Hacia una nueva gobernanza de recursos naturales en América Latina y el Caribe.* Santiago de Chile, CEPAl, 2016.

Assies, W. "David Versus Goliath in Cochabamba: Water Rights, Neoliberalism, and the Revival of Social Protest in Bolivia." *Latin American Perspectives* 30, no. 3 (May 1, 2003): 14–36. doi:10.1177/0094582x03030003003.

Brysk, A. *From Tribal Village to Global Village: Indian Rights and International Relations in Latin America.* Stanford (CA): Stanford University Press, 2000.

Ceppi, N. "Los hidrocarburos en el gobierno de Evo Morales: Extractivismo nacionalista con presencia extranjera." *Civilizar* 16.30 (2016), 175–190.

Comisión Interamericana de Derechos Humanos (CIDH). Informe "Pueblos indígenas, comunidades afrodescendientes y recursos naturales. Protección de derechos humanos en el contexto de actividades de extracción, explotación y desarrollo," 2016. http://www.oas.org/es/cidh/prensa/comunicados/2016/048.asp.

Comisión Nacional de Derechos Humanos (CNDH). RECOMENDACIÓN General No. 27/2016 sobre el derecho a la consulta previa de los pueblos y comunidades indígenas de la República Mexicana, 2016.

Constant, B. *Constant: Political Writings.* Cambridge, United Kingdom: Cambridge University Press, 1988.

Cunningham Kain, M. "La participación política de los pueblos indígenas. Escenarios, estrategias, modalidades y resultados." In *Los derechos indígenas tras la Declaración: El desafío de la implementación,* edited by Felipe Gómez Isa and Mikel Berraondo, 247–86. Bilbao: Universidad de Deusto, 2013.

"Conflicto en Las Bambas: gobierno levanta estado de emergencia." *La República*, 2015. Published electronically Oct 29 http://larepublica.pe/politica/714188-conflicto-en-las-bambas-gobierno-levanta-estado-de-emergencia.

"Declaran estado de emergencia en Apurímac por proyecto Las Bambas." *La República*, 2015a. Published electronically Sep 29 http://larepublica.pe/politica/706815-declaran-estado-de-emergencia-en-apurimac-por-proyecto-las-bambas.

"Declaran estado de emergencia por violencia en Las Bambas." *El Comercio*, 2015b. Published electronically Sep 29 http://elcomercio.pe/peru/apurimac/declaran-emergencia-violencia-bambas-222236.

Despouy, L. *Los derechos humanos y los estados de excepción.* Ciudad de México: Universidad Nacional Autónoma de México, 1999.

ECLAC. *Natural Resources: Status and Trends Towards a Regional Development Agenda in Latin America and the Caribbean. Contribution of the Economic*

Commission for Latin America and the Caribbean to the Community of Latin American and Caribbean States. Santiago de Chile: ECLAC, 2013.
Fowks, J. "Perú decreta el estado de emergencia por un conflicto minero." *El País*, 2015. Published electronically Sep 29 http://internacional.elpais.com/internacional/2015/09/29/actualidad/1443490267_288762.html.
Friedrich, C. *Constitutional Government and Democracy*. Boston: Ginn and Company, 1950.
García Gallegos, B. "Nuevas tendencias en la seguridad energética de América del Sur" In *La guerra del fuego: políticas petroleras y crisis energéticas en América Latina*, edited by Guillaume Fontaine and Alicia Puyana, 219–40. Quito: Flacso-Ecuador/Ministerio de Cultura, 2008.
Le Calvez, M. "El rediseño de los sistemas de gobernanza petrolera en el Ecuador y Venezuela" In *La guerra del fuego: políticas petroleras y crisis energéticas en América Latina*, edited by Guillaume Fontaine and Alicia Puyana, 219–40. Quito: Flacso-Ecuador/Ministerio de Cultura, 2008.
López Bárcenas, F. *El Derecho de los Pueblos Indígenas de México a la consulta*. Oaxaca: Servicios para una Educación Alternativa A.C., 2013.
Loveman, B. (1994) *The constitution of tyranny: Regimes of exception in Spanish America*. Pittsburgh: University of Pittsburgh Press.
Loveman, B. and Davies, T.M., eds. *The Politics of Antipolitics: The Military in Latin America*. Lincoln: Scholarly Resources Inc.,U.S., 1997.
Machiavelli, N. *Discursos Sobre la Primera Década de Tito Livio*. Madrid: Alianza, 2000.
Maduro, N. "Ganancias del Arco Minero del Orinoco se destinarán al Fondo de las Misiones y Grandes Misiones," 2016. Published electronically Aug 5 http://www.nicolasmaduro.org.ve/presidente/ganancias-arco-minero-orinoco-se-destinaran-fondo-misiones-grandes-misiones/#.V9HpMFdzORs.
Martínez Espinoza, M.I. "Reconocimiento sin implementación, Un balance sobre los derechos de los pueblos indígenas en América Latina." *Revista Mexicana de Ciencias Políticas y Sociales*, LX, 224 (2015), 251–78.
McGee, B. "The Community Referendum: Participatory Democracy and the Right to Free, Prior and Informed Consent to Development." *Berkeley Journal of International Law*, 27 (2009), 570.
McNeish, J.A. *Rethinking Resource Conflict*. n.p.: World Development Report Background Paper, 2010. https://www.cmi.no/publications/file/3852-rethinking-resource-conflict.pdf.
Monge, C. "La herencia del super ciclo. Una perspectiva regional." Ponencia presentada en el XI Foro Latinoamericano sobre Industrias Extractivas. El súper ciclo en América Latina: efectos y desafíos tras la caída del precio de los hidrocarburos y los minerales. Quito: Ecuador, 2015.
Narváez Q, I. *Petróleo Y Poder: El Colapso de Un Lugar Singular: Yasuní*. Quito, Ecuador: FLACSO Sede Ecuador, 2009.
Pérez Guadalupe, J.L. "Conflicto en Las Bambas: gobierno levanta estado de emergencia." *La República*, 2015. Published electronically Oct 29 http://larepublica.pe/politica/714188-conflicto-en-las-bambas-gobierno-levanta-estado-de-emergencia.
Perreault, T. "Extracting Justice: Natural Gas, Indigenous Mobilization, and the Bolivian State." In *The Politics of Resource Extraction*, edited by Suzana Sawyer and Edmund Terence Gomez, 75–102. UK: Palgrave MacMillan, 2012.
Portillo Riascos, L.H. Extractivismo clásico y neoextractivismo, ¿dos tipos de extractivismo diferentes? Primera parte. (2014) *Tendencias* (XV: 2), 11–29.

PNUD/FIIAPP. Diálogo y consulta previa. Los pueblos indígenas y la extracción de los recursos naturales. Informe Final. (2016). Retrieved from http://www.aecidcf.org.co/Ponencias/2016/junio/MI160616-1/Prod.3.InformeCartagena.pdf.

Martí i Puig, S., Wright, C., Aylwin, J. and Yáñez, N, eds. *Entre el desarrollo y el buen vivir. Recursos naturales y conflictos en los territorios indígenas.* Madrid: La Catarata, 2013.

Rea Granados, S.A. "Derecho a la consulta y la participación de los pueblos indígenas. La experiencia constitucional en los casos de México y Chile." *Boletín Mexicano de Derecho Comparado* nueva serie, XLVIII: 144 (2015), 1083–117.

Ross, M. L. "Does Oil Hinder Democracy?" *World Politics* 53, no. 03 (April 2001): 325–61. doi:10.1353/wp.2001.0011.

Ross, M.L. "What have we learned about the resource curse?" *Annual Review of Political Science* 18, (2015) 239–59.

Rossiter, C.L. and W.J Quirk. *Constitutional Dictatorship: Crisis Government in the Modern Democracies*. 2nd ed. New Brunswick, NJ: Transaction Publishers, 2002.

Rousseau, I. "La reorganización de Petróleos Mexicanos. Visiones encontradas sobre la gobernanza de una empresa pública." In *La guerra del fuego: políticas petroleras y crisis energéticas en América Latina.*, edited by Guillaume Fontaine and Alicia Puyana, 219–40. Quito: Flacso-Ecuador/Ministerio de Cultura, 2008.

Rousseau, J.J. *El Contrato Social*. 14th ed. Madrid: EDAF Antillas, 1999.

Schilling-Vacaflor, A., "Democratizing Resource Governance through Prior Consultations? Lessons from Bolivia's Hydrocarbon Sector." *GIGA Working Paper*, No. 184. Hamburg: GIGA, 2012.

Schmitt, C. *Dictatorship: From the Origin of the Modern Concept of Sovereignty to Proletarian Class Struggle*. Cambridge: Polity Press, 2013.

Servindi. "Sangre y cobre en Las Bambas," 2016a. Published electronically May 9 https://www.servindi.org/actualidad-informe-especial/08/05/2016/sangre-y-cobre-en-las-bambas.

Servindi. "Las Bambas: un conflicto latente en el sur andino," 2016b. Published electronically Aug 23 https://www.servindi.org/actualidad-noticias/23/08/2016/las-bambas-un-conflicto-latente-en-el-sur-andino.

Servindi. "Estado admite que Arco Minero no tiene estudio de impacto ambiental," 2016c. Published electronically Dec 8 https://www.servindi.org/actualidad-noticias/07/12/2016/venezuela-reconoce-en-cidh-que-no-ha-realizado-estudio-de-impacto.

Sieder, R. "Pueblos Indígenas y Derecho(s) en América Latina," In *El derecho en América Latina: un mapa para el pensamiento jurídico para el siglo XXI.*, edited by en César Rodríguez Garavito, 303–21. Buenos Aires: Siglo XXI, 2012.

Stavenhagen, R. "Pueblos Indígenas: retos después de la batalla." In *Los derechos indígenas tras la Declaración: El desafío de la implementación.*, edited by Felipe Gómez Isa and Mikel Berraondo, 15–38. Bilbao: Universidad de Deusto, 2013.

Taureck, R. "Securitization Theory and Securitization Studies." *Journal of International Relations and Development* 9, no. 1 (March 2006): 53–61. doi:10.1057/palgrave.jird.1800072.

United Nations Development Programme. "Extractive Industries for Sustainable Development. A Global Initiative, 2013–2017." 2017. Accessed January 16, 2017. http://www.undp.org/content/undp/en/home/librarypage/poverty-reduction.html?topic=focus%20areas%3Asustainable-development.

Wright, C. "Perú. El Estado de Emergencia Como Mecanismo de Represión de la Protesta Indígena En El Contexto de Conflictos Sobre Recursos Naturales." In

Entre el desarrollo y el buen vivir. Recursos naturales y conflictos en los territorios indígenas., edited by Salvador Martí i Puig, Claire Wright, José Aylwin, and Nancy Yáñez, 265–92. Madrid: La Catarata, 2013.

Wright, C. *Emergency Politics in the Third Wave of Democracy: A Study of Regimes of Exception in Bolivia, Ecuador, and Peru.* Lanham (MA): Lexington Books, 2015.

5. The bottom two billion: the global expansion of urban slums and second-class citizenship

Natasha Bennett

INTRODUCTION

In 2007 Paul Collier wrote of a "bottom billion" people caught in state-centric poverty traps. By 2030, there will be two billion people caught in localized, individual poverty traps created by the political and socio-economic conditions in urban slums (UN Habitat 2010). This global expansion of urban slums presents a critical challenge for human rights. Slums are highly populated informal settlements or shantytowns, generally on the outskirts of metropolitan areas, and are characterized by sub-standard housing and infrastructure.[1] As informal spaces, they have weak human rights accountability and are especially susceptible to state-based violations of human rights. Often, slum dwellers' personal integrity rights and rights to an adequate standard of living, such as the right to housing, are not protected or are actively violated.

Slums are "areas of limited statehood" (Risse-Kappen 2011), that lack an institutionalized rule of law; the state is often absent, and governance often relies on non-state actors or self-regulation. Urban slum dwellers live at the margins of political life, not fully incorporated into the city or the institutional arrangements that protect and fulfill human rights. Since cities are critical for the way that individuals access the state, and in turn human rights through state institutions, the absence of urban governance leads urban slum dwellers to fall through a "citizenship gap" (Brysk and Shafir 2004). The citizenship gap describes the gap between an individual's legal standing and his or her degree of access to human rights protection and fulfillment. Without access to state institutions and legal mechanisms, urban slum dwellers fall through this citizenship gap, despite often being citizens of states that comply with international human rights laws and norms.

This chapter argues that the global expansion of slums exacerbates two mutually reinforcing problems in the provision of human rights: fulfillment and accountability. State-centric mechanisms for human rights fulfillment often do not deliver at subnational levels of governance, particularly in economically weaker states (see Hertel and Minkler 2007). Furthermore, states may be unwilling or unable to require subnational governments to absorb responsibility for slums outside city limits. Additionally, slum dwellers tend to be stigmatized, or otherwise viewed as undesirable sectors of the population, and municipal elites rarely have incentives to formally incorporate them. In addition to this top-down problem of fulfillment, urban slum dwellers lack the ability to hold the state accountable. Slum residents on the whole are politically, socially, and economically excluded, often without resources for mobilization or access to formal claims-making mechanisms, such as the courts. Without a solution to the problems of fulfillment and accountability, the world faces a future in which two or three billion urban poor find themselves locked out of the human rights regime. This chapter discusses the extent of global slum formation, the nature of the relationship between human rights fulfillment and accountability, and then how this framework applies to one example: the human right to housing in India and Brazil.

GLOBAL SLUM FORMATION

The United Nations Population Fund estimates that as of 2012 approximately 863 million people live in urban slums around the world, which is about one quarter of the world's urban population. For urban populations in developing countries, roughly one-third of urbanites live in slums. In sub-Saharan Africa, the proportion is closer to three-fifths, at 62% (UN Habitat 2010). By 2030, the number of people living in slums is expected to grow to approximately 2 billion, mostly in low and middle-income counties. Some estimates say that number should grow to 3 billion by 2050 (UN Habitat 2010).

The projected increase of slum dwellers is a function of the increase in the rate of urbanization and the increase in global inequality and poverty. The rapid rate of urbanization, particularly in developing economies, transforms the global demographic landscape. For the first time in history, the majority of the world population (51%) lives in cities (UNFPA "Urbanization"). This proportion of urban dwellers worldwide is only expected to grow. UN Habitat estimates that by 2050, 66% of the world's population will live in cities, and approximately 90% of urban growth will occur in regions with economic constraints. The urban population in the world's poorest regions, South Asia and sub-Saharan Africa, is expected to double, placing considerable urban pressures and demands on cities in those regions, which often have not planned for a massive influx of internal migrants. As rapid economic development and subsequent urbanization continues, the increasing number of slum dwellers suggests that many countries, particularly in parts of Asia and sub-Saharan Africa, are unable to keep up with the pressures of urban population growth. In China, India, Pakistan, Bangladesh, the Philippines, and Vietnam, for example, the rapid rate of urbanization poses greater challenges; faster rates of urbanization make it more difficult to accommodate demands for social services and create urban plans (Ooi and Phua 2007). However, one study finds that the connection between economic growth and slum formation varies worldwide. Between 1990 and 2007, they find that some countries such as Mexico, Egypt and Indonesia experienced a decline in percentage of slum dwellers, whereas in others—Pakistan and Nigeria—the growth of urban slum dwellers accounts for most of the urban growth (Marx et al 2013).

THE GOVERNANCE AND FULFILLMENT PROBLEM

Rapid urbanization and uneven development present a series of governance challenges that can limit a state's ability and/ or desire to fulfill social and economic rights in urban slums. Human rights fulfillment, and social and economic rights fulfillment in particular, relies on effective governance and service delivery. The expansion of slums represents a series of governance failures at global, national, and local levels (UN Habitat 2010) that interact and create spaces of limited statehood and gaps for human rights. Together, the institutional arrangements present at global, national, and local levels create a set of incentive structures that leave slums at the edge of the state, in turn creating a human rights fulfillment gap.

Economic globalization at the global level drives increased urbanization and incentivizes state retrenchment. The international political economy encourages developing countries to liberalize their economies and reduce or eliminate protective subsidies and tariffs, driving agricultural workers to the cities in search of more sustainable employment. Additionally, as cities grow larger and economically stronger, they attract poor people and families from rural areas with the allure of greater economic opportunities. Information technology in places such as India, for example, has led to creation of urban information centers where knowledge is easily concentrated and exchanged (Glaeser 2009). Globalization also promotes retrenchment—or the reduction in welfare expenditures in order to be more competitive in international markets (Hay 2005). Nita Rudra's "race to the bottom" study argues that because countries consistently compete with one another to attract business, countries benefit from lifting business regulations and restrictions on trade. She argues that this kind of competition makes it difficult for developing countries to raise revenues, therefore it systematically affects the world's poor populations (Rudra 2008). Additionally, developing economies are encouraged to privatize state-owned industries and social services, further limiting the state's role in providing fulfilling human rights.

At the national level, urban slum formation can reflect policy failure where states do not consider the effect that their macroeconomic policies have on cities and their ability to fulfill human rights. It is the case, particularly in very poor countries, that growth-oriented macroeconomic policies can be necessary in order to protect and fulfill economic and social rights (Dicklitch and Howard-Hassmann 2007). However, the type of institutions and politics largely determines how developing economies spend and govern domestically—whether they give populations voice and implement welfare public policies. National governments may be persuaded by the neo-classical wisdom of "modernization" theories that prescribe economic growth as the central solution to all economic problems, including widespread poverty and economic inequality.

Governance failures at the local level largely include the lack of urban planning and the inability or lack of political will to meet the housing, infrastructure, and security needs of the populace, as well as the inability to secure property rights, perpetuating illegality and poor environmental conditions. At the local level, slums are geographically excluded from political decision-making bodies and processes as well as from formal economic activity and governance, all of which stop at municipal boundaries. Typically situated just outside of cities, they expand outward onto unincorporated lands. As such, public services—like waste collection, lighting, local police authority, transportation, and sanitation facilities—are rarely provided, taxes are not collected, and most of the infrastructure is of an informal, self-made, nature. Making matters worse, while they often benefit from the cheap labor force occupying the slums, municipal government officials rarely want to incorporate and govern informal land populated by sectors of the population they often consider to be undesirable. Furthermore, urban slum dwellers often lack property rights and legal residence. Without a physical, legal address, a slum dweller will face barriers to accessing hospitals, schools, or financial institutions (Khan et al 2009). Additionally, without ownership of property there is only a limited incentive for slum dwellers to improve upon their housing and neighborhood conditions because they fear that the slum will be demolished or that they will be evicted.

As marginalized physical spaces, slums fall outside the human rights

Figure 5.1 Governance gap

regime. While national governments have formalized processes for rural governance, the rapid growth of slums means that no such processes yet exist. As such they are dependent on city governments, which do not have the capacity or will to integrate them for rights protections. Even in democratic states that comply with international human rights at the state level, slums fall outside the formal legal protections. Figure 5.1 above illustrates this human rights fulfillment gap from a top-down approach, where slum governance is divorced from municipal governance. States bind cities to provide human rights in accordance with their international treaty obligations. But since slums exist outside of cities, the protections do not reach them.

This problem is especially visible in the realm of policing. Because they are formally ungoverned, slums must be policed, which becomes the state's responsibility, often one it is unwilling to accept. Policing activities are primarily limited to countering gang activity or carrying out forced evictions. These kinds of policing activities are bad policy in that they create greater human insecurity and constitute direct violations of human rights, such as the human right to housing. Forced evictions often lead to a significant loss of income because they uproot families from a place of informal employment. Evictions and relocations also break up social networks and ties that families may rely on for things like babysitting, or other forms of interpersonal assistance. Zimbabwe's "Operation Clean Up" in 2005 is a notable policy failure that involved uprooting 1.5 million members of Zimbabwe's urban poor. Government officials resorted to torching local infrastructure and bulldozing homes (Wines 2005). Human rights groups estimate that these actions left at least 200,000 people homeless, but that the actual figures could be several times that (Wines 2005). The UN Special Rapporteur on adequate housing at the time, Miloon Kothari, raised concerns about the effect of these policies on deaths from exposure and suicide. Although this approach is ineffective, forced eviction policies remain the norm in much of the developing world. For example, in Brazil, favela residents were evicted within days of the 2016 summer Olympics in Rio de Janiero. It is estimated that "beautification" projects for Olympic games in the past 20 years have displaced approximately 2 million people (Cohre and Ruig/Gian Joint Media Statement in Khan et al. 2009). The governance and fulfillment failures represent just one of the ways that urban slums exist in human rights limbo. The relative inability of those living in peri-urban residents to make effective claims and demand accountability present the second critical challenge.

SECOND CLASS CITIZENSHIP AND THE CLAIMS-MAKING PROBLEM

The informal nature of urban slums relegates residents to second-class citizenship through a lack of inclusion in state-based legal institutions. Holston and Appadurai (1996) point to the ways in which city life shapes national citizenship. In their understanding, "cities remain the strategic arena for the development of citizenship" (188) because cities provide the basis for social and political action. In this way, national citizenship is renegotiated at the city level, transforming the nature of substantive citizenship and the ways in which people access the state. Appadurai (2001) continues this line of argumentation in calling urban slum dwellers "citizens without cities." Other scholars have noted that neoliberal economic reforms are in large part responsible for the decentralization of citizenship (Postero 2006; Hale 2002). Goldstein (2012) also discusses the limits of national citizenship for those living in Bolivian urban slums. In his work, the term "phantom state" describes the perceptions of indigenous urban slums dwellers, because while they recognize their position as citizens, the state is absent in terms of services and infrastructure. In the case of Bolivia, Goldstein (2004) also recognizes the racialized component of urban exclusion that reinforces the borders between the city, where elites are in the positions of local power.

The ability of the urban poor to attenuate the citizenship gap is further constrained by their limited material resources. Resource mobilization

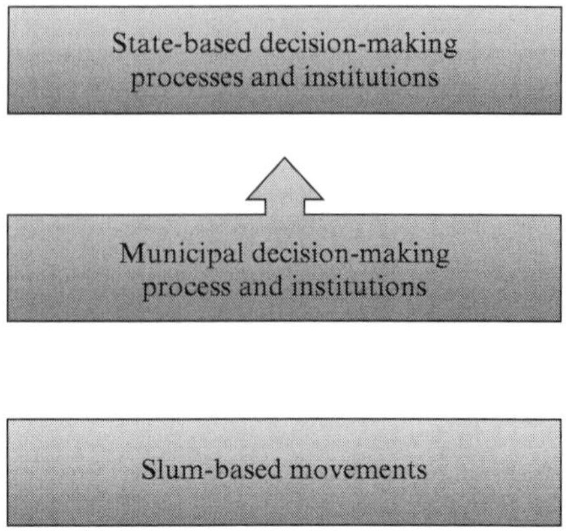

Figure 5.2 Globalization gap

theory (see McCarthy and Zald 1978) argues that without the material resources needed to organize and mobilize people, social movements are unlikely to sustain themselves. Urban slum residents are likely to have access to few of these resources without external aid. Indeed, Piven and Cloward (1973) show that poor people are often not able to dedicate the time or resources to sustain effective protests such as strikes or file legal claims; instead, they resort to disruptive tactics such as protest—as slum dwellers often do. Just as slums are vulnerable to falling out of the top-down human rights regime, mobilization efforts face barriers in tapping into the legal and political mechanisms theoretically available for bottom-up approaches for accountability for human rights at both local and national levels.

THE HUMAN RIGHT TO HOUSING IN INDIA AND BRAZIL

The human right to housing provides the most critical example of how the enjoyment of social and economic human rights for urban slum dwellers faces fulfillment and accountability problems. Municipal policies do not provide public goods to slums, and local social movements struggle to hold municipalities accountable. Both India and Brazil have ratified the International Covenant on Economic, Social and Cultural Rights (ICESCR), which commits states to implement and fulfill social and economic rights domestically. The right to housing in the ICESCR is almost identical to that in the UDHR: "the right of everyone to an adequate standard of living . . . clothing and housing, and to the continuous improvement of living condition" (ICESCR n.d.). According to the ICESCR committee, the human right to housing "should not be interpreted in a narrow sense which equates with it . . . Rather, it should be seen as the right to live somewhere in security, peace and dignity" (V. Annex 1, General Comment No. 4 on the right to adequate housing (Article 11, § 1), § 7, adopted December 13, 1991). In this way, the human right to housing mandates regular access to permanent dwelling, as housing serves as a basis for access to other social rights including medical services and education (Hoover 2016, Shue 1980).

Although the international community and many national governments recognize a human right to housing,[2] one of the central drivers of slum formation is the lack of affordable housing options that is in large part dictated by the market. Although subsidized government housing provides an alternative to informal settlements, national and municipal governments may not be want or be able to deliver in cases of housing crises in overcrowded cities. At the national level, the bulk of states that experience and will continue to experience slum expansion are developing/emerging economies that will prioritize growth without considering sustainable housing options. This occurs at local levels as well. Municipal governments may not prioritize sustainable growth and may have social or political incentives to discriminate against undesirable slum dwellers, and deliberately ignore their housing needs (Khan et al. 2009).

The slums of India and Brazil receive considerable international attention due to their size and density. Both of these countries are one of the five major emerging national economies in the world (BRICS), and as such have an increasing role in the global political economy. Despite similarities, there are key differences. Brazil is more urban than India, which in many ways is still largely rural with only about 33% of its population living in cities. Brazil has a longer history with the expansion of urban slums and subsequent urban policies (Saglio-Yatzimirksy and Landy 2014). Brazil's slums are more developed; the urban poor have higher living standards and better access to social services. However, higher levels of gang and police violence plague Brazil's slums. Although India's experience with urban slums is more recent, India's slums are almost twice as populous as Brazil's (Saglio-Yatzimirsky and Landy 2014). Table 5.1 overleaf briefly compares India and Brazil.

Through ratification of the ICESCR, both India and Brazil recognize a human right to housing, but face challenges fulfilling that right. They differ in their domestic commitment to the human right to housing as a standalone right. Brazil's constitution explicitly engages the human right to housing. In another chapter of the constitution, the state officially

Table 5.1 Urban slums in India and Brazil

	Poverty rate (headcount ratio)	Urban pop (% of total)	Urban rate	Right to housing laws	Slum policy efforts	Key movements
Brazil	5.5 (2011) 3.7 (2014)	86	1.2	ICESCR, Right to adequate housing recognized in constitution	Land regularization policies, slum upgrading, eviction policies, heavy policing	Popular contestation, Homeless Workers' Movement
India	21.2 (2011)	33	2.4	ICESCR, no national level adoption of human right to housing	2015— rehabilitation (Delhi); land regularization policy, police repression	Popular contestation, National Slum Dwellers Federation, SPARC, Indian Alliance

recognizes the role of municipalities when it comes to designing and implementing urban development policies (Gonçalves 2014). Despite Brazil's formal commitment, and adoption of the legal human rights framework for a human right to housing, recent eviction policies and slum conditions violate key components of the right. Favela eradication projects and evictions gained international media attention in the year leading up to the 2016 Olympic games in Rio. In order to construct the Olympic Park, the city began the demolition of Rio's favelas in 2009. One book on the subject estimates that more than 60,000 people lost their homes between 2009 and 2013 (Azevedo and Faulhaber 2015 in Phillips 2016).

Unlike in Brazil, India does not have clear public policies regarding housing at the national level. At best, the human right to housing can be found in Article 21 of the constitution, which guarantees protection of life and personal liberty, which leaves much room for juridical interpretation. Aside from this, there is no clear domestic adoption of the language of a human right to housing. However, there is some legal change, if not immediate results. One important Supreme Court ruling ruled in favor of slum dwellers, making it mandatory for local authorities to provide alternative housing in the event of slum demolitions (Chandran 2016). A government plan to provide 20 million new housing units by 2022 is slowly underway, but has led to increased evictions to destroy housing to make way for the project and the ruling has not been respected (Chandran 2016). The rate at which housing is being demolished is faster than the rate of construction of new units, leaving thousands displaced. According to the advocacy group, Housing and Land Rights Network (HLRN), other forms of human rights violations including police violence and arbitrary detention have also been reported at several evictions.

FULFILLMENT PROBLEM: MUNICIPAL POLICIES IN INDIA AND BRAZIL

With different levels of success, India and Brazil have implemented similar public policies over time. These national and local level public policies aim to bridge the fulfillment gap between slums and municipal governments. Land regularization policies, the most common type of policy, formalize and legalize slum lands. They might include the legalization of land titles, or simply the formal acknowledgement of the existence of a slum, with the ultimate intent to incorporate the claims of slum residents. These policies are alternatives to slum eradication policies or self-help policies. "Self-help housing" circumvents some of the issues surrounding the lack of political will, and limited financial resources (Tunas and Peresthu 2010), by ignoring slum development and informally allowing slum dwellers to build their homes with an understanding that forced evictions will not take place.

Land regularization policies in Brazil stand in tension with recent evictions across the country preceding the 2014 FIFA World Cup and the 2016 Olympic Games, and have had limited success overall. The land regularization process varied across municipalities and involved a series of different social actors, but generally aimed for permanent integration into the city planning process. Despite the laudable goals, the process largely failed. Both Sao Paulo and Rio de Janeiro provide illustrative examples of the problems cities face in governing slums. In each city, the incentives of entrenched interests resulted in a deficit of political will. Rio de Janeiro's policies made efforts to incorporate slums located on both private and public lands that were undermined by conflicts regarding land ownership (Gonçalves 2014). Sao Paulo attempted to do the same but eventually chose to focus on favelas on public lands after facing a similar backlash. Neither city had the political will to expropriate private land. Both cities also faced problems maintaining cooperation among various offices and levels of government that eventually led to an abandonment of regularization and a reversion to the previous policy of eradication in almost all instances (Goncalves 2014). The end result of this policy was slum dwellers who are uncertain of their status and unwilling to invest in their communities.

In contrast to Brazil, much scholarly work hails select Indian cities as success stories for land regularization policies. One study based on 157 slums in Bangalore finds that through the legal recognition of slums, households are more likely to behave as though they have private titles (Wibbels, Krishna and Sriram 2016), meaning that they are more likely to invest locally and build social networks for collective action purposes. Additionally, they find that land titling on its own has limited benefits, because possession of a title does not directly translate into improved access to financial markets (Wibbels, Krishna and Sriram 2016). Their study suggests that the act of formally recognizing the existence of slums provides residents with a certain degree of security, somewhat independently of whether it is accompanied by land titling efforts. From a human rights perspective, formal recognition is a first step towards improving the ability of urban slum dwellers to exercise their rights. Establishing that city governments have an obligation to formally recognize the existence of slums, assigns a concrete duty to a particular member. Additionally, formal recognition facilitates local investment in infrastructure, which can lead to a higher standard of living.

Other policies in India have not been as successful in advancing the right to adequate housing in large part due to the lack of funds. For example, enabling policies—or policies aimed at creating private-public networks—have not empowered slum residents, despite the presence of NGOs, due to financial constraints (Andavarapu and Edelman 2013). India's largest slum outside of Mumbai was specifically selected for reconstruction in 1988, with the help of the World Bank. Even the largest NGOs involved in the project struggled to finance the various projects, and were ultimately unable to provide the necessary collateral for loans to continue. When faced with economic hardships, the NGOs abandoned the project (Andavarapu and Edelman 2013). Today, India is at the forefront of attempts to address increasing urbanization. The government has launched a series of initiatives called the Rajiv Awas Yojana Program (RAY) designed to improve infrastructure though the 1) formal recognition of slums to facilitate basic service delivery and 2) address urban land shortages to discourage slum settlements (Andavarapu and Edelman 2013).

Even so, professionals are skeptical that the initiative will have long-term successes. These successes do not match the scope of the problem and only resolve issues in some cities; resulting in uneven slum incorporation and short-term solutions. Sheela Patel of the organization Shack/Slum Dwellers International notes that the infrastructure of the newly created units is poorly built, and the RAY initiative does not provide a space for municipal level dialogue between the slum communities and the municipality (Patel 2013 in Andavarapu and Edelman 2013). Municipal successes are unable to meet the scope of the problem, as it currently stands, much less the demographic shifts and increased projections in the numbers of the urban poor. Even in the best-case scenarios, internal migrants and the urban poor will continue to face exclusion from human rights protection policies.

ACCOUNTABILITY PROBLEM: SLUM-BASED SOCIAL MOVEMENTS IN INDIA AND BRAZIL

Despite challenges associated with mobilization of the poor, social movements and resistance efforts in India and Brazil are gaining some influence with the help of non-state actors and other activists. This perhaps provides more hope for bottom-up solutions to the human rights exclusions facing slum dwellers, but again these solutions are unlikely to meet the scope of the problem. Protest and disruption in response to specific policies, related to development or policing, characterize the majority of social movement activities in Brazil and India. These forms of popular contestation respond to slum conditions and management, but have limited influence because of the way slum dwellers are viewed by their governments, and because they lack sustained organization as well as access to legal and political channels for making claims on the state.

In Brazil, protests respond to police violence and evictions. In 2015, slum residents across Rio staged coordinated protests in response to the police shooting of a ten-year-old boy. The protests' messages broadly called attention to the violence that occurs during police raids of favelas aimed to arrest suspected drug traffickers. While people were mobilized to protest, these protests resulted in no changes in police behavior. In response to the favela evictions and demolitions preceding the Olympic games, protestors managed one small, bittersweet success. Residents of a small favela titled Vila Autodromo—home to about 600 families—actively fought to protect the neighborhood. The favela was eventually bulldozed. However, social pressure led residents and authorities to make an agreement to urbanize the area, but the city provided only the last twenty families to be actively engaged in protest, and who refused to leave, with one of the newly constructed bungalows (Phillips 2016). Other families had already fled.

Across India, protest movements respond to the latest wave of evictions. In late 2016, residents from Delhi slums staged three sets of protests in response to planned evictions that are part of the city's efforts to upgrade that sector of the city (Chandran 2016). Residents claim that they did not receive notice of the specifics of eviction and that they were not given the option of where they would like to be temporarily relocated (Chandran

2016). There is evidence that in some other evictions in years prior, alternative housing options were not provided (Chandran 2016).

There are a few instances of more organized efforts in India, aided by networks of professional non-state actors. India's National Slum Dwellers Federation, for example, was founded by several slum leaders and coordinates with other collective action organizations such as the Indian Alliance and the Society for the Promotion of Area Resource Centers (Bautes et al. 2014). The federation now represents more than seventy towns and cities across India, working on developing links with international funding agencies and building international and domestic credibility (Bautes et al. 2014). However, based on fieldwork in Delhi, scholars have demonstrated that these NGOs and human rights efforts have not been able to alter slum clearances (Bautes et al. 2014). They find that these efforts have made only limited impact in terms of awareness, with many slum dwellers still ignorant of their rights (Bautes et al. 2014). They also attribute the failure of these NGOs to lacking a unified and sustained social movement without broad-base support from municipalities or the middle-class base. Although there are some successful mobilization efforts, their successes are largely limited and they are unable to remedy the chronic problem facing the claims-making process for residents.

CONCLUSION: THE PRESSING CHALLENGE OF SLUMS

The slum experiences in India and Brazil are not unique, and in both cases the successes—whether they be the result of top down or bottom up efforts—are miniscule compared to the problem. India and Brazil are two key modernizing economies, with large cities and dense populations, and are somewhat characteristic of the countries that will face the bulk of the challenges that the global expansion of slums presents. They also represent states that generally respect international human rights but that will continue to face fulfillment and accountability problems affecting those populations that will end up living on the outskirts of cities.

If it is the case that the projections are accurate, that 2–3 billion people will be living in urban slums within the next 50 years, approximately 2–3 billion people may remain locked out of the human rights regime, trapped in conditions of second-class citizenship. As second-class citizens, they will be unable to fully enjoy their human rights. In regard to the specific example of the human right to housing as a key component of the human right to an adequate standard of living, there are some hopeful avenues in the form of the land formalization policies, and concentrated mobilization efforts, but these local efforts may not be enough to secure safer and more stable housing alternatives.

The international, national, and local level governance gaps are too extensive to adequately comply with social and economic rights fulfillment as slums continue to proliferate in part as a result of economic dynamics of these different levels. Furthermore, developing economies may be too financially constrained. Parts of Asia and sub-Saharan Africa will certainly face increased financial difficulties and may be unable to accommodate new urbanites, and other regions may not have political incentives to take into account these kinds of effects of uneven development. The variety of actors, such as municipal government offices and private landowners—most of who are not incentivized to incorporate slums—creates policy coordination problems in even the best-case scenarios.

Mobilization efforts also face key limitations. For one, the urban poor are vulnerable to being chronically disenfranchised, and often must rely on informal networks and governance. Second-class citizenship is most easily sustained when they lack access to the law and necessary resources to make grievances. The lack of legal, adequate housing is at the root of most of the human insecurity found in slums. Without formal processes and regular housing, second-class citizens living in urban poverty will continue to be limited in their abilities to exercise their civil/political rights in ways that place pressures on government and reclaim their status as full citizens.

Human rights fulfillment at subnational forms of governance and the relative inability of slum dwellers to hold states accountable to their responsibilities creates a mutually reinforcing chronic problem that the human rights institutional framework will have to confront in systematic ways. If it does not, the urban poor will continue to be some of the world's most vulnerable populations, and be left without much hope of enjoying an adequate standard of living. The future of human rights, and the fulfillment of social and economic rights in particular, will depend on how well the regime can accommodate the creation of new political boundaries and global demographic shifts that are occurring at more localized levels of governance.

NOTES

1. The term "slums" is debated, but generally refers to a wide range of urban informal settlements broadly characterized by poor living conditions. The UN agency for human settlements and sustainable urban development. Definition outlines six characteristics: lack of basic services, substandard housing, unhealthy living conditions, poverty and social exclusion, and high levels of violence.
2. Armenia, Belgium, Burkina Faso, Congo, Ecuador, Equatorial Guinea, Guyana,

Haiti, Honduras, Mali, Mexico, Nicaragua, Paraguay, Russia, Sao Tome and Principe, Seychelles, South Africa, Spain, and Venezuela. Other countries include adequate housing as a social or political goal: Argentina, Bahrain, Bangladesh, Colombia, Costa Rica, Dominican Republic, Finland, Greece Guatemala, India, Iran, Italy, Nepal, Netherlands, Nigeria, Pakistan, Panama, Peru, Philippines, Poland, Republic of Korea, Slovenia, Sri Lanka, Suriname, Switzerland and Turkey.

REFERENCES

Andavarapu, Deepika, and David J Edelman. "Evolution of Slum Redevelopment Policy." *Current Urban Studies* 1, no. 4 (2013): 185–92.

Appadurai, Arjun. "Grassroots Globalization and the Research Imagination." In *Globalization*, edited by Arjun Appadurai, 1–21. Durham: Duke University Press, 2001.

Bautes, Nicolas, Veronique Dupont, and Frederic Landy. "Acting from the Slums: Questioning Social Movement and Resistance." In *Megacity Slums: Social Exclusion, Space and Urban Policies in Brazil and India*, ed, Marie-Caroline Saglio-Yatzimirsky and Frederic Landy. New Jersey: Imperial College Press, 2014.

Brysk, Alison, and Gershon Shafir. *People out of Place: Globalization, Human Rights, and the Citizenship Gap*. New York: Routledge, 2004.

Chandran, Rina. "Hundreds Resist Eviction from Delhi Slum as New Housing Falls Short." *Reuters* (2016). December 22, 2016. http://www.reuters.com/article/us-india-landrights-slums-idUSKBN14B235.

Collier, Paul. *The Bottom Billion: Why the Poorest Countries Are Failing and What Can Be Done About It*. Oxford; New York: Oxford University Press, 2007.

Dicklitch, Susab, and Rhoda E. Howard-Hassmann. "Public Policy and Economic Rights in Ghana and Urganda." In *Economic Rights: Conceptual, Measurement, and Policy Issues*, eds Shareen Hertel and Lanse Minkler, 325–34. New York: Cambridge University Press, 2007.

Glaeser, Edward L. "Why Has Globalization Led to Bigger Cities." *New York Times* (2009). Published electronically 19 May. https://economix.blogs.nytimes.com/2009/05/19/why-has-globalization-led-to-bigger-cities/?_r=0.

Goldstein, Daniel M. *Outlawed Between Security and Rights in a Bolivian City*. Durham: Duke University Press, 2012.

Goldstein, Daniel M. *The Spectacular City: Violence and Performance in Urban Bolivia*. Durham: Duke University Press, 2004.

Gonçalves, Rafael Soares. "The Right of the City or the Right to the City?". In *Megacity Slums: Social Exclusion, Space and Urban Policies in Brazil and India*, edited by Marie-Caroline Saglio-Yatzimirsky and Frederic Landy. New Jersey: Imperial College Press, 2014.

Hale, Charles R. "Does Multiculturalism Menace? Governance, Cultural Rights and the Politics of Identity in Guatemala." *Journal of Latin American Studies* 34, no. 3 (2002): 485–524.

Hay, Colin. "Globalization's Impact on States." In *Global Political Economy*, edited by John Ravenhill. New York: Oxford University Press, 2005.

Hertel, Shareen, and Lanse Minkler. *Economic Rights: Conceptual, Measurement, and Policy Issues*. Cambridge; New York: Cambridge University Press, 2007.

Holston, James, and Arjun Appadurai. "Cities and Citizenship." *Public Culture* 8 (1996): 187–204.
Hoover, Joe. *Reconstructing Human Rights: A Pragmatist and Pluralist Inquiry in Global Ethics*. Oxford: Oxford University Press, 2016.
ICESCR. "International Covenant on Economic, Social and Cultural Rights." http://www.ohchr.org/EN/ProfessionalInterest/Pages/CESCR.aspx.
Khan, Irene, David Petrasek, and Kofi A. Annan. *The Unheard Truth: Poverty and Human Rights*. New York: W.W. Norton & Co., 2009.
Marx, Benjamin, Thomas Stoker, and Tavneet Suri. "The Economics of Slums in the Developing World." *Journal of Economic Perspectives* 27, no. 4 (2013): 187–210.
Ooi, Giok Ling, and Kai Hong Phua. "Urbanization and Slum Formation." *Journal of Urban Health* 84, no. 1 (2007): i27–i34.
Phillips, Dom. "Days before the Olympics, Rio Families Say Goodbye to Their Homes." *The Washington Post* (2016). Published electronically Aug 2, 2016. https://www.washingtonpost.com/world/the_americas/the-favela-next-to-rios-new-olympic-park-that-fought-to-survive-and-lost/2016/08/01/fc8496ce-55c2-11e6-b652-315ae5d4d4dd_story.html?utm_term=.e8dba9fb397b.
Piven, Frances Fox, and Richard A. Cloward. *Poor People's Movements: Why They Succeed, How They Fail* (in English). New York: Vintage Books, 1979.
Postero, Nancy Grey. *Now We Are Citizens: Indigenous Politics in Postmulticultural Bolivia*. Stanford: Stanford University Press, 2006.
Risse-Kappen, Thomas. *Governance without a State?: Policies and Politics in Areas of Limited Statehood*. New York: Columbia University Press, 2011.
Rudra, Nita. *Globalization and the Race to the Bottom in Developing Countries: Who Really Gets Hurt?* Cambridge; New York: Cambridge University Press, 2008.
Saglio-Yatzimirsky, Marie-Caroline, and Frèdèric Landy. *Megacity Slums: Social Exclusion, Space and Urban Policies in Brazil and India*. London: Imperial College Press, 2014.
Shue, Henry. *Basic Rights: Subsistence, Affluence, and U.S. Foreign Policy*. Princeton, N.J.: Princeton University Press, 1980.
Tunas, Devisari, and Andrea Peresthu. "The Self-Help Housing in Indonesia." *Habitat International* 34 (2010): 315–22.
UN Habitat. "Development Context and the Millnnium Agenda: 2010 Update." In *The Challenge of Slums: Global Report on Human Settlements 2003*, edited by UN Habitat, 2010.
UNFPA. "Urbanization Overview." http://www.unfpa.org/urbanization. Date accessed: 27 Dec 2016.
Wibbels, Erik, Anirudh Krishna, and M.S. Sriram. "Satellites, Slums and Social Networks: Evidence on the Origins and Consequences of Property Rights from 157 Slums in Bangalore." In *Workshop on Urban Poverty in Developing Countreis*. Stanford: Duke University Press, 2016.
Wines, Michael. "Zimbabwe's 'Cleanup' Takes a Vast Human Toll." *New York Times* (2005). Published electronically 11 June. http://www.nytimes.com/2005/06/11/world/africa/zimbabwes-cleanup-takes-a-vast-human-toll.html.
Zald, Mayer N., and John D. McCarthy. *The Dynamics of Social Movements: Resource Mobilization, Social Control, and Tactics* (in English). Lanham; London: University Press of America, 1988.

PART II

Backlash

6. The human rights costs of NGOs' naming and shaming campaigns

Clair Apodaca

INTRODUCTION

International human rights non-governmental organizations' (NGOs) advocacy campaigns of naming and shaming are intended to be a form of leverage against recalcitrant governments to encourage their compliance with legal and moral human rights standards. Naming and shaming campaigns are viewed by NGOs as a key component in the attempt to transform repressive government policy and eliminate human rights abuses. There is ample evidence that these campaigns can and do "save lives" (Brysk 1993: 274). However, these campaigns can have the opposite effect too (Hafner-Burton 2008; DeMeritt et al 2016). Criticism of a government's policy and behavior can put the NGO staff and public at risk of retaliatory violence. Naming offending governments may thus undermine rather than reinforce compliance with human rights norms. Unquestionably, the entity that perpetrates the human rights abuse is culpable[1] for the harm done. But NGOs must recognize and be held accountable for the impacts and consequences of their advocacy activities too. Finally, if the NGO employs a naming and shaming campaign as a deliberate strategy to stimulate state retaliation in order to further popular uprisings, then the NGO is complicit in the human rights abuse.

Although many NGOs and prominent scholars have tiptoed around this critical issue, I want to examine the philosophical arguments for and against NGOs' accountability for the unintended consequences of the naming and shaming campaigns on nonparticipants, that is to say, on those individuals who are not donors, staff, members, affiliates, associates, or direct beneficiaries of NGO activity. The purpose of this chapter is to review the various arguments that ascribe accountability to NGOs by moving beyond the commonly debated aspects of NGO accountability: the undemocratic nature of transnational NGOs, their debatable claim to speak for marginalized people, their assertion to convey inclusive global values, or their weak answerability to stakeholders.

NAMING AND SHAMING ADVOCACY

Naming and shaming is an advocacy strategy whereby the NGO fact-finds and drafts a report on a country's human rights conditions. The report is then made public, widely distributed to the press and other media outlets, and provided to various United Nations human rights bodies. The reports are also circulated among international political elites, and academics, and published on the NGO website in order to pressure the government to implement changes. Naming and shaming campaigns are, by definition, oppositional (Stoddard 2003).

Human rights naming and shaming campaigns have several disagreeable outcomes for targeted states. Research has indicated that naming and shaming campaigns increase the likelihood of economic sanctions (Murdie and Peksen 2013), result in a loss of reputation (Ausderan 2014), lead to a reduction in international financial institutional financing (Lebovic and Voeten 2009), to decreased trade (Peterson et al 2016), to less foreign aid (Lebovic and Voeten 2006), and to an increased possibility of a humanitarian intervention (Murdie and Peksen 2014). Furthermore, NGOs' naming and shaming campaigns can increase grievances and encourage antigovernment sentiments leading to protests and demonstrations (Dupuy et al 2016), which can then threaten the survival of authoritarian leaders (Wright and Escribà-Folch 2009).[2]

The backlash is more than a theoretical concern. States can and frequently do react negatively to naming and shaming campaigns. Brysk's (1993) early study on the effects of a social movement's mobilization of shame against Argentina's Dirty War revealed that there was an increase in the number of extrajudicial executions. In Chile, Pinochet's response to the 1977 naming and shaming campaign was to restrain opposition media coverage and to increase repression. With the continuing campaigns in the 1980s, "Pinochet increased repression in an effort to drive out opposition organizers . . . in 1987, the Chilean Human Rights Commission found the highest number of kidnappings, incidents of torture, and politically motivated killings in seven years" (Wright and Escribà-Folch 2009: 30). Sudan provides another example of the backlash of naming and shaming campaigns. Once NGOs turned their attention to the atrocities being committed against civilians in Darfur in the early 2000s, their campaigns eventually led to the indictment of President Omar Hassan al-Bashir. The United Nations anticipated an increase in repression as a result of the indictment. Simons and MacFarquhar (2009) quote Salah Gosh, head of the Sudanese Intelligence Agency, who called for the "amputation of the hands and the slitting of the throats of any person who dares bad-mouth al-Bashir" or supports the indictment. As a further illustration, Myanmar's response to the naming and shaming resulting from NGO reports following its submission of the Universal Periodic Review to the Human Rights Commission in 2011 has increased repression and killing (Beckstrand 2015). Local NGOs were reluctant to consult with the Myanmar National Human Rights Commission due to the fear of backlash (IBAHRI 2016). Statistical studies confirm the anecdotal evidence. Hafner-Burton (2008) found that states shamed by Amnesty International might actually increase their use of terror after being targeted. This is because "Governments . . . feel an urge for revenge against those opponents who just caused them so much grief" (Dupuy et al 2016: 303).

DeMeritt et al (2016) argue that, when IGOs and NGOs name and shame a government for one form of human rights violation, most typically the use of torture, governments use other forms of violations to hide the shamed repressive tactic. For example, if the regime is shamed for torture violations, the regime will increase the use of disappearances or imprisonments to hide its torturous activities. Conrad and DeMeritt (2014) find that shamed governments will violate empowerment rights, for example, the right to assemble and to associate, as well as free speech, in order to deny political opponents the opportunity to mobilize against the government or to block NGOs from publicizing the abuses. Shaming does not eliminate the reason the regime chose to employ repression in the first place; it simply changes the cost-benefit analysis or the repressive strategy. Thus, those governments will resort to increased repression and human rights abuses. Rubenstein acknowledges that, as political actors, NGOs and their activities can have unintended negative effects. She writes, "NGOs must decide how much and what kinds of negative effects to accept" (Rubenstein 2015: 70). In order to do their beneficial work, NGOs must be willing to accept that they may indirectly contribute to the harm but that this does "not shield them from moral responsibility for the predictable effects of their actions" (Rubenstein 2015: 104). With growing evidence that their advocacy strategies can have unintended human rights consequences, NGOs must be held accountable.

ANALOGY

Suppose I have a very long stick and I am using it to poke a tiger. Now suppose there are peasant farmers, whole families with elders and children, arduously laboring in their fields between the tiger and me. When the tiger attacks, I am responsible for the injuries to the farmers. Even if some of the farmers were joining in on the taunting of the tiger, either helping to direct my very long stick to its target or using short sticks themselves, I am still responsible for the injuries to the uninvolved farmers. Had I, an expert in tiger behavior, convinced those farmers taunting the tiger that the tiger would not attack, I am responsible for their injuries too.

Thus, if I am an NGO advocating against a repressive state for its human rights violations, I am poking a tiger. Since I am headquartered in London, New York, or Washington, my stick is very long. When the state retaliates for my advocacy efforts, I am responsible for the injuries to those nonparticipating group members who are not holding a stick but still suffer state retribution. For example, if an NGO is advocating for labor rights and organizes sweatshop labor unions to protest against the government, those labor union members who chose to participate are responsible for their own decisions. However, the NGO is responsible for the abuse inflicted on nonparticipating laborers and their families because it should have known that the government would retaliate, and perhaps retaliate indiscriminately, against all sweatshop workers, whether they are participants or not. In this case, the NGO failed to recognize—or simply ignored—the likely outcome of its human rights campaign that provoked government retaliation.

The NGO's intention to end human rights abuse does not absolve its responsibility for the suffering of the nonparticipating citizen. NGO naming and shaming campaigns can significantly impact the fate of nonparticipating individuals. There can be unintended consequences to using human rights advocacy that can result in harm to the very people whose rights they are seeking to protect. Yet, these NGOs may not be representative of them and may not be accountable to them.

ACCOUNTABILITY

The NGO's responsibility for the human rights of nonparticipants arises when its campaigns indirectly contribute to governmental abuse. Mackie reasons that "if B's action [retaliatory repression by the state, in our case], though neither defensible nor excusable, could be confidently anticipated as a response to A's [NGO campaign of naming and shaming], then A must take some responsibility for the result, and the more automatic B's response could be foreseen as being, the more of the responsibility for the result must be referred back to A's action" (1977: 164, as quoted in Gasper 1999). Ashford (2006) argues that a right, such as the right to physical integrity, generates not only a negative duty not to perpetrate torture, but also a negative duty not to reduce a person's security against being tortured.[3] Steigleder (2012) explains that, if an individual or group has an entitlement (in our situation, an internationally guaranteed right to physical integrity), others have a duty not to do anything that infringes on that entitlement. However, this is not an unqualified right as there may be justifiable reasons for taking actions that expose an individual or group to the risk of harm. But, there is little if any practical guidance on who determines whether the actions are worth the risks and which reasons are justifiable. This is where my concern in this chapter lies. There is an asymmetrical power relationship between those who impose the risk and those who are exposed to the risk. Perrow argues that risk is ultimately about "power; the power to impose risks on the many for the benefit of the few" (1999: 306). Oftentimes, the exposed do not get the opportunity to decide whether the risks are justifiable or not, and they are certainly not given the opportunity to withhold consent. Thus, NGOs should consider the unintended risks that may flow from their advocacy actions.

NGOs are significant independent influential global actors who have the power to affect state policies and actions. NGOs wield significant influence and their activities can have substantial consequences on people who are not affiliated with the NGO. The economic and political power of NGOs necessitates the development of a moral system of accountability.

NGOs need to be accountable for those they do not organize and represent, people I refer to as nonparticipants. This is particularly important since research indicates that NGOs' campaigns of naming and shaming are often the result of high visibility situations rather than actual human rights violations (Ron et al 2005). High profile states that receive a lot of media coverage will receive greater NGO attention in order for the NGO to further its own agenda, attract funding, increase its prestige, and maintain its "market share" (Mihr and Schmitz 2007). Research by Berkovitch and Gordon (2008) found that donor-provided funds encourage not only the type of rights the NGO promotes, but also the use of particular advocacy techniques. In addition, research indicates that strong political ties between a donor state and a targeted state reduces the likelihood of a shaming event (Terman and Voeten 2017).

Schmitz acknowledges that, frequently, "the initial impetus for mobilization does not originate on the local level and is not driven by domestic activists" (2010: 7198). Rather, the NGO determines the scope, nature, and target of the human rights campaign. Sharp argues that NGOs have the potential to "drown out, even if unintentionally, the voices and efforts of nationally-based organizations" for several reasons (2015: 81). NGOs have evolved in an elite professional class whose members are often elite educated lawyers, whose work is biased in favor of mobilizing shaming campaigns, thus legitimizing and generating power for the NGOs themselves. Human rights advocacy is frequently performed without extensive local NGO support or without any victim's engagement. Domestic NGOs tend to be less confrontational than their international counterparts and less focused on shaming.[4] The difference in strategies can put the domestic and international NGOs at odds, thus curbing cooperation and collaboration (Bell and Carens 2004).

NGOs have been criticized for using their domestic affiliates as a "channel into the national political arena, a justification for meddling in national affairs" of target states (Burgerman 1998: 916). Rubenstein (2014) refers to this as the "capacity to arbitrarily interfere," whereby powerful NGOs take actions that significantly affect others without taking into account the interests and preferences of the affected. NGOs must recognize their own possible contributions to human rights abuses, particularly when they place their agenda above the safety of nonparticipating individuals and groups. Thus, even if an NGO is the indirect cause of human rights violations (i.e., it does not directly inflict the human rights abuse), it should still be responsible for the harm created.

RISK IMPOSITION

A risk is a possibility or likelihood of experiencing a harm (an injury, loss, or death), the occurrence of which is not certain. Schroeder argues that it is permissible to impose certain risks on others. The human right to bodily integrity "undoubtedly constitutes a fundamentally important part of any definition of the individual; it may even be first among equals" (Schroeder 1986: 518). But it is not the only right an autonomous individual wishes to secure. Individuals also value the quality of their lives, and to live free of fear and government repression. The rights of the risk creator (in this situation, the local active participants seeking greater human rights protections for themselves and their peers) must be balanced with the rights of the nonparticipants not to have the risk of government retaliation imposed on them. Schroeder's conception of justice values individual autonomy but does not oblige an absolute restriction against risk. After all, both the local NGO's affiliated risk creator and the nonparticipant risk bearer have rights. The risk bearer has the right not to have risk imposed on him/her while the risk creator has a right to action. The restriction of all risk infringes on the rights of risk creators (Steigleder 2012). In each case, both the risk creator and the risk bearer wish to protect their right to bodily integrity. However, the risk creator is acting in response to actual human rights violations while the risk bearer has only a potential for being harmed. The risk creator, the local activist, is not culpable for the possible but unintended consequences of his/her activities.

Domestic actors who actively organize and mobilize against the government with the knowledge that they are placing themselves in harm's way are unambiguously taking a risk. Local NGOs are populated and led by "people who care enough about some issue that they are prepared to incur significant costs and act to achieve their goals" (Keck and Sikkink 1998: 14). The local NGO staff and participant stakeholders freely, courageously, and heroically accept the risk to their safety and security. Those citizens who decide for themselves to poke the tiger are putting themselves in danger; but they have consented to the risk of state retaliation. Consent to a risk makes the moral problem of risk imposition disappear: "the prima facie right not to be subject to risky behavior of others without consenting is a natural consequence of the rationale for finding consent important" (Hayenhjelm and Wolff 2011: e41). Local activists have the right to organize, protest, and participate in naming and shaming campaigns on their own behalf, even if this puts others in danger. NGOs, on the other hand, may not have the right to put local citizens at risk.

ARGUMENTS AGAINST NGO RESPONSIBILITY REFUTED

Utilitarianism

The utilitarian argument stipulates that NGOs' naming and shaming campaigns and the resultant repressive retaliation are justified by the promise that, in spite of the pain and disruption caused, the greater good of human rights attainment will be available for everyone. Schroeder explains that "utilitarianism emphasizes that risks are worth taking because of the potential gains associated with them" (1986: 505). Human action should be evaluated in terms of its ability to advance the general welfare. Thus, the ends justify the means. Schroeder continues: "the goal of maximizing some measure of utility . . . produces moral requirements that can trample an individual, if necessary, to maximize utility, since once the net effects of a proposal on the maximand have been taken into account, the individual is expendable" (1986: 508). A utilitarian would argue for the moral permissibility of collateral harm to nonparticipants, due to NGO naming and shaming campaigns, because this harm is outweighed by the benefits that are gained from having the state halt its use of human rights abuses. Regrettably, balancing the potential benefits versus the costs can lead to a callous indifference to the lives and safety of sacrificed individuals or groups to the benefit of the greater good.

Rawls (1999: 3–4) refutes the utilitarian argument when he writes:

> Each person possesses an inviolability founded on justice that even the welfare of society as a whole cannot override. For this reason justice denies that the loss

> of freedom for some is made right by a greater good shared by others. It does not allow that the sacrifices imposed on a few are outweighed by the larger sum of advantages enjoyed by many.

NGOs have a moral obligation to recognize the rights, needs, and claims of individuals and to make sure that the individual is not sacrificed to the long-term interests of society. Justifications such as the "greater good," or sacrificing some for the elimination of human rights abuses (with the consequence that nonparticipants are placed at risk for government retaliation to further the NGO agenda), are untenable. This is particularly true since NGOs are not democratic institutions and therefore may not be representative of the population or its interests.

Utilitarianism advocates a course of action that leads to the best possible consequences for the greatest number of people. Accordingly, even wrong actions may be permissible if these actions result in an overall gain in benefits and the maximization of the good. We all (the totality of humanity) benefit from a reduction in human rights abuse. Yet, Hayenhjelm and Wolff (2011) warn that the maximization of the good says little about the distribution of the risk. I believe we would be hard-pressed to find any real-world example where the rich and powerful were asked to assume torturous harm for the greater good. Accordingly, the theory of utilitarianism cannot be used to justify placing risk on nonparticipants for state retaliation for NGO's campaigns of naming and shaming.

The Principle of "Double Effect"

But what if the harm is a side effect of promoting a good end? After all, Rubenstein notes that "NGOs' contributions to harm or injustice are almost always unintended side effects of efforts to achieve a good outcome, rather than means to an end of achieving a good outcome" (2015: 99). The principle of "double effect" concerns the well-meaning intentions of the NGO, not an egregious state. McIntyre states that the principle of "double effect" is "directed at well-intentioned agents who ask whether they may cause a serious harm in order to bring about a good end of overriding moral importance when it is impossible to bring about the good end without the harm" (2014). The doctrine of "double effect" authorizes an action that could cause an unintentional harm as a side effect ("double effect") of promoting some good. Nevertheless, McIntyre (2014) advises that a morally permissible harm may be allowed if and only if the beneficial effects of an action are proportional to the harm caused. The principle of "double effect," unfortunately, is reliant on the agent causing the harm determining whether the harm is balanced by the good.

The principle of "double effect" has a long history in medical ethics. The principle's primary example is the care of a dying patient: is it morally acceptable to administer large doses of an opioid to relieve pain in a dying patient even if this act could hasten the patient's death? Death is a possible side-effect of a good, which is the alleviation of pain. In medical ethics debates, a single party—the patient—holds both the good end and the risk. However, in the case of NGOs' naming and shaming campaigns, the beneficiaries of the good end and the nonparticipating victims of the imposed risk are different parties. The good is provided for one at the expense of another. I believe that it is not morally acceptable to cause harm to nonparticipating citizens as a result of a naming and shaming campaign even if these effects (state retaliation) are not intended and the good (the reduction in overall abuse) is proportional to the harm.

In examining the principle of double effects in humanitarian interventions, Tesón (2003) argues that the unintentional harm caused to innocents—the double effect—may be morally justified if the intervening agent seeks to remedy an injustice. It is not simply a matter of sacrificing some to save others but an attempt to restore human rights and justice. However, as research has shown, NGOs do not necessarily target states with the greatest human rights abuses and their motives may not be pure at heart. Maybe the calculated political strategy employed by an NGO or IGO is supported by powerful donor states. NGOs' advocacy campaigns are heavily influenced by donor interests, substantial media coverage, and funding opportunities as well as the impetus to right a wrong or to remedy an injustice.

Collateral harms are rarely justified when they affect third parties with no voice in the activities of the more powerful actors, particularly if the third party is not the direct beneficiary of powerful actors' activities. It is merely wrong to unintentionally but foreseeably cause harm to an innocent person even if this would minimize overall abuse within the state, a good end.

ARGUMENTS USED TO HOLD NGOS ACCOUNTABLE

The "All Significantly-Affected" Principle

NGOs ought to be held accountable to all those upon whom they may have an impact whether or not the individuals are mobilized members or supporters of the NGO, intended beneficiaries of the NGOs' advocacy, or merely collateral bystanders. Unerman and O'Dwyer (2006) convincingly argue that, if an NGO's advocacy mobilizes the actions of others, it must assume the duties of accountability. Thus, even the unintended negative consequences of NGO discourse on people not considered direct stakeholders are the responsibility of the NGO.

The "all-affected" principle requires that NGOs be held accountable to all people who are affected by NGOs' decisions and actions. However, the "all-affected" principle "suffers from both practical and normative problems" (Uhlin 2010: 26). The problem with the "all-affected" principle, in the opinion of Näsström (2011), is the butterfly effect—namely, almost any action anywhere can affect anyone. Applying an "all-affected" principle can lead to paralysis. Nothing can ever be done because at some point someone somewhere will be hurt. Domestic NGOs and local activists have the right to assume the risk and advocate for the fulfillment of their human rights and fundamental freedoms even if their activities put nonparticipants at risk.

Consequently, the less rigid "all significantly-affected" principle has been established. Most scholars and NGOs themselves believe that an NGO should be accountable to its stakeholders, members, donors, and beneficiaries. Yet, little is said regarding the impacts on the nonparticipating individual. NGOs need to be accountable for their wider social impacts. In practice, NGOs have been most attentive to their accountability to donors, largely ignoring accountability to other affected individuals and groups (Peruzzotti 2006, Schmitz et al 2012). O'Dwyer and Unerman (2007) report that NGOs are rarely accountable to stakeholder groups other than their funders.

The "all-significantly affected" principle ought to be broadened to include the nonparticipating citizen who may be subject to state retaliation as a result of NGO activity. Whether or not campaigns aimed at naming and shaming abusive governments are successful, NGOs have a responsibility to ensure that those significantly affected by their activities are protected. If the "all-significantly affected" principle were accepted and practiced by NGOs, it could adequately protect nonparticipating civilians from retaliation by the state.

The "Do No Harm" Principle

A human right can be understood as an interest so fundamentally important to human dignity that it imposes duties onto others. Duties can be either negative duties (to "do no harm") or positive duties (to protect and fulfill). NGOs have a strong duty not to perform actions that cause harm. If the actions or advocacy policies of the NGO create an environment that causes a violation, the NGO is responsible for the resulting violation. Accordingly, NGOs have a moral obligation to abstain from actions that violate human rights. In addition, NGOs also have a duty to protect human rights, to reduce or eliminate dangers and threats to human rights within the scope of their authority or field of influence. This, I argue, includes not exposing the nonparticipant to the danger or risk of being harmed by a third party. Incongruously, the duty to fulfill or realize political and civil human rights, the objective of naming and shaming campaigns, is the exclusive obligation of states. Rubenstein (2015) believes that following a strict "do no harm" principle can have the effect of doing nothing in the face of human suffering. In order to prevent the sin of omission, she supports a balanced medium "do less harm" principle whereby NGOs can act when intervention outweighs the harm.

The "do no harm" principle basically means that one does not inadvertently create harm when doing good. Ruggie (2008) defines the "do no harm" principle as simply avoiding infringement on the human rights of others. Although Ruggie was speaking of multinational corporations, the guidance holds true for NGOs too. To "do no harm" requires an active commitment to "become aware of, prevent and address adverse human rights impacts" (Ruggie 2008: 199). This requires that an NGO practice due diligence in order to "manage the risk of human rights harm with a view to avoiding it" (Ruggie 2008: 194). Nonparticipants' interests in not being harmed are important enough to establish a negative duty on NGOs to "do no harm". The protection of nonparticipating citizens and communities against state retaliation is of critical importance.

The "do no harm" principle requires NGOs to do their due diligence before organizing a naming and shaming campaign. Taylor (2011) clarifies due diligence as an assessment that looks for harms to people (impacts) that arise, or could arise, from operations (activities and relationships) in a particular context and interprets these facts in light of international human rights standards (the existing body of national and international human rights law). In practice, due diligence involves reasonable precautions to avoid doing harm, specifically, a pre-assessment of state characteristics, monitoring of the campaign's fallout, and developing option for remediation if necessary. The NGO ought to carry out an investigation of the probable direct and indirect impacts that the naming and shaming campaign will have on the population of the target state. With such a study in hand, the NGO could then assess whether the collateral harm is proportional to the benefits. Collateral harm should be minimized or repaired. The "do no harm" principle, if accepted and observed by NGOs, would hold NGOs accountable for the protection of nonparticipants.

CONCLUSION

NGOs have a moral responsibility to take into account the potential harm their naming and shaming strategies may cause. Clearly, an ethic that accepts the responsibility to help victims of state repression must also consider whether actions help or harm nonparticipating third parties. NGOs need to be very attentive to the risk of potential harm of their advocacy activities. It would be grossly unethical to continue practices that cause inadvertent harm to people.

There are compelling philosophical arguments for developing a framework for placing indirect or limited responsibility for human rights abuses on NGOs. The moral arguments reviewed here maintain that NGOs cannot abrogate their responsibility to respect and protect the rights of nonparticipants, and that NGOs must be held accountable for the harm their naming and shaming campaigns inflict.

In those cases where NGO activity could increase the harm to nonparticipant third parties, what is the alternative to naming and shaming campaigns to persuade recalcitrant governments to comply with legal and moral human rights standards and avoid a backlash effect? Undeniably, the failure to intervene can also threaten the lives and security of nonparticipants. This chapter was meant to caution NGOs about the effects of their advocacy campaigns, to encourage the use of assessments before organizing a campaign, and to urge NGOs to partner (in more than a rhetorical sense) with local NGOs and marginalized groups. NGO advocacy has undoubtedly been successful within certain contexts. Because NGO human rights naming and shaming campaigns have had notable success in saving lives, it is important to not throw the baby out with the bath water. Rather than banning confrontational strategies, NGOs should be persuaded to perform thorough vulnerability risk assessments beforehand. Here the work of Oxfam could serve as a useful model. Oxfam's Vulnerability and Risk Assessment (VRA) uses a "participatory process of identification and prioritization of existing and future vulnerabilities, risks, capacities and ambitions" (Oxfam, online). The VRA takes pains to ensure that marginalized groups are included in the discussion and are not negatively impacted by either the frank discussion or the implantation of the agreed upon program.

In order to reduce their accountability for human rights violations due to naming and shaming advocacy, NGOs ought to "step back and let nationally based organizations take the lead, working not to develop their capacity, but acting in a purely supporting role, much as some national organizations have played a largely invisible and supporting role in the work of the NGOs for many decades" (Sharp 2015: 81). After all, local activists have the moral right and perhaps the duty to poke the tiger with or without international help.

NOTES

1. Culpability is to be blameworthy for a harm or injury. The state is morally and legally culpable for the human rights abuses it perpetrates. Because the NGO is not culpable for harm, I do not believe that there is any legal accountability.
2. Governments respond to political mobilization with greater levels of repression in order to maintain their leadership and control. The greater the level of organization and violence of the dissident activity, the greater the threat to government control, and consequently, the more severe the government's reprisal (Apodaca 2017).
3. NGOs are important participants in the international system and have a legal personality under international law. NGOs are autonomous subjects of international law with rights and duties and, therefore, are bound by customary law and peremptory norms. Nowrot writes: "NGOs can be regarded as at least partial subjects of international law with not only rights but also duties under the international legal system" (1999: 614). The legal role of NGOs can be established by the UN Charter's creation of consultative status for NGOs. NGOs also have observer and consultative status with many other specialized organizations of the UN family.
4. Local NGOs can and do disagree with their international partners and often attempt to modify, forestall, or prevent advocacy campaigns (Hertel 2006).

ACKNOWLEDGMENTS

The author thanks Mauro Caraccioli and Zehra Arat for their advice and suggestions on the chapter.

REFERENCES

Apodaca, Clair. (2017) *State Repression in Post-Disaster Societies*. New York: Routledge.

Ashford, Elizabeth. (2006) "The Inadequacy of our Traditional Conception of the Duties Imposed by Human Rights," *Canadian Journal of Law and Jurisprudence*, 19(2), 217–35.

Ausderan, Jacob. (2014) "How Naming and Shaming Affects Individual Human Rights Perceptions in the Shamed Country." *Journal of Peace Research*, 51(1), 81–95.

Beckstrand, M. (2015) "Recommendations, Rhetoric, and Reporting: State and NGO Behavior in the Universal Periodic Review of Human Rights." Dissertation. http://surface.syr.edu/cgi/viewcontent.cgi?article=1340&context=etd.

Bell, Daniel and Carens, Joseph. (2004) "The Ethical Dilemmas of International Human Rights and Humanitarian NGOs: Reflections on a Dialogue Between Practitioners and Theorists." *Human Rights Quarterly*, 26(2), 300–29.

Berkovitch, Nitza and Gordon, N. (2008) "The Political Economy of Transnational

Regimes: The Case of Human Rights." *International Studies Quarterly*, 52, 881–904.
Brysk, Allison. (1993) "From Above and Below: Social Movements, the International System, and Human Rights in Argentina." *Comparative Political Studies*, 26(3), 259–85.
Burgerman, Susan. (1998) "Mobilizing Principles: The Role of Transnational Activists in Promoting Human Rights Principles." *Human Rights Quarterly*, 20(4), 905–23.
Conrad, Courtenay and Jacqueline DeMeritt. (2014) "Unintended Consequences: The Effect of Advocacy to End Torture on Empowerment Rights Violations," in Tracy Lightcap and James Pfiffner (eds), *Examining Torture: Empirical Studies of State Repression*, New York: Palgrave MacMillan, 159–83.
DeMeritt, Jacqueline, Courtenay Conrad and Christopher Fariss. (2016) "How International Advocacy Can Worsen State Repression," https://www.researchgate.net/profile/Jacqueline_Demeritt/publication/304986271_Unintended_Consequences_The_Effect_of_Advocacy_to_End_Torture_on_Empowerment_Rights_Violations/links/5783184108ae5f367d3b69f1.pdf.
Dupuy, Kendra, James Ron, and Aseem Prakash. (2016) "Hands Off My Regime! Governments' Restrictions on Foreign Aid to Non-Governmental Organizations in Poor and Middle-Income Countries," *World Development*, 84, 299–311.
Gasper, Des. (1999) "'Drawing a Line' – Ethical and Political Strategies in Complex Emergency Assistance." *European Journal of Development Research*, 11(2), 87–115.
Hafner-Burton, Emilie. (2008) "Sticks and Stones: Naming and Shaming and the Human Rights Enforcement Problem," *International Organization*, 62(4), 689–716.
Hayenhjelm, Madeleine and Jonathan Wolff. (2011) "The Moral Problem of Risk Impositions: A Survey of the Literature," *European Journal of Philosophy*, 20(S1), e26–e51.
Hertel, Shareen. (2006) *Unexpected Power: Conflict and Change among Transnational Activists*, Ithaca: Cornell University Press.
International Bar Association's Human Rights Institute (IBAHRI). (2016) "The Role of the Universal Periodic Review in Advancing Human Rights in the Administration of Justice." *United Nations Programme Report*. http://www.ibanet.org/Article/NewDetail.aspx?ArticleUid=742c8431-9c25-4d0b-bb05-f7950b22b5c4.
Keck, Margaret and Kathryn Sikkink. (1998) *Activists Beyond Borders: Advocacy Networks in International Politics*, Ithaca: Cornell University Press.
Lebovic, James and Erik Voeten. (2006) "The Politics of Shame: The Condemnation of Country Human Rights Practices in the UNHCR," *International Studies Quarterly*, 50(4), 861–88.
Lebovic, James and Erik Voeten. (2009) "The Cost of Shame: International Organizations and Foreign Aid in the Punishing of Human Rights Violators," *Journal of Peace Research*, 46(1), 79–97.
Mackie, J.L. (1977) *Ethics: Inventing Right and Wrong*. Harmondsworth: Penguin Books.
McIntyre, Alison. (2014) "Doctrine of 'double effect,'" in Edward Zalta (eds) *The Stanford Encyclopedia of Philosophy*. http://plato.stanford.edu/archives/win2014/entries/double-effect/.
Mihr, Anja and Hans-Peter Schmitz. (2007) "Human Rights Education and Transnational Activism," *Human Rights Quarterly*, 29(4), 973–93.

Murdie, Amanda and Dursun Peksen. (2013) "The Impact of Human Rights NGO Activities on Economic Sanctions," *The Review of International Organizations*, 8(1), 33–53.
Murdie, Amanda and Dursun Peksen. (2014) "The Impact of Human Rights NGO Shaming on Humanitarian Interventions," *The Journal of Politics*, 76(1), 215–28.
Näsström, Sofia. (2011) "The Challenge of the All-Affected Principle," *Political Studies*, 59, 116–34.
Nowrot, Karsten. (1999) "Legal Consequences of Globalization: The Status of Non-Governmental Organizations Under International Law." *Indiana Journal of Global Legal Studies*, 6(2), 579–645.
O'Dwyer, Brendan and Jeffrey Unerman. (2007) "From Functional to Social Accountability: Transforming the Accountability Relationship between Funders and Non-governmental Development Organisations," *Accounting, Auditing and Accountability Journal*, 20(3), 446–71.
Oxfam. Online. *Policy and Practice: Vulnerability and Risk Assessment*. http://policy-practice.oxfam.org.uk/our-approach/toolkits-and-guidelines/vulnerability-risk-assessment.
Perrow, Charles. (1999) *Normal Accidents: Living With High Risk Technologies*, Princeton NJ: Princeton University Press.
Peruzzotti, Enrique. (2006) "Civil Society, Representation and Accountability: Restarting Current Debates on the Representativeness and Accountability of Civic Associations," in Lisa Jordan and Peter van Tuijl (eds), *NGO Accountability: Politics, Principles and Innovations*, London: Earthscan, 43–58.
Peterson, Timothy, Amada Murdie, and Victor Asal. (2016) "Human Rights NGO Shaming and the Exports of Abusive States." *British Journal of Political Science*, https://doi.org/10.1017/S0007123416000065.
Rawls, John. (1999) *A Theory of Justice* (Revised Edition), Cambridge: Harvard University Press.
Ron, James, Howard Ramos, and Kathleen Rodgers. (2005) "Transnational Human Rights Politics: Human Rights Reporting, 1986–2000," *International Studies Quarterly*, 49(3), 557–87.
Rubenstein, Jennifer. (2014) "The Misuse of Power, Not Bad Representation: Why It Is Beside the Point that No One Elected Oxfam." *The Journal of Political Philosophy*, 22(2), 204–30.
Rubenstein, Jennifer. (2015) *Between Samaritans and States: The Political Ethics of Humanitarian NGOs*, Oxford: Oxford University Press.
Ruggie, John. (2008) "Business and Human Rights: The Evolving International Agenda," Working Paper No. 38, Corporate Social Responsibility Initiative, Cambridge, MA: Harvard University John F. Kennedy School of Government.
Schmitz, Hans Peter. (2010) "Transnational Human Rights Networks: Significance and Challenges," in Robert Denemark (ed), *The International Studies Encyclopedia Volume XI*, Wiley-Blackwell, 7189–208.
Schmitz, Hans Peter, Paloma Raggo, and Tosca Bruno-van Vijfeijken. (2012) "Accountability of Transnational NGOs: Aspirations vs. Practice," *Nonprofit and Voluntary Sector Quarterly*, 41(6), 1175–94.
Schroeder, Christopher. (1986) "Rights Against Risks." *Columbia Law Review*, 86(29), 495–562.
Sharp, Dustin. (2015) "Human Rights Fact-Finding and the Reproduction of Hierarchies," in Philip Alston and Sarah Knuckey (eds.), *The Transformation of Human Rights Fact-Finding*. Oxford: Oxford University Press, 69–88.

Simons, M. and MacFarquhar, N. (2009) "Court Issues Warrant for Arrest of Sudan President." *New York Times* (March 4). http://www.nytimes.com/2009/03/05/world/africa/05court.html.

Steigleder, Klaus. (2012) *Risk and Rights: Towards a Rights-Based Risk Ethics.* http://www.ruhr-uni-bochum.de/philosophy/mam/ethik/content/steigleder_risk_and_rights.pdf.

Stoddard, Abby. (2003) "Humanitarian NGOs: Challenges and Trends," in Joanna Macrae and Adele Harmer (eds), *Humanitarian Action and the 'Global War on Terror': A Review of Trends and Issues*, London: Humanitarian Policy Group, 25–36.

Taylor, Mark. (2011) "The Ruggie Framework: Polycentric Regulation and the Implications for Corporate Social Responsibility." *Etikk i praksis. Nordic Journal of Applied Ethics*, 5(1), 9–30.

Terman, Rochelle and Voeten, Erik. (2017) "The Relational Politics of Shame: Evidence from the Universal Periodic Review." *Review of International Organizations.* DOI 10.1007/s11558-016-9264-x.

Tesón, F. (2003) "The Liberal Case for Humanitarian Intervention." In J. Holzgrefe, and R. Keohane (eds), *Humanitarian Intervention: Ethical, Legal, and Political Dilemmas*, Cambridge: Cambridge University Press.

Uhlin, Anders. (2010) "Democratic Legitimacy of Transnational Actors: Mapping Out the Conceptual Terrain," in Eva Erman and Anders Uhlin (eds), *Legitimacy Beyond the State? Re-examining the Democratic Credentials of Transnational Actors*, New York: Palgrave MacMillan, 16–37.

Unerman, Jeffrey and Brendan O'Dwyer. (2006) "Theorising Accountability for NGO Advocacy," *Accounting, Auditing and Accountability Journal*, 19(3), 349–76.

Wright, J. and Escribà-Folch, A. (2009) "Are Dictators Immune to Human Rights Shaming?" *IBEI Working Papers* 25, 3–39.

7. Perils of success: backlash and resistance to LGBT rights in domestic and international politics[1]

Phillip M. Ayoub

The sweeping successes we have observed in the spread of sexual minority rights worldwide have also provoked intense backlash in many corners of the globe. Lesbian, gay, bisexual and transgender (LGBT) human rights can do this because they are seen by some to challenge the coherence of national identity, calling into question sovereignty, values and self-understandings. This chapter explores why norms governing LGBT rights mobilize a backlash and/or enduring resistance in some cases and not in others. It explores the phenomena of resistance at two related levels. First, based on a comparison of Poland and Slovenia, I trace how differing perceptions of threat define the way international norms are received in distinct domestic realms. Threat perception is heightened in cases where religion is historically embedded in the essence of the popular nation. In these cases, the domestic opposition has a higher likelihood of successfully counter-framing a narrative that links LGBT rights to external forces threatening national values. Second, I explore threat perception and resistance as part of the emerging phenomena of "norm polarization" (Symons and Altman 2015) at the *global level*. Such polarization refers to a process in which states resist norms by purposively taking contradictory positions on the same norm, leading to norm indeterminacy. This involves one community of states rejecting the values of another, making LGBT rights part of a geopolitics in which states coopt the values that align with "their side". The chapter ends with some reflection on an increasingly intertwined politics of backlash at multiple levels of politics.

If any world region can boast the establishment of wide ranging successes concerning (LGBT) rights, it is Europe. While we have to take great caution with describing human rights "success"—improvements being limited to some aspects of LGBT life, for only some LGBT people and in only some regions—we do note positive changes in the legal standing of sexual minorities in many European countries. European actors—the

European Union (EU), Council of Europe institutions and a transnational network of activists—have fostered change by propagating LGBT human rights and by introducing the issues into the domestic discourse of various European states (Ayoub 2013; Paternotte and Kollman 2013). Yet even in this region we observe substantial variation in the domestic reception of the international norm. Furthermore, just as LGBT movements occur at multiple levels of world politics, we also observe multifaceted resistances promoted at local, national and transnational levels. This chapter explores resistance and backlash to LGBT rights in an era perceived as one of success for LGBT movements. Precisely, I ask why the expansion of LGBT rights mobilizes an active resistance in some cases and not others. Using a paired comparison design, I answer these questions by tracing the different trajectories of norm reception around LGBT rights.

The chapter's core compares the link between national identity and religion in Poland and Slovenia, finding that different perceptions of threat in distinct national contexts influence responses to the human rights norms championed by transnational LGBT movements. This is particularly relevant if we consider the varied roles played by the Catholic Church and the related impact on the strength and longevity of the anti-LGBT response. In Slovenia, activists were able to foster change in favor of LGBT people without a strong and resonant domestic resistance. In Poland, mobilized resistance to LGBT rights was routine. To explain this difference, I argue that state actors can use religion to contribute to counter-mobilization in cases where its moral authority is historically embedded in the popular idea of the nation. In Poland, the Catholic Church created a role for itself as a symbol of the nation. There, the domestic opposition succeeded in framing a narrative that linked LGBT rights to external forces threatening national values. By contrast, the Catholic Church in Slovenia could neither maintain nor (re-)establish similarly strong ties to the popular nation after the Second World War (WWII). LGBT rights norms provoke a lesser resistance in states where the Church[2] has lost its moral authority as a constitutive part of national identity.

Next, I look at threat perception and resistance as part of the emerging phenomena of "norm polarization" (Symons and Altman 2015) at the *global level*. Such polarization refers to a process in which states resist norms by purposively taking contradictory positions on the same norm, which both contracts and further challenges the validity of LGBT rights. As the new Russian paradigm of "traditional values" politics exemplifies, which also roots religion in the nation, states are increasingly framing LGBT rights as a global threat. This also involves one community of states refusing the values of another.

The argument is presented in four sections. Section one conceptualizes the differing perceptions of threat that derive from the ties between religion and nationalism in Europe. Section two traces these differences in the cases of Poland and Slovenia. Section three explores the dissimilar trajectories of mobilized resistance that varied threat perceptions produced in both domestic cases. Section four then thinks through how these dynamics play out at the global level. The analysis draws on data collected for a larger project that involved 25 months of fieldwork (2008–2012) in the EU (Ayoub 2016). The fieldwork included over 80 semi-structured interviews with LGBT activists and their opponents and participant observation at LGBT and anti-LGBT events.

PREDICTING RESISTANCE: DIFFERING PERCEPTIONS OF THREAT

Threat Perceptions

A central premise of the proposed theoretical framework is that the ability of movements to expand rights projections of LGBT people is moderated by differing perceptions of threat across national contexts. I define *threat* as the anticipation of danger to a set of values that defines a group and *perception* as the process of apprehending by means of the senses. It is important to note that this definition assumes that threat can have a symbolic value at the collective level, in that threat is socially constructed through discourse among political authorities and publics (Meyer 2009). This sociological interpretation of perceived threat stipulates that social understandings within the domestic realm define the way state actors respond to international pressures (Andrews 1975, 524–35).

Sociologists of sexuality and feminist and queer theorists have long argued that new forms of sexuality are threatening to national identity because they destabilize the narrative of nation. This argument builds on the work of Stychin (1998), Binnie (2004) and others, who trace a history of national policies intended to categorize and repress non-reproductive forms of sexual intimacy; homosexuality being historically "linked to conspiracy, recruitment, opposition to the nation, and ultimately a threat to civilization" (Stychin 1998, 9). Sexuality, like gender, is threatening to national narratives because it is not confined to national borders and challenges the fixity of categories of national identity (Conrad 2001, 125). This is not to say, as Binnie (2004) also notes, that the relationship between national identity and sexuality is determined. National narratives of sexuality do change, for better or for worse, across time and place.

In international relations (IR) literature, one understanding of national security is the "absence of threat to acquired values" (Bajpai 2000, 8). Katzenstein (2003, 736) argues that "conceptions of identity, of self versus other, are always part of threat perceptions . . . The threat perceptions of groups and states are embedded [. . .] in systems of meaning that affect what is and what is not defined as a threat." Indeed, some state actors do interpret the imposition of the EU's norms on sexual minorities as a threat that requires "self-defense" (Cârstocea 2006, 216). This is especially true if our understanding of societal security "concerns the sustainability . . . of traditional patterns of language, culture, and religious and national identity and custom" (Buzan 1990, 2). Furthermore, as championed by feminist IR scholars, *who* merits security and *what* entails a security threat must be unpacked to include issues such as poverty, rape, domestic violence and gender subordination (Sjoberg 2009, 4; Tickner 1992). Paradoxically, the security of women and LGBT individuals—who seek protection from the state and the social collective—is often framed as threatening to the security of nations (Mole 2011).

Religion and the Popular Nation

Religion connects to nationalism because national narratives often invoke a return to the purity of an imagined past, one that is rooted in religious tradition (Hayes 2000). Even in "secular Europe," religion continues to be a feature of the nation and it has an authoritative voice on issues of sexuality and societal security in global geopolitics. Religion on its own does not explain the resistance to social norms, however, and more secular states are not necessarily the first to adopt LGBT norms (Ayoub 2016). Echoing scholars that champion a complex understanding of religion's effect on politics (Berger 1993; Grzymala-Busse 2012), I argue that religion plays a role in moderating the effect of international LGBT norms, but only in contexts where it has become linked to the popular nation. The role of religion varies across national contexts and across time as the relationship between religion and nation changes and as the LGBT norm is deliberated and coopted by various social actors. These factors have shaped the discourse and the extent of the opposition to norms concerning LGBT rights at multiple levels. The primary level analyzed in this section is domestic: exploring how domestic movements resist human rights norms that are perceived as external. A similar process occurs at the international level, however; the proliferation of "traditional values" arguments peddled to protect global security also contribute to the backlash against LGBT rights—the Russian state's newfound alliance with the Orthodox Church in defending nations against the encroachment of unwelcome "Western" values is a case in point.

In post-socialist European states, the relationship between religion and nation has been established in part by democratic transition, in which "the Church" played vastly dissimilar roles. By looking at Poland and Slovenia, two Roman Catholic countries, I hold constant the separate effect that denomination could play and because Catholicism is transnational and hierarchical in its institutional structure. Yet Philpott (2007, 506) has warned that despite this transnational scope, "religions do not usually act singly or comprehensively in their politics," which is true of the role religious institutions play in domestic LGBT politics. Their influence on politics varies across contexts, depending on the intricacies of Church-society relations and its role in processes of national meaning-making. Politicization of LGBT human rights as a threat is at the core of fueling resistance and backlash.

Without trying to downplay the distinct Polish and Slovenian features in the historical ties between religious nationalism and LGBT rights and their placement on opposite ends of this "most different" case design, the general trends are informative of diffusion processes of other states in the region (see Ayoub 2014, 339–340). According to the co-president of the European Forum of LGBT Christian Groups, the historical ties between religion and nation offer a predominant explanation for resistance to LGBT rights (interview no. 104).

THREAT PERCEPTION IN POLAND AND SLOVENIA

Poland and Slovenia exemplify differences in LGBT socio-legal recognition, with Slovenia making gains at an earlier time. As part of the emerging civil rights movement, which helped topple communism in Yugoslavia, the two first Slovenian gay and lesbian organizations, Magnus and Lesbian Group (ŠKUC-LL), were founded in 1984 and 1987, respectively. These were the first gay and lesbian groups not only in Yugoslavia but also in Eastern Europe (Greif 2005, 150), and both were transnationally oriented early on. Poland's movement started with fewer formal transnational ties, but the presence of LGBT groups has grown rapidly since the turn of the century. The "Let Them See Us" campaign and the Cracow March of Tolerance in 2003 and 2004 were the earliest key moments for gay and lesbian visibility in Poland (Gruszczyńska 2007, 99). The Polish experience with state-sponsored homophobia—including bans on LGBT marches in several cities around the time of EU accession—also differs from that of Slovenia, where social attitudes and legislation changed at an accelerated pace. In 2000, about 60% of Poles felt that homosexuality was never justifiable, while only 40% of Slovenes agreed (EVS 2011). In direct contrast to

Poland, Slovenia also enacted some of the most far-reaching LGBT rights laws in Europe (Ayoub 2016, 168).

These differences persist despite the fact that both states have a majority Catholic population, with over 90% of Slovenes (Conway 2009) and Poles (Mizielińska 2010) self-identifying as Catholic in 1990.[3] Both countries are also ethnically and linguistically homogenous relative to their European counterparts. Finally, they attained independence at roughly the same time, joined the EU in 2004 and are among the countries ranked by Freedom House as having the most successful democratic transitions (Bunce 2003, 172). By virtue of their differences in LGBT recognition, these two historically Catholic countries merit in-depth consideration. In what follows, I trace these distinctions back to different degrees of resistance generated by different perceptions of threat in both contexts.

Threat Perception in Poland

In Poland, national identity is linked to a long history of being deprived of nationhood and to the collective memory of foreign intrusion and oppression. The Church, in the last two centuries, adopted most of the functions of a political organization. It "gave people faith and power to struggle against invaders: the Germans, the Russians and the Austrians," becoming a defining feature of the Polish nation and their identity (interview no. 141).

The German-Soviet occupation of Poland during WWII and the subsequent re-drawing of geographic borders and population transfer only strengthened the role of the Church in popular memory as resistant to external power. During the post-war period, the WWII narrative of "bad" Germans was expanded into a "dualistic societal structure: 'bad' communists, associated with the Communist Party and its apparatus; and 'good' Poles, patriots, associated with the Roman Catholic Church" (Borowik 2002, 239–41). Soured relations between Church and state were fueled by the internment of priests, including the Primate of Poland, Cardinal Stefan Wyszyński, in response to Church resistance in the 1950s and 1960s (Philpott 2007, 511). In 1981, after the state imposed martial law and imprisoned Solidarity activists, the Church again assumed its role as "a shelter for truth against political censorship . . . [as] a symbol of freedom" (Borowik 2002, 241). It is important to note here that the Church not only became an increasingly important political actor in terms of its actions, but that it became a symbolic force equated with autonomy and democracy.

Before and after democratic transition, Karol Józef Wojtyła, later Pope John Paul II, also played an exceptional role in the Church's particular relationship to Poland, to Europe and to LGBT people. A Polish activist echoed the scholarship that has cited the Pope's political vision for a "new East to West evangelism" that Poland could bring to the EU in its accession (Katzenstein and Byrnes 2006, 684) and the responsibility bestowed upon Polish society to maintain and spread Catholic values via their return to Europe. In her view, the obstacle behind this philosophy for the LGBT movement is that "'saving the world' is already a difficult enough task, and doing it with 'fucks' [LGBT people] is impossible, so you had to kick 'fucks' out of the country [to realize the Pope's political role for Poland]" (interview no. 9). The ramifications of this philosophy played out politically when the socially conservative coalition of the Law and Justice Party (PiS), the League of Polish Families (LPR) and the Self-Defense of the Polish Republic (SRP) came to power in 2005, making LGBT people the core symbolic "other" in their nationalist politics of morality.

Threat Perception in Slovenia

In stark contrast to Poland, the Roman Catholic Church in Slovenia failed to become a consolidating social force either before or after democratic transition. The opportunity presented by a "return to Europe" did little to restore the political legitimacy of the Church; Slovenes placed minimal emphasis on it as a vehicle for evangelizing the "West." Coming out of WWII, the state successfully attributed the early post-war tensions between itself and the Church—which involved the expropriation of church properties, prosecution of priests and removal of religious curricula from schools—to the wider punishment for the Church's collaboration with Nazi occupiers and its failure to support the Resistance (Radeljić 2011, 179). Society's skeptical attitude towards the Church thus dates back to this time and is in contrast with the Polish collective memory, where the Church was heralded for its great resistance to outside forces. In the Yugoslav context, the essence of nation did not depend on the Church as it entered the post-war period.

While the Church was generally suppressed under communism, it is false to paint church-state interactions or the level of suppression as uniform. Črnič and Lesjak (2003), for example, provide a series of incidents exemplifying what they call a tolerant relationship between the Church and the Yugoslav state that did not win the Church popular sympathy after the regime changed. Finally, during the dissolution of Yugoslavia, Slovenia's brief, ten-day involvement in the war did not cement religion—which was used to differentiate the other republics and justify militarism—with the national philosophy (Črnič and Lesjak 2003, 350).

Historical experiences had political consequences for the Slovenian collective memory of church-state relations. Contrary to the widely accepted suppression narrative in Poland, Slovenes do not remember the Church as a victim of the socialist state. The results of the "Aufbruch" survey showed that 25% of respondents "believed that the Church was not persecuted at all during this [40-year socialist] period" and another 45% said the Church was only occasionally persecuted (Črnič and Lesjak 2003, 357). Similarly, 84% of Slovenes believed that individual Catholics were not at all (43%) or only occasionally (41%) discriminated against (357). This memory diminished the ability of the Church to influence societal thinking on LGBT politics: "People have a critical attitude towards the Church and they believe strongly in the separation of church and state. People do not take church messages seriously anymore" (interview no. 107).

Mobilized Resistance, Frames and Arenas of Opposition

Dissimilar perceptions of threat manifest themselves in the rhetoric and forms of resistance. This section examines how different threat perceptions influence the makeup and mobilization of the anti-LGBT resistance in the Polish and Slovene contexts, resulting in the varied discourses, arenas and frames of mobilization used. In both cases, the frames selected are initially grounded in morality and "the laws of nature," in which non-heterosexuality is portrayed as a threat to the family and thus also to the nation. In Poland, the threat to the nation begins with the family, but then makes a leap to become associated with the invasion of the nation by outside forces. I call this the *defend the nation* frame, because it is rooted in a philosophy of defensive moral nationalism. The frame is potent, because it harps on the idea that the nation is under attack—as depicted in Figure 7.1—where "wholesome" Poles waving the Polish flag are juxtaposed with "the other" waving EU, rainbow and (ironically) Soviet flags. Thus, similarly to what Mole (2011) has shown in the case of Latvia, threat is framed as *external* and presented in a way that suggests expanding LGBT human rights can dismantle the many attributes of national identity. The frame creates an artificial binary between Polish values and the imagined European queer periphery.

By contrast, in Slovenia, non-heterosexuality is framed as a threat to children and reproduction. Adopting Kuhar's (2009) term, I use the *well-being of children* to define the Slovenian counter-movement's frame. The frame links LGBT rights to societal frustrations with change in social structures, such as that provoked by lower birthrates. While the *wellbeing of children* frame is also inherently about the nation, the argumentation is not extrapolated to threat via invasive external power. In Slovenia, the opposition has less public visibility, and nationalist and religious groups do not use the same narrative, differentiating itself from the vocal opposition

Translations: (clockwise from left) "These are Fascists?," "These are Poles?," "Gay is OK".

Source: DlaPolski TV [online], November 8, 2011, available from: http://www.dlapolski.pl/faszysci-polacy (accessed 1 December 2012).

Figure 7.1 The defend the nation frame

by Polish groups that define themselves as both national and religious. In what follows, I touch on how these frames were employed as well as the types of anti-LGBT actors who were mobilized in response to LGBT rights in the streets. For a deeper analysis of resistance in other arenas, such as conventional politics, in the media and in the education system, refer to an earlier articulation of this research (Ayoub 2014, 346–53).

Resistance on the Streets

Not only were marches for LGBT rights banned in several Polish cities around the time of EU accession, but also "various groups and politicians organize[d] marches of 'normalcy'" (interview no. 129). Among the most active groups in mobilizing demonstrations is the *Stowarzyszenie Kultury Chrześcijańskiej im. Ks. Piotra Skargi* (Father Piotr Skarga Association for Christian Culture), founded in Cracow in 1999 (Mizielińska 2010, 333). This group organized the *Marsz dla Życia i Rodziny* (March for Life and

Family) from 2006 to 2008, and participants donned the typical Polish national symbols, crosses and banners, calling to "Stop Perversion" and that "Marriage is One Man, One Woman." As is common in Poland, these chants are often complemented with nationalist versions: "Lesbians and faggots are ideal citizens of the EU" and "Healthy Poles are not like that" (Gruszczyńska 2007, 100). Another Catholic organization, the *Fundacja Mamy i Taty* (Foundation for Mothers and Fathers) is vocal in the public sphere and politically lobbies conservative politicians (interview nos. 129 and 141). Before EuroPride in 2010, it paid for a full-page newspaper advertisement outlining the "homosexual threat" and, together with the Catholic magazine *Fronda*, organized an online petition and counter protest. All three groups have a Catholic mandate, but deploy a clearly nationalist discourse around the defense of uniquely Polish values.

Extreme in this regard was the early opposition to LGBT rights by *Młodzież Wszechpolska* (All Polish Youth), a far-right nationalist and Catholic youth organization founded in 1922 and revived after independence in 1989. In response to Cracow's Festival of Culture for Tolerance in 2004, the group formulated their "Declaration of Ideas" as follows: "The Nation is the most important worldly value. First, after God, service is deserved by our own nation . . . [The Church] creates and strengthens Polish national identity" (Kubica 2009, 130). The organization, which had ties to PiS, was most active against LGBT mobilization from 2004 to 2007. Other Polish nationalist groups also mobilized against LGBT rights, making LGBT politics the focus of their "defense of nation" rhetoric. The groups *Narodowe Odrodzenie Polski* (NOP) (National Rebirth of Poland) and *Obóz Narodowo-Radykalny* (ONR) (National Radical Camp) both describe their mission as "spiritually motivated" nationalism and championing "the development and revival of national and Catholic values" (Obóz Narodowo-Radykalny 2011).[4] In practice, these groups mobilize extremists from around the country to gather and block LGBT marches, informally recruiting, for example, through soccer fan forums that bring together hooligans opposed to LGBT rights (interview no. 130).

In contrast, the *wellbeing of children* frame in Slovenia has not spurred public mobilization in the way the *defend the nation* frame has in Poland. The Slovenian state has not banned freedom of assembly since independence in 1991 (Fundamental Rights Agency 2009, 5). Furthermore, "there is no record of demonstrations against tolerance of LGBT people" (6). The two opposition groups that activists sometimes, though rarely, mentioned in interviews and surveys are *Tukaj je Slovenija* (Here is Slovenia) and the Slovenian branch of the group Blood and Honor. The former makes a reference to the Church on its website, but religion is not mentioned among its three fundamental goals. Neither group has organized counter protests, but they are responsible for sporadic violence directed at individuals or vandalizing organizational façades. The difference between Slovenia and Poland in public sphere opposition to LGBT rights is that Slovenian "nationalist groups are anti-religious, and quite strongly anti-religious" (interview no. 108).

Across the board, in parliament and on the streets, Poland's opposition has outpaced its Slovenian counterpart in degree and intensity. For much of the two decades following independence, the Polish Church could confidently brand LGBT people as a threat to the Polish nation and to European civilization. The *defend the nation* frame in Poland mobilized a fervent opposition uniting diverse actors under a narrative of nation, which equated LGBT rights with an invasion of the domestic sphere. For observers at Polish LGBT marches, this frame is evident in that "demonstrators [carry] mainly EU flags while their opponents [carry] only Polish ones" (Kubica 2009, 141). In Slovenia, the perceived threat was lower, and the *wellbeing of children* frame could not mobilize or unite a weak and fragmented domestic opposition. Slovenian LGBT actors commanded a discourse that LGBT rights were part of what it meant to return to Europe, and the Church was not in a position to "adopt the powerful rhetoric of being a 'traditional,' 'national' or 'state-Constitutional Church'" (Črnič and Lesjak 2003, 361).

Defending Civilizations: Global Resistance[5]

Outside of the EU, and beyond the specific case studies of Poland and Slovenia, we see a similar tendency for active resistance in states where threat perception is high. Indeed, the success in fueling national and populist sentiments by targeting LGBT people as a threat has, at least partly, similar trajectories in very different contexts. Furthermore, as LGBT rights have become more visible, states have paid more attention to them, in some cases offering to "defend" traditional values—by opposing LGBT human rights—in geopolitical contests. With norm polarization (Symons and Altman 2015), different spheres of influence impact LGBT rights and result in starkly different perceptions of the legitimacy of those rights. While Europe (broadly conceived) has become a champion of LGBT rights in the imaginations of many states, other powerful political entities having become vocal opponents of them, using the issue to champion a moral conservatism that purposefully distinguishes itself and other states from "Europe" and "the West." The Ukraine crisis that began in 2013 illustrates the situation of a state caught between the EU and Russia, where Russian authorities framed the Maidan protesters as "gay" and, as in Poland, westward alignment as an abandonment of Ukraine's moral and traditional values. As Alexei Pushkov, the Chairman of the Russian Duma's Foreign Affairs Committee, explained to Ukrainians, turning toward a de-masculinized "Gayropa" would mean "an expansion of the sphere of the so-called gay culture, which has now turned into the official policy of the EU" (Ayoub and Paternotte 2014, 1). Politics that "defend the nation" can thus also be championed by other states in contemporary world politics to defend tradition and civilization as a whole.

In many ways, this global process of constructing threat around LGBT human rights is similar to issues we have explored domestically in earlier sections. Like the tie between the Catholic Church and the notion of "Polishness" that heightened threat perception in Poland, "Russians today view [Orthodox] Church affiliation as a way to reaffirm their 'Russianness'" (Khazan 2013). While rates of religiosity are strikingly low in global comparison, much of the Russian population supports the Russian Orthodox Church as a national symbol of pride, and the Church wields considerable political might as a close ally to President Vladimir Putin's government. A defend the nation type of resistance is increasingly apparent in recent years. In June 2013, the Russian Duma extended various city ordinances banning LGBT "propaganda" by unanimously passing a federal law that fines individuals and organizations up to $31,000 for promoting homosexuality (Khazan 2013). Yet these politics are not isolated to just one nation. Contracting LGBT rights has found a central place in the contemporary geopolitics, portrayed as a feature of the cultural paradigm—distinct from the decadent West—that it can offer the world (Riabov and Riabova 2014).

In sum, much like the transnational innovations by LGBT actors, state actors have also been creative in promoting their ideologies transnationally. Whether in the United States or in Lithuania, they have also introduced and diffused novel bills intended to protect religious liberty, sanctify marriage, oppose "gender ideology" and ban the promotion of homosexuality. The language of protecting society from the gender and sexuality "threat" is apparent for example, in the religious opposition to the Colombian FARC peace accords (which claimed the deal promoted "gender ideology"), the U.S. based resistance to gender-neutral bathrooms and support for the religious "freedom" to refuse serving LGBT people, the French *Manif pour Tous* movement to oppose same-sex marriage and the notorious Ugandan "kill-the-gays" bill proposal.

Thus, the expansion of LGBT rights as part of universal human rights—for example in EU law, or in the United Nations' more recent rhetoric and declarations—does not go uncontested (Chase 2016). Resistance by governments creates an indeterminacy surrounding the legitimacy of LGBT norms that also fuels the fomentation of societal backlash. The more states perceive and politicize these issues to be "external," the more resistance they will provoke.

CONCLUSION

This chapter has explored the domestic responses to international norms governing LGBT rights. I have suggested that distinct contexts attach differing degrees of threat to an otherwise similar human rights norm. Threat perception concerning LGBT rights depends largely on the degree to which the moral authority of religious institutions is tied to national identity. The argument thus goes beyond religious morality, to place importance on the situational politicization of religion in national identity. It is the role of religion in people's identities—not religion itself—that matters for LGBT politics, which can result in distinctive political manifestations for LGBT resistance across states. In Poland, the intense collective reaction in society of a perceived threat from LGBT and reproductive rights, linked to the Church's historically deep ties to the popular nation, resulted in zealous resistance—a resistance that could frame LGBT rights as an external threat to the nation. Comparatively, in Slovenia, the weaker credibility of the Church hampered its ability to bring together an opposition around a national and moral narrative, which in turn limited its mobilizing potential against LGBT rights.

While much of the chapter looked at domestic resistance, constructing LGBT rights as a threat has also had currency at the international level. There are thus two ways to look at such resistance: perceived threat at the domestic level *and* at the international level, where states differentiate themselves from LGBT rights with the new traditional values paradigm. In both cases, the defense of some imagined past—the nation or "tradition"—rests at the center of such resistance. Various religions and denominations can inflate threat in similar ways when conditions are right. In doing so, networks of homophobia play an increasingly powerful role globally (Bob 2012; Weiss and Bosia 2013). Furthermore, with increasing norm polarization around LGBT rights, states may react according to how enmeshed they are in the norms of their distinct international communities. Where nationalist fervor is high and norms supporting LGBT rights are most indeterminate we should expect resistances to have the most success at challenging the expansion of LGBT rights.

In sum, resistance (in degree and scope) is deeply linked to society's perception of a possible threat. What does this all mean for LGBT human rights? It suggests a long and difficult struggle ahead for LGBT movements around the globe. Whether resistance is effectual, however, is a separate question. The pathway to LGBT rights in Slovenia has been smoother, but the active resistance in Poland will not necessarily yield success for opponents of these rights. While resistance fuels a political backlash, for states centered within international communities that clearly espouse LGBT rights norms, resistance can also be a pathway to visibility by making LGBT issues more salient than before (Ayoub 2016; O'Dwyer 2012). Contractions to human rights can also galvanize the very movements supporting those rights.

NOTES

1. This text is adapted with permission from an article published in the Journal of Human Rights (Ayoub 2014).
2. By "Church," I simply refer to the dominant religious institution, all of which happen to be Christian in the EU.
3. Beyond self-identification, Poles are far more likely to attend religious services. In 1990, 71% of Slovenes considered themselves adherent to the Catholic faith. Before WWII, 97% of Slovenes identified as Catholic.
4. Translated from the Polish.
5. The ideas and prose in this section are adapted from Ayoub (2016, 47–8 and 217–20).

REFERENCES

Andrews, Bruce. 1975. "Social Rules and the State as a Social Actor." *World Politics*, 27(4): 521–40.

Ayoub, Phillip M. 2013. "Cooperative Transnationalism in Contemporary Europe: Europeanization and Political Opportunities for LGBT Mobilization in the European Union." *European Political Science Review*, 5(2): 279–310.

Ayoub, Phillip M. 2014. "With Arms Wide Shut: Threat Perception, Norm Reception, and Mobilized Resistance to LGBT Rights." *Journal of Human Rights*, 13(3): 337–62.

Ayoub, Phillip M. 2016. *When States Come Out: Europe's Sexual Minorities and the Politics of Visibility*. New York: Cambridge University Press.

Ayoub, Phillip M., and David Paternotte, eds. 2014. *LGBT Activism and the Making of Europe*. Palgrave Macmillan.

Bajpai, Kanti. 2000. Human Security: Concept and Measurement. New Delhi, India: Kroc Institute Occasional Paper No. 19: OP:1.

Berger, Peter L. 1993. A Far Glory: The Quest for Faith in an Age of Credulity. New York: Anchor.

Binnie, Jon. 2004. *The Globalization of Sexuality*. London, UK: Sage Publications.

Bob, Clifford. 2012. *The Global Right Wing and the Clash of World Politics*. Cambridge: Cambridge University Press.

Borowik, Irena. 2002. "The Roman Catholic Church in the Process of Democratic Transformation: The Case of Poland." Social Compass, 49(2): 239–52.

Bunce, Valerie. 2003. "Rethinking Recent Democratization: Lessons from the Postcommunist Experience." *World Politics*, 55(2): 167–92.
Buzan, Barry. 1990. "The Case for a Comprehensive Definition of Security and the Institutional Consequences of Accepting It." Working Papers, 4(0): 1–17.
Cârstocea, Sinziana. 2006. "Between Acceptance and Rejection: Decriminalizing Homosexuality in Romania." In *The Gays' and Lesbians' Rights in an Enlarged European Union*, Brussels: Editions de l'Université de Bruxelles, 216–22.
Chase, Anthony. 2016. "Human Rights Contestations: Sexual Orientation and Gender Identity." *The International Journal of Human Rights*, 20(6): 703–23.
Conrad, Kathryn. 2001. "Queer Treasons: Homosexuality and Irish National Identity." *Cultural Studies*, 15(1): 124–37.
Conway, Brian. 2009. *Individual-Level Determinants of Religious Practice and Belief in Catholic Europe*. IRISS at CEPS/INSTEAD. IRISS Working Paper Series. http://ideas.repec.org/p/irs/iriswp/2009-14.html (February 8, 2013).
Črnič, Aleš, and Gregor Lesjak. 2003. "Religious Freedom and Control in Independent Slovenia." *Sociology of Religion*, 64(3): 349–66.
European Values Study. 1981–2008 (EVS). 2011. (Cologne, Germany: GESIS Data Archive), http://www.europeanvaluesstudy.eu/evs/data-and-downloads/ (January 1, 2012).
Fundamental Rights Agency (FRA). 2009. "The Social Situation Concerning Homophobia and Discrimination on Grounds of Sexual Orientation in Slovenia." Luxembourg: Publications Office of the European Union.
Greif, Tatjana. 2005. "The Social Status of Lesbian Women in Slovenia in the 1990s." In *Sexuality and Gender in Postcommunist Eastern Europe and Russia*, New York: The Haworth Press, 149–69.
Gruszczyńska, Anna. 2007. "Living 'La Vida' Internet: Some Notes on the Cyberization of Polish LGBT Community." In *Beyond the Pink Curtain*, eds. Roman Kuhar and Judit Takács. Ljubljana: Peace Institute, 95–115.
Grzymala-Busse, Anna. 2012. "Why Comparative Politics Should Take Religion (More) Seriously." *Annual Review of Political Science*, 15(1): 421–42.
Hayes, Jarrod. 2000. *Queer Nations: Marginal Sexualities in the Maghreb*. Chicago: University of Chicago Press.
Katzenstein, Peter J. 2003. "Same War: Different Views: Germany, Japan, and Counterterrorism." *International Organization*, 57(4): 731–60.
Katzenstein, Peter J., and Timothy A. Byrnes. 2006. "Transnational Religion in an Expanding Europe." *Perspectives on Politics*, 4(4): 679–94.
Khazan, Olga. 2013. "Why Is Russia So Homophobic?" *The Atlantic*. http://www.theatlantic.com/international/archive/2013/06/why-is-russia-so-homophobic/276817/ (June 15, 2013).
Kubica, Grażyna. 2009. "A Rainbow Flag against the Krakow Dragon: Polish Responses to the Gay and Lesbian Movement." In *Postsocialist Europe: Anthropological Perspectives from Home*, eds. Laszlo Kürti and Peter Skalnik. New York: Berghahn Books, 119–49.
Meyer, Christoph O. 2009. "International Terrorism as a Force of Homogenization? A Constructivist Approach to Understanding Cross-National Threat Perceptions and Responses." *Cambridge Review of International Affairs*, 22(4): 647–66.
Mizielińska, Joanna. 2010. "Poland." In *The Greenwood Encyclopedia of LGBT Issues Worldwide*, ed. Chuck Stewart. Westport, CT: ABC-CLIO/Greenwood, 321–37.

Mole, Richard. 2011. "Nationality and Sexuality: Homophobic Discourse and the 'national Threat' in Contemporary Latvia." *Nations and Nationalism*, 17(3): 540–60.
"Obóz Narodowo-Radykalny." 2011. *Obóz Narodowo-Radykalny*. http://www.onr.h2.pl/index.php?option=com_content&view=article&id=95&Itemid=28 (October 24, 2011).
O'Dwyer, Conor. 2012. "Does the EU Help or Hinder Gay-Rights Movements in Post-Communist Europe? The Case of Poland." *East European Politics*, 28(4): 332–52.
Paternotte, David, and Kelly Kollman. 2013. "Regulating Intimate Relationships in the European Polity: Same-sex Unions and Policy Convergence." *Social Politics*, 20(4): 510–33.
Philpott, Daniel. 2007. "Explaining the Political Ambivalence of Religion." *The American Political Science Review*, 101(3): 505–25.
Radeljić, Branislav. 2011. "Blessing the Collapse of Yugoslavia: The Vatican's Role in EC Policy-Making." *Serbian Studies Research*, 2(1): 177–204.
Riabov, Oleg, and Tatiana Riabova. 2014. "The Decline of Gayropa? – How Russia Intends to Save the World." *Eurozine*. http://www.eurozine.com/articles/2014-02-05-riabova-en.html (April 13, 2015).
Sjoberg, Laura, ed. 2009. *Gender and International Security: Feminist Perspectives*. London and New York: Routledge.
Stychin, Carl Franklin. 1998. *A Nation By Rights: National Cultures, Sexual Identity Politics, and the Discourse of Rights*. Philadelphia: Temple University Press.
Symons, Jonathan, and Dennis Altman. 2015. "International Norm Polarization: Sexuality as a Subject of Human Rights Protection." *International Theory*, 7(1): 61–95.
Tickner, Ann. 1992. *Gender in International Relations: Feminist Perspectives on Achieving Global Security*. New York: Columbia University Press.
Weiss, Meredith L., and Michael J. Bosia. 2013. *Global Homophobia: States, Movements, and the Politics of Oppression*. Urbana-Champaign, IL: University of Illinois Press.

Referenced Interviews:

9. Kampania Przeciw Homofobii (KPH), July 17, 2009.
104. European Forum of LGBT Christian Groups, October 29, 2010.
107. DIC Legebitra, October 30, 2010.
108. DIC Legebitra, October 30, 2010.
129. Kampania Przeciw Homofobii (KPH), October 12, 2011.
130. KPH Łódź, October 23, 2011.
141. All Polish Youth, November 25, 2011.

8. Human rights and democracy promotion in times of contraction: EU human rights and democratization policies in Egypt

Felipe Gómez Isa

INTRODUCTION

Since the end of the Cold War, the European Union (EU) has tried to accompany the so-called third wave of democratization processes in a number of countries, and has projected itself as what some scholars refer to as a "normative power Europe" (Manners, 2002). Accordingly, human rights and democratic principles have become essential pillars of the EU's identity both at internal and at external level (Barbé, 2014, p.395), at least as a proclamation of principles. With the adoption of the Treaty of Maastricht in 1992, the EU started to pay particular attention to human rights and democratization issues in its relations with third countries (Alston, 1999). Since then, the EU has significantly upgraded its human rights and democratization policies *vis-à-vis* third countries (Smith, 2008), and has placed human rights and democracy "at the heart of EU External Action" (European Commission and High Representative of the EU, 2011). As a clear manifestation of this commitment, the EU has adopted a wide range of instruments, policy statements, guidelines and programmes (both thematic and geographic) to support human rights and democracy as an integral dimension of the EU foreign policy.

Due to the new international scenario and the progressive decline of Western power (Piccone, 2015), there are increasing concerns about the capacity of the EU to have a significant impact on democratization processes taking place in different regions of the world. We are witnessing a global backlash against human rights and democracy that is weakening the key ingredients of the Western liberal order (Youngs, 2015). The access of Donald Trump to the US Presidency, and the emergence of populisms in Europe, are but reaffirming this global trend that is undermining the universal scope of values such as human rights and democracy (Aguirre, 2017). The aim of this paper is to shed light on the potential, shortcomings and contradictions of the EU as a human rights and democracy promoter in a strategically relevant context: post-Arab Spring Egypt.

A DECLINE OF WESTERN POWER?

In the last decades, a progressive decline of Western power has taken place, with an increasing economic and political relevance of emerging countries such as Brazil, Russia, India, China, South Africa (the so-called BRICS), the Gulf States and Turkey, to name but a few. While some emerging states are currently facing a strong economic crisis, they still pose a geopolitical challenge to the exercise of power by the West. This has led some commentators to proclaim that we have entered a "post-Western World" (Dennison and Dworkin, 2010), a new context in which the EU and the US cannot take the lead any more in issues that have to do with the promotion of a value-based international system. Contrary to the prophecy advanced by Francis Fukuyama (1989) with his idea of the *End of History* and the victory of the liberal democratic paradigm after the fall of communism, we are facing a troubling weakening of human rights and democracy as shared values of a universal scope (Magen, 2015). Against the background of this dramatic change in the global balance of power, Richard Youngs (2010) has alerted that the EU is running the risk of becoming globally irrelevant.

Moreover, some of these emerging countries have a rather different approach to human rights and democracy, thus questioning the legitimacy of the EU to promote its human rights and democracy agenda internationally (Walker, 2014). To some extent, the so-called *Beijing Consensus* is progressively substituting the *Washington Consensus* as a paradigm to be followed in many countries outside the West (Dennison and Dworkin, 2010, p.2).[1] The main consequence of this trend is that economic liberalization can go hand in hand with authoritarian or semi-authoritarian policies and practices (Keukeleire and Delreux, 2014, p.287). And some of these relatively powerful countries have initiated a calculated strategy of "autocracy promotion" (Burnell, 2010) in third countries to counter-react to Western efforts at human rights and democracy support when they perceive these efforts "as a threat to its own regime survival . . ., or as a threat to its geostrategic interests" (Risse and Babayan, 2015, p.385).[2]

A particular case is the strong support by Saudi Arabia and Qatar to authoritarian regimes in the MENA region to avoid any influence of the democratic wave brought about by the Arab Spring and to maintain the status quo (Sigillò, 2015). Saudi Arabia has been able "to buy influence and undermine Western leverage for political reforms" (Hassan, 2015, p.492). This counter-revolutionary role played by Saudi Arabia points to one of the greatest contradictions of the values-based foreign policies of both the EU and the US. Once again, the West has prioritized security and stability over democracy and human rights, very much in line with the strategic interests of Saudi Arabia (Greenfield and Balfour, 2012). We cannot but remember that Saudi Arabia is one of the closest allies of the West in the region, in spite of its manifestly poor record on human rights and democracy. This is a crystal-clear manifestation of one of the main deficits of the EU human rights and democracy policies: the *credibility gap*, the use of double standards when European strategic interests are at stake in third countries. Obviously, this lack of credibility strongly undermines the EU's legitimacy to pursue a human rights and democracy agenda, thus hindering the effectiveness and impact of its human rights and democracy promotion efforts.

The Arab Spring has acted as a wake-up call for an EU that for decades had supported the authoritarian regimes that offered stability and access to their natural resources in the region (Durac, 2009). These uprisings clearly illustrate the shortcomings of the interest-driven EU's approach to the promotion of human rights and democracy worldwide, paving the way to criticisms of selectivity and double standards.

Another telling illustration of this emerging autocratic wave is exemplified by Russia's support to authoritarian regimes in its neighbourhood (its "zone of influence" in the eyes of the Russian regime, reinvigorating the old language of the Cold War) to counteract democracy promotion by the EU and the US. Russia perceives human rights and democracy promotion as an orchestrated campaign by a number of actors in the West (the EU, the US, the Soros Foundation and other think-tanks) aimed at curtailing its influence in its neighbour countries, therefore undermining its strategic interests not only in the region but, ultimately, worldwide. This confrontational attitude adopted by Russia is based on its perception of the actions sponsored by the West as arrogant and based on a sense of moral superiority. In the end, Russia is suffering from what some scholars refer to as "imperial nostalgia" (Krickovic, 2014). As Nelli Babayan has rightly pointed out, Russia's strong reaction to human rights and democracy promotion from the outside is mainly based on "its ambitions of restoring its great power status and maintaining its regional influence" (Babayan, 2015, p.438). And in order to do so, Russia is prone to contain any attempt to challenge authoritarian rule and to promote democratic ideals. The accurate reflection by Christopher Walker (2014) speaks for itself:

> Russia's destabilization of Ukraine, where Moscow has annexed Crimea and provoked a debilitating separatist rebellion in the eastern part of that country, has dominated the news recently. But this action should be seen for what it is: a Kremlin containment effort to prevent Ukrainians from achieving a democratically accountable government that would threaten Russia's corrupt authoritarian system. The Ukraine example is just one small part of a vast containment ambition led by the regimes in Moscow, Beijing, Riyadh and Tehran, which may disagree on many things but share an interest in limiting the spread of democracy.

The rise of China as a competing economic power is also a source of concern in Western capitals due to the negative influence it may have on the EU and the US human rights and democracy promotion policies (Nathan 2015). China and the EU "compete for the same resources, markets and political influence" (Keukeleire and Delreux, 2014, p.285) in the Middle East, Africa, Latin America and other parts of the world. China's disregard for the human rights situations in the countries with which they cooperate is a relevant source of distrust and suspicion, since the EU firmly believes that it can pave the way to "undermining the EU's human rights, democracy and development policies" (Keukeleire and Delreux, 2014, p.286). China's approach to the EU's democracy promotion policies is dominated by pragmatism, and it will only react to those policies when regime survival at home is at risk. If Chinese strategic interests are at stake, China will definitively counter-react to human rights and democracy promotion from the outside. As the cases of Angola and Ethiopia in Africa show, "the presence of China has had limited influence on the implementation of the US and the EU's democracy promotion strategies" (Hackenesch, 2015, p.431). But, as Dennison and Dworkin (2010, p.11) have ironically emphasized, "instead of simply criticizing China's role in Africa as undermining Western efforts, Europeans should look critically at the record of their own governments and businesses".

THE EU'S HUMAN RIGHTS AND DEMOCRACY PROMOTION IN EGYPT BEFORE 2011

The *Barcelona Declaration* adopted at the Euro-Mediterranean Conference on November 1995 intended to establish a comprehensive partnership among the countries of the two shores of the *Mare Nostrum* (Blanc Altemir, 2012). The Euro-Mediterranean Partnership (EMP) was based on measures in the fields of political dialogue, economic and financial cooperation, and advancements in the social, cultural and human dimension. One of the underlying ideas of this process of cooperation was that "stability and prosperity requires a strengthening of democracy and respect for human rights".[3] The Association Agreement that was concluded between the EU and Egypt in 2001[4] included the ritual human rights clause that the EU requires of all third countries. As established in Article 2 of the Agreement:

> relations between the Parties, as well as all the provisions of the Agreement itself, shall be based on respect of democratic principles and fundamental human rights as set out in the Universal Declaration on Human Rights, which guides their internal and international policy and constitutes *an essential element of this Agreement.*
> (emphasis added)

The *European Neighbourhood Policy* (ENP) launched in 2004 is basically focused on economic integration and financial aid, but it also has a human rights and democracy component. As a manifestation of these strategic objectives, the *EU/Egypt Action Plan* (2007) prioritized cooperation in the areas of trade, investment and growth so that Egypt can better integrate in the EU economic structures, but it also established as priorities some ambitious actions dealing with key democracy and human rights issues in Egypt. In particular, the Action Plan foresaw specific actions on strengthening participation in political life, on fostering the capacity of civil society to participate and contribute to the political process, on opening a dialogue with the Egyptian Government on human rights and democracy, on ensuring the independence of the judiciary, on engaging in a dialogue on the death penalty, on the rights of women and children, on freedom of association and expression, and on fundamental social rights and core labour standards, among many others.

All these cooperation frameworks between the EU and Egypt insist on the relevance of human rights and democracy opening the door to the application of the principle of conditionality if the third country does not make sufficient progress. But we must recognize that the EU has been very reluctant to apply this principle, in spite of a significant deterioration of the situation of human rights and democracy in Egypt under President Mubarak. The EU supported for decades Mubarak's authoritarian regime that offered stability, access to their natural resources in the region, and an adequate management and control of the rise of political Islam (Silvestri, 2005, p.388).

THE EU'S HUMAN RIGHTS AND DEMOCRACY PROMOTION IN EGYPT AFTER THE ARAB SPRING

The unexpected uprisings that took place first in Tunisia and then in Egypt in 2010 and 2011, respectively, caught Europe "by surprise" (Khalifa Isaac, 2012, p. 7). A great sense of perplexity and confusion invaded European capitals, as they did not know what line of action to support in relation to their old "autocratic friends" (Askar Karakir, 2014, p.44). In the case of Egypt, given its geostrategic importance and its political weight in the region, initially the EU adopted a very cautious approach, and avoided any open criticism of the Mubarak regime. In the very beginning, the EU and some relevant Member States believed that the Mubarak regime could accommodate the demands of the protests that started on 25 January 2011 and pilot an ordered transition to democracy. From the EU's perspective, "political reform led by a friendly regime was more preferable . . ., rather than regime change in the form of an uncontrolled process" (Askar Karakir, 2014, p.44). But this strategy proved illusory very soon, as the protesters in Tahrir Square were determined to push for a radical change of regime. On 4 February 2011, the European Council adopted a *Declaration on Egypt and the Region*, and "called on the Egyptian authorities to meet the aspirations of the Egyptian people with political reform not repression" (European Council, 2011). Although the Council did not demand explicitly Mubarak's resignation, the EU changed its tone, trying to "distance itself from the Mubarak regime" (Askar Karakir, 2014, p.44).

The collapse of the Mubarak regime on 11 February 2011 sent a clear message to the EU and, as a consequence, it opened a process of reflection to adopt a new approach to the relations with Egypt. Some days later, the EU High Representative said that what Egypt and the whole region needed was "deep democracy", and that the EU had to develop a "fundamental review of the ENP" (EU High Representative, 2011, p.2). There was a significant rhetoric shift in the EU, since from that time onwards the EU insisted that democratic reforms and political reforms must go hand-in-hand; long-term stability cannot be achieved without the opening of political space to democratic reform. The new EU document outlining the main components of the reviewed ENP adopted in May 2011 stressed that the goal of the new approach is "to build and consolidate healthy democracies, and to pursue sustainable economic growth" (EU High Representative and European Commission, 2011, p.1).

One of the pillars of this new approach is the principle of *conditionality*. EU support "will depend on progress in building and consolidating democracy and respect for the rule of law. The more and the faster a country progresses in its internal reforms, the more support it will get" (*more for more*)

(EU High Representative and European Commission, 2011, p.3). On the contrary, for those countries that do not show a sufficient commitment to democratic reforms, "the EU will reconsider or even reduce funding" (*less for less*) (EU High Representative and European Commission, 2011, p.3). The EU promised a substantial increase in the funds allocated to the whole region, but they would be conditional on a sincere commitment to the promotion of deep democracy.

In spite of the initial rhetoric ambitions of the EU to radically change its approach to the promotion of human rights and democracy in Egypt and the whole region after the Arab Spring, we must recognize that only some cosmetic changes have taken place. The EU "has reverted to business as usual with Egypt, despite the country's return to authoritarian government" (Balfour *et al.*, 2016, p.6). The core tenets of the EU's policies towards Egypt have remained largely unaltered.

Ultimately, given the serious violations of human rights and democracy taking place in Egypt and the progressive deterioration of the situation, unfortunately we are inclined to share the pessimistic conclusions expressed by Tommaso Virgili (2014, p.45): "the EU has been both unable and unwilling to use negative and positive conditionality in order to drive the various Egyptian governments to build a deep democracy". Both the Morsi Government (2012–2013) and the Al-Sisi Government have been extremely reluctant to engage in an open and sincere dialogue on human rights and democracy with the EU. On the contrary, they have taken very restrictive measures to close spaces to those actors, both external and domestic, working on human rights and democracy. As explicitly recognized by an EU official, although the "politically correct response is that human rights and democracy are a core objective for the EU in its relations with Egypt", reality shows that these issues are "very sensitive"; the EU deals with these issues very carefully and "in a context of a region in crisis with an increasing problem of terrorism."[5]

The Democratization-Stability Dilemma

The relations between the EU and Egypt in the last decades have been conditioned by the dilemma of how to promote human rights and democracy without risking the stability and security in Egypt and in the whole region (Pace, 2012, p.58). The EU has tried to promote human rights and democracy but, simultaneously, it has aimed at preserving the political stability of the authoritarian regime due to its strategic and geopolitical significance, for its role in the fight against terrorism and illegal migration, for its importance to secure energy routes from North Africa, and for its ability to restrain the rise of political Islam in the country (Khalifa Isaac,

2012, p.5). In case of conflict between these seemingly competing interests, the EU opted without any doubt for supporting its authoritarian friend in the country of pharaohs.

The uprisings that led to the end of the Mubarak regime in January 2011 showed very clearly that lasting stability cannot be achieved to the detriment of human rights and democracy. In the end, the democratization-stability dilemma is a false dilemma, since the best way to guarantee long-term stability and security is through a firm commitment to democracy, human rights and social justice (Muñoz Nogal and Gómez Isa, 2016). This idea has been openly accepted, at least rhetorically, by senior EU officials. The words pronounced by the then President of the European Commission, José Manuel Durao Barroso (2011), in a speech at the Opera House in Cairo on 14 July 2011 are very illuminating, and sound like a confession of past mistakes on Egypt: "In the past too many have traded democracy for stability. But recent events have only proven that lasting stability can only be achieved through democratic and accountable governments".

Unfortunately, in spite of the *mea culpa* issued by some relevant EU officials, and in spite of the rhetorical shift developed by the EU through official statements and through the review of policies such as the ENP, we have to recognize that security and strategic considerations continue figuring prominently in the bilateral relations with Egypt. The EU continues considering Egypt a strategic partner in the region and continues offering substantial cooperation in spite of the manifest deterioration of the situation of human rights in Egypt and lack of progress in areas such as democratization, freedom of association and assembly, fight against corruption, independence of the judiciary, and the necessary space for CSOs (European Commission, 2015, p.3).

A very telling example is the EU's accommodation and implicit acceptance of the strong financial and political support offered by Saudi Arabia to Egypt to avoid any influence of the democratic wave brought about by the Arab Spring and to maintain the status quo in the region (Sigillò, 2015). Once again, Europe has prioritized security and stability over democracy and human rights. This contradiction was clearly illustrated when General Al-Sisi organized a coup d'État in July 2013 to oust the democratically-elected Islamist President Mohammed Morsi. Not only the EU did avoid the use of the term coup d'État, but it also offered an implicit approval.

Despite the recognition of past mistakes by the EU, and despite the new rhetoric about deep democracy, "the EU has not been distancing itself from old politics and attitudes" (Wouters and Duquet, 2013, p.23). The old dynamics of stability versus democracy are still a core ingredient of the EU's foreign policy on Egypt (Helmy, 2015, p.6), thus hindering the

EU's capacity to have a significant impact in Egypt's human rights and democracy performance.

Backlash Against Human Rights and Democracy Promotion in Egypt

As part of the new international climate brought about by the relative decline of Western power and the rise of emerging powers, many countries are expressing a growing hostility to the human rights and democracy support policies and programmes sponsored by the EU and other international donors (Carothers, 2006), "especially those that seek to empower civil society; promote free media; and strengthen democratic political parties, institutions, and processes" (Gershman and Allen, 2006, p.36). The root causes of the global phenomenon of backlash are complex, multifaceted, and inextricably linked to structural changes in global politics and global economy. In the view of Carothers and Brechenmacher (2013, p.23), two main factors help us understand the reactions against human rights and democracy promotion. First of all, after the post-Cold War decade in which democracy assistance was favourably perceived, the 2000s witnessed a "loss of democratic momentum", and power holders in many countries began to view such assistance as "excessively intrusive and politically threatening". This counter-reaction has also much to do with the "democracy rhetoric that accompanied the 2003 Iraq War" (Huber, 2013, p.105). This disastrous military intervention deepened the weakening of the credibility of the West and negatively affected global views on human rights and democracy support policies. Therefore, the democracy promotion discourse "became synonymous for Western-imposed regime change" (Carothers and Brechenmacher, 2013, p.25), something that faced radical opposition by many countries.

The second reason that explains this global pushback is the "greater recognition and fear on the part of many power holders of the capacity of independent civil society to challenge entrenched regimes, especially in light of ongoing advances in communications technology" (Carothers and Brechenmacher, 2013, p.61). The protagonist role of civil society in the uprisings that led to revolutionary changes in Egypt in January 2011 only reinforced this negative perception on the part of the elites in power (*demonstration effect*), paving the way for more repression and more obstacles to the activities of civil society organizations.

This troubling situation poses once again an old dilemma to the EU and other international donors, since they have to make a difficult choice in a continuously changing international environment: either to support the drivers of change (even against the wishes of local governments), or to continue with the traditional *business as usual* for the sake of stability.

Egypt is a case in point, since it is progressively erecting barriers to the activities of both local and international actors trying to promote human rights and democracy in its territory (Ruffner, 2015). Egypt has one of the most restrictive laws on NGOs in the region, Law 84/2002. The restrictions imposed by Egyptian authorities are increasingly sophisticated, and have taken the form of state control mechanisms to the operation of local and international NGOs, difficulties and limitations to access foreign funding, expulsion of human rights activists working for international organizations, creation of government-operated NGOs (the so-called GONGOs), obstacles to international election monitoring. Therefore, according to the European Commission, there is now much "less space" for CSOs working in Egypt, which has led many human rights NGOs "to decide to close their offices" (European Commission, 2015, p.3) in the country.

The protection and support for human rights defenders (HRDs) is one of the EU's strategic goals in the area of human rights and democracy promotion. As a clear manifestation of this priority, it adopted the *EU Guidelines on Human Rights Defenders* in 2004, and revised and updated them in 2008 (Council of the European Union, 2008). Along the same lines, the EU created in 2010 the position of *EU Liaison Officers on Human Rights Defenders* in a high number of EU Delegations, a very promising step forward if adequately used.

Along the same lines, the EU created the *European Endowment for Democracy* (EED) on 25 June 2012. Although the idea of setting up the EED was proposed by Poland in 2010 in the context of the significant deterioration of the human rights situation in Belarus, "the decisive momentum to create the EED . . . came in 2011, in the aftermath of the Arab Spring" (European Endowment for Democracy, 2015). The EED is an independent foundation created at the initiative of both the EU and Member States aimed at channeling funds to those local actors that work for democratic change, particularly young leaders, independent media and journalists, non-registered NGOs, and trade unions. Given the flexible procedure, the fast screening of the grant applications, the possibility of submitting applications in Arabic, and the intention to fund local initiatives with a great democratic potential, the EED could eventually play a major role in Egypt (Teti *et al.*, 2013, p.71).[6] Unfortunately, the current political climate and the reluctance of the Egyptian authorities to allow foreign support to critical CSOs (Ruffner, 2015) explain why the impact of the EED is still rather limited.

CONCLUSIONS

Due to the strategic nature of Egypt in the Southern Mediterranean, the EU offered significant political and economic support to Hosni Mubarak's authoritarian regime for the sake of stability and security. When the unexpected Arab Spring put an end to Mubarak's era in February 2011, the EU tried to accommodate the new scenario launching a reflection about its new role in a changing southern neighbourhood. The new approach to the Southern Mediterranean came full of rhetoric, very much in line with the EU's ambition to be considered as a human rights norms champion. Most of the announced changes in EU's policies and programmes on Egypt are mainly cosmetic, and do not alter the traditional approach that has dominated these relations since the 1990s. The reviewed ENP emphasized the relevance of the so-called "3 Ms" (money, market, and mobility). As we have demonstrated, these innovations point to more of the same, far from a highly needed paradigm shift.

One area in which the EU has tried to articulate a new vision is the focus on civil society organizations (CSOs) as essential ingredients of any meaningful promotion of human rights and democracy. The creation of the European Endowment for Democracy (EED), and the renewed impetus on supporting human rights defenders (HRDs), are modest but relevant signals of this new approach to the role to be played by CSOs in democratic transitions. Unfortunately, the current situation of Egypt does not allow the EU to constructively work with independent and critical CSOs. On the contrary, the dramatic crack down on human rights in the country is closing the limited spaces that CSOs had to push for democratic change. It seems that the old authoritarian habits and practices are back.

The EU is not reacting as strongly as it should against this deterioration of human rights and democracy in Egypt, paying lip service to the principle of conditionality. Once again, the EU is confronted with an old dilemma, and it prefers security and stability in Egypt over democracy and human rights, as in the old times. On the other hand, we also have to recognize that the EU's capacity to exert leverage on Egypt has dramatically reduced in the aftermath of the Arab Spring. The new geopolitical scenario, with new economic and political actors in Egypt such as Saudi Arabia, China or Russia, is leading the EU to become increasingly impotent and irrelevant. In this changing international context, the EU has to open a strategic reflection about its role in the whole Southern Mediterranean, particularly in Egypt. We are afraid that the Arab Spring has been a missed opportunity for the EU, and for the West in general, to rethink the relations with Egypt, and to base these relations on universal human rights and democratic principles.

NOTES

1. We could even think of an emerging *Trump–Putin Consensus* if they harmonize their approaches and policies in the field of human rights and democracy promotion. As an illustration of the risks associated with the new US Presidency, the Trump Administration has announced in March 2017 a cut of the total budget for the State Department and the United States Agency for International Development (USAid) by 28% in 2018 (Siddiqui and Quinn, 2017).
2. Some EU Members such as Hungary and Poland can also be considered as part of this tendency to resist to efforts to promote human rights and democracy within their borders (Von Bogdandy and Sonnevend, 2015).
3. Preamble of the *Barcelona Declaration* (1995).
4. *Euro-Mediterranean Agreement establishing an Association between the European Communities and their Member States, of the one part, and the Arab Republic of Egypt, of the other part*. Signed in 2001, it entered into force in 2004.
5. Interview with a high official working for the European External Action Service (EEAS) on Egypt, 27 January 2016.
6. So far, the EED has only supported a small number of projects (in 2015 there were 13 EED on-going initiatives), but some projects have great democratic potential if adequately implemented. The European Parliament made an evaluation of the overall EED's functioning and acknowledged "with satisfaction that despite its short period of activity and limited funds, and the challenges inherent in assessing the impact of democracy support actions. . .the EED is delivering added value to existing EU democracy support through fast, flexible, bottom-up and demand-driven funding provided directly to beneficiaries. . ." (European Parliament, 2015).

REFERENCES

Aguirre, Mariano (2017), "¿El orden atlantista bajo asedio?," *InfoMarruecos*, http://infomarruecos.ma/esglobal-el-orden-atlantista-bajo-asedio-mariano-aguirre/. (Accessed: 24 March 2017).

Alston, Philip (ed.) (1999), *The EU and Human Rights*, Oxford: Oxford University Press.

Askar Karakir, Irem (2014), "Limits of EU Democracy Promotion in the Arab Middle East: The Cases of Egypt and Morocco", *Uluslararasi Hukuk ve Politika*, 36, pp.33–67.

Babayan, Nelli (2015), "The return of the empire? Russia's counteraction to transatlantic democracy promotion in its near abroad", *Democratization*, 22(3), pp.438–58.

Balfour, Rosa, Fabbri, Francesca and Youngs, Richard (2016) *Report on Democracy Assistance from the European Union to the Middle East and North Africa* (EUSPRING Report), http://www2.warwick.ac.uk/fac/soc/pais/research/researchcentres/irs/euspring/euspring_eu_demo_assistance_on_template.4.pdf. (Accessed: 24 March 2017).

Barbé, Esther (2014), "La UE como promotora de los derechos humanos en

Naciones Unidas", in Esther Barbé (dir.), *La Unión Europea en las relaciones internacionales*, Madrid: Tecnos, pp.395–414.
Blanc Altemir, Antonio (2012), *La Unión Europea y el Mediterráneo. De los Primeros Acuerdos a la Primavera Árabe*, Madrid: Tecnos.
Burnell, Peter (2010), "Is There a New Autocracy Promotion?", *FRIDE Working Paper*, 96, pp.1–24.
Carothers, Thomas (2006), "The Backlash Against Democracy Promotion", *Foreign Affairs*, 85, pp.55–65.
Carothers, Thomas and Brechenmacher, Saskia (2013), *Closing Space. Democracy and Human Rights Support Under Fire*, Washington D.C.: Carnegie Endowment for International Peace.
Council of the European Union (2008), *Ensuring Protection-Updated European Union Guidelines on Human Rights Defenders*.
Dennison, Susi and Dworkin, Anthony (2010), *Towards an EU Human Rights Strategy for a Post-Western World*, London: ECFR.
Durac, Vincent (2009), "The impact of external actors on the distribution of power in the Middle East: the case of Egypt", *The Journal of North African Studies*, 14, pp.75–90.
Durao Barroso, José, Manuel (2011), "Partners in Freedom: The EU Response to the Arab Spring", Cairo, Egypt, SPEECH/11/523, 14 July.
EU High Representative (2011), *Remarks by the EU High Representative Catherine Ashton at the Senior Officials' Meeting on Egypt and Tunisia*, Brussels, 23 February.
EU High Representative and European Commission (2011), Joint Communication by the High Representative of the Union for Foreign Affairs and Security Policy and the European Commission, *A New Response to a Changing Neighbourhood. A Review of European Neighbourhood Policy*, COM(2011) 303, 25 May.
European Commission (2015), *Implementation of the European Neighbourhood Policy in Egypt. Progress in 2014 and recommendations for actions*, SWD(2015) 65 final, Brussels, 25 March.
European Commission and High Representative of the European Union for Foreign Affairs and Security Policy, Joint Communication to the European Parliament and the Council (2011), *Human Rights and Democracy at the Heart of EU External Action-Towards a More Effective Approach*, COM(2011) 886 final, December 12.
European Council (2011), EUCO 2/1/11, Annex II, 14.
European Endowment for Democracy (2015), *Supporting Democracy in the European Neighbourhood and Beyond, Annual Report*, Brussels.
Fukuyama, Francis (1989), "The End of History?", *The National Interest*, No. 16(Summer), pp.3–18.
Gershman, Carl and Allen, Michael (2006), "The Assault on Democracy Assistance", *Journal of Democracy*, 17(2), pp.36–51.
Greenfield, Danya and Balfour, Rosa (2012), *Arab Awakening: Are the US and the EU Missing the Challenge?*, Washington D.C.: Atlantic Council.
Hackenesch, Christine (2015), "Not as bad as it seems: EU and US democracy promotion faces China in Africa", *Democratization*, 22(3), pp.419–37.
Hassan, Oz (2015), "Undermining the transatlantic democracy agenda? The Arab Spring and Saudi Arabia's counteracting democracy strategy", *Democratization*, 22(3), pp.479–95.
Helmy, Abdallah (2015), *Exploring changes in the European Democracy Promotion*

Policy in Egypt after the 2011 Events. 'Same cocktail, different portions', Cairo: American University in Cairo.
Huber, Daniela (2013), "US and EU Human Rights and Democracy Promotion since the Arab Spring. Rethinking its Content, Targets and Instruments", *The International Spectator*, 48(3), pp.98–112.
Kamrava, Mehran (2012), "The Arab Spring and the Saudi-Led Counterrevolution", *Orbis*, 56 (1), pp.96–104.
Keukeleire, Stephan and Delreux, Tom (2014), *The Foreign Policy of the European Union*, Basingstoke: Palgrave Macmillan.
Khalifa Isaac, Sally (2012), "Europe and the Arab Revolutions. From a Weak to a Proactive Response in a Changing Neighbourhood", *KFG Working Paper*, 39.
Krickovic, Andrej (2014), "Imperial Nostalgia or Prudent Geopolitics? Russia's Efforts to Reintegrate the Post-Soviet Space in Geopolitical Perspective", *Post-Soviet Affairs*, 30, pp.503–28.
Magen, Amichai (2015), "The Democratic Entitlement in an Era of Democratic Recession", *Cambridge Journal of International and Comparative Law*, 4(2), pp.368–87.
Manners, Ian (2002), "Normative Power Europe: A Contradiction in Terms?", *Journal of Common Market Studies*, 40, pp.235–58.
Muñoz Nogal, Ester and Gómez Isa, Felipe (2016), "¡Pan, Libertad, Justicia Social! Las revueltas populares de Túnez y Egipto y la defensa de derechos económicos y sociales", in Jordi Bonet Pérez and Rosa Ana Alija Fernández (eds), *La exigibilidad de los derechos económicos, sociales y culturales en la sociedad internacional del siglo XXI: una aproximación jurídica desde el Derecho internacional*, Madrid: Marcial Pons, pp.219–41.
Nathan, Andrew J. (2015), "China's Challenge to Democracy", *Journal of Democracy*, 26, pp.156–70.
Pace, Michelle (2012), "Egypt", in Joel Peters (ed.), *The European Union and the Arab Spring. Promoting Democracy and Human Rights in the Middle East*, Lanham: Lexington Books, pp.49–64.
Piccone, Ted (2015), *Five Rising Democracies and the Fate of the International Liberal Order*, Washington D.C.: Brookings Institution Press.
Risse, Thomas and Babayan, Nelli (2015), "Democracy promotion and the challenge of illiberal regional powers: introduction to the special issue", *Democratization*, 22(3), pp.385–6.
Ruffner, Todd (2015), *Under Threat. Egypt's Systematic Campaign Against NGOs*, Washington D.C.: Project on Middle East Democracy.
Siddiqui, Sabrina and Quinn, Ben (2017), "Trump's funding cuts to diplomacy and aid would mark retreat from soft power", *The Guardian*, 16 March, https://www.theguardian.com/us-news/2017/mar/16/state-department-foreign-aid-funding-cuts-trump-budget. (Accessed: 24 March 2017).
Sigillò, Ester (2015), "Challenges to Normative power Europe in the Mediterranean. Impact on Arab civil societies and the role of Islamic donors", *Working Paper, ECPR General Conference*, Montreal.
Silvestri, Sara (2005), "EU Relations with Islam in the Context of the EMP's Cultural Dialogue", *Mediterranean Politics*, 10(3), pp.385–405.
Smith, Karen E. (2008), *European Union Foreign Policy in Changing World*, London: Polity Press.
Teti, Andrea; Thompson, Darcy and Noble, Christopher (2013), "EU Democracy

Assistance Discourse in Its New Response to a Changing Neighbourhood", *Democracy and Security*, 9(1–2), pp.61–79.
Virgili, Tommaso (2014), "The Arab Spring and the EU's Democracy Promotion in Egypt: A Missed Appointment?", *Perspectives on Federalism*, 6, pp.42–75.
Von Bogdandy, Armin and Sonnevend, Pal (eds) (2015), *Constitutional Crisis in the European Constitutional Area*, Baden-Baden: Nomos.
Walker, Christopher (2014), "Authoritarian Regimes are Changing How the World Defines Democracy", *The Washington Quarterly*, June 13, https://www.washingtonpost.com/opinions/christopher-walker-authoritarian-regimes-are-changing-how-the-world-defines-democracy/2014/06/12/d1328e3a-f0ee-11e3-bf76-447a5df6411f_story.html. (Accessed: 24 March 2017).
Wouters, Jan and Duquet, Sanderijn (2013), "The Arab Uprisings and the European Union: In Search of a Comprehensive Strategy", *Working Paper, Leuven Centre for Global Governance Studies*, 98, pp.1–33.
Youngs, Richard (2010), *Europe's Decline and Fall. The Struggle against Global Irrelevance*, London: Profile Books.
Youngs, Richard (2015), *The Puzzle of Non-Western Democracy*, Brussels: Carnegie Endowment for International Peace.

9. From lawless to secret law: the United States, the CIA, and extra-judicial killings

Arturo Jimenez-Bacardi

It is an act of insanity and national humiliation to have a law prohibiting the President from ordering assassination.[1]

Henry A. Kissinger, Secretary of State, 1975

INTRODUCTION

In 1997 United States ambassador to Israel, Martin Indyk, declared that the U.S., "is very clearly on the record as against targeted assassinations. They are extrajudicial killings, and we do not support that" (Mayer 2009). However, one year later, President Bill Clinton signed three memoranda authorizing the CIA to kill Osama bin Laden. Since 9/11 the U.S. has greatly expanded its "targeted killing" program, killing thousands through its premeditated lethal strikes in the war zones of Iraq, Afghanistan, and Eastern Pakistan, but also in lands far removed from the battlefield, including Yemen, Somalia, Syria, Libya, and the Philippines. In recent years, the U.S. government has consistently defended its targeted killing program as legal, legitimate, and moral, to the point where CIA director Leon Panetta boasted that lethal drones were "the only game in town" (Panetta 2009). How did the U.S. evolve from considering targeted killings as illegitimate extra-judicial killings to the only game in town?

With a focus on the Central Intelligence Agency (CIA), this chapter will show that the United States' intermittent obsession with assassinations has gone through three phases. The first phase covers the period from the establishment of the CIA in 1947 and ends in 1975. This era was marked by a lawless culture where controversial covert operations—including several assassination programs—were at best not vetted for their legality and at worst were approved even when they represented clear violations of the law.

The second phase begins in 1975 during the "year of intelligence" when a series of investigations on countless legally dubious CIA projects prompted a long list of proposed reforms (Johnson 2015, 259). For the purpose of this chapter, the most significant of these reforms was President Gerald Ford's 1976 Executive Order 11905 prohibiting assassinations. Other key reforms reorganized the national security bureaucracy and empowered a number of lawyers, most notably at the Department of Justice Office of Legal Counsel (OLC), and the CIA's General Counsel Office (CIA-GC), that would strengthen a legalized process meant to review the legality of covert actions. This second phase would last until the year 2000 and witnessed a relatively cautious U.S. approach to the law. Nonetheless, as the years passed, and new "crises" emerged, lawyers became more assertive and began chipping away at the scope of the assassination ban.

The final phase, which takes us to the present, began after al-Qaeda's terrorist attack on September 11, 2001. This phase has seen a highly legalized process dominated by the proliferation of secret law that consistently pushes the boundaries of legality at the expense of individual rights. Since 9/11 the OLC has written between eight and twelve secret legal opinions concerning extra-judicial killings (New York Times v. U.S. Department of Justice 2015, Savage 2015, 237). Only two of these opinions have been partially declassified pursuant to court orders (Barron 2010a, Barron 2010b). Notwithstanding the clear challenge of assessing secret law, since 2010 a growing array of evidence—ranging from the two partially declassified OLC opinions, a Department of Justice White Paper, speeches by administration officials, leaks to the press, and other government documents—has begun to clarify the U.S. legal position towards what it calls targeted killings. Here, the U.S. government has consistently rejected the applicability of International Human Rights Law (IHRL), and has instead pursued an International Humanitarian Law (IHL) centric approach. Furthermore, the U.S. has pushed a radical interpretation of what constitutes an armed conflict, and has stretched the legal limits of core IHL concepts, including the notion of "imminent threat" and "distinction."

A targeted killing, as Philip Alston, the former United Nations Special Rapporteur on Extrajudicial, Summary, or Arbitrary Executions has defined it, "is the intentional, premeditated and deliberate use of lethal force, by States or their agents acting under colour of law . . ." (Alston 2010, 4). From an international legal framework, extraterritorial targeted killings operations conducted by the U.S. as part of its global counterterrorism strategy are governed by three international law regimes: the law on interstate force (*Jus ad Bellum*), international humanitarian law (*Jus in Bello*), and international human rights law (Melzer 2008). For decades, the global trend has been to try and incorporate IHRL into IHL, in an attempt to continue to further humanize war (for a detailed discussion of a IHRL approach to targeted killings see Brunstetter *et al.* 2015, Melzer 2008). However, the U.S. has not only resisted this development, but it has also pursued its own legal counteroffensive: to push IHL into the IHRL space, in effect contracting rights.

One of the problems with the U.S. IHL-centric approach, as Melzer has noted is that, "the permissibility of extraterritorial targeted killings exclusively under the law of interstate force . . . seem to disregard the fact that that this law regulates only the relations between States, and not those between States and individuals" (Melzer 2008, 51–2). In order to protect the most basic individual rights, including the rights to life, Heyns (2013, 6) has argued that, "the most immediate protection for the right to life is provided by the international human rights law framework. This is the default legal regime from which deviations are permissible only when, and for as long as, those who justify the more permissive use of force under international humanitarian law can show that the requisite conditions have been fulfilled". More specifically, as Alston has explained, "In the legitimate struggle against terrorism, too many criminal acts have been re-characterized so as to justify addressing them within the framework of the law of armed conflict" (Alston 2010, 3). Given the U.S. insistence on maintaining its legal reasoning secret, the U.S. has failed to provide enough evidence to clearly indicate that, outside of the war zones in Iraq and Afghanistan, its targeted killing operations against suspected members of al-Qaeda, the Taliban, and a growing number of so-called "affiliated forces" are legally permissible. The lack of transparency makes legal accountability impossible and represents a key mechanism for contracting rights.

Today, the U.S. rejects the notion that IHRL applies to its targeted killing operations. Yet it acknowledges that it must abide by IHL, including some customary norms. As the next section will show, this was not always the case.

A LAWLESS WORLD: U.S. COVERT OPERATIONS, 1947–1974

The U.S. government defines covert action as, "an activity or activities of the United States Government to influence political, economic, or military conditions abroad, where it is intended that the role of the United States Government will not be apparent or acknowledged publicly" (U.S. Congress 1947, 503b(e)). In practice, this has involved everything from traditional espionage to psychological and paramilitary operations, coups, torture, and even assassinations (Prados 2006).

From a legal perspective, the CIA's turn to covert action was dubious in both a statutory sense as well as how the Agency saw the law constrain its actions. In its most specific section, the National Security Act of 1947 expected the CIA's main function to be, "coordinating the intelligence activities of the several Government departments and agencies in the interest of national security" (U.S. Congress 1947, 102(d)). To do so, the Act gave the CIA five tasks. The first four focused on intelligence analysis and dissemination; however, the final task—the most vague, and ironically, the most consequential, called on the Agency to, "perform *such other functions and duties* related to intelligence affecting the national security as the National Security Council may from time to time direct" (U.S. Congress 1947, 102(d)(5)). Such an indeterminate provision opened the door for abuse as proponents of covert action within the executive branch would argue that "other functions and duties" gave them the authority to conduct just about anything, including extra-judicial killings (Zegart 2000, 187).

The legislative record shows that Congress did not intend to authorize covert actions, and that "other functions" referred to intelligence coordination (Stuart 2008, 230–73). In its extensive investigation of the CIA, the Church Committee's final report concluded that "there is no reference to covert action in the 1947 National Security Act, nor is there any evidence in the debates, committee reports, or legislative history of the 1947 Act to show that Congress intended specifically to authorize covert operations" (U.S. Congress 1976, 149).

Although it appears that even President Truman did not intend for the CIA to engage in covert actions, once the Act was passed, he immediately moved to approve such operations (Zegart 2000, 188). The same week as the National Security Act took effect, members of the National Security Council began discussing covert operations (Houston September 25, 1947, 622). The issue came to CIA General Counsel Lawrence Houston, who was hearing arguments claiming that Section 102(d)(5) of the Act which authorized the CIA to conduct "such other functions and duties" as the NSC determined, was tantamount to sanctioning covert action. However, Houston was clear in his assessment that "commando type functions," "ranger and commando raids," "behind-the-lines sabotage," "support of guerrilla warfare," "black propaganda," and "subversion," were not legally covered by the Act, "In our opinion, however, either activity would be an unwarranted extension of the functions authorized in Sections 102 (d) (4) and (5)" (Houston September 25, 1947, 622–3). Houston further warned that if "taken out of context and without knowledge of its history," Section 102(d)(5), "could bear almost unlimited interpretation, provided the service performed could be shown to be of benefit to an intelligence agency or related to national intelligence" (Houston September 25, 1947, 622).

Houston's warning and legal judgement was ignored (Prados 2006, 37). Shortly thereafter, the covert operations spigot was left wide open. From 1949 to 1967, according to CIA numbers, 556 projects were approved. In 1975, the Church Committee found that, "the CIA has conducted some 900 major or sensitive covert action projects plus several thousand smaller projects since 1961" (U.S. Congress 1976, 445).

The use of covert action was at least in part a way to have a mechanism for bypassing the law. This sentiment was best captured by the 1954 Report on the Covert Activities of the Central Intelligence Agency, which concluded "It is now clear that we are facing an implacable enemy whose avowed objective is world domination by whatever means and at whatever cost. *There are no rules in such a game. Hitherto acceptable norms of human conduct do not apply*" (Emphasis added, Doolittle *et al.* 1954, 6–7). A lawless covert action structure and culture had been set and it was only a matter of time until someone at the CIA conjured up the use of extrajudicial killings as a way to deal with America's enemies.

The first proposed CIA assassination program took place in Guatemala as part of the Agency's larger operation to overthrow President Jacobo Arbenz from 1953 to 1954 (Central Intelligence Agency, n.d.(a), Cullather 2006). To prepare for the project, the CIA issued a "Study of Assassination," that covered everything from morality concerns to what are the most efficient and inconspicuous tools for killing someone (Central Intelligence Agency, Undated(a)). The one thing missing from the study was any discussion over the legality of such actions. On March 31, 1954, the CIA created a "selection of individuals for disposal by Junta Group," which included the names of more than fifty individuals, or "disposees" (Central Intelligence Agency, n.d.(b)). After the success of the coup in Guatemala, the CIA would also initiate assassination programs against the heads of state in Cuba, the Congo, and the Dominican Republic (U.S. Congress 1975).

By the late 1960s, during the Vietnam War, the U.S. set up its largest targeted killing program of the Cold War in an attempt to destroy the civilian infrastructure of the National Liberation Front (NLF). In 1967, MACV Directive 381–41, established the Intelligence Coordination and Exploitation Program (ICEX). ICEX was to emphasize intelligence coordination, but also the "elimination of the VC infrastructure" (Prugh 1975). A CIA report explained the distinct task of ICEX in the larger pacification campaign as, "*also involves the 'negative' task of identifying and eradicating the Communist politico-military control apparatus known as the Viet Cong Infrastructure*" (Jimenez Bacardi 2015, 163).

By "Viet Cong Infrastructure," U.S. officials meant the NLF's "shadow government," or the civilian political leadership and administration of the NLF, as well as members of the Communist Party structure in South Vietnam (Moyar 1997, 11). Therefore, to "eliminate" or "destroy" the NLF infrastructure, ICEX intended to "neutralize"—capture, kill, or convert—the civilian political leadership and activists of the NLF (Andrade and Willbanks 2006, 19). Directive 381–41 explained the approach as one intended to resemble, "a 'rifle shot' rather than a shotgun approach to the real target—key, important political leaders and activists in the VC infrastructure" (Prugh 1975). The program turned out to be anything but a precise "rifle shot," as thousands of innocent South Vietnamese were tortured and killed, at least in part due to the fact that a significant amount of ICEX intelligence was based on information obtained through torture (Kalyvas and Kosher 2007, Rejali 2009, 472).

In December 1967, ICEX was renamed Phoenix. In early 1968, the U.S. introduced a plan for an "Accelerated Pacification Campaign," with a special focus on "neutralizing" members of the NLF leadership. It is important to stress that the main targets for "neutralization" under Phoenix were not combatants (the military focused on them), they were mainly civilians—NLF political leaders and activist—as well as clandestine operatives (Thayer 1985, 208). As non-combatants, U.S. legal policy asserted that these groups were not covered by the Geneva Conventions (MACV Directive Number 381–46). Phoenix killed at least 15,000 people, where less than five percent of these were actually "confirmed" members of the NLF, according to U.S. government records (Kalyvas and Kosher 2007). In fact, even William Colby, the CIA's authority on Phoenix, admitted during a Congressional hearing when confronted about the possible arbitrary nature of the program, that "I have never been highly satisfied with the accuracies of our intelligence on the VCI [NLF Infrastructure]" (Prados 2009, 236).

The one office charged with making sure CIA operations were consistent with the law, the Office of General Counsel, was kept in the dark. During his testimony for the Rockefeller Commission, Lawrence Houston, the CIA's top lawyer acknowledged that he had not been included in a number of legally questionable covert operations, including extra-judicial killings. Houston was asked by a member of the Commission whether "it was a rather widespread practice that when they wanted to do something that they knew was questionable, they did not talk to the General Counsel, and they only talked to him when they were not quite sure whether they wanted to do it or not." Houston replied by stating, "well, that is a little unfair," and suggested that "we would say no, no, don't get into that or something like that. You won't find a memo from you to us, you won't find a record, but we were often consulted on that basis," yet he failed to provide any concrete examples (Quoted in Jimenez Bacardi 2015, 116).

Further, as noted above, when Houston questioned the legality of covert operations, he was simply ignored.

By late 1974, the legal excesses of these programs began to be exposed in the press, which led to a series of Congressional and other investigations followed by a number of key reforms.

REFORM AND CAUTION: THE ASSASSINATION BAN AND THE LEGALIZATION OF COVERT ACTION, 1975–2000

After the Church Committee finished its investigation into illegal CIA activities, it called for an "omnibus legislation" that would replace the vague National Security Act of 1947. The proposed law was to create a comprehensive intelligence charter that would clearly delineate the limits of each intelligence agency and outlaw several covert actions, including assassinations (U.S. Congress 1976, 426–50).

Concerning assassinations, the Church Committee recommended that legislation should clearly prohibit such actions. The Committee proposed language that would ban the killing of foreign officials but also members of an "insurgent force, an unrecognized government, or a political party" (U.S. Congress 1975, 283). In an attempt to preempt Congress, President Ford issue an executive order (E.O.) that included a prohibition on assassinations (Prados and Jimenez-Bacardi 2016). However, while Ford's executive order, 11,905 banned "political assassinations" it failed to define the term, sowing confusion for future government employees and also provided an opening for government lawyers to set the scope of the ban (Schmitt 1992). The White House strategy worked as Congressional delays and a successful lobbying effort against legislation by the intelligence community and its allies destroyed the proposed intelligence charter (Prados 2006, Chapter 18). The first legislation on intelligence activities after the Church Committee passed in 1980. At four pages long, the Intelligence Oversight Act of 1980 failed to create a clear intelligence charter, and while it banned assassinations, they adopted the non-definitional model of Ford's E.O.

President Jimmy Carter amended Ford's E.O. by eliminating the qualifier "political" and instead banning all "assassinations." However, Carter also failed to define assassinations, opening the door for Executive Branch lawyers to step in and set the boundaries of the law. Such lawyers have for decades been coming up with rationales to limit the scope of the ban.

Under Ford, CIA-GC underwent some significant reforms. In 1975, the CIA-GC had 14 lawyers and most of their work dealt with logistics and management (Jimenez Bacardi 2015). The Church Committee had concluded that:

> the participation of the General Counsel in determining the legality or propriety of CIA activities was limited; in many instances the General Counsel was not consulted about sensitive projects. In some cases the Director's investigative arm, the Inspector General, discovered questionable activities that often were not referred to the General Counsel for a legal opinion. Moreover, the General Counsel never had general investigatory authority.
>
> (U.S. Congress 1976, 459)

CIA Director George H. W. Bush established several new internal CIA procedures designed to empower the CIA-GC, including an extensive list of specific covert activities that needed to be reviewed by the lawyers before they were approved (Central Intelligence Agency 1976).

To provide additional legal cover, the Department of Justice's OLC was also brought in to assess the legality of controversial covert actions. OLC has become the most significant legal bureaucracy in the Executive Branch. OLC's power derives from three sources: (1) it is the final arbiter of legal disputes in the executive; (2) Courts and Congress rarely challenge OLC opinions; (3) its legal opinions often bestow an advance pardon or a "get out of jail-free card" for actions taken by U.S. government personnel (Goldsmith 2007, 149–50).

By the mid-1980s U.S. government officials began to question the policy wisdom behind the assassination ban as the threat of international terrorism began to rise. Before any policy shift, the legal scope of the assassination ban had to be settled. All OLC opinions dealing with the assassination ban from this period remain classified, however a Department of Defense opinion from 1989 offers a useful guide to how U.S. government legal interpretations have evolved. The memo was drafted by Marine lawyer W. Hays Park, who had served as a law consultant in preparing the 1986 bombing mission that indirectly targeted Libya's Muammar Qaddafi. The paper argues that while the Executive ban:

> prohibits assassinations as a matter of national policy . . . It concludes that the employment of military force against a terrorist or terrorist organization to protect U.S. citizens or the national security of the United States is a legitimate exercise of the international legal right of self defense and does not constitute assassination.
>
> (Parks 1989, 1)

However, the memo did set some limits by highlighting that individuals engaged in terrorism had to be part of a well-structured terrorist organization as, "the terrorist organizations envisaged as appropriate to necessitate or warrant an armed response by U.S. military forces are well financed, highly organized paramilitary structures engaged in the illegal use of force" (Parks 1989, 9). The memo also presents a definition of self-defense that its authors recognized went beyond what is accepted by the United Nations. Several of the arguments found in this memo are echoed in the post-9/11 memos, but without the qualifications.

THE RISE OF SECRET LAW: POST-9/11 TARGETED KILLINGS

Less than a week after the 9/11 attacks, President George W. Bush signed a Memorandum of Notification authorizing the CIA to capture or kill "persons who pose a continuing, serious threat of violence or death to U.S. persons and interests or who are planning terrorist activities" (U.S. Congress 2014, 11). Behind a veil of secrecy, the Executive Branch would be the sole arbiter of who those persons were, what legal protections they had, and what possible constraints might limit the U.S. global militarized response to the terrorist threat. On November 5, 2002, the U.S. carried out its first known successful targeted killing outside a warzone in the post-9/11 period. The operation took place in Yemen as missiles launched from a drone destroyed a moving vehicle with a suspected al-Qaeda operative, along with five other passengers including an American citizen (Savage 2015, 281). Since then, as of January 2017, between 866–1,184 individuals have been killed in Yemen, 2,501–4,003 have been killed in Pakistan, 301–449 have been killed in Somalia, and countless others have been killed in Syria, Libya, and other undeclared battlefields by U.S. forces (Bureau of Investigative Journalism 2017).

Such a massive "targeted killing" campaign has been justified under a structure of secret law that includes: a series of secret legal memos, Presidential directives, policy guidelines, and agreements with foreign governments (Goitein 2016). In addition, every intelligence authorization bill passed by Congress includes a classified annex—a literal addendum of secret law. More than a decade and a half after President Bush authorized to kill suspected members of al-Qaeda and the Taliban, few details are known about that administration's legal positions on extra-judicial killings (Savage 2015, Chapter 6). President Bush authorized both "personality strikes" where the identity of an individual is known, and also the more controversial and legally dubious, "signature strikes," where people are intentionally killed based on their "patterns of life," but without knowing who they are (Savage 2015, 255).

While all of the Bush era secret legal memos remain classified, two

OLC opinions from the Obama administration have been partially declassified. Both of these opinions along with a DOJ White Paper provide a glimpse into the U.S.'s legal positions towards not just targeted killings worldwide, but also the extra-judicial killing of an American citizen. In the first legal opinion of February 2010, Assistant Attorney General David Barron responded to a request from an unknown source asking if a CIA proposal to kill Shaykh Anwar Aulaqi, a U.S. citizen residing in Yemen, who was believed to be a member of al-Qaeda in the Arabian Peninsula (AQAP), was lawful. Barron concluded that, "Under the conditions and factual predicates as represented by the CIA in the materials provided to us from the Intelligence Community, we believe that a decision-maker, on the basis of such information, could reasonably conclude that the use of lethal force against Aulaqi would not violate the assassination ban in Executive Order 12333 or any applicable constitutional limitations due to Aulaqi's United States citizenship" (Barron 2010a, 1). The available snippets of the memo suggest that part of the argument that Barron makes for why such an operation would not violate the assassination ban is that "killing in self-defense are not assassinations . . ." (Barron 2010a, 4).

Concerning Aulaqi's U.S. citizenship, Barron argues that "being a U.S. person [redacted] does not give a member of al-Qa'ida a constitutional immunity from attack," citing in part the 2004 Supreme Court decision in Hamdi v. Rumsfeld (Barron 2010a, 5–6). The memo acknowledges that Aulaqi's rights under the Fourth Amendment, as well as the Fifth Amendment's Due Process Clause, "likely applies in some respects, even while he is abroad" (Barron 2010a, 6). However, these rights are presumably outweighed by the "Government's asserted interests," especially given that, "on the battlefield, the Government's interests and burdens preclude offering a process to judge whether a detainee is truly an enemy combatant [redacted]. In the case of a member, associate, or affiliate of al-Qai'da operating abroad in circumstances where capture is infeasible, and it is known that the individual [redacted] continued an imminent threat [redacted]" (Barron 2010a, 6–7). With one secret legal opinion that would not be challenged by any U.S. court, the OLC effectively contracted Aulaqi's Constitutional rights as well as any protections he might have had under IHRL.

Barron authored a second opinion in July 2010 that expanded on some of the government's legal interpretations of the law. This memo presents a number of legal justifications where the U.S. government is permitted to kill its own citizens including through the "public authority justification," which is admittedly a doctrine that is "understandably rare . . . and thus there is little case law," but nonetheless, "can render lethal action carried out by a governmental official lawful in some circumstances" (Barron 2010b, 15). The memo also argues that the 2001 Congressional Authorization for Use of Military Force which authorized the president to "use all necessary and appropriate force" against those states, organizations or individuals "he determines planned, authorized, committed or aided the terrorist attacks that occurred on September 11, 2001 . . ." can be expanded to include organizations that did not exist in 2001, including AQAP. Finally, pertaining to the fact that the proposed operation would be carried out in Yemen, a "location that is far from the most active theater of combat . . . That does not affect our conclusion, however" (Barron 2010b, 24). In other words, the Executive Branch could secretly expand the geographic reach of its war and unilaterally designate what organizations and individuals could be lethally targeted, without any outside check on its interpretation of the law.

In November 2011, a Department of Justice White Paper expanded on the government's assertion that an extra-judicial killing is lawful as long as the targeted individual constitutes an "imminent threat." The paper stressed that imminence "does not require the United States to have clear evidence that a specific attack on U.S. persons and interests will take place in the immediate future" (Department of Justice 2011, 7). Having interpreted the imminence standard to the point of irrelevance, the paper then argues that capturing a suspected terrorist:

> would not be feasible if it could not be physically effectuated during the relevant window of opportunity or if the relevant country were to decline to consent to a capture operation. Other factors such as undue risk to U.S. personnel conducting a potential capture operation also could be relevant. Feasibility would be a highly fact-specific and potentially time-sensitive inquiry.
>
> (Department of Justice 2011, 8)

Put together, the two OLC opinions from 2010 plus the 2011 White Paper all but render the Constitutional, IHRL, and even IHL protections against the unlawful use of lethal force meaningless.

In 2013 President Obama issued a series of detailed procedures for killing individuals located outside of areas of active hostilities that set a number of constraints on such operations (White House 2013). The guidelines were eventually made public representing an important step towards some transparency. Additionally, several of the guidelines take a much more restrictive approach towards the use of lethal force than the legal opinions made available. However, the policy guidelines are not legal interpretations of the law. Meaning that at any moment the President could choose to override his own guidelines, and any future President could simply revoke or reform them as he or she pleases. As such, the OLC legal opinions that have contracted the rights of countless individuals in the never ending global war on terror remain the law of the land.

CONCLUSION

Since the early days of the Cold War, the U.S. has employed a number of extra-judicial assassination programs. For three decades after WWII, American assassination programs were executed under a lawless structure, where legal-review was non-existent or simply disregarded. As a result of those early excesses, a number of reforms were enacted that legalized the covert action approval process. Some of those reforms certainly constrained U.S. behavior. Yet, others—especially the advent of secret law—created a new mechanism for contracting rights. This growing body of secret legal opinions (and possibly secret legislation), has provided legal cover for those who authorize and carry out these lethal operations. But for the victims, their rights have been abrogated without legal review or any avenue for legal recourse.

The second half of the twentieth century saw the expansion of human rights, the curtailment of state sovereignty, and the beginning of legal accountability for those engaged in state crimes. These advancements were made possible at least in part due to the globalization of human rights law (Brysk and Jimenez 2012). However, during the twenty-first century states have begun to fight back, looking for new mechanisms to legitimize their repression of basic rights, including the most rudimentary right of all, the right to life. Since the 9/11 attacks the U.S. has played a leading role in the broader campaign by states to contract rights in the name of national security. Among democracies, Britain, Israel, the Philippines, Russia, Turkey, and others have also contributed to this global rights contraction and the expansion of extra-judicial killings. Two main mechanisms have made this possible: state secrecy coupled with the legalization or the reappropriation of the law by the executive. Transparency and legal checks on the executive are two cornerstones of democratic governance. Human rights groups, legal advocacy organizations, and individuals need both information and avenues to legally challenge the executive, hold governments accountable, and guarantee basic rights. The U.S. has set the democratic model for contracting rights. Global civil society will now have to find new ways to challenge it.

NOTE

1. Quoted in Prados and Jimenez-Bacardi 2015.

REFERENCES

Alston, Philip. 2010. *Report of the Special Rapporteur on extrajudicial, summary or arbitrary executions*. edited by Human Rights Council. New York, NY: United Nations General Assembly.

Andrade, Dale, and James H. Willbanks. 2006. "CORDS/Phoenix: counterinsurgency lessons from Vietnam for the future." *Military Review*, (March–April): 9–23.

Barron, David J. 2010a. Memorandum for the Attorney General Eric Holder, "Re: Lethal Operations Against Shaykh Anwar Aulaqi," February 19, 2010.

Barron, David J. 2010b. Memorandum for the Attorney General Eric Holder, "Re: Applicability of Federal Criminal Laws and the Constitution to Contemplated Lethal Operations Against Shaykh Anwar al-Aulaqi," July 16, 2010.

Brunstetter, Daniel R, and Arturo Jimenez-Bacardi. 2015. "Clashing over drones: the legal and normative gap between the United States and the human rights community." *The International Journal of Human Rights*, 19 (2): 176–98.

Brysk, Alison, and Arturo Jimenez. 2012. "The Globalization of Law: Implications for the Fulfillment of Human Rights." *Journal of Human Rights*, 11 (1): 4–16.

Bureau of Investigative Journalism. 2017. "Drone Warfare." Available (accessed April 1, 2017): https://www.thebureauinvestigates.com/projects/drone-war.

Central Intelligence Agency. n.d.(a). "Study at Assassination." In National Archives and Records Administration, RG263, Studies on other records relating to the activities of the CIA in Guatemala 52-54, Box 1, Folder, "Documents used in Compiling, CIA & Guatemala assassination proposals, 1952–1954."

Central Intelligence Agency. n.d.(b). Memorandum from [redacted] to All Staff Officers, "Selection of Individuals for disposal by Junta Group." National Archives and Records Administration, RG263, Studies on other records relating to the activities of the CIA in Guatemala 52-54, Box 1, Folder, "Documents used in Compiling, CIA & Guatemala assassination proposals, 1952–1954."

Central Intelligence Agency. 1976. "Restrictions of Intelligence Activities," April 24, 1976. In Gerald Ford Presidential Library, Ann Arbor, Michigan, Leo Cherne Papers: IOB Series, Box 8, Folder, "CIA Inspector General and General Counsel Organizations."

Cullather, Nick. 2006. *Secret History: The CIA's classified account of its Operations in Guatemala, 1952–1954*: Stanford University Press.

Department of Justice. 2011. White Paper, "Lawfulness of a Lethal Operation Directed Against a U.S. Citizen Who Is a Senior Operational Leader of Al-Aq'ida or An Associated Force," November 8, 2011.

Doolittle, James H., William B. Franke, Morris Hadley, and William Pawley. 1954. Report on the Covert Activities of the Central Intelligence Agency. edited by Central Intelligence Agency.

Goitein, Elizabeth. 2016. *The New Era of Secret Law*. New York, NY: Brennan Center for Justice, New York University School of Law.

Goldsmith, Jack L. 2007. *The Terror Presidency: Law and Judgment Inside the Bush Administration*. New York: W. W. Norton & Company.

Heyns, Christof. 2013. Report of the Special Rapporteur on Extrajudicial, Summary, and Arbitrary Execution. In *23rd Session, April*. New York: Human Rights Council, United Nations.

Houston, Lawrence R. September 25, 1947. CIA Authority to Perform Propaganda and Commando Type Functions. edited by Central Intelligence Agency: Foreign Relations of the United States, 1945–1950, Emergence of the Intelligence Establishment.

Jimenez Bacardi, Arturo. 2015. *Speaking Law to War: International Law, Legal Advisers, and Bureaucratic Contestation in US Defense Policy*. University of California, Irvine.

Johnson, Loch K. 2015. *A season of inquiry revisited: the Church committee confronts America's spy agencies*. Lawrence, KS: University Press of Kansas.

Kalyvas, Stathis N., and Matthew Adam Kosher. 2007. "How 'Free' is Free Riding in Civil Wars? Violence, Insurgency and the Collective Action Problem." *World Politics*, 59 (2): 177–216.

Mayer, Jane. 2009. "The Predator War: What are the risks of the C.I.A.'s covert drone program?" *The New Yorker*, October 26, 2009.

Melzer, Nils. 2008. *Targeted killing in international law*. Oxford; New York: Oxford University Press.

Moyar, Mark. 1997. *Phoenix and the Birds of Prey: the C.I.A's Secret Campaign to Destroy the Viet Cong*. Annapolis, MD: Naval Institute Press.

New York Times v. U.S. Department of Justice, "Brief for Defendants-Appellees," No. 14–4432, 2nd Circuit, April. 2, 2015.

Panetta, Leon E. 2009. Remarks of Director of Central Intelligence Agency, Leon E. Panetta, at the Pacific Council on International Policy. edited by Central Intelligence Agency.

Parks, W. Hays. 1989. "Memorandum on Executive Order 12333 and Assassination." *Department of the Army Office of the Judge Advocate General of the Army* DAJA-IA (27–1A): 1–9.

Prados, John. 2006. *Safe for Democracy: The Secret Wars of the C.I.A.* Chicago, IL: Ivan R. Dee.

Prados, John. 2009. *William Colby and the CIA: the secret wars of a controversial spymaster*. Lawrence, Kan.: University Press of Kansas.

Prados, John, and Arturo Jimenez-Bacardi. 2015. White House Efforts to Blunt 1975 Church Committee Investigation into CIA Abuses Foreshadowed Executive-Congressional Battles after 9/11. *National Security Archive Electronic Briefing Book No. 522*. Accessed August 20, 2015.

Prados, John, and Arturo Jimenez-Bacardi. 2016. Gerald Ford White House Altered Rockefeller Commission Report in 1975; Removed Section on CIA Assassination Plots. *National Security Archive* National Security Archive Briefing Book No. 543. Accessed January 15, 2017.

Prugh, George S. 1975. *Law at War: Vietnam, 1964–1973*, *Vietnam Series*. Washington, D.C.: Department of the Army.

Rejali, Darius. 2009. *Torture and democracy*. Princeton, New Jersey: Princeton University Press.

Savage, Charlie. 2015. *Power Wars: Inside Obama's Post-9/11 Presidency*. New York, NY: Little, Brown and Company.

Schmitt, Michael N. 1992. "State-Sponsored Assassination in International and Domestic Law." *Yale Journal of International Law*, 17 (2): 610–85.

Stuart, Douglas T. 2008. *Creating the national security state: A history of the law that transformed America*. Princeton, NJ: Princeton University Press.

Thayer, Thomas C. 1985. *War without fronts: The American experience in Vietnam*. Westwood, MA: Westview Press.

U.S. Congress. 1947. "The National Security Act of 1947." Public Law 253, 80th Congress; Chapter 343, 1st Session; S. 758.

U.S. Congress, Senate. 1975. An interim report of the Select Committee to Study Governmental Operations with Respect to Intelligence Activities: Alleged assassination plots involving foreign leaders. Washington: U.S. Government Print Office.

U.S. Congress, Senate. 1976. Final Report of the Select Committee to Study Governmenta Operations with Respect to Intelligence Activities: Book I, Foreign and Military Intelligence. Washington, D.C.: United States Senate.

U.S. Congress, Senate. 2014. *Committee Study of the CIA's Detention and Interrogation Program, Findings and Conclusion*. Washington, D.C.: Senate Select Committe on Intelligence.

White House. 2013. "Procedures for Approving Direct Action Against Terrorist Targets Located Outside the United States and Areas of Active Hostilities," May 22, 2013.

Zegart, Amy. 2000. *Flawed by Design: The Evolution of the C.I.A., J.C.S., and N.S.C.* Stanford, CA: Stanford University Press.

PART III

Accountability

10. Whither accountability? Counter-terrorism and human rights at the United Nations Security Council

George Andreopoulos

The variety of measures adopted by the United Nations Security Council (UNSC) in response to the terrorist attacks of September 11, have generated a plethora of questions concerning its role within the normative architecture of the UN Charter. In particular, questions have been raised concerning the "legislative" role of the UNSC and the legitimacy of UNSC's initiatives in the area of counter-terrorism. Closely related to such a role is the critical issue of the relevance of human rights in this endeavor, and the extent to which the UNSC is subject to international legal rules. More specifically, does the UNSC have human rights obligations? If yes, what are these, how has the UNSC sought to address them in the context of counter-terrorism, and how can it be held accountable in situations of non-adherence? It is important to clarify here that the question refers to obligations that apply to the UNSC, as a separate and distinct (though related) issue from the corresponding obligations of member states.[1]

Counter-terrorism is an issue area which has registered a noticeable contraction of human rights[2] in at least two ways: (1) the 9/11 attacks have provided an opportunity to member states to become more open about repressive policies and practices that, in previous years, were engaged in but would not openly admit to doing so. In this sense, there is a considerable continuity between the pre- and post-9/11 eras; and (2) the collective processes of international law have been engaged in a way that have legitimized many of these practices under the legislative activism of the UNSC and the 1373 process. The reach of this activism and its implications for human rights are examined in this chapter in an attempt to critically discuss the key parameters of the accountability gap.[3] It is a story of the dynamic interplay between normative erosion and normative resistance that has tested the strengths and limitations of the international legal process.

This chapter will begin by situating the examination within the normative architecture of the UN Charter and the complex interplay between the legal regimes that shape two of the organization's main purposes: the maintenance of international peace and security and human rights. It will then proceed with the UNSC's shift into legislative activism on the immediate aftermath of 9/11. This legislative activism and the resulting practices have raised issues of legality and legitimacy, especially in the context of the 1373 reporting process and the 1267 sanctions regime.[4] By employing content analysis and process tracing, it will examine member states' country reports submitted under the 1373 process and explore the factors that have constrained the "humanization" of the UNSC's counterterrorist discourse.[5] In this context, it will analyze and assess some of the key legislative and administration of justice practices of member states. While some progress has been achieved since the initial stages of the "global campaign against terrorism," serious accountability challenges persist and the chapter will conclude by identifying these challenges and offer suggestions on how to address them.

THE UN CHARTER: PURPOSES AND PRINCIPLES

A review of the legislative history of the Charter reveals that, from the Organization's very inception, the maintenance of international peace and security was envisaged as hierarchically superior to all the other purposes, including the promotion and encouragement of respect for human rights and fundamental freedoms.[6] What linked human rights to the hierarchically superior purpose of peace maintenance were situations in which human rights violations were occurring in such a scale that, upon UNSC determination under Chapter VII, would constitute either a threat to the peace or breach thereof.

The intersections between peace maintenance and human rights in the context of terrorism are extensive. On the one hand, terrorist acts constitute violations of fundamental human rights (in particular, physical integrity rights); on the other hand, counter-terrorism measures, especially on the aftermath of 9/11, have exhibited serious disregard for certain fundamental human rights protections (among others, privacy, due process rights and freedom of movement). In addition, the UNSC has repeatedly identified terrorist acts as constituting threats to international peace and security and, in the process, has invoked its powers under Chapter VII of the UN Charter. These intersections have generated a series of questions relating to the nature of UNSC's human rights obligations in its adoption of such measures when acting under Chapter VII.[7]

Due to space limitations, this question will be examined in the context of the UN Charter, though such an examination by no means exhausts this complex issue.[8] There are a variety of positions on this issue ranging from the view that the UNSC is only bound by the law of the Charter and nothing else (I would call this the thin legalist position) to the view that the UNSC is bound by human rights law (I would call this the thick legalist one); in between these two are situated arguments that the UNSC is bound by jus cogens norms only, and that the UNSC should be presumed to act in accordance with international law, unless it explicitly authorizes actions that are in violation of international legal norms.[9]

There are several provisions of the UN Charter that affect the relations between peace maintenance and human rights: article 24 which stipulates that the UNSC bears "primary responsibility for the maintenance of international peace and security" and that, in discharging its duties, the UNSC "shall act in accordance with the Purposes and Principles of the United Nations;"[10] article 25 which states that member states "agree to accept and carry out the decisions of the Security Council in accordance with the present Charter;" article 39 which provides that the UNSC "shall determine the existence of any threat to the peace, breach of the peace, or act of aggression and shall make recommendations, or decide what measures shall be taken . . . to maintain or restore international peace and security;" and article 103 which notes that "In the event of a conflict between the obligations" of member states "under the present Charter and their obligations under any other international agreement, their obligations under the present Charter shall prevail."[11]

No matter which approach to treaty interpretation one subscribes to, there can be little argument with the proposition that, from an international legal perspective, the UNSC's capacity to make determinations as to what constitutes a threat to international peace and security and to decide on the corresponding measures is subject to very few limitations. The only express limitation is that such action should be in accordance with the purposes and principles of the organization, which include human rights. This, however, does not take us very far because the Charter offers no guidance as to how a commitment to the promotion and encouragement of respect for human rights is supposed to constrain the UNSC when it acts under Chapter VII. Here, the thin legalist position would advance the argument that the Charter's approach to peace maintenance is political, not legal; in this context, human rights and humanitarian law norms should be viewed as guidelines at best that do not "establish precise limits for enforcement actions."[12]

This position, however, provides an incomplete picture of UNSC's role. It does not take into consideration the extensive case law of this organ which is clearly central to any interpretation of its legal obligations.[13] UNSC practice, both before as well as after 9/11, points to the linkages between respect for human rights and peace maintenance, even if these linkages often appear ad hoc; something to be expected from the political organ par excellence of the UN system. Moreover, the UNSC's foray into the area of international justice—primarily manifested in the establishment of ICTY and ICTR—not only reinforces the said linkages, but also raises a troubling question for thin legalism proponents: how can the UNSC demand accountability for human rights violations, while remaining impervious to human rights obligations in its own conduct?

It is through this lens that the debate surrounding the interpretation of article 103 should be viewed. While states' obligations under the Charter are supposed to trump obligations under any other international agreement, such obligations cannot entail the willful violation of human rights; articles 24 and 25 in conjunction with the UNSC's own evolving case law render such a reading difficult to sustain. This interpretation, leaning towards thick legalism, is conditioned by two interrelated questions: (1) what will happen in situations in which the UNSC undertakes extraordinary measures and authorizes actions to maintain international peace and security that violate human rights and (2) under these circumstances, can it derogate from whatever constraints it may be subjected to under article 24, akin to what states do when they declare states of emergency and seek to reestablish "order"? The Charter is silent on this issue, and there is no precedent for such a course of action. Having said that, it is difficult to argue that if states are entitled to derogate from certain human rights obligations in times of public emergency, the UNSC cannot.[14] However, this leads us to the question of what exactly the UNSC is derogating from which takes us back to the original question of what human rights norms are binding upon the UNSC.

In light of the above, it is quite obvious that the issue is not whether human rights norms are binding upon the UNSC, but which ones. Probably, the most plausible argument here is that the UNSC is bound at least by those human rights norms that have reached the status of jus cogens norms. Leaving aside for the moment the question of which norms are included in such a list, this view both acknowledges and demarcates the contours of the accountability gap. In a nutshell, the accountability gap emerges because the human rights obligations of the UNSC are underspecified and this issue has emerged in the context of a situation that constitutes a threat to international peace and security; a situation that enables states to either declare or perpetuate ongoing states of emergency with all the abuses/excesses associated with such a course of action.

UNSC "LEGISLATIVE" MEASURES AND THE QUESTION OF LEGITIMACY

The UNSC had adopted resolutions on terrorism before 9/11 (UNSC 1992a, 1992b on Libya, 1998 on the Embassy bombings, 1999 on Afghanistan);[15] however, it is with the adoption of Security Council Resolution (hereinafter SCR) 1373, and later on with SCR 1540, that the question of the legitimacy of UNSC's legislative role became an issue. The key argument here, advanced by several analysts, is that, beginning with UNSCR 1373, the UNSC, with the US at the forefront, embarked on a legislative agenda (Szasz 2002).[16] While previous resolutions had included some temporal or geographic limitations (or both), or had included references to the conditions that had to be met before terminating the obligations imposed by them, UNSCR 1373 imposed binding orders on all states without any time limits and conditions attached (Alvarez 2003).[17] The driving force behind the adoption of this resolution was the United States; UNSCR 1373 appeared unconstrained by treaty and customary law obligations and rekindled the debate about the resurgence of hegemonic international law (HIL).[18] Even analysts, who have avoided the designation of legislative action, have acknowledged the "far reaching" nature of these initiatives.[19]

This UNSC foray into the issue area of counter-terrorism raises three interrelated questions: (1) can the UNSC engage in such "legislative" action (2) if it can, should it do so and (3) if such actions raise questions of legitimacy, what are the means through which determinations as to legitimate UNSC action should be made?

As noted earlier, the legislative history of the UN Charter, as well as subsequent practice, have demonstrated that, once the UNSC decides to take action under Chapter VII, there are very few restrictions on its powers. The main goal of the drafters was to ensure "rapid and effective action to maintain international peace and security."[20] This view was reaffirmed by the Appeals Chamber of the ICTY when it noted the UNSC's "wide margin of discretion" in choosing a particular course of action, once a determination has been made that the said course of action is in response to a threat to or breach of the peace, or an act of aggression.[21] More specifically, in the context of combating terrorism, it is important to remember that both UNSC resolutions 1368 and 1373 were adopted unanimously and without any expressions of concern registered in the UNSC or in the United Nations General Assembly (UNGA).

Having said that, as one analyst has noted, the fact that the UNSC has the legal authority to engage in such practices, it does not mean that it should.[22] There are several reasons for not engaging in such practices that include the institutional balance between the UNSC and the UNGA; the circumvention of the treaty-making process which is the main mechanism by which states express their willingness to be bound by an international legal rule; and the concern about the non-representative nature of the UNSC.[23] The latter issue will reinforce hegemonic tendencies within the international system, an outcome consistent with a realist/neorealist reading of such developments (human rights as second-order issues in the context of UNSCR 1373).[24]

The validity of these reservations notwithstanding, to argue against the assumption of greater decision-making powers on the part of the UNSC constitutes a tricky path for those concerned with the advancement of human rights. After all, one of the key goals of many human rights advocates during the early post-cold war period was to ensure that the UNSC would transcend its traditional understanding of security threats and render itself more receptive to non-military challenges that could undermine human welfare and the maintenance of international peace and security. Given the centrality of the UNSC within the organization, its embodiment of power differentials, as well as the concomitant and ongoing danger of cooptation of normative pursuits, the critical issue here was to enhance the legitimacy of the said assumption.

Legitimacy is a key attribute of authority, which is a form of power distinguished from coercive forms of power. As several analysts have noted, legitimacy is the basis for establishing claims of authority.[25] Claims of authority are premised on the existence of a "legitimate social purpose;" "it is this social purpose (as opposed to purely private gain) that facilitates recognition and legitimacy by the members of a community."[26] While authority entails legitimacy, the reverse is not true. An entity is considered authoritative if the rules and decisions that it issues are complied with due the fact that they originate from it.[27] Thus, and in the context of our study, a UNSC action would be considered legitimate by member states, if it is in accordance with the purposes and principles of the organization, and authoritative if it is complied with by them due to the fact that it is issued by a hierarchically superior, but rule-abiding council. While the degree to which the UNSC possesses legitimacy is a matter of dispute, even less of a consensus surrounds its exertion of political authority.[28]

What are the mechanisms that will assist in the determination of the legitimacy of UNSC actions? Two such key mechanisms are precedent and consensus.[29] The value of precedent, an important concept in legal argumentation, has been increasingly used as a key indicator of the acceptability of a particular course of action by the community of states. The UNSC has repeatedly drawn from previous decisions to justify current or intended courses of action; precedent legitimizes such courses of action by demonstrating consistency (like cases treated alike; deviations have to be explained) and coherence in reasoning.[30]

Consensus relates to the existing normative frameworks that shape discussions during a particular period and which "provide both a grammar and set of principles upon which the Council can draw" either in the determination of policies, or in the justification of those already chosen. These include the aforementioned purposes and principles of the Organization, those of the broader international community, as well as emerging norms.[31]

The United Nations' immediate response to the terrorist attacks of 9/11 was indicative of the challenges confronting pro-legitimacy efforts. Very early on, and with the certainty of a U.S. response in mind, there was a lot of discussion concerning the role of the United Nations in the global antiterrorist campaign. UN officials used arguments relating to both precedent and consensus to justify engagement in the unfolding campaign. References to precedent included the previous UNSC resolutions dealing with terrorism, which reaffirmed the link between the suppression of terrorism and the maintenance of international peace and security; references to consensus included the adoption of the twelve (at that time) international conventions which were developed under the auspices of the United Nations and its specialized agencies and the International Atomic Energy Agency (IAEA). These conventions constituted key elements of the normative framework that demarcated the necessary and appropriate policies and practices in addressing the various terrorist threats.[32]

These references were shaped by a very selective understanding of the nature of the said commitments.[33] The arbitrary confinement of human rights concerns to the human rights organs of the United Nations constitutes a telling example of such a selective understanding.

From the very beginning, the Counter-Terrorism Committee (CTC) consistently refused to address the human rights implications of its policies. The tone was set early on with Sir Jeremy Greenstock's statement that the mandate of the CTC did not include the monitoring of the human rights performance of member states.[34] During a UNSC meeting, he stated that "Monitoring performance against other international conventions, including human rights law, is outside the scope of the Counter-Terrorism Committee's mandate." He then went on to note "But we will remain aware of the interaction with human rights concerns, and we will keep ourselves briefed as appropriate."[35] This minimalist approach (simply remaining aware of such concerns), while framed as an issue of jurisdiction (the task of other organs in the UN system), clearly went against the UNSC's recent engagement in human rights issues. Such a compartmentalization reflected a perspective that sought to relegate human rights issues to second-order status.

Thus, very early on, the stage was set for organizational responses and measures that reinforced this direction and accentuated the tensions between the UNSC and the human rights organs in the organization.

ADDRESSING MEMBER STATES' LEGISLATION AND ADMINISTRATION OF JUSTICE PRACTICES

The CTC, which was established on the basis of UNSC resolution 1373, monitors the implementation of resolution 1373 by all states; the resolution "requested countries to implement a number of measures intended to enhance their legal and institutional ability to counter terrorist activities at home, in their regions and around the world."[36] All states were expected to report to the Committee on measures taken or planned to implement resolution 1373.[37] This task provided an opening to many member states to use the 1373 process in order to validate legislative initiatives and related practices that violated fundamental tenets, as well as basic procedural guarantees, of human rights law and criminal law. The submission of actual or proposed legislation by member states to the CTC, as well as certain practices in the administration of justice, were reflective of the challenges posed by the lack of human rights-sensitive control mechanisms in the early phases of the 1373 process.

Concerning legislation, a key principle in the adoption of legislation is its compliance with the principle of legality. This principle, which requires precision in legislation and prohibits the adoption of ex post facto laws (article 15 of the International Covenant on Civil and Political Rights-ICCPR), is a non-derogable right in international human rights law, as per article 4(2) of the ICCPR.

There are at least two factors which have facilitated member states' abuse of the said process. First, and as mentioned earlier, the CTC consistently refused over a certain period of time to address in any serious manner the human rights implications of the campaign against terrorism. The second flowed from the first: as a result of this approach, there was a manifest lack of interest on the part of the CTC to scrutinize member states' records on human rights.

These observations are validated as a result of a preliminary research conducted on two key databases: (1) the list of reports submitted by member states to the CTC during the period 2001–2006; and (2) the list of reports submitted by member states to the Human Rights Committee (HRC), which is the monitoring organ of the International Covenant on Civil and Political Rights (ICCPR). The HRC has the most extensive record of monitoring member states' human rights performance among treaty-based monitoring organs. The end year is 2006 because after that year, the CTC switched into another system of monitoring states' compliance, the Preliminary Implementation Assessments (PIAs), a matrix-type system which ostensibly facilitated a more dialogic approach between the CTC and member states. From September 2001 to 2006 period, 56 reports were submitted to the HRC, while the CTC received 709 reports.[38] The reports were analyzed on the basis of how they addressed: (1) the definition of terrorism in their criminal law code/statutes; (2) legal provisions about detention; and (3) the jurisdictional reach of special tribunals.

The country reports submitted to the CTC and the HRC were subjected to content analysis. Since fewer reports were submitted to the HRC than to the CTC during this period, the reports submitted to the HRC were used as the basis to identify the corresponding country reports to the CTC. While the responses of the CTC to the country reports (contra to the responses of the HRC to the country reports) are not publicly available, follow-up reports to the CTC were examined to see if there were any significant variations, on the above mentioned issue areas, from one report to the next. For example, if a country had adopted a questionable (from a human rights-based perspective) definition of terrorism, a definition criticized by the HRC, was that definition subjected to any changes in the follow-up report to the CTC? If not, we inferred that either the CTC did not raise any critical remarks about such a definition in its response to the initial country report, or that the reporting state's response reflected such an understanding (i.e. absence of a critical perspective).[39] Preliminary results show that there is wide variation in the responses between the HRC and the CTC to these issues in country reports. These results seem to confirm (so far) our basic hypothesis that the HRC review process would subject human rights-related issues to close scrutiny, while the CTC review process would exhibit near absence of such scrutiny.

For example, Egypt's definition of terrorism contained in Act no. 97 of 1992 included, among other things, "any use of force or violence or any threat or intimidation to which the perpetrator resorts in order to . . . prevent or impede the public authorities in the performance of their work; or thwart the application of the Constitution or of laws or regulations." In fact, when the HRC examined Egypt's periodic report in November 2002, it expressed alarm at "the very broad and general definition of terrorism given in Act No. 97 . . . ."[40] No such concern was apparently raised by the CTC when it reviewed Egypt's initial report, submitted in December 2001, which contained the very same definition.[41]

What were some of the key issues that appeared in subsequent reports submitted by Egypt to the CTC? among these issues were: the need for greater clarity on the decisions of the Central Bank regarding the freezing of funds; more information on border controls to prevent terrorist mobility; progress reports on the ratification and domestic implementation of international counter-terrorist conventions; improved screening at border points and the adoption of measures to counter extremism.[42] There is hardly any discussion of the impact of existing legislation, in particular of emergency laws, and of the variety of adopted measures on the human rights situation in the country.[43]

Likewise, there is no evidence that the CTC registered any objections or concerns over Algeria's definition of terrorism included in Article 1 of Decree No. 93–03; the Decree defines as a terrorist act "any offence targeting State security, territorial integrity or the stability or normal functioning of institutions through any action seeking to," among other things, "Disrupt traffic or freedom of movement on roads and obstruct public areas with gatherings; Damage national or republican symbols and profane graves;" and "Harm the environment, means of communication or means of transport."[44] In fact, all subsequent reports to the CTC, save one, did not address at all definitional issues of terrorist acts. Instead, they addressed issues ranging from the financing of terrorist activities and the obligations of lawyers and notaries "to report suspicious transactions," to the freezing of assets of non-residents held in Algerian banks and the legal and administrative arrangements for the registration of charitable organizations.[45] In the only subsequent report in which the definition of terrorist act is addressed, the phrasing is near identical to the one included in the initial report, thus raising serious questions about the legislation's potential for abuse, given some of its very broadly phrased and vague provisions.[46]

As expected, the HRC had a different reaction. In its concluding observations on Algeria's third periodic report,[47] the HRC noted that "While it understands the security requirements associated with the fight against terrorism," it "expresses concern at the lack of details on the particularly broad definition of terrorist and subversive acts given in the Criminal Code . . ."[48] The Committee emphasized that:

> The State party should ensure that counter-terrorism measures are consistent with the Covenant. In addition, the definition of terrorist and subversive acts should not lead to constructions whereby the terrorist acts can be invoked to deny the legitimate expression of rights established in the Covenant.[49]

Turning to another region, the CTC expressed no misgivings about the pending legislation related to terrorism, when it reviewed the initial report submitted by the Philippines.[50] This attitude was in sharp contrast to the reaction of the HRC when it reviewed the country's consolidated second and third periodic reports. In its concluding observations, the HRC noted, inter alia, that:

> While the Committee is mindful of the security requirements associated with efforts to combat terrorism, it is concerned by the exceedingly broad scope of the proposed legislation, as acknowledged by the delegation. The draft legislation includes a broad and vague definition of acts of terrorism which could have a negative impact on the rights guaranteed by the Covenant.[51]

And it concluded: "The State party should ensure that legislation adopted and measures taken to combat terrorism are consistent with the provisions of the Covenant."[52]

The most recent (2016) Global Survey on the Implementation of UNSCR 1373, prepared by the CTC, confirms that problems in this area persist.[53] In particular, the survey noted that:

> One core issue that remains a major matter of concern, more than 14 years after the adoption of Security Council resolution 1373 (2001), is the question of the legal definition of terrorist acts. . .The Counter-Terrorism Committee Executive Directorate is aware of situations in several States, in various regions, in which terrorism charges or administrative designations have been framed in vague terms, allowing for their misuse against legitimate conduct, such as the expression of political dissent or human rights advocacy. . ..[54]

Failure to address this issue can have adverse normative as well as policy implications. Imprecise/vague legislation not only undermines key norms and may lead to abusive conduct; "clearly defined and mutually-consistent offenses" can render extradition requests less contentious, thus facilitating effective international cooperation in counter-terrorism.[55]

Concerning the administration of justice, an equally troubling picture emerges. While bringing those suspected of terrorist-related offenses to justice is a fundamental objective of UNSCR 1373, this goal has to be addressed within a framework that reflects adherence to internationally recognized rules and standards. Some of the critical issues involved here include provisions for investigative detention, access to counsel, the use of military or other special tribunals for terrorism-related cases, and the existence of "independent judicial oversight at all stages of terrorist investigations and prosecutions."[56] A related issue is whether the country in question has declared a state of emergency. In such a case, it is important to ensure that (1) non-derogable rights are respected; (2) that adopted measures derogating from human rights obligations adhere to the principles of necessity and proportionality and are non-discriminatory; and (3) that derogations from certain rights do not undermine adherence to non-derogable rights.

The last point is particularly important since the record of states of exception has shown that non-compliance with derogable rights (for example, minimum fair trial guarantees as per article 14 of the ICCPR) often lead to violations of non-derogable rights (for example, right to life). The relation between derogable and non-derogable rights was highlighted in General Comment 29 issued by the HRC:

> It is inherent in the protection of rights explicitly recognized as non-derogable in article 4, paragraph 2, that they must be secured by procedural guarantees,

> including often, judicial guarantees. The provisions of the Covenant relating to procedural safeguards may never be made subject to measures that would circumvent the protection of non-derogable rights . . . Thus, for example, as article 6 of the Covenant is non-derogable in its entirety, any trial leading to the imposition of the death penalty during a state of emergency must conform to the provisions of the Covenant, including all the requirements of articles 14 and 15.[57]

In this context, the CTC did not express any concern about Colombia's draft legislative act No.10 of 2002 which sought to amend key provisions dealing with the administration of justice. On the contrary, the HRC registered its serious concern with the said act, while reviewing the country's fifth periodic report:

> The State party should take into consideration the fact that some of the provisions of this draft act would be in clear contradiction with provisions of the Covenant, in particular articles 2, 4 and 14. If it were to be adopted, such fundamental remedies as amparo proceedings could be jeopardized.[58]

Likewise, the CTC did not raise issues relating to the administration of justice when reviewing Tajikistan's third periodic report submitted under the 1373 process. In particular, the conditions of detention and trial procedures for members of groups which had "engaged in particularly serious State crimes"[59] did not seem to register with the Committee. On the other hand, a few months later the HRC, when reviewing Tajikistan's initial report, expressed serious concern, among other things, over "the apparent lack of independence of the judiciary" and the extensive jurisdiction of military courts.[60]

In the previous global survey (2011), the administration of justice was highlighted as another problematic area:

> An issue that has recently drawn attention is the application of states of emergency or other states of exception in some States, purportedly on the basis of the terrorism threat. For States that are parties to the International Covenant on Civil and Political Rights . . . the application of emergency measures is subject to strict requirements and may in no case infringe on non-derogable rights, such as those set out in article 4 of the Covenant.[61]

A similar concern was echoed in the 2016 survey which noted that "compliance with international standards of due process and fair treatment also remains a matter of concern . . .."[62]

While member states clearly bore responsibility for these developments, it would be a mistake to underplay the UNSC's contribution to the problem and concomitant responsibility. To be sure, many of these legislative acts and administration of justice practices antedated 9/11. After all, then Egyptian President Hosni Mubarak famously declared that U.S. policy measures adopted after 9/11 proved "that we were right from the very beginning in using all means, including military tribunals, to combat terrorism."[63] However, by compartmentalizing jurisdictional issues (human rights as concerns of other UN organs) the UNSC enabled the legitimization of questionable state practices through the 1373 process. By denuding, during its early phase, the 1373 process from any human rights-related scrutiny,[64] the UNSC failed to uphold its human rights obligations even within the most restrictive understanding of what such obligations would entail.

The overwhelming narrative of a "global war on terror" demanding security-oriented responses notwithstanding, the first signs of resistance appeared as soon as some of its excesses became known. What began to turn the tide towards a more human rights-sensitive counter-terrorist approach?

It was a combination of endogenous (to the UN system) and exogenous factors. Early signs of resistance emerged from within the UN, as well as from prominent human rights organizations. These were primarily manifested in the form of repeated requests by human rights officials and experts in the UN for quality control mechanisms and greater collaboration between the CTC and various human rights organs. These efforts were reinforced by critical NGO reports highlighting aspects of the said human rights deficit and calling for adherence to international human rights norms and standards.[65] In addition, the appointments of a Human Rights Officer in CTC's CTED and of a Special Rapporteur on the promotion and protection of human rights and fundamental freedoms while countering terrorism by the then Commission on Human Rights,[66] contributed to a more robust and coordinated response to the excesses of counter-terrorism.[67]

CONCLUDING REMARKS

Some analysts have been perplexed at UNSC's slow response to the necessity of taking human rights seriously.[68] Is this a puzzle? From a perspective that subscribes to the notion that the collective processes of international law and the corresponding normative framework matter, this can indeed be a puzzle. From a realist/hegemonic law perspective though, in which the UNSC is perceived as a vehicle for the interests of its most powerful member(s), this is clearly not a puzzle.[69] However, there are other arguments, consistent with the rationalist optic, as to why, from the very beginning, the UNSC should and could have been more human rights-sensitive in its responses to the terrorist challenge. Taking human rights norms seriously would have rendered cooperation (in extradition) among states easier, and thus would have contributed to one of the key goals of the counter-terrorism effort. Such arguments would also be consistent with a social institutional reading of hegemony emphasizing the importance of legitimacy.

To be sure, the 1373 process is only part of the problem. A lot of ink has been shed on the 1267 Sanctions Committee and its listing and de-listing practices that have raised serious concerns about the lack of adequate due process standards in its operations.[70] Arguably, the overarching notion that underscores the initial responses of these two key subsidiary organs was that human rights issues were the responsibility of other organs in the UN system, not that of the UNSC. Such a notion could not be expressed in terms of an alleged second-order status for human rights within the security discourse despite the fact that the conduct of these bodies was consistent with such reading. Instead, the initial reluctance to take human rights seriously had to be framed as an issue of jurisdiction (an indication in itself that some importance should be attached to human rights).

For those who subscribe to the notion that the collective processes of international law matter, the non-conformity to human rights norms undermines the organization's legitimacy and the prospects for accountability. There are two other factors that antedate the 1373 process and have reinforced its impact on norm erosion and accountability: the first relates to the status of the UNSC within the UN and the second to states of emergency. The former points to long-standing issues of institutional design and the second to the "price" that the human rights regime had to pay in order to ensure state adoption of the major human rights treaties.

More specifically, the first points to two main problems: the underspecified human rights obligations of the UNSC and the corresponding lack of mechanisms and procedures to address human rights issues. This lack of mechanisms and procedures has, as one analyst noted, adversely impacted the protection of targeted individuals under the sanctions regime.[71] As the preliminary examination of state reports under the 1373 process has demonstrated, the problem is not confined to the sanctions regime; it has affected the interaction of the CTC with member states, not just with targeted individuals. While the situation has improved since the adoption of a more dialogic approach with the implementation of PIAs, problems in some of the key issue areas persist, as confirmed in the most recent Global Survey (2016).[72]

The second issue relates to the concept of emergency which first appeared, more than 60 years ago, in a regional and subsequently in a global human rights instrument.[73] As has been well-documented, this concept has provided governments with wide latitude to engage in often widespread and/or systematic abuses against their own citizens.[74] Attempts to subject determinations, as to the existence of a public emergency and of the derogations made under it, to some type of stricter judicial scrutiny has proven to be a rather elusive quest.[75] The concept of emergency "has turned out to be the Achilles' heel of the human rights doctrinal corpus."[76]

This brings us to the last point. Turning the effort to combat terrorism into an ongoing global war without geographic or temporal limitations has privileged the securitization of counter-terrorism measures at the expense of human rights and has contributed to the normalization of emergency situations.[77]

In an effort to enhance accountability, two suggestions are advanced: (1) that the UNSC authorize the CTED to conduct human rights impact assessments on all draft resolutions dealing with counter-terrorism;[78] and (2) that the CTED submit a request to member states to conduct such assessments on their proposed counter-terrorism legislation and related administrative measures. The review of such assessments should be included in countries' DIS compiled by the CTED. Such a process would provide additional entry points for the human rights organs of the UN system to have an input in the assessment of draft UNSC resolutions and for national human rights institutions and NGOs to do the same in their respective countries.

While there is no magic bullet here, these initiatives could build on the momentum generated by the work of the UN's human rights bodies (such as OHCHR and HRC); the advocacy of key human rights NGOs; the applications filed by affected individuals and entities before regional courts (such as the ECFI/General Court, the ECJ, and the ECtHR); pertinent issues raised and debated in normatively-oriented intergovernmental fora (CoE);[79] and legal challenges before domestic courts. All these factors have raised the "legitimacy stakes" and in the process have increased the pressure on the UNSC to adjust its relevant policies and procedures by reinforcing the abovementioned consensus, as well as advancing a different interpretation of the applicable precedent.

These developments, though modest, have registered an impact at the discursive level.[80] It is nowadays routine to see UNSC resolutions and statements reaffirming states' obligations under international human rights law, international humanitarian law and refugee law, when countering terrorism; the Global Surveys of the implementation of resolution 1373 confirm this trend. Changes at the discursive level constitute the first step towards the creation of additional pathways to human rights scrutiny and accountability, using platforms generated by the interactions among entities inside and outside the UN system. In an issue area exposed to the perpetual risk of human rights backsliding, the synergy among various entry points to accountability could and should constitute a sustainable form of resistance.

NOTES

1. The main point here is that states may, and occasionally do, violate their human rights obligations while implementing mandatory UNSCR resolutions. The question arises as to the responsibility incurred by the UNSC when states commit violations in observance of its resolutions. In addition, as one analyst has noted, challenges to UNSCR resolutions have been directed at states that have ratified human rights treaties; Vera Gowlland-Debbas (in Fassbender 2011: 73).
2. See Alison Brysk's Introduction in this volume.
3. On the concept of accountability and its role in limiting abuses of power in international affairs, see Ruth W. Grant and Robert O. Keohane (2005).
4. While some references will be made to the 1267 sanctions regime, the focus here is on the 1373 process.
5. By humanization, I refer to the process of rendering the discourse more receptive to human rights norms and standards.
6. As the ICJ noted in the *Certain Expenses* case, "The primary place ascribed to international peace and security is natural, since the fulfillment of the other purposes will be dependent upon the attainment of that basic condition;" ICJ Reports (1962).
7. In recent years, increasing attention has focused on the question of the human rights obligations of organs and specialized agencies of the UN system. For a recent treatment of this issue in the context international financial institutions (Apodaca 2017).
8. For a useful attempt to synthesize the different threads of this debate, see Karima Bennoune, "The Interplay of Legal Regimes Governing International Peace and Security and the Protection of Persons Under International Law," (on file with the author).
9. Bennoune, pp.2–14.
10. This of course takes us back to articles 1 and 2 on the Purposes and Principles of the Organization.
11. Needless to say, this is not an exclusive list, but it includes the main provisions relevant to the argument that follows. One could add here articles 55(c) and 56 of the Charter.
12. Bennoune, supra note 8, p.8.
13. This argument is consistent with the ordinary meaning contextual approach to treaty interpretation.
14. For a similar view, see Dapo Akande (2009). I do differ with Akande though on the idea that art. 103 only becomes relevant when the question arises as to whether ultra vires UNSC resolutions create any obligations for UN members.
15. United Nations Security Council Resolution 731 of January 21, 1992, and United Nations Security Council Resolution 748 of March 31, 1992 (Libya); and United Nations Security Council Resolution 1189, S/RES/1189, August 13, 1998 (on the Embassy bombings) and United Nations Security Council Resolution 1267, S/RES/1267, 15 October 1999 (on Afghanistan).
16. Paul Szasz, "The Security Council Starts Legislating," *American Journal of International Law*, vol. 96 (4), 2002, pp.901–905.
17. See Jose Alvarez, "Hegemonic International Law Revisited," *American Journal of International Law*, vol. 97(4), 2003, pp.873–88.
18. Alvarez, 2003, p.875. This was not the only development that rekindled the debate, but it was a key contributing factor. For a discussion of the key characteristics of Hegemonic International Law and the way that dominant states interact with international law, see Vagts (2001) and Krisch (2005).

19. For more on this, see Johnstone (in Bruce Cronin and Ian Hurd 2008).
20. Bruno Simma *et al.* (2002).
21. Prosecutor v. Dusko Tadic aka "DULE," Decision on the Defense Motion for Interlocutory Appeal on Jurisdiction, para. 31.
22. Johnstone (2008: 82).
23. These reasons are discussed in Johnstone (2008: 82–4).
24. This reading is reflective of an understanding of hegemony based on material resources, as opposed to an understanding resting on shared norms that bind states as members of an international society. In the latter context, hegemony is anchored on legitimacy; see Clark (2011) and Haas (1999).
25. For more on this, see Rodney Bruce Hall and Thomas J. Biersteсker (2002) and Cronin and Hurd (2008).
26. Cronin and Hurd (2008: 6).
27. Allen Buchanan, "Political Legitimacy and Democracy" (cited in Lowe, Roberts, Welsh and Zaum, 2008: 30).
28. See also remarks in Lowe *et al.*, (2008: 31).
29. The list is not exhaustive. One study on UNSC authority included deliberation and delegation to the list; Cronin and Hurd, "Assessing the Council's authority" (in Cronin and Hurd 2008: 202–206). Part of the following discussion on precedent and consensus draws from that study to which the author was one of the contributors.
30. UNSC action to protect civilian populations and to establish accountability mechanisms, the International Criminal Tribunals for the Former Yugoslavia (ICTY) and Rwanda (ICTR), are examples of this.
31. Cronin and Hurd (2008: 206).
32. For the texts of the International Conventions dealing with terrorism issues, see http://www.un.org/en/sc/ctc/laws.html.
33. Here is where arguments about Hegemonic International Law (HIL) become relevant.
34. Sir Jeremy Greenstock, (UNSC 2002: 5). See also Human Rights Watch (2004: 6).
35. Greenstock, ibid.
36. https://www.un.org/sc/ctc/about-us/ The discussion that follows on the requirements of the resolution draws in part on George Andreopoulos, "United Nations Counterterrorist Strategies and Human Rights," (in Andreopoulos, Barberet and Levine 2011).
37. There is wide variation in the reports submitted by states. By the end of 2006, which is when the CTC decided not to make public anymore the reports submitted by states, all (at that time) 192 member states had submitted reports, for a total of 706 reports (if one adds the Cook Islands, the total number of reports is 709). The reports vary widely in number (for example, Chad submitted only one report during this period, while Argentina six), in length (from a few pages to more than a hundred) and in quality; for the texts of these reports, see http://www.un.org/en/sc/ctc/resources/1373.html (UNSC 2001a) and appendix. In addition to member states, two regional organizations, OSCE and EU, and one UN Mission (UNMIK), submitted reports.
38. UNSC 2001a. The HRC received 55 country reports and one report from UNMIK.
39. From the reports examined so far (thirty reports to the HRC and 127 reports to the CTC), we found only one case, Paraguay, in which the reporting state indicated resistance to the implementation of the recommendations due to their adverse human rights implications; S/2004/375, May 10, 2004. This communication reinforces our argument about CTC's insensitivity to human rights issues.
40. Human Rights Watch (2004: 8).
41. UNSC 2001b; https://documents-dds-ny.un.org/doc/UNDOC/GEN/N01/714/85/PDF/N0171485.pdf?OpenElement; and Human Rights Watch, pp.8–9.
42. See subsequent reports by Egypt: S/2002/601, https://documents-dds-ny.un.org/doc/UNDOC/GEN/N02/408/44/PDF/N0240844.pdf?OpenElement; S/2003/277, https://documents-dds-ny.un.org/doc/UNDOC/GEN/N03/276/05/PDF/N0327605.pdf?OpenElement; S/2004/343, https://documents-dds-ny.un.org/doc/UNDOC/GEN/N04/345/04/PDF/N0434504.pdf?OpenElement; S/2005/288, https://documents-dds-ny.un.org/doc/UNDO

C/GEN/N05/338/02/PDF/N0533802.pdf?OpenElement; S/2003/351, https://documents-dds-ny.un.org/doc/UNDOC/GEN/N06/370/14/PDF/N0637014.pdf?OpenElement (UNSC 2001a).

43. UNSC 2001a; and Shelby Prue, Assessment of the Impact of UN Treaty Bodies in post 1373 Counter-terrorist Strategy through the Counter-Terrorism Committee and Human Rights Treaty Bodies; The Center for International Human Rights, John Jay College of Criminal Justice, 2013 (on file with the author).
44. Report submitted by Algeria to the Security Council Committee pursuant to resolution 1373 (2001), S/2001/1280, 27 December 2001; https://documents-dds-ny.un.org/doc/UNDOC/GEN/N02/205/90/IMG/N0220590.pdf?OpenElement.
45. See subsequent reports submitted by Algeria: S/2002/972 and S/2003/723; (UNSC 2001a).
46. United Nations Security Council, Letter dated 20 April 2004 from the Chairman of the Security Council Committee established pursuant to resolution 1373 (2001) concerning counter-terrorism addressed to the President of the Security Council, S/2004/324, 23 April 2004, https://documents-dds-ny.un.org/doc/UNDOC/GEN/N04/329/60/PDF/N0432960.pdf?OpenElement.
47. United Nations International covenant on civil and political rights. Examination of Reports Submitted by States Parties under Article 40 of the Covenant. Third Periodic Report. People's Democratic Republic of Algeria, CCPR/C/DZA/3, November 7, 2006.
48. United Nations International covenant on civil and political rights. Consideration of Reports submitted by States Parties under Article 40 of the Covenant. Concluding Observations of the Human Rights Committee. Algeria, CCPR/C/DZA/CO/3,12 December 2007.
49. United Nations 2003, *Concluding Observations of the Human Rights Committee*. Algeria, 2007.
50. United Nations Security Council. Letter dated December 27, 2001 from the Chairman of the Security Council Committee established pursuant to resolution 1373 (2001) concerning counter-terrorism addressed to the President of the Security Council Philippine Action and Initiatives Against Domestic and International Terrorism, December 27, 2001, S/2001/1290.
51. United Nations. International Covenant on Civil and Political Rights. Consideration of Reports Submitted by States Parties Under Article 40 of the Covenant. Concluding observations of the Human Rights Committee. The Philippines, CCPR/CO/79/PHL, 1 December 2003.
52. Concluding observations of the Human Rights Committee. THE PHILIPPINES, 2003.
53. United Nations Security Council Counter-Terrorism Committee Executive Directorate (CTED). Global survey of the implementation of Security Council resolution 1373 (2001) by Member States, S2016/49, 20 January, 2016.
54. Global survey of the implementation of Security Council resolution 1373 (2001) by Member States, S2016/49, 20 January, 2016.
55. See Edward Flynn, *Pushing the Limits: Human Rights at the United Nations Counter-Terrorism Committee* (unpublished paper, on file with the author). The key principle in this context is dual criminality according to which a person may only be extradited if her/his actions constitute offenses under the criminal law of both the requesting and the requested state.
56. Flynn, *Pushing the Limits*.
57. International Covenant on Civil and Political Rights. General Comment No 29. States of Emergency (Article 4); http://www.unhchr.ch/tbs/doc.nsf/898586b1dc7b4043c1256a450044f331/71eba4be3974b4f7c1256ae200517361/$FILE/G0144470.pdf.
58. United Nations. International Covenant on Civil and Political Rights. Consideration of reports submitted by states parties under article 40 of the Covenant. Concluding observations of the Human Rights Committee. Colombia; CCPR/CO/80/COL, 26 May 2004.
59. United Nations Security Council. Report of the Republic of Tajikistan submitted to the United Nations Counter-Terrorism Committee pursuant to paragraph 6 of resolution

1373 (2001); S/2004/992, December 22, 2004. According to the report, these crimes included terrorism and sabotage.

60. United Nations. International Covenant on Civil and Political Rights. Consideration of Reports Submitted by States Parties Under Article 40 of the Covenant. Concluding observations of the Human Rights Committee. Tajikistan; CCPR/CO/84/TJK, 18 July 2005.
61. Global survey of the implementation of Security Council resolution 1373 (2001) by Member States. Compiled by the Counter-Terrorism Committee 2011; http://www.un.org/en/sc/ctc/docs/2011-globalsurvey1373.pdf.
62. Global survey of the implementation of Security Council resolution 1373 (2001) by Member States, supra note 53.
63. Author's emphasis; quoted in Huq (2006: 32).
64. Although our research of all the state reports has yet to be completed, there is nothing that has been found so far that would challenge this admittedly preliminary finding.
65. Examples of such reports are Human Rights Watch (2004), and Lawyers Committee for Human Rights (2003).
66. Both appointments were made in 2005.
67. Space does not allow for a more detailed treatment of these issues. I have dealt with some of these issues before (Andreopoulos 2011).
68. See, for example, Nigel Rodley's separate individual opinion (concurring) in the Sayadi and Vinck case (United Nations 2008).
69. It is important to reemphasize that though there is a lot of blame that could be laid on the hegemon's doorstep, there were many willing accomplices among member states, as their reports to the CTC indicate.
70. See Post (2012).
71. Salvatore Zappala, "Reviewing Security Council Measures in the Light of International Human Rights Principles," in Fassbender (2011: 185–6).
72. See supra, note 53. In 2013, PIAs were replaced by an assessment document called Detailed Implementation Survey (DIS).
73. The European Convention on Human Rights and Fundamental Freedoms (1950) and the International Covenant on Civil and Political Rights (UN 1966).
74. United Nations Economic and Social Council (1982; 1996).
75. Oren Gross and Fionnuala Ni Aolain (2001) and Scott P. Sheeran (2013).
76. Balakrishnan Rajagopal (2003: 176).
77. See Lawyers Committee for Human Rights (2003).
78. See also Bennoune, supra note 8.
79. Parliamentary Assembly. Council of Europe (2008); available at: http://assembly.coe.int/nw/xml/XRef/Xref-XML2HTML-en.asp?fileid=17618&lang=en.
80. At this stage, it is difficult to validate empirically progress beyond the discursive level.

REFERENCES

Akande, Dapo. The Security Council and Human Rights: What is the role of Art. 103 of the Charter? EJIL: Talk! Posted on March 30, 2009.

Alvarez, Jose. Hegemonic International Law Revisited. *American Journal of International Law*, vol. 97(4), 2003, 873–88.

Andreopoulos, George. United Nations Counterterrorist Strategies and Human Rights. In Andreopoulos, George, Barberet, Rosemary and Levine, James P. (eds). *International Criminal Justice: Critical Perspectives and New Challenges*. Springer 2011, 153–68.

Apodaca, Clair. Expanding Responsibilities: the consequences of World Bank and IMF policies on child welfare. In Alison Brysk and Michael Stohl (eds). *Expanding human rights: 21st century norms and governance*. Cheltenham; Northampton: Edward Elgar, 2017, 215–35.

Bennoune, Karima. The Interplay of Legal Regimes Governing International Peace and Security and the Protection of Persons Under International Law. *Working paper prepared for Hague Expert Group on Counter-terrorism Strategies, Human Rights and International Law*, n.d.

Clark, Ian. *Hegemony in International Society*. Oxford University Press, 2011.

Cronin, Bruce and Hurd, Ian (eds). *The UN Security Council and the Politics of International Authority*, Routledge, 2008.

European Court of Human Rights / Council of Europe. European Convention on Human Rights and Fundamental Freedoms. 1950.

Fassbender, Bardo (ed.). Securing Human Rights? Achievements and Challenges of the UN Security Council. Oxford: Oxford University Press, 2011.

Flynn, Edward. *Pushing the Limits: Human Rights at the United Nations Counter-Terrorism Committee* (unpublished paper, on file with the author).

Global survey of the implementation of Security Council resolution 1373 (2001) by Member States. Compiled by the Counter-Terrorism Committee 2011; http://www.un.org/en/sc/ctc/docs/2011-globalsurvey1373.pdf.

Grant, Ruth W. and Keohane, Robert O. Accountability and Abuses of Power in World Politics. American Political Science Review, 99(1), February 2005, 29–43.

Gross, Oren and Ni Aolain, Fionnuala. From Discretion to Scrutiny: Revisiting the Application of the Margin of Appreciation Doctrine in the Context of Article 15 of the European Convention on Human Rights. *Human Rights Quarterly*, 23(3), 2001, 625–49.

Haas, Richard N. What to do with American Primacy. *Foreign Affairs*, 78(5), 1999, 37–50.

Hall, Rodney Bruce and Bierstecker, Thomas J. (eds). *The Emergence of Private Authority in Global Governance*. Cambridge University Press, 2002.

Human Rights Watch. *Hear No Evil, See No Evil: The U.N. Security Council's Approach to Human Rights Violations in the Global Counter-Terrorist Effort*. Human Rights Watch Briefing Paper, August 10, 2004.

Huq, Aziz Z. Extraordinary Rendition and the Wages of Hypocrisy. *World Policy Journal*, 23(1), 2006, 25–35.

International Court of Justice (ICJ). *Certain Expenses*. 1962.

International Covenant on Civil and Political Rights. General Comment No 29. States of Emergency (Article 4); http://www.unhchr.ch/tbs/doc.nsf/898586b1dc7b4043c1256a450044f331/71eba4be3974b4f7c1256ae200517361/$FILE/G0144470.pdf.

Johnstone, Ian. The Security Council as Legislature. In Bruce Cronin and Ian Hurd (eds). *The UN Security Council and the Politics of International Authority*, Routledge, 2008, 80–104.

Krisch, Nico. International Law in Times of Hegemony: Unequal Power and the Shaping of the International Legal Order. *European Journal of International Law*, 16(3), 2005, esp. 369–408.

Lawyers Committee for Human Rights. Assessing the New Normal. Liberty and Security for the Post-September 11 United States. 2003.

Lowe, Vaughan, Roberts, Adam, Welsh, Jennifer and Zaum, Dominik (eds). *The United Nations Security Council and War. The Evolution and Practice since 1945*. Oxford University Press, 2008.

Parliamentary Assembly. Council of Europe. Resolution 1597(2008). United Nations Security Council and European Union blacklists. Text adopted by the Assembly on 23 January 2008. Available at http://assembly.coe.int/nw/xml/XRef/Xref-XML2HTML-en.asp?fileid=17618&lang=en.

Post, Kimberly. Fair Process and the Security Council: A Case for the Office of the Ombudsperson. In Salinas De Frias, Ana Maria, Samuel, Katja and White, Nigel (eds). *Counter-Terrorism. International Law and Practice*. Oxford University Press, 2012, 409–23.
Prue, Shelby. "Assessment of the Impact of UN Treaty Bodies in post 1373 Counter-terrorist Strategy through the Counter-Terrorism Committee and Human Rights Treaty Bodies." The Center for International Human Rights, John Jay College of Criminal Justice, 2013 (on file with the author).
Rajagopal, Balakrishnan. International Law from Below. Development, Social Movements and Third World Resistance. Cambridge University Press, 2003.
Sheeran, Scott P. Reconceptualizing States of Emergency under International Human Rights Law: Theory, Legal Doctrine and Politics. *Michigan Journal of International Law*, 34 (3), 2013, 491–557.
Simma, Bruno, Khan, Daniel-Grasmus, Nolte, Georg, Paulus, Andreas, and Wessendorf, Nikolai, (eds). *The Charter of the United Nations: A Commentary*. Oxford University Press, 2002, 75.
Szasz, Paul. The Security Council Starts Legislating. *American Journal of International Law*, 96 (4), 2002, 901–5.
United Nations Economic and Social Council. Question of the Human Rights of Persons Subjected to Any Form of Detention or Imprisonment. Study of the implications for human rights of recent developments concerning situations know as states of siege or emergency. Special Rapporteur: Mrs. N. Questiaux; E/CN.4/Sub.2/1982/15, 27 July 1982.
United Nations Economic and Social Council. The Administration of Justice and the Human Rights of Detainees. Question of Human Rights and States of Emergency. Final Report of the Special Rapporteur, Mr. Leandro Despouy; E/CN.4/Sub.2/1997/19/Add.1, 9 June 1996.
United Nations. International Covenant on Civil and Political Rights. 1966.
United Nations. International Covenant on Civil and Political Rights. CONSIDERATION OF REPORTS SUBMITTED BY STATES PARTIES UNDER ARTICLE 40 OF THE COVENANT. Concluding observations of the Human Rights Committee. THE PHILIPPINES, CCPR/CO/79/PHL, 1 December 2003.
United Nations. International Covenant on Civil and Political Rights. Consideration of reports submitted by states parties under article 40 of the Covenant. Concluding observations of the Human Rights Committee. Colombia; CCPR/CO/80/COL, 26 May 2004.
United Nations. International Covenant on Civil and Political Rights. Consideration of Reports Submitted by States Parties Under Article 40 of the Covenant. Concluding observations of the Human Rights Committee. Tajikistan; CCPR/CO/84/TJK, 18 July 2005.
United Nations International covenant on civil and political rights. Examination of Reports Submitted by States Parties under Article 40 of the Covenant. Third Periodic Report. People's Democratic Republic of Algeria, CCPR/C/DZA/3, 7 November 2006.
United Nations International covenant on civil and political rights. Consideration of Reports submitted by States Parties under Article 40 of the Covenant. Concluding Observations of the Human Rights Committee. Algeria, CCPR/C/DZA/CO/3,12 December 2007.
United Nations. International covenant on civil and political rights. Communication

No. 1472/2006 Nabil Sayadi and Patricia Vinck v. Belgium, CCPR/C/94/D/1472/2006, 29 December 2008.

United Nations Security Council. Letter dated December 27, 2001 from the Chairman of the Security Council Committee established pursuant to resolution 1373 (2001) concerning counter-terrorism addressed to the President of the Security Council Philippine Action and Initiatives Against Domestic and International Terrorism, December 27, 2001, S/2001/1290.

United Nations Security Council. Resolution 731, 21 January 1992a.

United Nations Security Council. Resolution 748, 31 March, 1992b (Libya).

United Nations Security Council. Resolution 1189, S/RES/1189, 13 August 1998 (on the Embassy bombings).

United Nations Security Council. Resolution 1267, S/RES/1267, 15 October 1999 (on Afghanistan).

United Nations Security Council. Reports by Member States pursuant to Security Council resolution 1373, 2001a. http://www.un.org/en/sc/ctc/resources/1373.html, S/2002/601 https://documents-dds-ny.un.org/doc/UNDOC/GEN/N02/408/44/PDF/N0240844.pdf?OpenElement; S/2003/277 https://documents-dds-ny.un.org/doc/UNDOC/GEN/N03/276/05/PDF/N0327605.pdf?OpenElement, S/2004/343 https://documents-dds-ny.un.org/doc/UNDOC/GEN/N04/345/04/PDF/N0434504.pdf?OpenElement, S/2005/288 https://documents-dds-ny.un.org/doc/UNDOC/GEN/N05/338/02/PDF/N0533802.pdf?OpenElement, S/2003/351 https://documents-dds-ny.un.org/doc/UNDOC/GEN/N06/370/14/PDF/N0637014.pdf?OpenElement.

United Nations Security Council, Report submitted by Egypt to the Security Council Committee established pursuant to resolution 1373 (2001), S/2001/1237, 2001b. https://documents-dds-ny.un.org/doc/UNDOC/GEN/N01/714/85/PDF/N0171485.pdf?OpenElement.

United Nations Security Council, Report submitted by Algeria to the Security Council Committee established pursuant to resolution 1373 (2001), S/2001/1280, https://documents-dds-ny.un.org/doc/UNDOC/GEN/N02/205/90/IMG/N0220590.pdf?OpenElement.

United Nations Security Council. Letter dated 27 December 2001 from the Chairman of the Security Council Committee established pursuant to resolution 1373 (2001) concerning counter-terrorism addressed to the President of the Security Council Philippine Action and Initiatives Against Domestic and International Terrorism, 27 December 2001, S/2001/1290.

United Nations Security Council, Letter dated 20 April 2004 from the Chairman of the Security Council Committee established pursuant to resolution 1373 (2001a) concerning counter-terrorism addressed to the President of the Security Council, S/2004/324, 23 April 2004, https://documents-dds-ny.un.org/doc/UNDOC/GEN/N04/329/60/PDF/N0432960.pdf?OpenElement.

United Nations Security Council. Report of the Republic of Tajikistan submitted to the United Nations Counter-Terrorism Committee pursuant to paragraph 6 of resolution 1373 (2001b); S/2004/992, 22 December 2004.

United Nations Security Council. 4453rd meeting, 18 January 2002, S/PV.4453, p.5.

United Nations Security Council Counter-Terrorism Committee Executive Directorate (CTED). Global survey of the implementation of Security Council resolution 1373 (2001) by Member States, S2016/49, 20 January, 2016.

Vagts, Detlev F. Hegemonic International Law. *American Journal of International Law*, 95 (4), 2001, 843–8.

11. Backlash and international human rights courts

Wayne Sandholtz, Yining Bei and Kayla Caldwell

International human rights courts constantly confront states that reject or fail to comply fully with court judgments. Non-compliance with, and even criticism of, the decisions of international human rights courts are normal forms of resistance to adverse rulings. But sometimes states strike at international human rights courts (IHRCs) with more far-reaching forms of resistance that we label "backlash." "Backlash" refers to actions that aim to curtail a court's authority. It can include a range of actions, from pruning a court's competences, to withdrawing from a court's jurisdiction, to shutting a court down altogether. We examine instances of backlash against three prominent international courts devoted to the protection of human rights. The first two are the most active of the regional human rights courts, the European Court of Human Rights (ECtHR) and the Inter-American Court of Human Rights (IACtHR). The third court, the International Criminal Court (ICC), covers the flip side of international judicial protection of human rights, namely, individual accountability for grievous rights violations.

Our central claim is that governments are more likely to deem the costs of joining an international human rights court excessive the more its decisions are seen by national leaders as harming their domestic political interests, creating what we call "regime costs." Recent instances of backlash raise the specter of contagion that could undermine the legitimacy and effectiveness of international human rights courts.

BACKLASH

States routinely criticize, or refuse to comply with, ECtHR and IACtHR rulings. The ECtHR is the most influential human rights court in the world, having generated a sophisticated, expansive jurisprudence that shapes "the

Table 11.1 Types of actions that qualify as resistance

Resistance
When a state engages in: 1. Criticism of a specific judgment or judgments 2. Non-compliance with a specific judgment or judgments 3. Failure or refusal to cooperate with an international court in specific cases 4. General criticism of a court or its jurisprudence

Table 11.2 Types of actions that qualify as backlash

Backlash
When a state acts, or threatens, to: 1. Cease completely to cooperate or comply with the court 2. Narrow the court's jurisdiction 3. Restrict access to the court (limit standing) 4. Withdraw from the court's jurisdiction or denounce its underlying treaty 5. Abolish the court

nature and content of fundamental rights in Europe" (Stone Sweet and Keller 2008, 3). Yet even the ECtHR "faces a substantial minority of cases in which compliance is partial for quite extended periods" (Hawkins and Jacoby 2010, 66). The average rate of compliance with specific ECtHR orders is 48 percent (Hillebrecht 2014, 48–51). For the Inter-American Court of Human Rights (IACtHR), partial compliance with judgments is the norm, occurring in 83 percent of cases (Hawkins and Jacoby 2010, 37). At the more detailed level of specific remedies, the rate of compliance is 34 percent (Hillebrecht 2014, 48–51). For the ICC, non-compliance with judgments is not the issue. Rather, the problem has been non-compliance with requests from the ICC Prosecutor for cooperation in apprehending indictees and transmitting evidence. The case against Omar al-Bashir, for example, has been suspended in part because no state has been willing to detain al-Bashir and hand him over for trial (Berlin 2013). The case against Uhuru Kenyatta has likewise been adjourned because Kenya has declined to produce the documentary evidence requested by the Prosecutor (International Criminal Court 2014).

Non-cooperation and non-compliance are perennial forms of resistance to international courts. We are concerned with actions that go beyond resistance and aim to reduce the authority, competence, or jurisdiction of the court. To clarify this distinction, we list the types of actions that qualify as resistance and then those that count as backlash (Alter, Gatthi *et al.* 2016; Vinjamuri 2016).

The most drastic form of backlash – abolishing a human rights court – is not just a theoretical possibility. It has happened. The Southern Africa Development Community (SADC) came into being in 1992; the SADC Tribunal opened in 2005. In the wake of the Tribunal's first major judgment – a rights case decided against Zimbabwe in 2008 – the member states first crippled the Tribunal and then effectively shut it down in 2012 (Alter, Gatthi et al. 2016; Nathan 2013).

We frame our analysis of backlash in terms of the perceived benefits and costs of court membership. The benefits of human rights court membership vary by types of states. Strong democracies value IHRC membership for its expressive role (communicating support for international human rights) and from its expected effects in improving rights in other countries. Promoting rights abroad can contribute to regional or even global stability. Transitional democracies – those seeking to move from civil war or repressive regimes towards democracy – see IHRC membership as a means of enhancing the credibility of their commitment to democracy, rights, and the rule of law (Moravcsik 2000; Simmons 2009). Authoritarian governments might hope for a short-term reputational gain from joining an IHRC. We assume that the benefits of IHRC membership will generally remain stable for strong democracies, but that they can diminish over time for transitional democracies (after democratic consolidation, there is less ongoing need to "lock in" the commitment to human rights) and are likely to shrink rapidly for authoritarian regimes. Similarly, when a government seeks the help of an international court in resolving internal conflicts (as in the self-referrals of Uganda and DRC to the ICC), the perceived benefits of membership might decline once the domestic situation has stabilized.

Joining a human rights court also entails potential downstream costs. For instance, a government on the losing end of an IHRC judgment will generally have to take domestic action – legislative, judicial, executive, or administrative – to correct the situation that led to violations or to implement remedies ordered by the court. Such adaptation costs are a constant feature of IHRC membership and can lead to various forms of resistance (criticism, non-compliance). Backlash, however, is more likely when the IHRC is perceived by a government to be imposing regime costs. Regime costs arise when a government perceives that an international court's actions weaken its domestic hold on power, either by: (1) reducing public support for the government, (2) reducing support for the government within the governing coalition (the regime's elite constituencies), or (3) empowering or emboldening regime opponents. By the same token, if the international court becomes unpopular with the public or political elites (or both), the government will seek to preempt regime costs by engaging in backlash against the international court. We argue that backlash is more likely to occur when a government perceives that regime costs are rising or are about to rise. Backlash is especially likely where the perceived regime costs of IHRC membership are rising and the benefits are seen as declining.

Before proceeding, however, we should emphasize that the costs and benefits of IHRC membership are subjective. They are matters of perception, perspective, and interpretation, and are therefore malleable. Because the cost-benefit balance exists in the minds of people, actors – government officials, political party leaders, judges, legislators, editors and other media figures, activists – can work to tip it.

BACKLASH AND THE INTER-AMERICAN COURT OF HUMAN RIGHTS

The Inter-American Court has always faced criticism and resistance from various governments and domestic courts (Huneeus 2010; Huneeus 2011). Resistance has sometimes grown into backlash.

1. Trinidad and Tobago

In the early 1990s, Trinidad and Tobago, along with Jamaica and other Caribbean countries, had not only retained the death penalty but had expanded its use in response to rising rates of violent crime tied to the increasing role of Caribbean states as transshipment points for drugs moving from South America to the United States. Capital punishment was strongly supported by both governments and publics (Helfer 2002, 1868). In 1993, a death penalty case from Jamaica reached the Privy Council in London, which at the time functioned as a final court of appeal for British Commonwealth states in the Caribbean. The Privy Council ruled that an extended stay on death row violated international rules prohibiting inhuman or degrading treatment or punishment (the "death row phenomenon") and declared that a delay of more than five years from death sentence to execution would require commutation of a death sentence to life imprisonment (Helfer 2002, 1869–72).

Trinidad and Tobago, which also had death penalty cases pending, found that the five-year limit was too short to permit the completion of cases in the Inter-American Court, meaning that the Privy Council decision amounted to "a near de facto abolition of the death penalty in Caribbean states" (Helfer 2002, 1879). The de facto ban on capital punishment became increasingly unpopular with publics and governments in several

Caribbean states, and Trinidad denounced the American Convention on Human Rights in May 1998 (Helfer 2002, 1880–4). From the perspective of the government in Trinidad, remaining in the IACtHR would entail substantial regime costs because it would mean giving up the death penalty when the public and political elites strongly favored retaining it.

2. Venezuela

Following the election of Hugo Chávez as president of Venezuela in 1998, his opponents began to turn to the Inter-American System as a means of pushing back against "Chavismo." High-powered lawyers represented Chávez critics – generally from Venezuela's economic elite – at the Commission and the Court, particularly in claims regarding violations of freedom of expression and judicial independence. The IACtHR ruled against Venezuela in prominent cases, but the Venezuelan courts "increasingly rejected the recommendations and rulings of the Inter-American Commission and Court" (Huneeus 2016, 199–200). In fact, between 2000 and 2008, the Constitutional Chamber of Venezuela's Supreme Tribunal of Justice (STJ) blocked six judgments of the IACtHR from being applied in Venezuela. In addition, the STJ rejected decisions of the Inter-American Commission as unacceptable intrusions in the internal affairs of the country. Venezuela angrily denounced a critical 2009 Commission report and threatened to withdraw from the Commission (Serbin and Serbin Pont 2013, 241–2). The Supreme Court ruled that Commission precautionary measures were not binding in Venezuela, refused to implement the Inter-American Court's judgment in high profile cases,[1] and urged the government to withdraw from the American Convention.

Chávez finally renounced the American Convention (and the jurisdiction of the IACtHR) in 2012, on the grounds that the Commission and the Court had exceeded their authority, exhibited bias against Venezuela, and made themselves subservient to the United States. Chávez again threatened again to exit the Commission (which is an organ of the Organization of American States, not of the American Convention on Human Rights) (Serbin and Serbin Pont 2013, 241–2).

From the perspective of the Chávez government, the Commission and the Court were siding with regime opponents in the freedom of expression cases and intervening in Venezuela's domestic judicial structures. Chávez clearly viewed the Court's judgments as a danger to his Bolivarian revolution, raising perceived regime costs.

3. The Dominican Republic

The IACtHR decision in *Expelled Dominicans and Haitians v. Dominican Republic* (August 2014) held far-reaching domestic implications for the Dominican Republic.[2] The application submitted to the IACtHR claimed that the denial of identity documents and Dominican nationality to Haitians born in the Dominican Republic and Dominicans of Haitian descent, as well as their detention and expulsion, violated the American Convention. The Court agreed. The judgment was immediately criticized by Dominican lawmakers as a violation of the country's sovereignty. One senator asserted that the decision was not binding on the Dominican Republic and invoked Chávez's example of withdrawal (BBC 2014). Months later, the Dominican Constitutional Tribunal issued a decision that placed the country's IACtHR membership in question.

The Dominican Republic had accepted the contentious jurisdiction of the IACtHR in February 1999 through an Instrument of Recognition signed by then-president Leonel Fernández. That instrument had been under constitutional review since November 2005. The gist of the challenge was that it had not been approved by the congress, in violation of the Dominican constitution. The Constitutional Tribunal ruled in November 2014 that the Instrument of Recognition was unconstitutional and therefore not binding on the Dominican Republic. Though the Tribunal did not directly state that the Dominican Republic was no longer subject to the jurisdiction of the IACtHR or that the Court's decisions were no longer binding on the Dominican Republic, the judgment has been seen as implying those effects (Calcaneo Sánchez 2015). The government of the Dominican Republic has not clarified the country's position vis-à-vis the IACtHR. But the government places a high priority on the policies condemned by the IACtHR and those policies have the support of other political elites (legislators and the Supreme Court). The IACtHR judgment in Expelled Dominicans thus raised the perceived regime costs for the DR government.

Backlash against the Inter-American Court has come from states where regime costs were seen as rising, with no offsetting increase in the benefits of membership. In Trinidad and Tobago, Venezuela, and the Dominican Republic, governments perceived that IACtHR judgments were undermining their public support, their elite support, or both. The loss of member states weakens the Inter-American Court and limits its reach. But in recent years, Ecuador (BBC 2012), Bolivia (Woods 2013; Nuño 2013), and Argentina (Contesse 2017) have all taken actions that represent steps away from resistance and towards backlash. The potential for a backlash trend that would seriously undermine the IACtHR worries human rights advocates.

BACKLASH AND THE EUROPEAN COURT OF HUMAN RIGHTS

The European Court of Human Rights is widely seen as the most effective and influential human rights court in the world (Helfer 2008, 126). Membership in the Court is mandatory for members of the Council of Europe (COE). What distinguishes recent years from past decades is that resistance has on occasion developed into backlash.

1. Russia

Russia applied in 1992 to join the COE as part of its post-Soviet move to integrate more closely with Europe so as to gain economic benefits and signal its commitment to democratic governance. Though Russia's war in Chechnya produced large-scale human rights violations, the hope on the European side was that admitting Russia would bind it to the West and bring about human rights improvements (Parliamentary Assembly of the Council of Europe 1996).

Although Russia failed to carry out many of the commitments it had made upon its accession to the COE (Jordan 2003), it did ratify Protocol 11 of the Convention, thereby subjecting itself to the ECtHR's compulsory jurisdiction and giving its citizens the right of individual petition. The Russian people took advantage of that right. The number of applications from Russian nearly doubled from 971 in 1999 to 2108 just two years later, giving it the highest number among all member states (European Court of Human Rights 2002, 77). This trend persisted throughout the following decade and in 2013 Russia accounted for a staggering 12,328 cases, out of the Court's overall caseload of 65,790 (European Court of Human Rights 2016, 195). Polls also indicated steadily growing interest in the Court from the public. Whereas only 2–3 percent of Russians knew of their access to the ECtHR in 2001, a year and a half later, 19 percent did. In 2008, the Public Opinion Foundation found in its nationwide poll that 61 percent of respondents knew of their access to the Court and 29 percent were prepared to go to the Court to defend their rights (Trochev 2009, 148).

Despite (or perhaps because of) public interest, the attitude of the Russian government towards the Court has been cold. The Russian government has sometimes taken measures to stop its citizens from resorting to the Court, especially in cases related to the ongoing human rights violations in Chechnya. For example, Russian applicants who appealed to the ECtHR after the death or disappearance of their relatives in Chechnya met with death threats, forced disappearances, and even murder (Finn 2005). Russian officials have invoked national sovereignty, stating that they object to seeing domestic issues being settled outside the country. Even Vladimir Lukin, the political activist who once served as Human Rights Commissioner of Russia, said: "I prefer to see our problems, including burning issues of Chechnya, settled within this country, rather than in Strasbourg" (Hillebrecht 2012, 288). The government has also attempted to settle cases by offering applicants financial compensation, provided that they withdraw their applications from the Court (Trochev 2009, 152).

Russia's resistance to the ECtHR has recently developed into backlash. Following the ECtHR judgment in *Yukos v. Russia*, which ordered 2.51 billion dollars in compensation to Yukos shareholders for unfair tax proceedings (Alpert 2014), President Putin signed a law that gave the Constitutional Court of Russia the authority to decide whether to comply with ECtHR judgments (Sims 2015). Moreover, the Russian government can request the Constitutional Court to reevaluate ECtHR judgments in individual cases (Moscow Times 2015). The legislation effectively enables the Russian government to choose when the ECtHR will interpret the European Convention for Russia. In the words of Alexei Kravtsov, chairman of the Moscow Court of Arbitration, it also signals "the beginning of the end of Russia's ties with the Council of Europe" (Moscow Times 2015).

For the Russian government, the costs of ECtHR membership had been rising for years with a constant stream of ECtHR judgments finding Russian violations of the European Convention on Human Rights. The Yukos judgment was a tipping point, not just because of the real financial cost but because it placed in question the Kremlin's manipulation of major Russian economic assets. Standing up to "Europe" would also have a domestic regime payoff, enhancing Putin's image as the defender of Russian sovereignty.

2. The United Kingdom

Over a span of more than five decades, the ECtHR has issued 1,795 judgments regarding applications from the United Kingdom (European Court of Human Rights 2016, 5), with far-reaching effects on the development of individual rights in the UK.

The UK has generally complied with judgments, albeit grudgingly (Hillebrecht 2012, 285). Indeed, in Hillebrecht's analysis, the United Kingdom has the fourth best rate of compliance with ECtHR orders (71 percent), tied with Sweden and trailing only the Netherlands and Ireland (Hillebrecht 2014, 48). The British government has not been hesitant to criticize the Court for unfavorable rulings. But never, until recent years, have the attacks directed towards the Court targeted not just individual cases but also the fundamental legitimacy of the Court.

A pair of controversial cases swung both public opinion and a portion of elite opinion against the ECtHR. The first was the judgment in *Hirst v. United Kingdom* (which ruled that a blanket denial of the right to vote for prison inmates violated the Convention). Public opinion was sharply against the decision. In one poll, 76 percent of respondents agreed that prisoners "should not be allowed to vote." Half of respondents agreed that "[t]he government should refuse to implement the ruling" (YouGov 2010). By the following year, only 19 percent of those surveyed believed that the ECtHR had been a "good thing" for Britain and only 24 percent agreed that the UK should remain a member of the Court. In 1996, 71 percent of the British public had supported the ECtHR (Voeten 2013, 418). The House of Commons rejected by 234–22 a proposed law that would have complied with the Hirst decision (Voeten 2013, 419; Donald, Gordon et al. 2012, 174). The second case was *Othman (Abu Qatada) v. United Kingdom* in 2012, which held that Britain could not legally deport Abu Qatada – arrested in the UK and accused of having links to terrorist organizations – to Jordan because of the risk that he would be subjected to torture. In a November 2012 poll, a majority of Britons thought that Abu Qatada should be deported regardless of whether he would be guaranteed a fair trial in another country; 81 percent of Conservative voters shared that view (Rogers 2012). Then, Prime Minister David Cameron declared that the ECtHR was harming the fight against terror and making it harder for the UK government to protect British citizens (Donald *et al.* 2012, 154, n.469). The then Home Secretary (now Prime Minister) Theresa May called the Court's decision a "crazy interpretation of our human rights laws" and suggested that withdrawal from the European Convention should remain an option (Donald *et al.* 2012, 58).

The backlash against the ECtHR has been fueled by grossly misleading tabloid reporting. For instance, the *Telegraph*, *The Sun* and the *Daily Mail* have all published stories with headlines claiming (erroneously) that the UK loses either three out of four or three out of five cases in the Strasbourg-based Court (Hough and Whitehead 2012).[3] Public opinion shifted against the ECtHR. By July 2013, 48 percent of survey respondents agreed that Britain should withdraw from the European Convention on Human Rights (and thus also the Court) (Jordan 2014).

With the public, members of Parliament, and cabinet ministers intensely critical of the Court, the Conservative government in Britain perceived rising regime costs to membership in the ECtHR.

3. The Brighton Conference

The mounting British backlash against the Court found a broader European forum in the High Level Conference at Brighton in 2012. The conference was intended to find ways of dealing with the Court's immense backlog of applications (Helfer 2012), which by the beginning of 2012 had reached 151,600 (European Court of Human Rights 2013, 6). The United Kingdom held the chairmanship of the Council of Europe (COE) in 2012 and British leaders hoped not just to reform the Court but to curtail its powers. The British government's draft conference declaration, leaked to the press prior to the meeting, "contained a blueprint for clipping the Strasbourg Court's wings and weakening supranational review of member states' human rights practices" (Helfer 2012). In the end, the final Brighton Declaration included a number of statements to the effect that states should have more leeway in interpreting and applying Convention rights. Though the Brighton Declaration did not propose measures that would shrink the ECtHR's jurisdiction or authority, it did signal to the Court that some member states wanted the Court to be less assertive in its jurisprudence and more deferential to states.

The COE subsequently adopted Protocol 15 to the European Convention on Human Rights. To reduce the Court's caseload, Protocol 15 reduces the time limit to apply to the ECtHR from six months to four and establishes a stricter "significant disadvantage" test for admissibility. The principle of subsidiary and the margin of appreciation were included explicitly in the Convention for the first time, but only in the preamble. The Brighton Conference and the protocols that followed from it did not, then, curtail the ECtHR's authority in any substantive way. But they did reveal that the British backlash against the Court resonated with concerns being felt in some other states.

BACKLASH AND THE INTERNATIONAL CRIMINAL COURT

Criticism of and resistance to the ICC have recently turned into backlash, especially from African states.[4]

1. Kenya

Following the disputed 2007 election in Kenya, thousands of people were killed and hundreds of thousands displaced by post-election violence. Three years later, the ICC prosecutor opened a *proprio motu* investigation focusing on six high-level officials suspected of crimes against humanity. Two of the accused were then Minister of Higher Education William Ruto and then Minister of Finance Uhuru Kenyatta.[5] A week after the ICC prosecutor opened the investigation, the Kenyan parliament voted to withdraw from the ICC. The Minister of Energy declared that "it is only Africans from former colonies who are being tried at the ICC. No American or British will be tried at the ICC and we should not willingly allow ourselves to return to colonialism" (Rugene 2010). Kenya undertook various forms of resistance, including an appeal to the UN Security Council to defer the case, a challenge to the case's admissibility, and attempts to transfer the case to another court. These maneuvers failed. Kenya's approach changed dramatically when ICC indictees Kenyatta and Ruto won the March 2013 election and took office as, respectively, President and Deputy President of Kenya. Kenya again threatened to withdraw (BBC News 2013), and obstructed the ICC process by interfering with witnesses and refusing to hand over documentary evidence. The prosecutor was forced to drop the charges against Kenyatta in December 2014 and those against Ruto in April 2016.

The Kenyan government's backlash against the ICC did not necessarily represent Kenyans as a whole. An Afrobarometer survey conducted in 2014 found that only 34 percent of Kenyans were in favor of withdrawal from the ICC, with a 55 percent majority against it. Moreover, 55 percent of respondents perceived the ICC to be impartial, while 35 percent viewed it as biased against Kenya and other African countries (Lekalake and Buchanan-Clarke 2015). Rather, the Kenyan backlash against the ICC was driven primarily by the political self-interest of the two most prominent indictees, Kenyatta and Ruto, who perceived clear regime costs from ICC activities.

2. The African Union

At the 12th African Union Summit in January 2009, the AU called for a deferral of the case of Sudanese President Omar al-Bashir at the ICC in the interest of peace-building (Assembly of the African Union 2009, para. 1–3). The ICC Prosecutor nonetheless proceeded in March 2009 to issue an arrest warrant for war crimes and crimes against humanity, and followed up with a second one in July 2010 for genocide. In addition, the ICC issued an arrest warrant for Libyan leader Muammar Gaddafi in June 2011, shortly before he was killed. The AU urged member states to uphold customary diplomatic immunity by refusing to execute ICC arrest warrants. In October 2013, shortly after the Kenya trial began, the AU resolved in an Extraordinary Session that "no charges shall be commenced or continued before any International Court or Tribunal against any serving AU Head of State or Government" and declared that the Ruto and Kenyatta trials should be suspended (Assembly of the African Union 2013, para. 10(i)). Immunity for heads of state was incorporated into the proposed African Court of Justice and Human Rights, which was being seen as an alternative to the ICC (African Union 2014, Art. 46A bis).

The next AU summit in January 2016 coincided with the opening of the trial of the former Côte d'Ivoire President Laurent Gbagbo at the ICC, which contributed to the perceived pattern of bias against Africa. The summit agreed on "the urgent development of a comprehensive strategy including collective withdrawal from the ICC" (Assembly of the African Union 2016, para. 10(iv)). At the July 2016 Summit, the AU voted to move forward with a collective withdrawal strategy, though four states entered reservations on this clause (Assembly of the African Union 2016, para. 5(3)(b)).

The AU backlash against the ICC is partly a reaction against the Court's focus on African cases (see Ainley, Chapter 12), though fueled in particular by ICC prosecutions that raised regime costs for sitting African heads of state (al-Bashir, Kenyatta). In the states that have taken concrete steps to withdraw, governments faced the prospect of rising regime costs.

3. The 2016 withdrawals

Burundi

The 2015 decision of Burundi's President Pierre Nkurunziza to seek a third term in office, despite a constitutional two-term limit, prompted mass protests, which were met with violent repression. As tensions escalated, Nkurunziza withstood a coup attempt and was re-elected in July 2015. By the end of the year, hundreds of Burundians had been killed, thousands had been arrested, and hundreds of thousands had fled the country. The ICC opened a preliminary examination of the situation (International Criminal Court 2016). In response, First Vice-President Gaston Sindimwo characterized the ICC as a "political tool used by the international community to oppress African countries" (Jeune Afrique 2016). Days later, in October 2016, Parliament overwhelmingly passed a bill to withdraw from the ICC (Voice of America 2016). With ICC cases possible against high national officials, including Nkurunziza himself, Burundi's action was clearly a reaction to rising regime costs of the ICC.

South Africa

On October 19, 2016, President Jacob Zuma signed an executive order withdrawing South Africa from the ICC. The background to this move was that when Omar al-Bashir attended the 25th African Union Summit in Johannesburg in June 2015, the South African government declined to arrest him and hand him over to the ICC. Subsequently the North Gauteng High Court ruled that South Africa had violated its international obligation to arrest al-Bashir, a decision that was upheld by the Supreme Court of Appeals in March 2016. The Constitutional Court was scheduled to hear the case on appeal in November 2016. Upon leaving the ICC, the executive branch withdrew this appeal, thereby sidestepping a potentially unfavorable judgment that would be politically damaging to the government.

Regarding the ICC, South Africa is split along party lines, with the backlash against the ICC primarily coming from Zuma's governing party, the African National Congress (ANC). The opposition Democratic Alliance (DA) sharply criticized the "unconstitutional, irrational, and procedurally flawed" withdrawal that "shows the depth of impunity and disregard for the rule of law within the ruling African National Congress" (Freedom Online 2016). The opposition DA is also challenging the withdrawal in the courts (Democratic Alliance 2016). As of late 2016, with debate ongoing in parliament, the High Court reserved judgment on the matter (IOL 2016).

Zuma's government anticipated regime costs connected to the ICC, through an unfavorable ruling in the Constitutional Court. By the same token, withdrawal from the ICC could enhance Zuma's standing among ANC supporters, a domestic political payoff.

Gambia

The government of President Yahya Jammeh announced on 25 October 2016 that Gambia would withdraw from the ICC, declaring that "the International Criminal Court is in fact an International Caucasian Court for the persecution and humiliation of people of color, especially Africans" (Reuters 2016). Significantly, the withdrawal announcement came in the midst of a hotly contested presidential election campaign, in which the Jammeh government had brutally cracked down on the media and the opposition (Human Rights Watch 2016a). Jammeh had reason to fear ICC prosecution. His government – in power since 1994 – had been a chronic abuser of human rights, including enforced disappearance, torture, and arbitrary detention (Human Rights Watch 2016b). If Jammeh were to win the election, the ICC could open an investigation of his regime. If he lost the election, his successor could cooperate with an ICC prosecution. Jammeh therefore perceived potential regime costs from the ICC.

The opposition candidate Adama Barrow defeated Jammeh in the December 2016 election and Jammeh refused to accept the results. Barrow immediately promised to cancel Gambia's withdrawal from the ICC. In late January 2017, Jammeh fled the country under intense international pressure. He took refuge in Equatorial Guinea, a choice that is further evidence that Jammeh contemplated the prospect of an ICC prosecution. Equatorial Guinea was not an ICC member and would therefore be under no obligation to hand Jammeh over to the Court if he were to be indicted (National Public Radio 2017). Barrow, as the new president, informed the United Nations that Gambia was canceling its request to withdraw from the ICC (National Public Radio 2017).

The ICC faces additional backlash from states in Africa. Namibia, for instance, has threatened to withdraw (Reuters 2016), and two states that referred their own situations to the ICC, Uganda and DRC, have openly discussed it. If the withdrawal movement continues, the ICC's legitimacy and reach will diminish.

CONCLUSIONS

International human rights courts have always faced resistance, in the form of criticism and non-compliance. Occasionally, states have moved beyond resistance to take actions intended to reduce the authority, competence, or jurisdiction of the court, a phenomenon we have labeled "backlash." All three courts examined here have experienced some form of backlash, ranging from efforts to curtail the court's jurisdiction (the ECtHR and the Brighton Conference) to states' withdrawal from the court (IACtHR, ICC). The fear among human rights advocates is not that these courts are in imminent danger of collapse but rather that backlash could spread, undermining their legitimacy and effectiveness.

We argued that rising domestic regime costs are a primary driver of backlash behavior by states. Regime costs occur when an IHRC action either weakens support for the government in the general public or among elite constituencies, or strengthens the political opposition. Backlash, in this perspective, aims to shore up the government's domestic position by undermining the international court or withdrawing from its jurisdiction. A test of hypotheses derivable from this argument would require a much broader empirical analysis, encompassing varying regime costs (low to high) connected with state responses (compliance, resistance, backlash), while controlling for other potential causal factors. That analysis is beyond the scope of this contribution. Rather, our goal has been to demonstrate the link between domestic regime costs and backlash behavior. The empirical cases, we suggest, establish the general plausibility of our argument.

The implications of backlash vary across the courts. For the ECtHR, the impact of the Russian backlash is minimal, as Russia has an increasingly autocratic regime and chronic human rights violations. The UK backlash is potentially more troubling as it comes from a state with a strong human rights record. Still, the UK effort at Brighton to trim the ECtHR's powers did not bear fruit. The IACtHR is more vulnerable. The withdrawals, combined with efforts by additional states (Bolivia and Ecuador) to weaken the Inter-American System (Nuño 2013; Woods 2013) and the Argentine Supreme Court's recent rejection of an IACtHR judgment (Contesse 2017), raise serious concerns about the system's future ability to promote human rights in the region. For the ICC, if the threat of large-scale African withdrawals becomes a reality, the Court's legitimacy and effectiveness will be seriously diminished.

International human rights courts recognize these dangers. They must constantly walk a fine line between their desire to expand rights through assertive rulings and their recognition of the real political limits that states can impose. When backlash increases, international courts are likely to show that they recognize states' concerns. The ICC has opened (or reopened) preliminary examinations in Iraq (involving the United Kingdom), Palestine, and Ukraine, and announced an investigation into the situation in Georgia. The ECtHR appears to be demonstrating a greater degree of deference in cases involving the United Kingdom (Madsen 2016, 261). Indeed, the number of judgments against the UK has been strikingly small and declining in recent years, with 28 in 2008, eight in 2013, and only four in 2014. The UK in 2014 was the COE member state with the "highest number of judgments (10) finding no violation of the Convention" (United Kingdom 2015, 7). We would expect the IACtHR likewise to explore ways of opening dialogues with national courts, or to signal an increased willingness to grant leeway to states as they interpret and apply American Convention rights. Like all courts, international courts are political, not just judicial, actors. The current environment may test their ability to take into account, and respond to, the concerns of states and other constituencies while at the same time promoting the fulfillment of rights.

NOTES

1. *Apitz Barbera et al. ("First Court of Administrative Disputes") v. Venezuela* (2008); *López Mendoza v. Venezuela* (2011).
2. *Expelled Dominicans and Haitians v. Dominican Republic* (2014).
3. The reports overlooked the huge share of UK applications that were declared inadmissible. Taking into account applications found inadmissible, the proportion of applications in which the UK ended up losing in the ECtHR was "closer to 1%" United Kingdom (2015), 6.
4. The discussion here complements that of Ainley, Chapter 12.
5. For more detail, see Ainley (Chapter 12) and Nichols (2015).

REFERENCES

African Union (2014). Protocol on Amendments to the Protocol on the Statute of the African Court of Justice and Human Rights. 27 June 2014. Available at https://http://www.au.int/web/sites/default/files/treaties/7804-treaty-0045_-_protocol_on_amendments_to_the_protocol_on_the_statute_of_the_african_court_of_justice_and_human_rights_e.pdf. Accessed 14 March 2017.

Alpert, Lukas I. (2014). "Russia Must Compensate Yukos Shareholders, European Court Rules." *The Wall Street Journal*. 28 July 2014. Available at https://http://www.wsj.com/articles/russia-must-compensate-former-yukos-shareholders-court-rules-1406536768. Accessed 14 March 2017.

Alter, Karen J., James T. Gatthi, and Laurence R. Helfer. (2016). "Backlash against International Courts in West, East, and Southern Africa: Causes and Consequences." *European Journal of International Law* 27(2): 293–328.

Apitz Barbera et al. *("First Court of Administrative Disputes") v. Venezuela* (2008). Inter-American Court of Human Rights. Preliminary Objections, Merits, Reparations and Costs. Series C, No. 182. Decided 5 August 2008.

Assembly of the African Union (2009). Decision on the Application by the International Criminal Court (ICC) Prosecutor for the Indictment of the President of the Republic of the Sudan. Assembly/AU/Dec.221(XII). 1–3 February 2009. Available at https://http://www.au.int/web/sites/default/files/decisions/9559-assembly_en_1_3_february_2009_auc_twelfth_ordinary_session_decisions_declarations_message_congratulations_motion.pdf. Accessed 14 March 2017.

Assembly of the African Union (2013). Decision on Africa's Relationship with the International Criminal Court (ICC). Ext/Assembly/AU/Dec.1(Oct. 2013). 12 October 2013. Available at https://http://www.au.int/web/sites/default/files/decisions/9655-ext_assembly_au_dec_decl_e_0.pdf. Accessed 14 March 2017.

Assembly of the African Union (2009). Decision on the Application by the International Criminal Court (ICC) Prosecutor for the Indictment of the President of the Republic of the Sudan. Assembly/AU/Dec.221(XII). 1–3 February 2009.

BBC (2012). "Bolivia: Regional Group Aligns against OAS, Media, Human Rights Commission." *BBC Worldwide Monitoring*. Lexis-Nexis. 7 June 2012.

BBC News (2013). "Kenya MPs Vote to Withdraw from ICC." Available at http://www.bbc.com/news/world-africa-23969316. Accessed 14 March 2017.

BBC (2014). "Dominican Republic Lawmakers to Snub Human Rights Court." *BBC Worldwide Monitoring*. Lexis-Nexis. 24 October 2014.

Berlin, Mark S. (2013). "Why (not) Arrest? Explaining Third-Party State Compliance and Noncompliance with International Criminal Tribunals." *Journal of Human Rights* 15(4).

Calcaneo Sánchez, Alfonso (2015). "The Dominican Withdrawal from the Jurisdiction of the Inter-American Court of Human Rights." Faculty of Law. Master's Thesis, University of Oslo.

Contesse, Jorge (2017). "Judicial Backlash in Inter-American Human Rights Law?" *I-CONnect*: Blog of the International Journal of Constitutional Law and Constitution Making. Accessed 14 March 2017.

Democratic Alliance (2016). "ICC Withdrawal: DA's Challenge Will be Heard in North Gauteng High Court." Available at https://http://www.da.org.za/2016/11/icc-withdrawal-das-challenge-will-heard-north-gauteng-high-court/. Accessed 14 March 2017.

Donald, Alice, Jane Gordon, and Philip Leach. (2012). *The UK and the European Court of Human Rights. Research Report 83*. Equality and Human Rights Commission. London. Available at http://www.equalityhumanrights.com/sites/default/files/83._european_court_of_human_rights.pdf. Accessed 17 January 2017.

European Court of Human Rights (2002). *Annual Report 2001*. Registry of the European Court of Human Rights. Available at http://www.echr.coe.int/Documents/Annual_report_2001_ENG.pdf. Accessed 16 January 2017.

European Court of Human Rights (2013). *Analysis of Statistics 2012*. Available at http://www.echr.coe.int/Documents/Stats_analysis_2012_ENG.pdf. Accessed 16 January 2017.

European Court of Human Rights (2016). *Annual Report 2015*. Registry of the European Court of Human Rights. Available at http://www.echr.coe.int/Documents/Annual_Report_2015_ENG.pdf. Accessed 16 January 2017.

European Court of Human Rights (2016). Overview 1959 – 2015: ECHR. March 2016. Available at http://www.echr.coe.int/Documents/Overview_19592015_ENG.pdf. Accessed 17 January 2017.

Expelled Dominicans and Haitians v. Dominican Republic (2014). Inter-American Court of Human Rights. Preliminary Objections, Merits, Reparations and Costs. Series C, No. 282. Decided 28 August 2014.

Finn, Peter (2005). "Russians' Appeals to Court Bring Intimidation, Death." *Washington Post*. 3 July 2005. Available at https://http://www.washingtonpost.com/archive/politics/2005/07/03/russians-appeals-to-court-bring-intimidation-death/b87918f0-cd36-4bec-a9ab-706f800d956a/. Accessed 14 March 2017.

Freedom Online (2016). "South African Lawmakers Welcome Decision to Withdraw from ICC; Opposition Party Threatens Court Action over Withdrawal." Available at http://freedomonline.com.ng/south-african-lawmakers-welcome-decision-to-withdraw-from-icc-opposition-party-threatens-court-action-over-withdrawal/. Accessed 14 March 2017.

Hawkins, Darren and Wade Jacoby (2010). "Partial Compliance: A Comparison of the European and Inter-American Courts of Human Rights." *Journal of International Law and International Relations* 6(1): 35–85.

Helfer, Laurence R. (2002). "Overlegalizing Human Rights: International Relations Theory and the Commonwealth Caribbean Backlash against Human Rights Regimes." *Columbia Law Review* 102(7): 1832–911.

Helfer, Laurence R. (2008). "Redesigning the European Court of Human Rights: Embeddedness as a Deep Structural Principle of the European Human Rights Regime." *European Journal of International Law* 19(1): 125–59.

Helfer, Laurence R. (2012). "The Burdens and Benefits of Brighton." *ESIL Reflections. European Society of International Law*. Available at http://esil-sedi.eu/node/138. Accessed 2 December 2016.

Hillebrecht, Courtney (2012). "Implementing International Human Rights Law at Home: Domestic Politics and the European Court of Human Rights." *Human Rights Review* 13(3): 279–301.

Hillebrecht, Courtney (2014). *Domestic Politics and International Human Rights Tribunals: The Problem of Compliance*. Cambridge: Cambridge University Press.

Hough, Andrew and Tom Whitehead (2012). "ECHR: Britain Loses 3 in 4 Cases at Human Rights Court." *The Telegraph*. 12 January 2012. Available at http://www.telegraph.co.uk/news/worldnews/europe/9008904/ECHR-Britain-loses-3-in-4-cases-at-human-rights-court.html. Accessed 14 March 2017.

Human Rights Watch (2016a). "Gambia: Crackdown Threatens Presidential

Election." Available at https://http://www.hrw.org/news/2016/11/02/gambia-crackdown-threatens-presidential-election. Last updated 2 November 2016. Accessed 14 March 2017.

Human Rights Watch (2016b). "World Report 2016: Gambia." Available at https://http://www.hrw.org/world-report/2016/country-chapters/gambia. Accessed 14 March 2017.

Huneeus, Alexandra (2010). "Rejecting the Inter-American Court: Judicialization, National Courts, and Regional Human Rights." *Cultures of Legality: Judicialization and Political Activism in Latin America*. Javier Couso, Alexandra Huneeus and Rachel Sieder, ed. Cambridge, Cambridge University Press: 112–38.

Huneeus, Alexandra (2011). "Courts Resisting Courts: Lessons from the Inter-American Court's Struggle to Enforce Human Rights." *Cornell Int'l LJ* 44(3): 493–534.

Huneeus, Alexandra (2016). "Constitutional Lawyers and the Inter-American Court's Varied Authority." *Law and Contemporary Problems* 79(1): 179–207.

International Criminal Court (2014). *Statement of the Prosecutor of the International Criminal Court, Fatou Bensouda, on the status of the Government of Kenya's cooperation with the Prosecution's investigations in the Kenyatta case*. Available at https://http://www.icc-cpi.int/Pages/item.aspx?name=otp-stat-04-12-2014.

International Criminal Court (IOL) (2016). *Preliminary Examination: Burundi*. Available at https://http://www.icc-cpi.int/burundi. Accessed 14 March 2017.

IOL (2016). "Judgment Reserved in DA Bid to Halt Withdrawal from ICC." Available at http://www.iol.co.za/news/politics/judgment-reserved-in-da-bid-to-halt-withdrawal-from-icc-7110982. Last updated 6 December 2016. Accessed 14 March 2017.

Jeune Afrique (2016). "Burundi: Un Projet de Loi au Parlement pour Quitter la CPI." Jeune Afrique. Available at http://www.jeuneafrique.com/363744/politique/burundi-projet-de-loi-parlement-quitter-cpi/. Last updated 7 October 2016. Accessed 14 March 2017.

Jordan, Pamela A. (2003). "Does Membership Have its Privileges? Entrance into the Council of Europe and Compliance with Human Rights Norms." *Human Rights Quarterly* 25(3): 660–88.

Jordan, William (2014). "Scepticism about Human Rights as Well as the ECHR." *YouGov UK*. Available at https://yougov.co.uk/news/2014/07/20/scepticism-about-human-rights-well-echr/. Last updated 20 July 2014. Accessed 17 March 2017.

Lekalake, Rorisang and Stephen Buchanan-Clarke (2015). Support for the International Criminal Court in Africa: Evidence from Kenya. Policy Paper No. 23. Afrobarometer. August 2015. Available at http://afrobarometer.org/sites/default/files/publications/Policy papers/ab_r6_policypaperno23_kenya_anti_corruption.pdf. Accessed 14 March 2017.

López Mendoza v. Venezuela (2011). Inter-American Court of Human Rights. Merits, Reparations, and Costs. Series C, No. 223. Decided 1 September 2011.

Madsen, Mikael Rask (2016). "The European Court of Human Rights and the Politics of International Law." *Handbook on the Politics of International Law*. Wayne Sandholtz and Christopher A. Whytock, ed. Cheltenham, UK: Edward Elgar.

Moravcsik, Andrew (2000). "The Origins of Human Rights Regimes: Democratic Delegation in Postwar Europe." *International Organization* 54(2): 217–52.

Moscow Times (2015). "Russian Constitutional Court Determines Moscow Not Bound to All Human Rights Court Rulings." *The Moscow Times*.

Nathan, Laurie (2013). "The Disbanding of the SADC Tribunal: A Cautionary Tale." *Human Rights Quarterly* 35(4): 870–92.
National Public Radio (2017). "Under New Leader, Gambia Cancels Withdrawal from International Criminal Court." Available at http://www.npr.org/sections/thetwo-way/2017/02/14/515219467/under-new-leader-gambia-cancels-withdrawal-from-international-criminal-court. Accessed 14 March 2017.
Nichols, Lionel (2015). *The International Criminal Court and the End of Impunity in Kenya*. Cham, Switzerland: Springer.
Nuño, Alejandra (2013). "Los Desafíos del Sistema Interamericano de Derechos Humanos: Las OSC Internacionales y el SIDH." *Pensamiento Propio* 38(July–December): 287–318.
Parliamentary Assembly of the Council of Europe (1996). Russia's Application for Membership of the Council of Europe. Committee on Legal Affairs and Human Rights. Doc. 7463. 18 January 1996. Available at http://assembly.coe.int/nw/xml/XRef/Xref-DocDetails-en.asp?FileID=7397&lang=en. Accessed 16 January 2017.
Reuters (2016). "Gambia Announces Withdrawal from International Criminal Court." Available at http://www.reuters.com/article/us-gambia-icc-idUSKCN12P335?il=0. Last updated 26 October 2016. Accessed 14 March 2017.
Reuters (2016). "Namibia Will Stay in ICC -- If United States Joins, Says President." Available at http://www.reuters.com/article/us-namibia-economy-president-idUSKBN13Q5L0. Last updated 1 December 2016. Accessed 14 March 2017.
Rogers, Joel Faulkner (2012). "Public Says No to Prison Votes." *YouGov UK*. Available at https://yougov.co.uk/news/2012/11/25/public-says-no-prison-votes/. Accessed 17 March 2017.
Rugene, Njeri (2010). "Parliament Pulls Kenya from ICC Treaty." Daily Nation. 22 December 2010. Available at http://www.nation.co.ke/news/politics/Parliament-pulls-Kenya-from-ICC-treaty/1064-1077336-us2knmz/index.html. Accessed 14 March 2017.
Serbin, Andrés and Andrei Serbin Pont (2013). "La Política Exterior de las República Bolivariana de Venezuela y el Sistema Interamericano de Derechos Humanos como Obstáculo." *Pensamiento Propio* 38(July–December): 235–54.
Simmons, Beth A. (2009). *Mobilizing for Human Rights: International Law in Domestic Politics*. Cambridge: Cambridge University Press.
Sims, Alexandra (2015). "Vladimir Putin Signs Law Allowing Russia to Ignore International Human Rights Rulings." *Independent*. 15 December 2015. Available at http://www.independent.co.uk/news/world/europe/vladimir-putin-signs-law-allowing-russian-court-to-overthrow-international-human-rights-rulings-a6773581.html. Accessed 14 March 2017.
Stone Sweet, Alec and Helen Keller (2008). "The Reception of the ECHR in National Legal Orders." *A Europe of Rights*. Helen Keller and Alec Stone Sweet, ed. Oxford: Oxford University Press: 3–28.
Trochev, Alexei (2009). "All Appeals Lead to Strasbourg? Unpacking the Impact of the European Court of Human Rights on Russia." *Demokratizatsiya: The Journal of Post-Soviet Democratization* 17(2).
United Kingdom (2015). Seventh Report, Human Rights Judgments. Human Rights Joint Committee. HL Paper 130/HC 1088. 11 March 2015. Available at http://www.publications.parliament.uk/pa/jt201415/jtselect/jtrights/130/130.pdf. Accessed 16 January 2017.

Vinjamuri, Leslie (2016). "The International Criminal Court and the Paradox of Authority." *Law and Contemporary Problems* 79(1): 275–87.
Voeten, Erik (2013). "Public Opinion and the Legitimacy of International Courts." *Theoretical Inquiries in Law* 14(2): 411–36.
Voice of America (2016). "Burundi Votes to Leave ICC." Available at http://www.voanews.com/a/burundi-lower-house-votes-to-leave-icc/3547324.html. Last updated 12 October 2016. Accessed 14 March 2017.
Woods, Cindy (2013). "Bolivia Announces Plans to Leave the Inter-American Commission of Human Rights." *PulseAmérica*. Available at http://www.pulsamerica.co.uk/2013/03/human-rights-bolivia-announces-removal-from-inter-american-commission-of-human-rights/. Accessed 7 January 2017.
YouGov (2010). "YouGov / The Sun Survey Results." Available at https://d25d2506sfb94s.cloudfront.net/today_uk_import/YG-Archives-Pol-Sun-PrisonersVoting-021110.pdf. Last updated 2 November 2010. Accessed 17 March 2017.

12. Retreat or retrenchment? An analysis of the International Criminal Court's failure to prosecute presidents

Kirsten Ainley

INTRODUCTION

The establishment of the International Criminal Court (ICC) in 2002 was seen by many as game changing in its challenge to power politics and state sovereignty. Human Rights Watch (2002) called the ICC: 'potentially the most important human rights institution created in 50 years.' The Court was intended to end impunity through its rejection of the doctrine of Head of State Immunity and to have almost universal jurisdiction through the powers afforded to the United Nations Security Council (UNSC) to refer situations over which the Court did not already have treaty-based jurisdiction. Through the ICC, human rights were to be protected more aggressively and more consistently than ever before. However, the Court now stands accused of having failed in its first decade of operation to overcome the challenges of operating in an environment of great power politics. Critics of the Court argue that rather than upholding human rights for all, the Court has only prosecuted Africans, and has proved toothless in the face of some of the most appalling human rights violations in recent times – in Sri Lanka, Syria, and Yemen. Further, there is no evidence that the ICC is acting as a general deterrent to mass human rights abuses.[1] The United Nations Secretary General (Ban Ki Moon 2016, citing Melander 2015) has acknowledged that 'in 2014 the number of deaths caused by armed conflict and atrocity crimes exceeded 100,000 — its highest level since 1994 — driven in large measure by the increased targeting of civilians'. The situation at the ICC reached crisis point with the threatened withdrawal from the Rome Statute of South Africa, Burundi and the Gambia in October 2016, in opposition to the attempts by the Office of the Prosecutor (OTP) to prosecute heads of state in Sudan and Kenya.

The Court is facing a sovereignty backlash among some sections of the Global South and many of the states which it relied upon to underwrite its authority have failed to support the Court ideologically or materially in its most challenging situations.

This chapter examines the Court's attempts to prosecute sitting heads of states, and their repercussions, to establish the extent to which the ICC is failing or dysfunctional. In examining the cases, the chapter highlights aspects of ICC process which, perhaps unexpectedly, give reasons for optimism about the Court's ability to uphold human rights in the future. I argue that, while the OTP would clearly have preferred to be able to move forward in its prosecutions of Presidents Bashir and Kenyatta, its failure to do so demonstrates the ways which the Court is maturing.

THE DARFUR CASE

The situation in Darfur was the first to be referred to the ICC by the Security Council under its Chapter VII powers. The referral, in 2005, granted the ICC jurisdiction over Sudan, despite Sudan not being a State Party to the Rome Statute. The referral followed reports of genocidal attacks on the civilian population in Darfur, orchestrated by a Janjaweed militia working alongside or under the control of the Sudanese government, and allegedly resulting in hundreds of thousands of deaths prior to the referral.

The OTP investigated the situation in Sudan enthusiastically, with some seeing the Council's referral as validation of the Court. Warrants of arrest were issued in May 2007 for Sudanese humanitarian affairs minister Ahmad Harun and Janjaweed militia leader Ali Kushayb, along with summons to appear for three Darfuri rebel commanders. Two years later the Pre-Trial Chamber (PTC) authorised the Prosecutor's request to issue an arrest warrant for Sudanese President Omar al-Bashir, on charges of crimes against humanity and war crimes in Darfur, and in July 2010 the PTC issued a separate arrest warrant for Bashir on charges of genocide.

The situation in Sudan should have progressed to trial. It was referred to the ICC by the most powerful body in world politics – the UNSC – and the gravity of the crimes (if not the details of their commission) is virtually undisputed. The civil war has now killed hundreds of thousands (300,000 deaths were estimated by the UN in 2008, the last time reliable figures could be gathered) and displaced more than three million (Internal Displacement Monitoring Centre 2017), and there are credible recent reports of more war crimes (Amnesty International 2016). Yet the arrest warrants have not been executed, and Bashir has successfully repositioned himself from international pariah to controversial cause celebré of the African Union (AU). And on 12 December 2014 the Prosecutor announced that, despite the increased brutality of crimes and the deteriorating conditions in Darfur, she was suspending the entire investigation into the situation.

This decision was applauded by the AU which called for the UNSC to withdraw its referral entirely (African Union 2015, 3). Rather than running a flagship prosecution against an allegedly genocidal President, the OTP has ceased investing any resources in the case, to the great disappointment of victims' groups and human rights campaigners.

THE KENYA CASE

Accusations of fraud following the 2007–2008 elections in Kenya led to widespread and systematic violence – around 1300 deaths, widespread sexual violence and the displacement of hundreds of thousands (Waki Commission 2008) – in the worst political crisis in the country since its independence. The violence was brought to an end after an emergency mediation effort by the AU, and the AU, along with a range of other states, called for prosecutions to end the impunity long enjoyed by politicians responsible for political violence in Kenya. A Commission of Inquiry into Post-Election Violence was established, and recommended that a Kenyan Special Tribunal be created to try those senior political figures accused of organising the violence. The Commission noted that if the Kenyan government failed to establish the tribunal, the case should be passed to the ICC. The Kenyan Parliament twice voted down a bill to establish a tribunal and the evidence gathered by the Commission was subsequently passed to the ICC Prosecutor on 9 July 2009. On 5 November 2009, the Prosecutor announced he intended to seek authorisation from the Pre-Trial Chamber to proceed with the first OTP investigation launched under its *proprio motu* powers. The Chamber authorised the investigation and, in January 2012, authorised the OTP to move to trial on charges of crimes against humanity in two cases against four individuals (Francis Muthaura and Uhuru Kenyatta on the one hand and William Ruto and Joshua Sang on the other).

Given the scale of the violence in Kenya and the evidence gathered by the Commission of Inquiry, one would have expected linear progress to trials. In fact, the Kenyan cases faced crisis after crisis. Two of the accused – Kenyatta and Ruto – teamed up in the Jubilee Alliance (dubbed the 'Coalition of the Accused' by critics) and won the Presidency and Vice-Presidency respectively in the 2012 Kenyan elections. This made Kenyatta the second sitting head of state to be accused of war crimes at the ICC. The case against Francis Muthaura collapsed after evidence from a key witness turned out to be compromised. More dramatically still, on 5 December 2014 the Prosecutor issued a statement withdrawing charges against Kenyatta, stating that 'I [do] not consider the available evidence to be sufficient to prove Mr Kenyatta's alleged criminal responsibility beyond reasonable doubt as is required at trial' (Bensouda 2014a). The Prosecutor blamed this failure to procure evidence on the Kenyan government's failure to comply with the OTP's requests for financial and phone records, the death of (allegedly seven) key witnesses and the withdrawal of other witnesses due to their fear of testifying or claims to have lied in earlier statements to the OTP. Thus, the centrepiece case in the OTP's first *proprio motu* investigation turned into a farce. A year and a half later, the other major case – against Ruto and Sang – also collapsed. On 5 April 2016, the Trial Chamber, in a 2–1 majority decision, terminated the case and vacated the charges against the accused, as they ruled that the evidence against the two was weak and the prosecution's case had broken down.[2]

I examine below what these failures to prosecute tell us about the Court more broadly. First, I analyse whether the cases are examples of institutional dysfunction, looking at whether material or ideational features of the ICC itself, or the environment it operates within, might satisfactorily explain the Court's actions. Second, I compare these explanations to an alternative view: that the decisions made to suspend or withdraw cases are signs that the Court (in particular the OTP) is moving towards institutional maturity, showing an increasing ability to use its place in the international system to bolster its efficiency and legitimacy and to achieve its institutional objectives.

Barnett and Finnemore (1999) suggest a useful framework for analysing institutional dysfunction, focused on four possible determinants of institutional behaviour:

1) material features of the institution itself (for instance processes of internal bargaining or turf wars within the institution);
2) material features of the environment of the institution (for instance the preferences of powerful states);
3) ideational features of the institution itself (in particular pathologies brought about by the bureaucratic nature of the institution);
4) ideational features of the environment of the institution (for instance a quest for legitimacy leading to a failure to behave efficiently, or a clash of contradictory principles in the environment leading to contradictory institutional behaviour).

Unlike Barnett and Finnemore, who use this framework to analyse instances already determined to be examples of institutional dysfunction, I use it to ascertain if the OTP's actions are in fact examples of institutional dysfunction. By using their framework, I am assuming that the Court has power independent of the states that created it, via its legal authority. The analysis in the chapter bears out this assumption – the Court's behaviour cannot be persuasively explained simply by reference to state preferences. The material external environment of the Court is powerful, but not determinative.

THE DARFUR SITUATION AS ICC INSTITUTIONAL DYSFUNCTION

The suspension of the investigation in Darfur looks to be a severe embarrassment for the Court. It seems to have shown itself, in this and the Kenya cases, to be incapable of ensuring accountability at the highest levels of government. Bashir has revelled in what he perceives to be his victory: 'They wanted us to kneel before the International Criminal Court but the ICC raised its hands and admitted that it had failed' (Abdelaziz 2014).

This triumphalism was entirely predictable given the history of Sudanese non-cooperation with the ICC subsequent to the Harun and Kushayb arrest warrants being issued. So why did the prosecutor make the decision to suspend investigations? Is this a case of institutional dysfunction?

Material features of the environment of the Court suggest dysfunction. The Court is fairly severely constrained by state interests in the Darfur case as it cannot rely on the cooperation of Sudan. Sudan is not a State Party to the Rome Statute, and opposed the UNSC referral. Experience from previous international and hybrid criminal courts and tribunals demonstrates the dependence of these courts for their success on the material support of states in the form of security, economic inducements to cooperation and the enforcement of arrest warrants. Without the cooperation of Sudan, the ICC relies heavily on the support of other states to enable it to do its work. As Barnett and Finnemore (1999, 717) explain, international organisations (IOs):

> do not have the luxury of choosing the optimal policy but rather are frequently forced to choose between the bad and the awful because more desirable policies are denied to them by states who do not agree among themselves and/or do not wish to see the IO fulfil its mandate in some particular instance.

These dynamics are clearly visible here, and the Prosecutor made plain the need for UNSC states to support the Court in her statement announcing the hibernation of investigations:

> Not only does the situation in Darfur continue to deteriorate, the brutality with which crimes are being committed has become more pronounced . . . But this Council is yet to be spurred into action . . . In the almost ten years that my Office has been reporting to this Council, there has never been a strategic recommendation provided to my Office, neither have there been any discussions resulting in concrete solutions for the problems we face in the Darfur situation . . . What is needed is a dramatic shift in this Council's approach to arresting Darfur suspects.
>
> (Bensouda 2014b)

Yet this is not quite the straightforward example of dysfunction it may at first seem. The Prosecutor has risked enraging states rather than persuading them to assist. She has moved the OTP from passive recipient of (very) occasional UNSC assistance, to public denouncer of the lack of UNSC commitment to its own referral. The implications of this move will be discussed below.

In addition to Sudan and the UNSC member states, there is another group of states who have a vested interest in the Darfur (and Kenya) investigations, and who have taken an increasingly combative stance to the ICC: the African Union. Of 54 African States, 34 are State Parties to the Rome Statute, most of them sub-Saharan, making the African grouping the largest regional grouping of State Parties. African states were central in negotiating the Rome Statute and were particularly enthusiastic about the inclusion of the crime of aggression in the jurisdiction of the Court, given the experience of most African states with military or political domination by more powerful states. The Court was imagined as an institution that could be used by weaker states to hold stronger states to account (Bekou 2014, 88; Ainley 2011). Yet the experience of sub-Saharan African states of the ICC so far is suggesting to them that the Court is just one more institution used by states with structural power to impose that power over others. Of the 10 investigations currently being undertaken by the Court, 9 are in Africa, and 8 are sub-Saharan. Georgia, where an investigation was opened in January 2016, is the only non-African situation under investigation. Yet there are various other conflicts in which evidence suggests the commission of Rome Statute crimes: the situations in Syria, Sri Lanka and North Korea, for instance, surely merit ICC attention.

African states are concerned not just about the failure of the Court to investigate crimes outside their continent, but also about the level of power they perceive European ex-colonial states to hold over the Court via funding. The biggest contributors to the ICC are EU states, specifically Germany, the UK, Italy, France and Spain, with EU states paying more than half of the ICC's budget (ICC Assembly of States Parties 2016). There is no direct evidence to suggest that providing funding to the Court buys European states' influence over where investigations are opened, but it is not surprising that African states balk at the power the Europeans seem to have here. Finally, African states note that, outside Europe, very few powerful states are subject to the jurisdiction of the court. The US, China, Russia and India are all yet to accede to the Rome Statute system.

Nevertheless, until the ICC began seeking to prosecute sitting Presidents of African states, it had broad support from African governments. Most requests for cooperation were complied with, and states used the Court to further their interests (for instance by referring their own cases to the Court to attempt to control rebel activity on their territories). The breakdown in relations between African states and the ICC started when the ICC issued arrest warrants for Bashir.

In July 2009, the AU passed a decision forbidding its Member States from cooperating with the ICC over Bashir and later reminded its Member States of the ability of the AU to impose sanctions on members who did not comply.[3] The AU rejects the UNSC's power, via its referral of a non-State party to the ICC, to end the immunity for sitting heads of state found in customary international law. AU states have responded to this decision with uncomfortable fervour. Both ICC State Parties (including Chad, Djibouti, Kenya, Nigeria and South Africa) and Non-State Parties (including Algeria, Egypt, Ethiopia and Libya) have failed to arrest Bashir when he visited their territories (Bashir-Watch 2017). Very few states have rejected the AU's position: only Malawi (which reversed its previous toleration of Bashir) and Botswana have refused Bashir entry or threatened him with arrest. The likelihood of the material environment of AU opposition explaining the Darfur case is discussed together with Kenya below, as the two are closely linked.

THE KENYA SITUATION AS ICC INSTITUTIONAL DYSFUNCTION

The material environment is even more difficult for the ICC in the Kenya situation. As in Darfur, the Court lacks the support of the state under investigation, the states in its region and the UNSC (which is not opposed to the ICC investigation, but is unwilling to take any positive actions to support it). However, in this case, as Kenya is a State Party to the Rome Statute, its non-compliance is more of a threat to the Court.

As a State Party, Kenya is under an obligation to comply with ICC decisions and cooperate fully with the Court. While there was an initial show of compliance by Kenya, and while Kenyatta attended a status hearing at the Court in 2014 to avoid an arrest warrant being issued for him, the relationship between Kenya and the Court has significantly deteriorated since the investigation was launched. Kenyatta and Ruto used the ICC as part of their election campaign in 2012, claiming that they were standing up against foreign interference in Kenya's domestic affairs and Kenya has attempted to undermine the Court in a number of ways. It has, for instance, campaigned for a UNSC/ Article 16 deferral of the OTP's investigation (which the African Union requested but has not been granted – see below) and made (unsuccessful) efforts to amend the Rome Statute and the Rules of Procedure and Evidence at the Assembly of State Parties in 2014 to provide immunity to sitting heads of state. The Prosecutor outlined the extent of Kenya's non-cooperation after withdrawing the charges from Kenyatta, citing the Trial Chamber's 3 December 2014 finding of non-compliance against the Government of Kenya:

> the Kenyan Government's non-compliance has not only compromised the Prosecution's ability to thoroughly investigate the charges, but has ultimately impinged upon the Chamber's ability to fulfil its mandate under Article 64, and in particular, its truth-seeking function . . . Contrary to the Government of Kenya's public pronouncements that it has fully complied with its legal obligations in this case, the ruling has confirmed that in fact it has breached its treaty obligations under the Rome Statute by failing to cooperate with my investigation. [Other challenges to my office] include:
> A steady and relentless stream of false media reports about the Kenya cases;
> An unprecedented campaign on social media to expose the identity of protected witnesses in the Kenya cases;
> Concerted and wide-ranging efforts to harass, intimidate and threaten individuals who would wish to be witnesses.
>
> (Bensouda 2014c)

Kenya has also appealed to the African Union to assist in its efforts to undermine the Court, for instance describing the Court in October 2013 as 'the toy of declining imperial powers . . . a fetid insult [to Africa]' (Latiff 2013). The support of the AU for the Kenyan position – a more wholehearted support than the AU has shown for the Sudanese position – has quite radically changed the material environment of the ICC.

The AU requested in 2013 that the UNSC defer the cases against Kenyatta and Ruto to enable them to deal with the aftermath of attacks on a Nairobi mall by al-Shabab militants. The UNSC vote to defer failed as 8 UNSC members abstained, denying the motion the majority of 9 it needed to pass, subject to the veto not being used. Of these 8, 7 were non-African ICC members (the final one being the US). The 7 who voted in favour – China, Russia, Togo, Azerbaijan, Rwanda, Morocco and Pakistan – are not members of the ICC. This split was seen as having serious consequences. Kenyan Ambassador to the UN, Macharia Kamau, said after the vote African states wanted to see reform of the UNSC to avoid powerful states imposing their will on the rest of the world. Kenya's Ministry of Foreign Affairs said in a statement that the UNSC had failed to act in the interests of the security and stability of the African continent, and 'humiliated the continent and its leadership' (Nichols 2013).

The AU followed up this failure with an Extraordinary Session of its Assembly in October 2013 to discuss its relationship with the ICC. The feared mass-withdrawal from the Court did not happen, but the AU did call on the ICC to amend the Rome Statute such that no charges are brought against AU Heads of State or Government during their terms of office, citing concerns that such charges put states at risk of instability (African Union 2013, 2). They also started to work on an 'African solution' to the ICC problem through a proposed criminal chamber of the African Court of Justice and Human Rights, which will be used to prosecute individuals accused of Rome Statute crimes. In June 2014, the AU adopted an amendment to the Protocol on the Statute of the African Court of Justice and Human Rights. According to Article 46A bis of the Protocol: 'No charges shall be commenced or continued before the Court against any serving African Union Head of State or Government, or anybody acting or entitled to act in such capacity, or other senior state officials based on their functions, during their tenure of office' (African Union 2014).

The relationship between the ICC and the AU appears to have broken down over the Kenya case (with the caveat that the AU did not call for a mass withdrawal of African States Parties from the Rome Statute in 2016, as was feared). President Museveni of Uganda, the first person to refer a situation to the ICC, has called on African states to withdraw, as the Court has become a 'tool to target' the continent. Gambia, South Africa and Burundi announced in 2016 that they would indeed withdraw, though Gambia and South Africa were in the process of reversing these withdrawals by early 2017.

Can the attitudes and actions of the AU explain Court behaviour, thus demonstrating institutional dysfunction (in terms of the Court doing the bidding of states rather than pursuing justice)? The argument of this chapter is that the Court's actions in these cases are not symptoms of institutional dysfunction brought about by the material environment of the ICC. Rather than trying to appease Kenya, Bensouda has been outspoken in her criticism of its failure to comply with Court requests. And the Assembly of State Parties refused to even debate Kenya's proposed amendments to the Rome Statute. It may be that AU action has forced the ICC to cease prosecutions of sitting heads of state for now, but Bensouda has laid the blame for the Court's inability to bring these cases at the feet of the UNSC and the ICC Assembly of States Parties, rather than the AU.

Thus, while the literature on the ICC provides strong evidence to suggest that the material external environment of the Court, in the shape of powerful state interests, may influence Court behaviour (Bosco 2014), such evidence in these two cases is thin. There is significant evidence of states resisting the sovereignty costs of the ICC regime, but little reason to think this has forced the Court to behave according to state demands. Further, there is countervailing evidence that the ICC is resisting environmental pressures by provoking the most powerful states in the system in the form of the UNSC permanent members.

Some suggest that the ideational external environment of the Court could impact its behaviour in other cases, for instance the goals of peace and justice may be in tension in Colombia, leading to the ICC prevaricating on its course of action.[4] However, in the Kenya and Darfur situations, we see something quite unexpected: the legitimacy of the Court has been put on the line by the Court and, as argued below, doing so has bolstered the Court's standing, rather than providing evidence of its dysfunction. We also see, in both situations, the opposite of Barnett and Finnemore's 'irrationality of rationalization' pathology. Institutions may pursue particular processes – in an OTP one might expect those processes to be investigations and prosecutions – as ends in themselves. But the situations examined here demonstrate the opposite – the Prosecutor has shelved prosecutions or suspended investigations rather than irrationally pursuing them. So, the explanations for the situations as dysfunctional behaviour are contradictory and unconvincing. The behaviour of the Court seems to run counter to UNSC state interests (as states would rather pretend that something is being done – particularly in the Kenya and Bashir cases) and counter to external cultural or normative forces that suggest it must seek legitimacy.

INSTITUTIONAL MATURITY

What happens if we assess the situations as signs of the Court's power? Could they be indicators of a new pragmatism and a new flexibility, demonstrated by the OTP in particular, to pursue the objectives of the Court, broadly conceived (i.e. with a view to the success of the institution as a whole rather than the success of any individual case) in creative and provocative ways?[5]

The actions of the OTP have real practical benefit to the Court in the case of Darfur. First, they free up the resources of the Court for other investigations. The Court needs successful prosecutions under its belt to build legitimacy in the international system, and freeing up resources to devote to investigations likely to result in such prosecutions makes good sense. It also demonstrates a change in the power dynamic between the UNSC and the Court. The ICC is acting like an institution relatively sure of its place in the international system rather than one that must mould itself to state – or UNSC interests to enable its survival. It is therefore starting to assert itself quite significantly. It has demonstrated through the hibernating of the Darfur investigation that the UNSC cannot soak up the Court's resources by referring cases to it without increasing its funds, and Bensouda has thrown the responsibility for accountability in Darfur back to the UNSC by requiring that the Council arrest suspects. She has also kept pressure on the UNSC with repeated referrals of Sudan to the UNSC, via the ICC Pre-Trial Chamber, for non-compliance, and threatened another direct referral (Office of the Prosecutor 2014).

The Kenya situation is more difficult to read as an assertion of Court interests, however it is at least facilitating the development of innovative policies in the ICC to avoid witness tampering in future, for instance through a new rule that permits introduction of a witness's 'prior recorded testimony' if he is no longer available because of intimidation or death (Roth 2014).

Where the OTP's pragmatism (and courage) is apparent is in the new Prosecutor's handling of the AU crisis. Bensouda has showed some sensitivity to the issues raised about the Court by the African Union, without capitulating to them. She has defended the Court for opening investigations to bring justice to African victims, but has made sure to open preliminary examinations elsewhere – Iraq, Palestine and Ukraine – even in the face of obviously opposed powerful state interests. Most significantly, she signalled in October 2016 her intention to open an investigation into alleged crimes in Afghanistan (Bosco 2016). This is the first time that an international criminal tribunal has targeted US nationals, and the first time the ICC has moved against UNSC permanent 5 interests. The Prosecutor has also responded to the position into which the AU has manoeuvred the Court by transferring at least some pressure on to the UNSC, even as she undertook the distasteful task of halting the investigations of the Darfur suspects and withdrawing charges from Kenyatta. In both of these cases, the OTP looks to have pragmatically cut its losses for now, leaving nowhere for the AU to go, except perhaps to keep working on the development of an African court to apply international criminal law.

CONCLUSION

The examination of the situations of Darfur and Kenya at the ICC suggests that the Court is less constrained by the material environment created by state interests than might be expected. It also shows distinct signs that the OTP, as the body of the Court that has the most frequent and extensive contact with states, is learning to use its legal and political power in practical and creative ways.

This is not to say that state power is unimportant in international justice. The ICC was created in an international system with conflicting and combined histories of colonialism, liberal pioneering and impunity (particularly for sitting heads of state); a system dominated at the time of the ICC's establishment – and to some extent ever since – by a global war on terror. States' interests in justice and their support for, or opposition to, the Court have fluctuated over time, and the ICC – which the history of international criminal justice would suggest requires state support to be effective – has had to navigate some difficult terrain. The vulnerability of the Court to powerful states (now including the collective power of the African Union) can be identified in the cases discussed above, but so too can the OTP's increasing willingness to rhetorically sanction states and the UNSC when support is denied. States, for their part, have shown themselves through these cases to have a relatively thin commitment to the principles of international justice and to be largely unwilling to accept the political costs of pursuing it.

This said, the two situations may help to foster a growing commitment of states to international justice by exposing the vulnerability of the project itself. States have shown some propensity to defend the project by refusing to support calls for the UNSC to defer the Kenya prosecutions or withdraw the Sudan situation. Even in its attempts to undermine the ICC, the African Union has shown an interest in ending impunity for all but sitting heads of state via an African Court of Justice and Human Rights. But this support does not go far enough. There is little hope of the Court ever successfully trying cases in more powerful states if it doesn't have enough support from states to try cases in less powerful, Global South states. African States Parties could help the Court to move out of Africa by supporting it more vociferously – by lending it their weight – rather than by undermining it through threats to leave, failures to fulfil their responsibilities under the Rome Statute (e.g. by failing to arrest indictees on their soil) or quietism. States had the chance to demonstrate their commitment to the Court and its goals at the 2016 Assembly of States Parties (ASP), and there was widespread relief at the number of states (including a reasonably large number of African states) which professed their support for the Court rather than threatening to withdraw from it.[6] But the Court needs substantive and material support rather than just rhetorical statements if it is to withstand the sovereignty backlash and narrow the impunity gap.

The aim of the chapter was to examine the extent to which the ICC's failures in Sudan and Kenya were indicative of a deep-lying institutional dysfunction, signalling a contraction of human rights protections. The situations discussed illuminate the challenges faced by the ICC, but also show its increasing ability to use its political power to refuse responsibility for the failures of its States Parties or its referring body (the UNSC). In addition, and somewhat unexpectedly, the situations give reason for some optimism for the Court's success in the years ahead, if (and only if) the state supporters of the Court at least minimally fulfil their responsibilities to facilitate its work.

NOTES

1. There is some evidence emerging that the ICC might act as a deterrent in specific situations. Jo and Simmons (2016) show a reduction in civilian killing by government actors when states implement statutes consistent with Rome Statute law into their domestic criminal codes. See also Hillebrecht 2016 on the ICC and Kim and Sikkink (2010) on the deterrent effect upon states of human rights prosecutions more broadly.
2. The ruling of a mistrial rather than a positive no-case-to-answer decision leaves the door open to future prosecution if new evidence comes to light, though this is very unlikely (Kersten 2016a).
3. State Parties to the ICC are under an obligation to comply with the Bashir arrest warrants, but Non-State parties are only 'urged' to cooperate under Resolution 1593 rather than obliged to do so.
4. Hayner (2014) discusses the tension between the interests of peace and of justice in ICC decision-making. Ainley (2016) commends the ICC for its careful, if unconventional, approach to the Colombia situation.
5. See Kersten (2016b) for discussion of the institutional interests of the ICC. Institutional maturity is used instead of institutional autonomy here as the ICC was set up explicitly to act autonomously. Nevertheless, there is significant overlap with Loescher's (2001) discussion of institutions.
6. Russia announced its withdrawal during the ASP, but it had never ratified the Rome Statute, so was simply withdrawing its signature, as the US had done previously. This caused an unwarranted amount of attention as the withdrawal of a signature has virtually no practical significance.

REFERENCES

Abdelaziz, K. (2014) 'Sudan's President Omar al-Bashir claims victory over ICC after it drops Darfur war crimes investigation', *Independent*. Available at http://www.independent.co.uk/news/world/africa/sudans-president-omar-al-bashir-claims-victory-over-icc-after-it-drops-darfur-war-crimes-9924471.html.

African Union (2013) 'Extraordinary Session of The Assembly Of the African Union, 12 October 2013, Addis Ababa, Ethiopia: Decisions, Declarations and Resolutions'.

African Union (2014) 'Protocol on Amendments to the Protocol on the Statute of the African Court of Justice and Human Rights'.

African Union (2015) 'Assembly of the Union Twenty-Fourth Ordinary Session, 30–31 January 2015, Addis Ababa, Ethiopia: Decisions, Declarations and Resolutions'.

Ainley, K. (2011) 'The International Criminal Court on Trial' *Cambridge Review of International Affairs* 24 (3): 309–33.

Ainley, K (2016) 'The great escape? The role of the International Criminal Court in the Colombian peace process', *Justice in Conflict*, Available at: https://justiceinconflict.org/2016/10/13/the-great-escape-the-role-of-the-international-criminal-court-in-the-colombian-peace-process/.

Amnesty International (2016) *Scorched Earth, Poisoned Air* (London: Amnesty International Limited).

Ban Ki Moon (2016) 'Mobilizing Collective Action: The Next Decade of The Responsibility To Protect', A/70/999, 22 July 2016.

Barnett, M. N. and M. Finnemore (1999) 'The Politics, Power, and Pathologies of International Organizations', *International Organization* 53(4) 699–732.

Bashir-Watch (2017) 'Bashir Travel Map'. Available at: http://bashirwatch.org/.

Bekou, O. (2014) 'Mainstreaming Support for the ICC in the EU's Policies' (European Parliament Directorate-General for External Policies Policy Department).

Bensouda, F. (2014a) 'Statement of the Prosecutor of the International Criminal Court, Fatou Bensouda, on the withdrawal of charges against Mr. Uhuru Muigai Kenyatta'.

Bensouda F. (2014b) 'Statement to the United Nations Security Council on the Situation in Darfur, pursuant to UNSCR 1593 (2005)'.

Bensouda F. (2014c) 'Statement of the Prosecutor of the International Criminal Court, Fatou Bensouda, on the status of the Government of Kenya's coopera tion with the Prosecution's investigations in the Kenyatta case'.

Bosco, D. (2014) *Rough Justice* (Oxford: Oxford University Press).

Bosco, D. (2016) 'International Criminal Court Poised to Open Investigation into War Crimes in Afghanistan' *Foreignpolicy.com*, 31 October 2016. Available at http://foreignpolicy.com/2016/10/31/exclusive-international-criminal-court-poised-to-open-investigation-into-war-crimes-in-afghanistan/.

Hayner, P. (2014) 'Does the ICC advance the interests of justice?' *Open Democracy*. Available at: https://www.opendemocracy.net/openglobalrights/priscilla-hayner/does-icc-advance-interests-of-justice.

Hillebrecht, C. (2016) 'The Deterrent Effects of the International Criminal Court: Evidence from Libya' *International Interactions* 42(4): 616–43.

Human Rights Watch (2002) 'International Criminal Court a Reality', 11 April 2002, available at: http://www.hrw.org/news/2002/04/11/international-criminal-court-reality.

ICC Assembly of States Parties (2016) 'Report of the Committee on Budget and Finance on the Work of its Twenty-Seventh Session' ICC-ASP/15/15.

Internal Displacement Monitoring Centre (2017) 'Sudan'. Available at: http://www.internal-displacement.org/database/country/?iso3=SDN.

Jo, H., and Simmons, B. (2016). 'Can the International Criminal Court Deter Atrocity?' *International Organization* 70(3): 443–75.

Kersten, M. (2016a) 'A Missed Trial or a Mistrial? The End of the ICC Cases against Ruto and Sang'. Available at: https://justiceinconflict.org/2016/04/07/a-missed-trial-or-a-mistrial-the-end-of-the-icc-cases-against-ruto-and-sang/.

Kersten, M. (2016b) *Justice in Conflict* (Oxford: Oxford University Press).

Kim, H. and K. Sikkink (2010) 'Explaining the Deterrence Effect of Human Rights Prosecutions for Transitional Countries' *International Studies Quarterly* 54(4): 939–93.
Latiff, E. (2013) 'ICC toy of declining imperial powers – Uhuru' *CapitalNews* 12 October 2013. Available at: http://www.capitalfm.co.ke/news/2013/10/icc-toy-of-declining-imperial-powers-uhuru/.
Loescher, G. (2001) *The UNHCR and World Politics: A Perilous Path* (New York: Oxford University Press).
Melander, E. (2015) 'Organized Violence in the World 2015: An Assessment by the Uppsala Conflict Data Program', (Uppsala: Uppsala Conflict Data Program).
Nichols, M. (2013) 'Africa fails to get Kenya ICC trials deferred at United Nations' *Reuters* 15 November 2013. Available at: http://www.reuters.com/article/us-kenya-icc-un-idUSBRE9AE0S420131115.
Office of the Prosecutor (2014) 'Prosecution's request for a finding of non-compliance against the Republic of the Sudan', ICC-02/05-01/09-219.
Roth, K. (2014) 'Africa Attacks the International Criminal Court', *New York Review of Books* 6 February 2014.
Waki Commission (2008) *Report of the Commission of Inquiry into Post-Election Violence* (Nairobi, Kenya).

13. Searching for accountability of the private sector: civil liability of corporations for trafficking in human beings for the purpose of labour exploitation in the European context

Julia Planitzer, Nora Katona, Barbara Linder and Karin Lukas

INTRODUCTION

This chapter shows how companies can be held accountable for trafficking in human beings (THB) for labour exploitation in Europe.[1] Based on the Council of Europe Convention on Action against Trafficking in Human Beings[2] and the European Union's Directive on Preventing and Combating Trafficking in Human Beings,[3] State Parties have to establish liability of corporations for THB. This liability can be either criminal, civil or administrative and should lead to effective, proportionate and dissuasive sanctions.[4] The following analysis focusses on civil liability of companies since information in this area is scarce compared to corporate criminal liability linked to THB.[5] This chapter contributes to research on the application of civil liability of companies as a tool to hold them accountable for THB. A further analysis of the implementation of corporate criminal law in comparison to civil liability would be beyond the scope of this chapter. The authors discuss liability for labour exploitation within one company and when liability takes place in subcontracting or in a subsidiary. Concerning labour exploitation within one company, the specific situation of undocumented workers is discussed. Furthermore, a case study from the United Kingdom (UK) has been chosen, since this case is the first decision of the UK High Court against a corporation for THB in which exploited workers claim compensation from this corporation. The chapter also outlines whether current liability regimes are conducive for exploited workers to have access to remedy. Concerning labour exploitation in subcontracting, the analysis of the European Union (EU) legal framework is complemented by an assessment of the application of the framework at national level. For showing how the framework is implemented in practice, the Member State Austria has been chosen.

CIVIL LIABILITY OF COMPANIES FOR THB

Overview of Current Debate

The legally non-binding 'Protect, Respect and Remedy' Framework of SRSG Ruggie[6] requires that corporations should act with due diligence in order to avoid causing or contributing to adverse human rights impacts through their activities.[7] The Guiding Principles on Business and Human Rights, implementing the 'Protect, Respect and Remedy' Framework, do not specify how States have to ensure that businesses implement due diligence.[8] One approach would be to implement criminal or civil liability for failures to act with due diligence.[9] The following analysis shows to which extent States use this approach in relation to THB.

Literature on civil liability of corporations for exploitation of workers is predominantly available concerning the situation in the US. The US system under the Trafficking Victims Protection Act of 2000 (TVPA) allows for a private right of legal action.[10] This civil action can be filed by a trafficked person against the perpetrator or whoever knowingly benefits, financially or by receiving anything of value from participation in a venture which that person knew or should have known has engaged in the case of THB.[11] As shown by Bang though, the numbers of THB cases filed under this civil action are surprisingly low, with only forty cases since the implementation of this possibility in 2003.[12]

Further types of civil action in relation to THB are relevant cases filed under the US Alien Tort Claims Statute (ATS). The ATS can be used in order to subject corporations to civil liability in US courts,[13] also for actions related to the corporation that take place outside the US. However, cases under the ATS did not lead to any decisions in favour of victims of human rights abuse by corporations so far.[14] In *Flomo v. Firestone Natural Rubber* (2011), children from Liberia sued Firestone because of hazardous child labour on Firestone's rubber plantations. Firestone itself did not employ children, but it implemented very strict production quotas and therefore workers used their children as helpers.[15] The court held that a company can be held liable under the ATS for child labour. However, no violation of customary international law could be proven[16] since the provisions under the UN Child Rights Convention (CRC) were too vague in order to create an 'international legal norm'.

The still ongoing case *Doe I et al. v. Nestle USA*[17] deals with children who were allegedly forced to harvest cocoa on farms in the Ivory Coast; one plaintiff claims to have been trafficked from Mali for this purpose. In 2010 the court decided that in order to establish a liability of Nestle, it would be necessary to prove that Nestle had purposefully contracted with farmers in Mali that exploited children to produce cocoa.[18] Nestle would have needed to act with a special intent ('i.e., for the purpose) of substantially assisting the commission of that crime'.[19] The Ninth Circuit Court of Appeals[20] decided in 2014 that Nestle would have had the means to stop or limit child slavery, which it did however not do. Additionally, Nestle allegedly benefitted from the lower costs based on labour exploitation.[21] Furthermore, the Court clarified that 'prohibition against slavery applies to state actors and non-state actors alike'.[22]

As shown in the US, there are entry points for a private right of action. Nevertheless, the enforcement of the available liability regimes, in particular civil enforcement, is to a large extent lacking. Concerning the TVPA, the numbers of civil law claims have not been significantly increasing in relation to the number of trafficked persons in the US.[23] Civil liability regimes have been neglected so far, inter alia, due to higher resources for legal services and due to the direct confrontation with businesses.[24]

Piercing the Corporate Veil and Duty of Care

At European level, attempts to hold corporations in a chain accountable for THB related to labour exploitation under tort law have predominantly drawn on the concepts of 'piercing the corporate veil' and the 'duty of care'.

The first one has grown out of the area of corporate law which has traditionally built on the principle of the separation of corporate identities implying that a parent company is generally not responsible for its subsidiaries' conduct.[25] Yet, under specific circumstances the corporate veil of the subsidiary can be pierced which means that the subsidiary is considered as an 'alter ego' of the parent.[26] This enables victims of human rights abuses to hold the parent corporation accountable and to obtain redress for the harm suffered by the subsidiary.[27]

The exact conditions for piercing the corporate veil of the subsidiary differ among EU Member States.[28] Generally, the parent needs to exercise actual direct or indirect control over its activities, e.g. by coordinating or directing them; mere ownership of the shares is not enough. Further indicators include the facts that the parent's and subsidiary's assets are mixed, the subsidiary's legal assets or personality are abused in bad faith or as a means to commit unlawful activities e.g. labour exploitation and non-payment of wages.[29] In practice, however, courts have only very exceptionally accepted the piercing of the corporate veil.[30] Tests were inconsistently applied and human rights victims were often not able to fulfil the high standards of proof of the parent's control over the subsidiary.[31] The concept of piercing the corporate veil appears therefore as a fairly difficult pathway for exploited workers to gain redress from corporations higher up in the chain, such as the parent corporation.

The second pathway to obtain redress is based on the argument that the parent was negligent in its own conduct vis-à-vis the subsidiary. In practice, this so called 'duty of care' constitutes a much more frequent basis for filing claims against the parent than the concept of piercing the corporate veil.[32] The parent corporation becomes liable for the conduct of the subsidiary when it breached its duty of care that it owes for instance to workers of its subsidiaries or to local communities, and when this breach harmed these individuals.[33] It focuses thus directly on the parent's own responsibility.

In *Lubbe and Ors v. Cape PLC*, a case dealing with allegations of employees who were exposed to asbestos in a South African subsidiary of a British parent corporation, the British Court of Appeal referred explicitly to the duty of care and the requirements for establishing it. It assessed:

> whether a parent company which is proved to exercise de facto control over the operations of a (foreign) subsidiary and which knows, through its directors, that those operations involve risks to the health of workers employed by the subsidiary and/or persons in the vicinity of its factory or other business premises, owes a duty of care to those workers [. . .].[34]

The court concluded that the British parent corporation had breached its duty of care by a negligent exercise of effective control of health and safety over its subsidiary's operations in South Africa.[35]

The standards of European jurisdictions for recognizing a parent corporation's duty of care vis-à-vis a subsidiary are however fairly high. The exact requirements differ again from country to country. Yet, two elements seem to be key: first, the parent needs to have the majority of the subsidiary's shares, and second, it needs to control the activities of the subsidiary.[36] Given that these preconditions are fulfilled, the parent may become liable in two situations: first, when its instructions to the subsidiary are a direct cause of the human rights violations committed by the latter. Second, when the parent corporation fails to prevent human rights violations by the subsidiary. In this case, three indicators have to be assessed in order to decide whether the corporation was supposed to interfere in the activities of the subsidiary or not: the parent's actual control over the subsidiary, whether it 'knew or ought to have known of the risk' and the magnitude of the risk caused by the subsidiary's conduct.[37]

Until to date, there are only few cases in which courts have affirmed such a duty of care. In *Chandler v. Cape* for example the British High Court acknowledged a breach of the duty of care. It argued that the parent corporation had knowledge of the working conditions in the subsidiary.[38] Bueno and Scheidt indicate in their assessment that there still exists no case law in Austria, Switzerland and Germany.[39] However, progress concerning the application of a duty of care can be traced in Europe. In 2015, a Dutch court indicated in the still ongoing Dutch Shell Nigeria case a possible application of the duty of care.[40] Based on the serious consequences of the oil spillages of one of Shell's subsidiaries, the parent corporation may have responsibilities to prevent spillages.[41]

CIVIL LIABILITY OF CORPORATIONS FOR THB IN EUROPE

It is shown that claiming payments of unpaid wages in the civil justice system in Europe is often more burdensome for trafficked persons than claiming compensation in criminal proceedings. Compensation claims in criminal proceedings are still rare, and if so they are transferred to civil courts, leading to further obstacles for trafficked persons such as lack of legal aid for civil proceedings.[42] An analysis of the EU Fundamental Rights Agency on severe labour exploitation in the EU comes to the conclusion that access to justice for persons who were exploited is in a significant number of EU Member States 'at best [,] precarious'.[43] The following section discusses various aspects of the application of obligations of EU Member States in order to ensure workers' access to compensation for unpaid wages from their employers. First, it analyses the specific situation of undocumented workers in Europe and discusses the application of EU Member States' obligations in practice based on the EU Employers' Sanctions Directive. Second, a case study shows one successful example in which exploited workers were able to receive compensation in a civil procedure from the company that exploited them. It furthermore shows how liability regimes for wages in subcontracting are applied. In order to be able to discuss the application of liability regimes in subcontracting in more detail at national level, one Member State, Austria, has been chosen. This part elaborates on the effectiveness of Austria's legal framework on liability for wages in subcontracting.

Liability of Employers for THB

Undocumented workers claiming unpaid wages

Apart from sanctioning employers, the Employers' Sanctions Directive[44] also requires that EU Member States ensure access for undocumented workers to procedures in order to claim unpaid wages. This requires that 'illegally employed third-country nationals' are first of all able to introduce a claim against an employer for outstanding remuneration.[45] Furthermore, EU Member States have to facilitate the complaints process and establish effective mechanisms so that undocumented workers for instance get support from trade unions to file complaints.[46] As shown in an assessment of the European Commission, only four States implemented a specific right for undocumented workers to file a complaint against the employer for unpaid wages.[47] The majority of States refer to general rules on bringing a case before civil or labour courts.[48] There are however barriers with regard to access to courts including the lack of access to legal advice and the lack of information about rights. PICUM concludes that 'it remains commonplace to deport undocumented workers instead of or before examining the violation of labour rights'.[49] An assessment in a few EU Member States shows that the mechanism to file complaints to get unpaid wages is ineffective due to close cooperation with immigration authorities. This deters people from complaining.[50] Due to a lack of data collection mechanisms, it is not clear how many complaints have been lodged and in how many cases compensation was received.[51]

Case study: exploited workers in the United Kingdom claiming unpaid wages from employer in civil procedure

The Chicken Catcher case[52] is the first UK High Court decision against a corporation for THB. The plaintiffs were employed between 2008 and 2012 by DJ Houghton Catching Services Ltd, a company supplying labour to chicken farms. The claimants stated that they were trafficked from Lithuania to the UK. Since there is no recognised tort of THB and no legislation in the UK that provides for civil remedy for victims of THB, the case was based on a breach of contract, torts such as negligence, and breaches of regulations such as those relating to employment. The claim was brought for lost wages, and compensation for personal injuries and harassment. In May 2016, the High Court heard an application brought by the claimants to strike out Houghtons' defence. They raised that they often worked around the clock for days at a time without facilities to rest, wash, eat or drink. Their wages were based on the number of chickens they caught and did not take into account the number of hours they were travelling and working.[53] The company did not pay the claimants according to the legally binding minimum wage laws for agricultural workers.[54] Furthermore, illegal deductions were made for rent and a work-finding fee. On 10 June 2014, the High Court found that there was 'no real prospect of successfully defending' most of the claims, and ordered the defendants to immediately pay £100,000 in part payment of compensation. On 20 December 2016, Leigh Day, the lawyers acting for the claimants, announced they had achieved a full settlement from the Houghton Defendants resulting in a very substantial compensation package.

While the claimants were able to pursue a civil claim, there was no criminal prosecution in the UK. The police arrested the Houghton Defendants, but no subsequent prosecution took place. Consequently, the case was based on civil claims exclusively like breach of contract or compensation for personal injuries and harassment. There are however no specific legal measures for civil law cases for crimes related to trafficking in the UK.[55] As the claimants had not been introduced to civil lawyers proceedings did not start before 2014. They faced certain challenges, such as the costs of the procedure as well as the risk that they might be required to pay the costs of the defendants if the claims were not successful. In this case, the lawyers worked under a conditional fee agreement, meaning that the claimants would not have to pay the lawyers even if they would lose. In the UK, when a case is based on personal injuries, there is protection against the risk of paying the other side's costs. However, since the case raised issues that go beyond personal injuries, the lawyers sought to ensure protection from this risk by obtaining legal aid.[56]

Liability Regimes for Wages in Subcontracting in Europe

The following focuses on liability regimes for wages in subcontracting. Research shows that work arrangements such as seasonal work, bogus self-employment, posted work and work in a subcontracting chain add to the risk of being exploited. Workers in subcontracting chains often do not know against which corporation they would have a claim in case of exploitation. This is paired with major challenges in monitoring these workplaces.[57] Cases dealing with liability in subcontracting are rare because workers tend not to report out of fear of losing the job. Although the EU enacted several legal instruments that should ensure regimes of liability and access to unpaid wages for workers in subcontracting chains,[58] major shortcomings exist.

In general, joint and several liability mechanisms in subcontracting processes to claim wages are not widespread throughout the EU. Joint and several liability means that next to a subcontractor also the contractor higher up in the subcontracting chain can be held liable. Research shows that only seven EU Member States have implemented a more or less elaborated system of general joint and several liability for aspects related to wages.[59] Often employees refrain from taking actions, since they fear the loss of employment, the high costs of litigations. Getting accurate information is also challenging.[60] In relation to undocumented workers, the EU legislator introduced for the first time a mechanism of joint and several liability for unpaid wages in the Employers' Sanctions Directive. Not only the employer can be held directly liable but also the contractor of the direct subcontractor (who is an employer at the same time) is liable to pay.[61] The full chain including the principal contractor and any intermediate subcontractor can be held liable when 'they knew that the employing subcontractor employed illegally staying third-country nationals'.[62] Furthermore the contractor needs to have failed to fulfil due diligence obligations.[63] Most of the EU Member States implemented a regulation on this due diligence obligation,[64] but many left the term 'due diligence' undefined or refer to general provisions of contract or civil law.[65]

Liability for Wages in Subcontracting in Austria

The Austrian legal system allows for liability of employers or contractors in a chain and foresees a couple of specific legal obligations regarding the liability for principal contractors using sub-contracting companies. In general, there are three different legal possibilities to hold contractors in a chain liable for unpaid wages.

The first possibility is regulated in the Combating Wage and Social Dumping Act (CWSD-A)[66]. It aims at ensuring equal conditions on the Austrian labour market and adequate wages for all employees working in Austria. The CWSD-A allows posted workers, who are workers that are employed in one EU Member State (sending State) but work in a different one (receiving State), to hold the contractor higher up in the subcontracting chain in the receiving State liable for unpaid wages. However, the contractor is only liable when he knew that the employer would not pay the wages or when it was obvious that he would not pay wages.[67] This provision is however only applicable to posted workers in the construction sector. A practitioner assessed its relevance as rather small and underlined that proving a violation of the duty of care was challenging. He noted that the requirements for holding a contractor liable were too complex in order to play a more significant role in practice.[68]

The second legal path to hold contractors liable for unpaid wages of subcontractors or suppliers is the Act on Combating Social Fraud.[69] Since January 2016, this Act intends to promote free competition and the protection of rights of employees in Austria by combating bogus companies. The principal contractor is held liable for unpaid wages in case of using a bogus company as supplier or sub-contractor, if he knew or must have known that it is a bogus company.[70] Currently there are no experiences with the application of this young provision yet. Its potential to achieve payments before the competent labour courts seem to be limited. Although the Act on Combating Social Fraud might assume an employment relationship and establish a liability for unpaid wages, this does not necessarily lead to an automatic assumption of an employment relationship under labour law.[71] Hence a labour court could decide that there was no employment relationship and consequently no access to unpaid wages for the worker.

The third legal possibility can be found in the Employment of Aliens Act (EAA). The contractor of another subcontractor can be held liable for unpaid wages of undocumented workers, if the contractor knew that the subcontractor unlawfully employed undocumented workers.[72] In theory, the workers could turn to the contractor in order to receive unpaid wages when the direct employer, the subcontractor, does not pay. However, cases in which this had been applied successfully, seem not to exist in Austria.

The Austrian practice shows that there are challenges in having access to unpaid wages. Especially in the construction sector many of those that recruit workers – e.g. at filling stations or crossroads – are not authorized to represent the company and the unwritten employment contract is thus not legally established between the company and the worker.[73] Yet, according to established case law by the Austrian Supreme Court, workers cannot rely on the presumption that a person is authorized to legally represent a company if the contract was agreed outside company premises.[74] While it could be argued that the workers have put themselves in this precarious position by starting work without assuring themselves of the correctness of the documents, this does certainly not reflect the daily reality of migrant workers, who often cannot find jobs via regular channels.[75] In the case of trafficked persons, the assumption that they should have verified the correctness of the documents and the contract concluded, becomes even more theoretical.

CONCLUSIONS

Various legal regulations exist in the EU which should ensure that workers have a possibility to claim unpaid wages from employers and in very limited cases also from a contractor higher up in the subcontracting chain. However, implementation in practice faces numerous challenges. Established legal mechanisms are limited in their function, hence, creating an accountability gap. Exploiting workers without paying wages still remains to a large extent without further consequences for corporations in Europe. The Council of Europe and the EU oblige Member States to implement liability of corporations for THB by establishing legal frameworks. Practical application of these frameworks at national level seems however to lag behind.

In order to improve claims to compensation and unpaid wages in civil procedures, it should be possible to conduct and effectively claim compensation on a civil law basis independent from a prior criminal conviction – since those are still rare. Proceedings before an employment tribunal can play an essential role to ensure some immediate compensation. However, challenges arise as employment tribunals are only competent for work-related questions and the existence of an employment relationship under labour law might be difficult to prove.

Claims are currently based on specific civil law breaches like a breach of contract or personal injuries leading to pecuniary and non-pecuniary damages. There should be the possibility for a stand-alone claim for the losses and damages that are linked to the exploitation. A much simpler process is needed to ensure immediate remedies in the form of repayment and compensation. Otherwise, proceedings are far too long, giving the victims the feeling that there is no timely justice.

NOTES

1. The research for this chapter is supported by funds of the Oesterreichische Nationalbank (Oesterreichische Nationalbank, Anniversary Fund, project number 16101). The authors would like to thank Hsin-Yu (Cynthia) Wang and Stefanie Lietze for comments on earlier drafts and editorial assistance. All interviews mentioned in this chapter were conducted in confidentiality, and the names of interviewees are withheld by mutual agreement.
2. Council of Europe Convention on Action against Trafficking in Human Beings, CETS No. 197 (hereinafter 'CoE Convention against THB').
3. Dir 2011/36/EU of the European Parliament and of the Council of 5 April 2011 on preventing and combating trafficking in human beings and protecting its victims, and replacing Council Framework Decision 2002/629/JHA.
4. CoE Convention against THB, Art. 22 (3) and 23 (2) and Dir 2011/36/EU, Art. 5 and 6.
5. See for instance on corporate criminal liability the analysis of S. Rodríguez-López, 'Criminal Liability of Legal Persons for Human Trafficking Offences in International and European Law', *Journal of Trafficking and Human Exploitation 1* (Paris Legal Publishers 2017).
6. UN Human Rights Council, 'Report of the Special Representative of the Secretary-General on the Issue of Human Rights and Transnational Corporations and Other Business Enterprises, John Ruggie – Protect, Respect and Remedy: A Framework for Business and Human Rights', A/HRC/8/5, 7 April 2008, https://documents-dds-ny.un.org/doc/UNDOC/GEN/G08/128/61/PDF/G0812861.pdf?OpenElement (accessed 10 January 2017).
7. UN Human Rights Council, 'Guiding Principles on Business and Human

Rights – Implementing the United Nations "Protect, Respect and Remedy" Framework', A/HRC/17/31, Guiding Principles 11, 13 and 17, March 21, 2011, accessed 10 January 2017 https://documents-dds-ny.un.org/doc/UNDOC/GEN/G11/121/90/PDF/G1112190.pdf?OpenElement.
8. de Schutter *et al.*, 'Human Rights Due Diligence: The Role of States', 3.
9. de Schutter *et al.*, 'Human Rights Due Diligence: The Role of States', 60.
10. Naomi Jiyoung Bang, 'Justice for Victims of Human Trafficking and Forced Labor: Why Current Theories of Corporate Liability Do Not Work,' *The University of Memphis Law Review*. 43 (2013): 1048; Karin Dryhurst, 'Liability up the Supply Chain: Corporate Accountability for Labor Trafficking' *N. Y. U. Journal of International Law and Politics* 45 (2013): 660.
11. 18 U.S.C. § 1595 cited after Karin Dryhurst, 'Liability up the Supply Chain: Corporate Accountability for Labor Trafficking' 661.
12. Naomi J. Bang, 'Justice for Victims of Human Trafficking', 1050–51. See for example *David et al. v. Signal International*, LLC, *et. al.*, No. 08–1220, (Eastern Dist. Louisiana, 3 January 2013).
13. Ashley Feasly, "Eliminating Corporate Exploitation: Examining Accountability Regimes as Means to Eradicate Forced Labor from Supply Chains", *Journal of Human Trafficking* 2, no. 1 (2016): 26.
14. Justine Nolan, 'All Care, No Responsibility? – Why Corporations have Limited Responsibility and no Direct Accountability for Human Rights Violations under International Law' in *Corporate Responsibility for Human Rights Impacts,* ed. Lara Blecher, Nancy Kaymar Stafford and Gretchen C Bellamy (Section of International Law, American Bar Association 2014): 22.; Ashley Feasly, 'Eliminating Corporate Exploitation: Examining Accountability Regimes as Means to Eradicate Forced Labor from Supply Chains' 26.
15. 643 F.3d 1013 (7th Cir. 2011), accessed 9 December 2016, https://www.crin.org/en/library/legal-database/flomo-v-firestone-natural-rubber-co-llc.
16. Ashley Feasly, 'Eliminating Corporate Exploitation' 27; 'Flomo v. Firestone Natural Rubber Co LLC', last accessed 9 December 2016, https://www.crin.org/en/library/legal-database/flomo-v-firestone-natural-rubber-co-llc.
17. The court in 2014 decided to remand the case so that the plaintiffs can amend the complaint in light of the case, *Kiobel et al. v. Royal Dutch Petroleum Co. et al.*, 569 U.S. 2003. Cited after Ashley Feasly 'Eliminating Corporate Exploitation' 27. See also Chimème I Keitner, 'Remarks on Complicity Under the Alien Tort Statute' *Proceedings of the Annual meeting (American Society of International Law)* 109 (2015): 176. The latest development in this case concerns the US Supreme Court's decision to reject Nestle's petition to throw out the lawsuit against Nestle, *Nestle U.S.A., Inc., et al., v. John Doe I et al.*, No. 15–349 (petition denied on 11 January 2016).
18. *Doe v. Nestle*, S.A., 748 F. Supp. 2d 1057 (C.D.Cal.2010), cited after Naomi J. Bang 'Justice for Victims of Human Trafficking: Why Current Theories of Corporate Liability Do Not Work' 1060.
19. *Doe v Nestle*, S.A., 748 F. Supp. 2d 1057 (C.D.Cal.2010).
20. *Doe I et al. v. Nestle USA*, No. 10-56739, (9th Cir., 2014): 22, accessed 12 December 2016, http://cdn.ca9.uscourts.gov/datastore/opinions/2014/09/04/10-56739.pdf.
21. *Doe I et al. v. Nestle USA*, No. 10-56739 (9th Cir., 2014): 24.
22. *Doe I et al. v. Nestle USA*, No. 10-56739 (9th Cir., 2014): 18.
23. Karin Dryhurst, 'Liability up the Supply Chain: Corporate Accountability for Labor Trafficking' 672.
24. Ashley Feasly 'Eliminating Corporate Exploitation: Examining Accountability Regimes as Means to Eradicate Forced Labor from Supply Chains' 28; Karin Dryhurst 'Liability up the Supply Chain: Corporate Accountability for Labor Trafficking' 673.
25. Cees van Dam, 'Tort Law and Human Rights: Brothers in Arms – On the Role of Tort Law in the Area of Business and Human Rights', *Journal of European Tort Law* 2, no. 3 (2011): 247.

26. Gwynne Skinner, 'Parent Company Accountability' ICAR (2015): 15, http://icar.ngo/wp-content/uploads/2015/06/ICAR-Parent-Company-Accountability-Project-Report.pdf.
27. Daniel Augenstein, 'Study of the Legal Framework on Human Rights and the Environment Applicable to European Enterprises Operating Outside the European Union' (University of Edinburgh, 2010): 62, 63.
28. Daniel Augenstein, 'Study of the Legal Framework on Human Rights and the Environment Applicable to European Enterprises Operating Outside the European Union' 62, 63; Gwynne Skinner, 'Parent Company Accountability', ICAR, (2015): 15, http://icar.ngo/wp-content/uploads/2015/06/ICAR-Parent-Company-Accountability-Project-Report.pdf.
29. Daniel Augenstein, 'Study of the Legal Framework on Human Rights and the Environment Applicable to European Enterprises Operating Outside the European Union' 62, 63.
30. Cees van Dam, 'Tort Law and Human Rights: Brothers in Arms – On the Role of Tort Law in the Area of Business and Human Rights' 248.
31. Gwynne Skinner, 'Parent Company Accountability', ICAR, (2011): 15, http://icar.ngo/wp-content/uploads/2015/06/ICAR-Parent-Company-Accountability-Project-Report.pdf.
32. Cees van Dam, 'Tort Law and Human Right : Brothers in Arms – On the Role of Tort Law in the Area of Business and Human Rights' 248.
33. Richard Meeran, 'Tort litigation against Multinationals (MNCs) for Violation of Human Rights: an Overview of the Position outside the US' Business and Human Rights (2011): 4, accessed 9 January 2017, https://business-humanrights.org/sites/default/files/media/documents/richard-meeran-tort-litigation-against-mncs-7-mar-2011.pdf.
34. UK, H.L., Lubbe and Others and Cape Plc. and Related Appeals [2000] UKHL 41 (20 July 2000), http://www.bailii.org/uk/cases/UKHL/2000/41.html, para 6.
35. Richard Meeran, 'Tort litigation against Multinationals (MNCs) for Violation of Human Rights: an Overview of the Position outside the US' *Business and Human Rights* (2011)' 5. See also Karin Lukas, *Labour Rights and Global Production* (NWV, 2013), 119–20.
36. Cees van Dam, 'Tort Law and Human Rights: Brothers in Arms – On the Role of Tort Law in the Area of Business and Human Rights' 248, 249.
37. Cees van Dam, 'Tort Law and Human Rights: Brothers in Arms – On the Role of Tort Law in the Area of Business and Human Rights' 249, 250.
38. *Chandler v. Cape plc*. No. (2012) EWCA Civ 525, England and Wales App., accessed 6 January 2017, http://www.bailii.org/ew/cases/EWCA/Civ/2012/525.html.
39. Nicolas Bueno and Sophie Scheidt, *Die Sorgfaltspflichten von Unternehmen im Hinblick auf die Einhaltung von Menschenrechten bei Auslandsaktivitäten* (Netzwerk Soziale Verantwortung, 2015): 10, 18.
40. Cees van Dam, 'Preliminary Judgments Dutch Court of Appeal in the Shell Nigeria Case' (2016), para. 19.
41. Ibid., para. 16.
42. European Union Agency for Fundamental Rights, *Severe Labour Exploitation: Workers Moving within or into the European Union (2015)*: 82.
43. European Union Agency for Fundamental Rights, *Severe Labour Exploitation: Workers Moving within or into the European Union (2015)*: 84.
44. Directive 2009/52/EC of 18 June 2009 providing for minimum standards on sanctions and measures against employers of illegally staying third country nationals.
45. Dir 2009/52, Art. 6(2).
46. Dir 2009/52, Art. 13.
47. European Commission, 'Communication from the Commission to the European Parliament and the Council on the Application of Dir 2009/52/EC of 18 June 2009 Providing for Minimum Standards on Sanctions and Measures against Employers of Illegally Staying Third Country Nationals', COM(2014) 286 final, Brussels (2014): 7.
48. Ibid., 7.

49. Kadri Soova *et al.*, 'Employers' Sanctions: Impacts on Undocumented Migrant Workers' Rights in Four EU Countries', *PICUM Position Paper* (2015): 11 <http://picum.org/picum.org/uploads/publication/EmployerSanctions_Final.pdf>.
50. Katarzyna Słubik, 'Implementation of the Employers' Sanctions Directive in the Czech Republic, Hungary, Poland, Romania and Slovakia' (2014): 18 http://interwencjaprawna.pl/en/files/employers-sanctions-directive-overview.pdf.
51. Kadri Soova, *et al.*, 'Employers' Sanctions: Impacts on Undocumented Migrant Workers' Rights in Four EU Countries', *PICUM Position Paper* 11.
52. *Galdikas and Ors v DJ Houghton Catching Services Ltd and Ors*, High Court of Justice of the UK [2016] EWHC 1376 (QB).
53. Interview with a lawyer/UK, 16 June 2016.
54. *Galdikas and Ors v DJ Houghton Catching Services Ltd and Ors*, para. 25.
55. Ibid.
56. Interview with a lawyer/UK, 16 June 2016.
57. European Union Agency for Fundamental Rights, 'Severe Labour Exploitation': 50, 67.
58. See for example Directive 96/71/EC of the European Parliament and of the Council of 16 December 1996 concerning the posting of workers in the framework of the provision of services.
59. Yves Jorens *et al.*, 'Study on the Protection of Workers' Rights in Subcontracting Processes in the European Union': (2012): 144, 153, http://business-humanrights.org/en/pdf-study-on-the-protection-of-workers-rights-in-subcontracting-processes-in-the-european-union.
60. Yves Jorens *et al.*, 'Study on the Protection of Workers' Rights in Subcontracting Processes in the European Union': 156–7.
61. Ibid., 14; Dir 2009/52, Art. 8 (1) lit. b.
62. Dir 2009/52, Art. 8 (2).
63. Dir 2009/52, Art. 8 (3).
64. European Commission – Communication 22.5.2014: 6, 7.
65. Yves Jorens *et al.*, 'Study on the Protection of Workers' Rights in Subcontracting Processes in the European Union': 147–8; European Commission – Communication 22.5.2014: 6.
66. Federal Law Gazette I No. 44/2016. The CWSD-A enters into force on 1 January 2017.
67. CWSD-A, s. 9 (1).
68. Interview with Trade Union/Austria, 24 June 2016.
69. Act on Combating Social Fraud, Federal Law Gazette I No. 44/2016 as amended by Federal Law Gazette I No. 44/2016.
70. Act on Combating Social Fraud: 9.
71. Interview with Trade Union/Austria, 24 June 2016.
72. EAA s. 29a. See Christoph Wiesinger, *ASoK-Spezial Sozialbetrugsbekämpfungsgesetz (SBBG)*: 75.
73. Interview with a lawyer/Austria, 9 June 2016.
74. See for instance decisions of the Austrian Supreme Court (OGH) 1Ob188/98y and 1Ob547/86. In practice, this is particularly relevant in cases were a (bogus) company goes bankrupt and denies that an employment relationship existed.
75. Interview with a lawyer/Austria, 9 June 2016.

REFERENCES

Augenstein, Daniel, 'Study of the Legal Framework on Human Rights and the Environment Applicable to European Enterprises Operating Outside the European Union', (University of Edinburgh, 2010), http://en.frankbold.org/sites/default/files/tema/101025_ec_study_final_report_en_0.pdf.

Bang, Naomi Jiyoung, 'Justice for Victims of Human Trafficking and Forced Labor: Why Current Theories of Corporate Liability Do Not Work' *The University of Memphis Law Review* 43 (2013): 1047–96.

Bueno, Nicolas and Sophie Scheidt, 'Die Sorgfaltspflichten von Unternehmen im Hinblick auf die Einhaltung von Menschenrechten bei Auslandsaktivitäten', Netzwerk Soziale Verantwortung, 2015.

Communication from the Commission to the European Parliament and the Council on the Application of Directive 2009/52/EC of 18 June 2009 providing for minimum standards on sanctions and measures against employers of illegally staying third country nationals, Brussels, 22.5.2014 COM(2014) 286 final.

de Schutter Olivier, Anita Ramasastry, Mark B. Taylor, and Robert C. Thompson, 'Human Rights Due Diligence: The Role of States', December 2012, https://static1.squarespace.com/static/583f3fca725e25fcd45aa446/t/58671817d2b857fd0d14182 0/1483151386977/Human-Rights-Due-Diligence-The-Role-of-States.pdf.

Dryhurst, Karin, 'Liability up the Supply Chain: Corporate Accountability for Labour Trafficking' *N. Y. U. Journal of International Law and Politics* 45 (2013): 641–75.

European Union Agency for Fundamental Rights, 'Severe Labour Exploitation: Workers Moving within or into the European Union' (2015), http://fra.europa.eu/en/publication/2015/severe-labour-exploitation-workers-moving-within-or-european-union.

Feasly, Ashley, 'Eliminating Corporate Exploitation: Examining Accountability Regimes as Means to Eradicate Forced Labor from Supply Chains' *Journal of Human Trafficking* 2, no. 1 (2016): 15–31.

Jorens, Yves, Saskia Peters, and Mijke Houwerzijl, 'Study on the Protection of Workers' Rights in Subcontracting Processes in the European Union' (2012) http://business-humanrights.org/en/pdf-study-on-the-protection-of-workers-rights-in-su bcontracting-processes-in-the-european-union.

Keitner, Chimème I, 'Remarks on Complicity under the Alien Tort Statute' *Proceedings of the Annual meeting (American Society of International Law)* 109 (2015): 175–7.

Lukas, Karin, 'Labour Rights and Global Production' (Vienna/Graz: NWV, 2013).

Meeran, Richard, 'Tort litigation against Multinationals (MNCs) for Violation of Human Rights: an Overview of the Position outside the US', Business and Human Rights (2011), accessed 9 January 2017, https://business-humanrights.org/sites/default/files/media/documents/richard-meeran-tort-litigation-against-mncs-7-mar-2011.pdf.

Nolan, Justine, 'All Care, No Responsibility? – Why Corporations Have Limited Responsibility and No Direct Accountability for Human Rights Violations under International Law' in *Corporate Responsibility for Human Rights Impacts*, edited by Lara Blecher, Nancy Kaymar Stafford, and Gretchen C. Bellamy, 3–25. Section of International Law, American Bar Association, 2014.

Rodríguez-López, Silvia, 'Criminal Liability of Legal Persons for Human Trafficking Offences in International and European Law', *Journal of Trafficking and Human Exploitation 1* (Paris Legal Publishers 2017): 95–114.

Skinner, Gwynne, 'Parent Company Accountability, Ensuring Justice for Human Rights Violations', ICAR, September 2015, http://icar.ngo/wp-content/uploads/2015/06/ICAR-Parent-Company-Accountability-Project-Report.pdf.

Słubik, Katarzyna, 'Implementation of the Employers' Sanctions Directive in the Czech Republic, Hungary, Poland, Romania and Slovakia', (paper as a part of

the project For Undocumented Migrants` Rights in Central Europe, supported by the EPIM, 2014) http://interwencjaprawna.pl/en/files/employers-sanctions-directive-overview.pdf.
Soova Kadri, Lilana Keith, and Michele LeVoy, 'Employers' Sanctions: Impacts on undocumented migrant workers' rights in four EU Countries', *Picum Position Paper*, April 2015.
UN Human Rights Council, 'Report of the Special Representative of the Secretary-General on the Issue of Human Rights and Transnational Corporations and Other Business Enterprises, John Ruggie – Protect, Respect and Remedy: A Framework for Business and Human Rights', A/HRC/8/5, 7 April 2008, https://documents-dds-ny.un.org/doc/UNDOC/GEN/G08/128/61/PDF/G0812861.pdf?OpenElement.
UN Human Rights Council, 'Guiding Principles on Business and Human Rights – Implementing the United Nations "Protect, Respect and Remedy" Framework', A/HRC/17/31, Guiding Principles 11, 13 and 17, 21 March 2011, https://documents-dds-ny.un.org/doc/UNDOC/GEN/G11/121/90/PDF/G1112190.pdf?OpenElement.
van Dam, Cees, 'Tort Law and Human Rights: Brothers in Arms – On the Role of Tort Law in the Area of Business and Human Rights', *Journal of European Tort Law*. 2: 3 (2011), 221–54.
van Dam, Cees, 'Preliminary Judgments Dutch Court of Appeal in the Shell Nigeria Case' (2016), http://www.ceesvandam.info/default.asp?fileid=643.
Wiesinger, Christoph, ASoK-Spezial Sozialbetrugsbekämpfungsgesetz (SBBG), Linde Verlag, 2015.

PART IV

Opportunities

14. Business and human rights: exploring the limits of an expanding agenda on corporate responsibility

Anne Vestergaard and Michael Etter

INTRODUCTION

In response to globalization's challenges to the nation state, the private sector is increasingly construed as a key agent for transnational societal change. While the world economy may be global, law and politics are still largely national, only slowly emerging from the bounds of the international states system (Kobrin 2009). The lack of a comprehensive political and legal framework in the global arena, has confronted multinational corporations with a need to redefine their role and deal with increasing expectations regarding their involvement in the development and enforcement of global rules and standards (Whelan 2012; Scherer and Palazzo 2011; Kobrin 2009; Matten and Crane 2005). Recent years have seen if not a surge, at least a distinct movement towards leveraging human rights norms for such global standards of corporate responsibility.

Despite obvious common concerns, there has until recently been little overlap between public agendas on human rights and Corporate Social Responsibility (CSR) (e.g., Stohl and Stohl 2017; Wettstein 2012; Campbell 2006; Cragg 2000; Whelan, Moon and Orlitzky 2009). From a human rights perspective, corporations have been seen as potential perpetrators rather than potential instruments for the protection of human rights (Wettstein 2012). From a CSR perspective, human rights, binding by international law, have been viewed as falling out of the sphere of voluntariness, which was for many years definitional to the notion of CSR (Stohl and Stohl 2017; Wettstein 2012). The last decade has, however, shown the beginning of a shift by which these agendas are increasingly coming into alignment.

Bringing the notion of human rights into conceptions of Corporate Social Responsibility, entails a shift from a conception of CSR as voluntary and philanthropic towards a conception of CSR as rights and justice-based, and thus entails a considerably larger demand and obligation on corporations. While such a more rights-oriented conception of responsibility is increasingly infusing CSR discourse in academia as well as among practitioners, it remains a topic of great controversy, whether the human rights obligations of business should be limited to the passive duty to respect human rights – do no harm – or include active responsibilities and positive obligations, to take proactive steps towards protecting human rights also outside the business' most immediate sphere of influence (Wettstein 2012).

Motivated by these controversies, this study sets out to examine the evolution of business and human rights discourse in news and CSR reports since the launch of UN Global Compact in 2000. This is done with a view to explore to what extent the expanded understanding of corporations' responsibility for human rights is shared by crucial actors – the corporations themselves on the one hand and on the other hand the news media, as watchdogs and primary sources of public information on corporate conduct.

THE BUSINESS AND HUMAN RIGHTS DEBATE

The question with which this chapter is concerned pertains specifically to the features of corporations' human rights responsibilities, that is, the legal status, nature, and scope of corporations' responsibility for human rights. While these features always occur in combinations and debates primarily revolve around a limited subset of these combinations, we review the dimensions in isolation.

The Legal Status of Business' Responsibility for Human Rights: Voluntary or Mandatory?

At the very basis of debates around business and human rights is the question of whether or not businesses can feasibly and meaningfully be held accountable for human rights. Opposition to business' human rights responsibilities tends to be based on the argument that states are the only subjects of international law, the only entities, which possess international legal personality and the capacity to have international duties and rights. Consequently, it is the responsibility of the nation state to oversee how organizations and individuals within their boundaries impact human rights (Weissbrodt and Kruger 2003; Brenkert 2016).

Thus, according to this perspective, although transnational corporations (TNCs) like any other social entity are required to respect basic human rights, they are accountable for this to national, not international laws. From such a point of view, business can never be legally accountable for human rights, although they may take on such responsibility voluntarily, e.g. in the interest of their reputation or legitimacy. The counter-position tends to be based on the argument that TNCs are becoming comparable to states in terms of power and, thus, can and should be held legally accountable by international law similarly to states (Wettstein 2010; Kobrin 2009; Scherer and Palazzo 2011).

For Which Type of Human Rights are Businesses Responsible: Economic/ Social or Political/Civil?

The more restrictive views on business and human rights (BHR) hold that businesses are responsible only for a limited list of human rights. Such subsets of rights tend to be based on distinctions between right types – political and civil rights on the one hand, and social-economic (and cultural) on rights, on the other. Political-civil rights are usually achieved through the absence of an action (do not torture, for example), whereas economic-social rights are broader and dependent on resources to be actualized (Whelan 2014). Restrictive views on BHR tend to derive subsets of rights for which business is accountable from basic political and civil rights (Donaldson 1989; Arnold 2010, Sen 2004). Proponents of a more expansive BHR position contend that businesses are potentially responsible for all human rights, depending on their relationship to the persons involved and/or how the actions the business takes may impinge upon their human rights (Brenkert 2016).

The Nature of Business' Responsibility for Human Rights: Negative or Positive Obligations?

The third dimension that distinguishes more restrictive positions in the BHR debate from the more expansive ones, concerns whether or not businesses are required to do more than simply respect human rights. 'Respect' is a negative obligation in that it simply requires business to 'do no harm'. Positive obligations, on the other hand, require businesses to take active measures to protect human rights. The distinction is most clearly exemplified with the response to human rights violations in the supply chain of a transnational corporation (for the distinction between direct and indirect, see p.214). A transnational corporation, which sees its responsibility as limited to respecting human rights, will (all else being equal) honor this responsibility by terminating collaborations with the perpetrating party. A transnational corporation, which sees its responsibility as extending to protecting human rights, will use whatever means it has at its disposal to induce the perpetrator to change its practices to comply with human rights norms (Wettstein 2010).

The Scope of Business' Responsibility for Human Rights: Direct or Indirect?

The fourth and final dimension that distinguishes more restrictive positions in the BHR debate from the more expansive ones, concerns whether businesses are responsible only for those direct impacts produced by their business activities, or whether their responsibilities extend to indirect human rights effects. Responsibility for direct impact includes responsibility for one's own actions. Responsibility for indirect impact extends responsibility to third parties' actions, such as those of suppliers (MacDonald 2011, Brenkert 2016). The latter conceptualization of responsibility has been criticized for being too broad and ambiguous, partly because it does not differentiate between impact and leverage (Ruggie 2008).

The framework developed in this chapter, makes this distinction through the intersecting dimension of negative (impact) versus positive (leverage) obligation. It is when such responsibilities are neglected that the issue of complicity arises, in the former case often termed "direct complicity", in the latter "indirect complicity" (Arnold 2016; Wettstein 2012). Complicity refers to instances where the corporation's activities do not directly contribute to the violation of human rights, but rather support the ability of the perpetrator to carry out systematic human rights violations (Wettstein 2010).

Businesses actively using (or indeed failing to use) their power of influence on human rights violations of third parties, or the issue of 'leverage', is arguably where the question of responsibility is the most controversial and where the potential for politicization is the greatest. The issue of leverage is closely tied to the notion of silent complicity, which reflects the expectation that companies raise systematic or continuous human rights abuses with the appropriate authorities, wherever they may have leverage (Wettstein 2010; MacDonald 2011; Hoffman and McNulty 2009). From an expansionist point of view this politicization is exactly what legitimates and indeed necessitates the introduction of human rights into CSR. Resistance, however, is based on that same argument as well as on the observation that the idea of 'leverage' leaves responsibility boundless and thus renders true accountability impossible.

UN INITIATIVES FOR BUSINESSES AND HUMAN RIGHTS

Since the 1990s, the UN has produced several initiatives to develop a human rights framework in relation to business and guide TNCs with respect to human rights norms. Two millennial milestones in this development are the UN Global Compact (UNGC) and the UN guiding principles (Bilchitz and Deva 2013; Rasche 2009).

The UNGC is a sustainability network and platform, the purpose of which is to encourage business worldwide to adopt environmentally and socially sustainable policies. UNGC relies explicitly on human rights and has as its pronounced goal "to transform the world through business" (UN Global Compact, ND). With this transformative aspiration, the UNGC clearly alludes to positive obligations beyond simply "do no harm", as well as explicitly mentioning indirect responsibility (complicity). It is, however, a governance mechanism, which operates exclusively on the basis of voluntariness employing neither monitoring nor sanctioning.

The "Guiding Principles on Business and Human Rights" provide a framework of "global standard for preventing and addressing the risk of adverse impacts on human rights linked to business activity" (UN Human Rights Office, n.d.). It is based on the "Protect, Respect and Remedy" framework that comprises three core principles: (1) the State duty to protect against human rights abuses by third parties, including business, through appropriate policies, regulation, and adjudication; (2) the corporate responsibility to respect human rights, which means to act with due diligence to avoid infringing on the rights of others; and (3) the need for greater access by victims to effective remedies, judicial and non-judicial (Ruggie 2008). The guiding principles (GP) were grounded on the recognition that business is, "required to comply with all applicable laws and to respect human rights" ("Guiding Principles," 2011, p. 1), but stressed that no additional obligations were being imposed or ratified but rather the guidelines were based on existing laws. In other words, Ruggie's tripartite framework defines human rights obligations of business exclusively in negative terms as duties to respect human rights, while assigning all duties in the positive realm to the state alone.

CSR REPORTING AND HUMAN RIGHTS

With the beginning of the new millennium the public pressure on business organizations to take responsibility for social and environmental issues has substantially increased. Corporations started to publish CSR reports that provide non-financial information relating to the environment (Hackston and Milne 1996; Eccles and Krzus 2010). In 2005, 52 percent of the Global Fortune 250 companies published an annual CSR report, compared to 12 percent ten years earlier (KPMG 2005). Over the years, CSR reports have become a major instrument for corporations in their efforts to build good relationships with their stakeholders (Idowy and Papasolomou 2007), gain trust (Podnar and Golob 2007), increase reputation (Bhattacharya *et al.* 2009), and maintain legitimacy (Hooghiemstra 2000).

However, the rise in CSR reporting was accompanied by increased skepticism and scrutiny among stakeholders (Waddock and Googins 2011). Critical scholars have argued that CSR reports are mainly public relations efforts that remain merely on a ceremonial level with little practical consequences (Bromley and Powell 2012). To counter this criticism and with the aim to institutionalize CSR, a number of initiatives, such as the UNGC policy on communicating progress (COP) and the Global Reporting Initiative (GRI), have undertaken work to develop global standards for CSR reporting. These initiatives prescribe a range of CSR topics, which companies should address in their reports.

The institutionalization through global standards has led to a certain degree of harmonization among CSR reports, while such factors as country of origin still seem to have an effect on the weighting of certain issues over others (e.g., Einwiller *et al.*, 2016). Nevertheless, studies provide evidence for harmonization in reporting for those companies that adhere to global CSR standards, such as the UNGC (Fortanier *et al.*, 2011). The issue of human rights finds consideration by most global CSR initiatives and in particular by the UNGC and GRI guidelines. While the UNGC addresses the issue of BHR more generally, the GRI guidelines are more specific as to how organizations may impact human rights, focusing on negative obligations ("respect") but including both direct and indirect impacts. Despite extensive research on CSR reporting, little is known about how the issue of BHR has been approached in CSR reports.

CSR IN THE NEWS MEDIA

There is little research into the coverage of BHR in news media. However, studies show that news media have always had a certain interest in the topic of CSR more generally. The term "corporate social responsibility" declined in major news media after its initial spike in the early 1970s, but remained at a high level in the second half of the twenty-first century (Hamilton 2003). More generally, in the U.S. business news coverage there has been a significant increase in the reporting about ethical issues (Hannah and Zatzick 2008).

CSR, however, competes for media attention with many other issues (McCombs and Zhu 1995). The motivation to cover ethical issues and CSR is related to the role of journalist, but also to the fact that news media have to stay attractive for audiences. Indeed, journalists are typically driven by their role as public watchdogs (Hanitzsch 2011), which encourages investigation about ethical issues related to CSR, such as corporate wrongdoing. Corporate scandals are of high news value and attract readers, and therefore are often covered (Etter and Vestergaard 2016). When reporting on CSR and ethical issues related to businesses, news media have proven to frame the responsibilities of businesses towards society as broad obligations that exceed legal and economic expectations (Zhang and Swanson 2006; Guthey and Morsing 2014).

ANALYTICAL FRAMEWORK AND CODING FRAME

In the review of the BHR debate above, we showed that the debate is oriented around three dimensions of controversy concerning the extent and nature of businesses' responsibility for human rights, namely the scope of impact, the type of responsibility and the type of right for which business is thought to have human rights responsibilities. In order to assess how the BHR discourse of corporations and news relate to the BHR debate, an analytical matrix based on these dimensions was developed, as shown in Table 14.1. An additional dimension was added to reflect whether the corporation is presented as playing a negative or positive role in relation to human rights:

1. Scope of Impact: Direct vs. indirect human rights impact of corporate activities
2. Type of responsibility: Negative (passive responsibility) vs. positive obligation (active)
3. Type of right: Political-civil rights vs. social-economic rights (as this distinction cuts across all categories, it is not included in the matrix in Table 14.1)
4. Framing of role: Positive vs. negative framing of the corporation's role in the human rights issue described (in the matrix leading to four categories: respect/protect –violate/neglect)

Table 14.1 Conceptual and analytical framework for BHR to be used as coding frame

	Direct impact	Indirect impact
Negative obligation: The duty to avoid depriving people of rights		
Respect	Corporation is not in its direct actions in violation of human rights	Corporation does not have dealings with governments, suppliers or contractors who violate human rights
Violate	Corporation is directly contributing to a human rights violation	Corporation aids and abets human rights abuse committed by third parties *(direct complicity)*
Positive obligation: The duty to take action to protect and further human rights		
Protect	Corporation is taking active steps to protect human rights	Corporation is putting pressure or otherwise uses its leverage for third parties to not violate
Neglect	Corporation is failing to take direct action to protect human rights	Corporation is failing to use its leverage as above within its sphere of influence (indirect complicity)

METHOD

To analyse and compare how human rights are portrayed by businesses and news media over time, we conducted content analyses of the CSR reports of ten transnational corporations as well as major news media coverage of human rights issues in relation to these companies. In order to select the companies with the greatest potential for influence, the ten TNCs were chosen based on consistent top performance on the Financial Times Global 500 list (Table 14.2).

The years 2005 and 2015 were used as chronological focus points from which data were collected. The year 2005 was chosen as this was the first year when all ten case corporations had established a CSR report.

To collect relevant news articles, individual searches for each company in the database Factiva during the allotted time periods were conducted, including all major regional and national English language publications.[1] Search words were "name of company" AND "human rights." For companies with less than 30 news articles, all were analysed. When the number of articles exceeded 30, every second article was analysed. The unit of analysis for news sources was the news article. We chose to include all forms of news media coverage to cover the overall representation of BHR in the

Table 14.2 Top Transnational Corporations from 2000–2016 (according to the Financial Times Global 500)

Name:	Industry:	Headquarters:	U.N. Global Compact member since:	No. of news articles:	No. of coded articles:
Microsoft	Software & Computers	U.S.A.	Nov 2006	85	43
British Petroleum	Oil & Gas	U.K.	Jul 2000	157	72
Coca-Cola	Beverages	U.S.A.	Mar 2007	74	37
Toyota	Automobiles & Parts	Japan	Mar 2013	16	16
IBM	Software & Computers	U.S.A.	Not member	13	13
Walmart	General Retailer	U.S.A.	Not member	87	44
General Electric	General Industries	U.S.A.	Dec 2008	9	9
Royal Dutch Shell	Oil & Gas	Netherlands	Jul 2000	108	54
Nestle	Food & Drink	Switzerland	Feb2001	27	27
HSBC	Financial Services	U.S.A.	Nov 2000	25	25

news, such that the sample includes not just general news articles but also commentaries and editorials. The total number of news articles manually coded was 340.

CSR reports from each of the ten companies were collected from company websites. Since the average report ranged between 100–200 pages, each report was coded per section if it contained content related to human rights. The total number of sections manually coded was 239.

The data were analysed using qualitative content analysis (Schreier 2014; Kripendorff 2013) comprised of a deductive two-step analysis including, first, an interpretative step by which texts were assigned to theoretically derived categories, and a second, quantitative step, by which category occurrences and co-occurrences were calculated. In the interpretative step, the BHR framework developed above was applied as the coding frame. CSR reports and news articles were coded manually in Nvivo using the coding frame described above. Each article and relevant section of CSR reports was annotated with a category from each of the four analytical dimensions listed above. In the second stage of analysis, data were examined for patterns and co-occurrences. Occurrence and co-occurrence frequencies corresponding to the matrix of the coding frame were calculated in order to enable comparisons between the first (year 2005) and second (2015) focus points. As it is not the aim of this chapter to test hypotheses and as this type of qualitative approach has inherent subjective properties, we have not conducted statistical analyses of significance.

RESULTS

Human Rights Framing in CSR Reports

In CSR reports, use of the phrase "human rights" tripled in the ten-year period. At the same time, as is clear from Figure 14.1, distinct shifts in context take place in the CSR reports between 2005 and 2015. Figure 14.1 shows the frequency of each analytical category, as a percentage of the total frequency of the dimension to which it belongs. Mentions of responsibility for indirect impact increase from only 13 percent in 2005 to 49 percent in 2015. Reference to positive duties increase from 22 percent to 31 percent and references to civil-political rights rise from 14 percent to 25 percent.[2]

Figures 14.2–14.4 show select frequencies of co-occurrences of certain categories for CSR reports. The figures show co-occurrences of categories as percentages of total number of texts (as opposed to percentages of dimensions in Figure 14.1 and 14.5) in order to show which combinations dominate in the data sets. Note however, that all categories overlap.

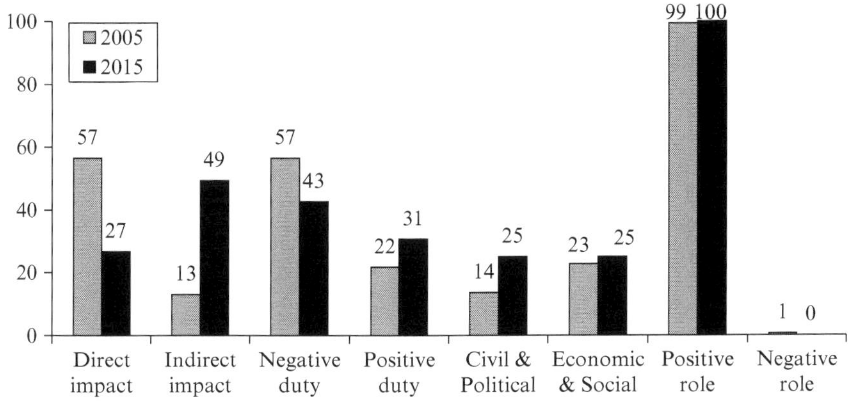

Figure 14.1 CSR reports; category frequencies in % relative to dimension

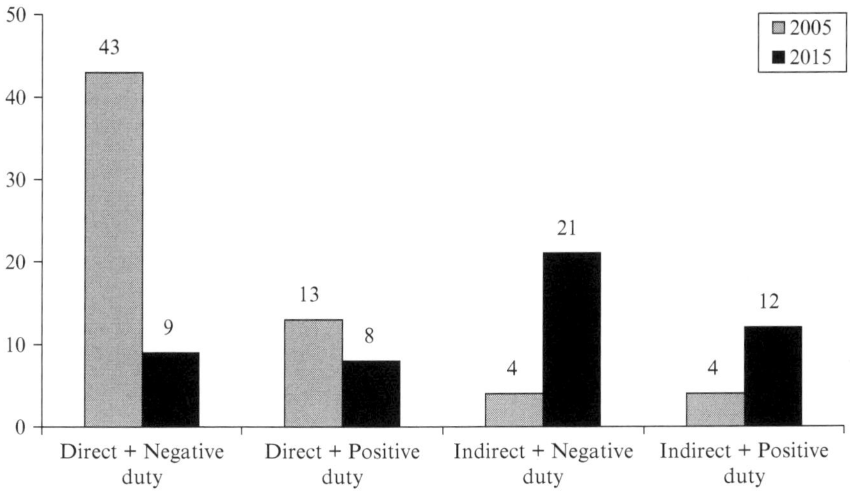

Figure 14.2 CSR reports; co-occurrence frequencies of impact scope and responsibility type (percentages of total)

In general, references to human rights in CSR reports tend to be quite generic, that is, in many cases they leave scope, responsibility type and right type unspecified. This is particularly pronounced in 2005. In spite of this, a clear picture emerges that CSR reports in 2005 were dominated by commitments to negative duty concerning the direct human rights impact of the corporations' activities, or in other words, with commitments to

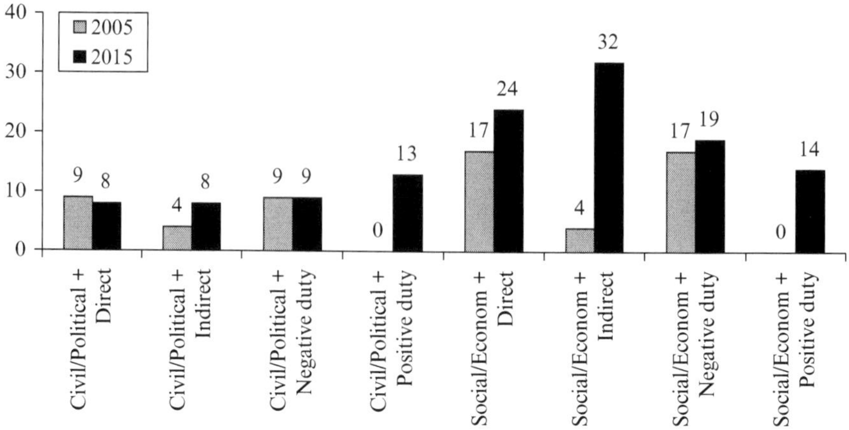

Figure 14.3 CSR reports; co-occurrence frequencies of rights type with other categories (percentages of total)

respect human rights within their immediate sphere of influence. By 2015, a substantially different pattern has emerged. Not only are corporations to a significantly greater extent making commitments to indirect impact, this also extends beyond negative duty. In 2015, as much as 12 percent of human rights commitments made by corporations involved taking active steps to protect human rights outside of their immediate sphere of influence.

When it comes to the types of human rights addressed, a similarly clear development emerges. The level of commitment to basic civil/political rights is unchanged between 2005 and 2015 when it comes to the more restrictive responsibility for direct impact and negative duty (see Figure 14.3). This testifies, simply, to corporations' commitment to not directly violate basic human rights. However, in 2015 commitments to civil/political rights have come to include more expansive indirect and positive responsibilities, meaning that CSR reports indicate a willingness to accept responsibility for protecting basic human rights outside of corporations' own immediate sphere of influence.

Social/economic rights do, however, dominate in 2005 and even more so in 2015. As shown in Figure 14.4, this owes to a great extent to an increased focus on labor rights. In 2015, 32 percent of references to human rights in CSR reports concern indirect responsibility for labor rights and 8 percent to positive duties concerning labor rights, i.e., corporations making commitments to respect and protect labor rights in their supply chains. In 2005, such commitments were not made in a single instance.

In sum, from 2005 and 2015 there is a clearly detectable change not

Figure 14.4 CSR reports; co-occurrence frequencies of labor rights with other categories (percentages of total)

only as regards the extent to which human rights language is used in the CSR reports of these influential TNCs, but also in how encompassing and specific the commitments made are. In 2015, human rights commitments are to a significantly larger extent both indirect and positive, involving commitments to take responsibility for indirect impact on labor rights and positive, proactive responsibility for political and civil rights.

Human Rights Framing in the News

In the news, contrary to CSR reports, the frequency of references to human rights did in fact not go up between 2005 and 2015, but marked changes in the way news uses human rights to frame corporate responsibility are none the less apparent. Mentions of positive duties increase from 17 percent to 40 percent and a similarly vast increase in stories which frame business as playing a positive role for human rights can be found (see Figure 14.5). Contrary to CSR reports, however, the concern with the indirect human rights impacts of business was already high in 2005 and does not further increase towards 2015. In addition, the concern with political-civil rights in the news in fact decreases between 2005 and 2015.

Figure 14.6, which shows category frequencies of co-occurrence, displays a pattern similar to the CSR reports, with an increase in positive duties for both direct and indirect impact. In 2015, as much as 28% of all news references to human rights pertained to the most expansive notion of BHR, positive responsibility for indirect impact.

News media overall pay considerably more attention to civil and political rights than CSR reports. It is noteworthy, however, that concern with civil/political rights in news has decreased quite markedly between 2005 and 2015.

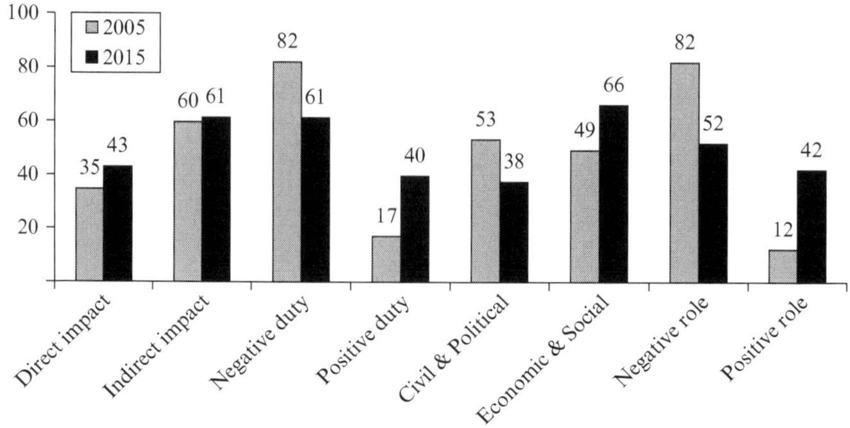

Figure 14.5 *News articles; category frequencies in % relative to dimensions*

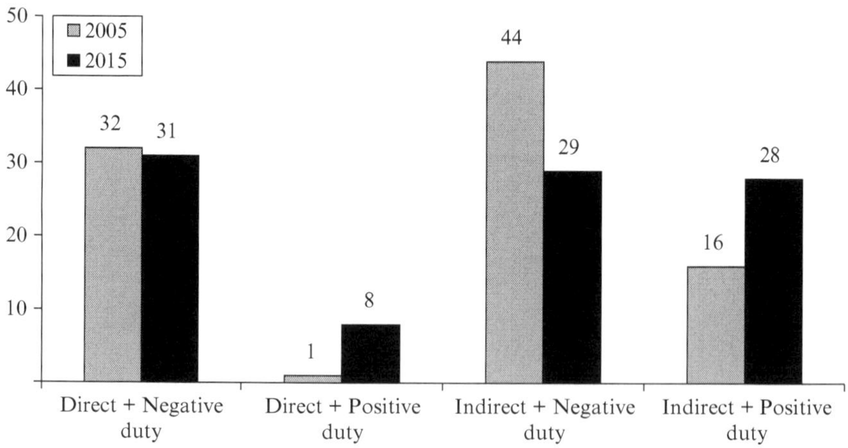

Figure 14.6 *News; co-occurrence frequencies of impact scope and responsibility type (percentages of total)*

Only when it comes to the positive responsibility to actively protect civil/political rights do we see a small increase (Figure 14.7). Conversely, news media have increased their attention to social and economic rights in the ten-year period. In particular positive obligation concerning social and economic rights has seen a surge, with its references having almost quadrupled in the period. The vast increase in positive duties for social/economic rights owes, as Figure 14.8 shows, almost exclusively to a concern with labor rights.

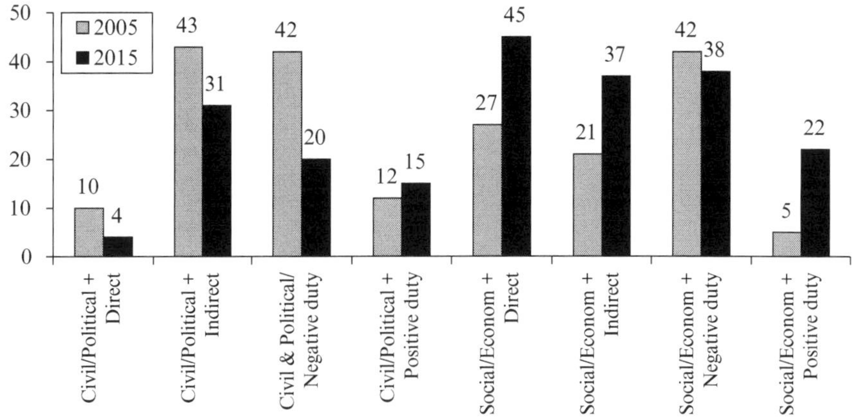

Figure 14.7 *News; co-occurrence frequencies of rights type with other categories (percentages of total)*

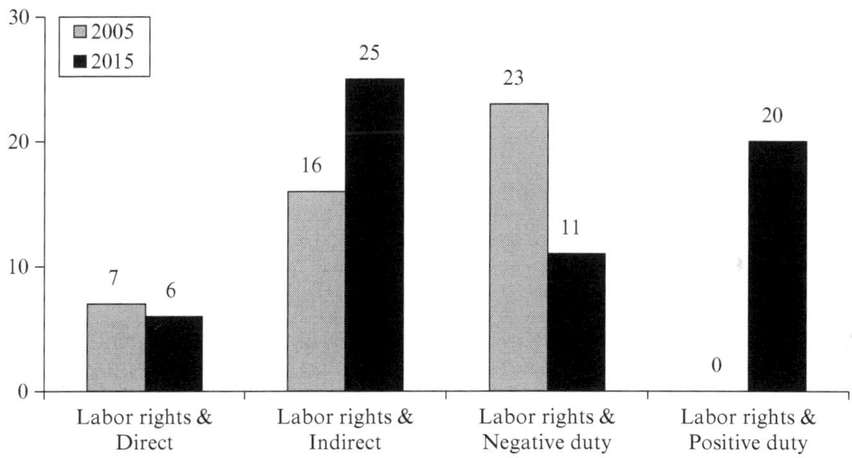

Figure 14.8 *News; co-occurrence frequencies of labor rights with other categories (percentages of total)*

Finally, a remarkable change can be observed in terms of how news portrayed the role played by business in relation to human rights (see Figure 14.9). While there was hardly any positive news coverage on BHR in 2005, in 2015 rather than criticizing corporations, almost half of the articles portrayed corporations as playing a positive role i.e., as protecting rather than violating or neglecting human rights norms. The positive stories predominantly describe corporations taking on positive duties.

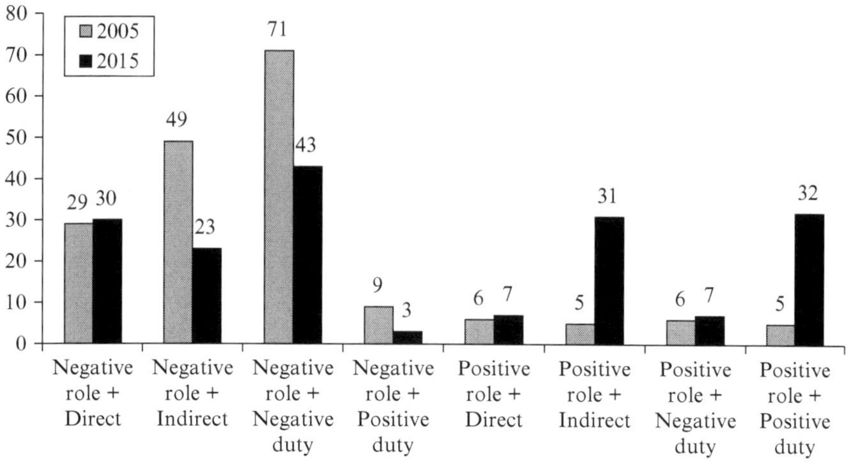

Figure 14.9 News; co-occurrence frequencies of positive/negative role with other categories (percentages of total)

Criticism, the negative stories, pertains only to negative duties, that is, when corporations are clearly violating human rights. In addition, contrary to negative news stories in 2005, in 2015 negative stories were overwhelmingly on social-economic rights. Whereas the majority of negative stories in 2005 were stories on violation of civil and political rights, in 2015 very few were.

In sum, the analysis indicates that news journalists show substantially greater attention to businesses' positive obligations now than ten years ago, but that this new attention is mostly restricted to labor rights. In addition, and surprisingly perhaps, stories on positive obligations are to a great extent stories about businesses actually taking this responsibility, rather than stories reporting on neglect. Negative stories on business and human rights in fact never critically address the lack of responsibility on the part of TNCs for indirect complicity, for failing to take active responsibility for their indirect impacts. So, while there seems to be news-worthiness in corporations taking active measures to protect human rights, the expectation for them to do so does not seem sufficiently strong for news to report on corporations neglecting such a responsibility.

DISCUSSION

The analyses show a distinct development in the use of human rights to frame corporate responsibility. This development is detectable across industries and regions, although more pronounced in some than others. Across the board, large corporations are, at least discursively, accepting responsibility for human rights beyond the minimal responsibility of respecting human rights in their immediate practices. While negative duties and responsibility for direct impact still dominate CSR reports, the greater inclusion of more expansive notions of responsibility is unquestionable. Companies, which are members of the UNGC, are required to report in accordance with its ten principles and thus it is not unlikely that this development owes to some extent to the UNGC. Two factors point to direct causality being an overly simplistic interpretation, however. First, it is worth noting that the same development toward an expansive notion of BHR can be observed for companies which are not members of the UNGC (see Table 14.2). Second, whereas the UNGC puts most emphasis on labor rights, this emphasis is not mirrored in CSR reports, where concern with labor rights is rather limited. Thus, although standards defined by the UN are highly influential, there is no ground for making claims about a unidirectional relationship between governance initiatives and corporate reporting.

The fact that human rights norms are increasingly being used in the reporting of transnational corporations, strictly speaking, tells us nothing about the extent to which these corporations are indeed paying more attention to the role they might play in protecting human rights, putting more effort and resources into doing so and having more substantial impacts. What it can, minimally, tell us is that expectations of corporate responsibility are developing beyond mere philanthropy and voluntariness and corporations are responding to these expectations. At least in the discursive realm, highly influential TNCs have shifted their focus to acknowledge responsibility for the indirect impacts of their activities, those that are not within their most immediate sphere of influence. With this shift, these corporations are contributing to opening up an infinite and indeterminable reach for businesses' human rights responsibilities. While the type of indirect responsibilities most often mentioned by the corporations themselves are social-economic (specifically labor rights), it is noteworthy that when it comes to positive obligations, doing more than simply avoiding harm, CSR reports overwhelmingly focus on political and civil rights. These are basic, first generation rights and ordinarily most closely associated with state power. When TNCs in their CSR reports acknowledge their role in protecting such basic citizen rights, this is an indication of a rising expectation that corporations take on a political role and use their leverage when governments are failing their citizenry.

Analysis of news articles similarly shows a clear expansion of the use of human rights terminology. News media's concern with positive responsibility has intensified markedly over the past decade. In 2015, almost a third of all news articles mentioning human rights in relation to the largest TNCs did so with the most expansive understanding of human rights, that is, as positive obligation in relation to indirect impact. In other words, a substantial part of BHR reporting is about business' responsibility to use their leverage to influence third parties, that is, to play an active role as political actors. As such news and CSR reporting seem to reflect the same development. It is crucial to note, however, that in the news the responsibility of business to use their leverage pertains primarily to social and economic rights, not basic civil, political rights. In this sense, then, the results of the analysis seem to indicate that CSR reports are indeed acknowledging responsibilities, which go a step beyond what the news media seems to expect of the corporate sector.

This result must be seen in the light of the parallel increase in positive news attention regarding the human rights role corporations may potentially play. Importantly, positive news stories overwhelmingly concern corporations using their leverage politically. The neglect to do so, on the other hand, virtually never leads to critical news stories. This indicates a clear acknowledgment by news journalists that there is a political role to be played by business, but no strong expectation or requirement that corporations use their leverage in such a manner. In other words, this responsibility is treated by the news media as morally voluntary. To the extent, then, that news media can be understood as reflecting wider public discourses, it is clear that while public discourse on business and human rights has gained prominence and expanded its scope, there is no public pressure for corporations to use their leverage politically. This conception mirrors that of the mentioned UN governance initiatives.

The question remains, however, whether positive attention is sufficient to drive an expansive BHR understanding forward and make TNCs use their leverage to protect human rights; or whether further development in this direction requires intensified societal expectation and risk of negative exposure. As long as there is not only legal, but also moral voluntariness in the minds of the wider public and TNCs are not held accountable for using their considerable power to the benefit of human rights, it could be argued that the expansion of human rights is of greater benefit for business than for constituencies, whose rights are at risk. While this study points to indications that interstate aspirational platforms, such as the UN Global Compact and the Sustainable Development Goals do indeed contribute to expanding perceptions of business' responsibility for human rights, and the voluntary nature of this expanded responsibility is a likely barrier to truly leveraging private sector power to the benefit of human rights. In fact, the positive discourse about private sector contributions to human rights may create the public illusion that business is already doing what it can, and therefore that we cannot and should not expect more.

NOTES

1. We used the setting for the commonly used "Major News and Business Sources" by Factiva database, which is described as the "Key sources from various regions covering general and business news".
2. Unsurprisingly, companies' CSR reports do not portray themselves as playing a negative role in relation to human rights in either of the years.

REFERENCES

Arnold, D. (2010). Transnational Corporations and the Duty to Respect Basic Human Rights, *Business Ethics Quarterly*, 20(3), 384f.

Arnold, D. G. (2016). Corporations and Human Rights Obligations. *Business and Human Rights Journal*, 1, 255–75.

Bhattacharya, C. B., Korschun, D., and Sen, S. (2009). Strengthening stakeholder–company relationships through mutually beneficial corporate social responsibility initiatives. *Journal of Business Ethics*, 85(2), 257–72.

Bilchitz, D., and Deva, S. (2013). The human rights obligations of business: a critical framework for the future. Human Rights Obligations of Business: Beyond the Corporate Responsibility to Respect, 271–94.

Brenkert, G. G. (2016). Business Ethics and Human Rights: An Overview. *Business and Human Rights Journal*, 1(02), 277–306.

Bromley, P., and Powell, W. W. (2012). From smoke and mirrors to walking the talk: Decoupling in the contemporary world. *The Academy of Management Annals*, 6(1), 483–530.

Campbell, T. (2006). A human rights approach to developing voluntary codes of conduct for multinational corporations. *Business Ethics Quarterly*, 255–69.

Cragg, W. (2000). Human rights and business ethics: Fashioning a new social contract. In Sójka, J. and Wempe, Johan, *Business Challenging Business Ethics: New Instruments for Coping with Diversity in International Business* (pp. 205–14). Springer Netherlands.

Donaldson, T. (1989). *The Ethics of International Business*. New York: Oxford University Press.

Eccles, R. G., and Krzus, M. P. (2010). *One report: Integrated reporting for a sustainable strategy*. Hoboken, N.J.: John Wiley & Sons.

Einwiller, S., Ruppel, C., and Schnauber, A. (2016). Harmonization and differences in CSR reporting of US and German companies: Analyzing the role of global reporting standards and country-of-origin. *Corporate Communications: An International Journal*, 21(2), 230–45.

Etter, M. and Vestergaard, A. (2016). Third level agenda setting during a corporate crisis. In L. Guo and M. McCombs (eds), *The Power of Information Networks: New Directions for Agenda Setting*. New York: Routledge.

Fortanier, F., Kolk, A., and Pinkse, J. (2011). Harmonization in CSR reporting. *Management International Review*, 51(5), 665–96.
Guthey, E., and Morsing, M. (2014). CSR and the mediated emergence of strategic ambiguity. *Journal of Business Ethics*, 120(4), 555–69.
Hackston, D., and Milne, M. J. (1996). Some determinants of social and environmental disclosures in New Zealand companies. *Accounting, Auditing and Accountability Journal*, 9(1), 77–108.
Hanitzsch, T. (2011). Populist disseminators, detached watchdogs, critical change agents and opportunist facilitators: Professional milieus, the journalistic field and autonomy in 18 countries. *International Communication Gazette*, 73(6), 477–94.
Hannah, D., and Zatzick, C. (2008). An examination of leader portrayals in the U.S. business press following the landmark scandals of the early 21st century. *Journal of Business Ethics*, 79(4), 361–77.
Hamilton, J. T. (2003). Media coverage of corporate social responsibility. *The Joan Shorenstein Center on the Press, Politics and Public Policy working paper series. Cambridge, MA: Harvard University*.
Hoffman, W. M., and McNulty, R. E. (2009). International business, human rights, and moral complicity: A call for a declaration on the universal rights and duties of business. *Business and Society Review*, 114(4), 541–70.
Idowu, S. O., and Papasolomou, I. (2007). Are the corporate social responsibility matters based on good intentions or false pretences? An empirical study of the motivations behind the issuing of CSR reports by UK companies. *Corporate Governance: The International Journal of Business in Society*, 7(2), 136–47.
Hooghiemstra, R. (2000). Corporate communication and impression management–new perspectives why companies engage in corporate social reporting. *Journal of Business Ethics*, 27(1), 55–68.
Kripendorff, K. (2013). *Content Analysis: An introduction to its methodology*. Thousand Oaks, CA: SAGE Publications, Inc.
Kobrin, S. J. (2009). Private political authority and public responsibility: Transnational politics, transnational firms, and human rights. *Business Ethics Quarterly*, 19(03), 349–74.
KPMG (2005). KPMG international survey of corporate responsibility reporting 2005, available at: https://commdev.org/userfiles/files/1274_file_D2.pdf, accessed on 27th November 2016.
Macdonald, K. (2011). Re-thinking 'spheres of responsibility': business responsibility for indirect harm. *Journal of business ethics*, 99(4), 549–63.
Matten, D., and Crane, A. (2005). Corporate citizenship: Toward an extended theoretical conceptualization. *Academy of Management Review*, 30(1), 166–79.
McCombs, M. E., and Zhu, J. H. (1995). Capacity, diversity, and volatility of the public agenda: Trends from 1954 to 1994. *Public Opinion Quarterly*, 59(4), 496–525.
Podnar, K., and Golob, U. (2007). CSR expectations: the focus of corporate marketing. *Corporate communications: An international journal*, 12(4), 326–40.
Rasche, A. (2009). "A Necessary Supplement": What the United Nations Global Compact Is and Is Not. *Business and Society*, 48(4), 511–37.
Ruggie, J. (2008). Clarifying the Concepts of 'Sphere of influence' and 'Complicity'. Geneva: UN Doc A/HRC/8/16.
Scherer, A. G., and Palazzo, G. (2011). The new political role of business in a globalized world: A review of a new perspective on CSR and its implications

for the firm, governance, and democracy. *Journal of management studies*, 48(4), 899–931.
Schreier, M. (2014). Qualitative content analysis. *The SAGE handbook of qualitative data analysis*, 170–83. London: Sage.
Sen, A (2004). Elements of a Theory of Human Rights. *Philosophy and Public Affairs*, 32(4), 315–356.
Stohl, M. and Stohl C. (2017). Expanding Responsibilities: Human Rights and Corporate Social Responsibility. In Brysk, A. and Stohl, M. *Expanding Human Rights: 21st Century Norms and Governance*; London: Edward Elgar. Pp. 115-136.
Un Global Compact (n.d.). *The ten principles of the UN Global Compact*, available at https://www.unglobalcompact.org/, accessed on 20th July 2016.
UN Human Rights Office (n.d.). *Business and human rights*, available at http://www.ohchr.org/EN/Issues/Business/Pages/BusinessIndex.aspx, accessed on 21st October 2016.
United Nations (2011). *Guiding Principles on Business and Human Rights*, available at http://www.ohchr.org/Documents/Publications/GuidingPrinciplesBusinessHR_EN.pdf, accessed on 20th November 2016.
Waddock, S., and Googins, B. K. (2011). The paradoxes of communicating corporate social responsibility. *The handbook of communication and corporate social responsibility*, 23–44.
Weissbrodt, D., and Kruger, M. (2003). Norms on the responsibilities of transnational corporations and other business enterprises with regard to human rights. *The American Journal of International Law*, 97(4), 901–922.
Wettstein, F. (2010). The duty to protect: Corporate complicity, political responsibility, and human rights advocacy. *Journal of Business Ethics*, 96(1), 33–47.
Wettstein, F. (2012). CSR and the debate on business and human rights: Bridging the great divide. *Business Ethics Quarterly*, 22(04), 739–70.
Whelan, G. (2012). The political perspective of corporate social responsibility: A critical research agenda. *Business Ethics Quarterly*, 22(04), 709–37.
Whelan, G., Moon, J., and Orlitzky, M. (2009). Human rights, transnational corporations and embedded liberalism: What chance consensus? *Journal of Business Ethics*, 87(2), 367–83.
Whelan, D. J. (2014). The Emerging Jurisprudence of Human Dignity. *International Studies Review*, 16(1), 129–132.
Zhang, J., and Swanson, D. (2006). Analysis of news media's representation of corporate social responsibility (CSR). *Public Relations Quarterly*, 51(2), 13–22.

15. Digital media and human rights: Loomio, Statistics New Zealand, and gender identity[1]

Cynthia Stohl, Michael Stohl and Shiv Ganesh

In 2011 the UN Human Rights Council convened "The Human Voice of Freedom: The Internet and Human Rights." At that meeting experts in the field of social media joined activists in discussing the centrality of internet freedom for human rights and the proposition that the information society must be based on respecting and upholding the standards laid down in the UN charter and the Universal Declaration of Human Rights. The experts also addressed how emerging digital media could help activist groups monitor and protect human rights. In the same year, during a speech to the League of Arab States, Minister Gunilla Carlsson of Sweden (2011, para. 11) argued, "In my view, these tools [information communication technologies] are technologies of liberation, symbols of a world that has irreversibly changed" (cited in Christiansen, 2011). In this chapter, we examine how digital technologies are harnessed in public deliberations about human rights issues by way of a case study involving discussions of what appropriate categories of gender identity, (e.g. transgender, gender diverse, gender-nonconforming) should be implemented in the 2018 New Zealand census, We first provide an overview of the relationship between digital technologies and human rights, followed by a discussion on digital technologies and deliberative democracy in particular. We then discuss the specifics of the case and its implications for how we view the relationships among technology, human rights, and public deliberative processes.

DIGITAL TECHNOLOGIES AND HUMAN RIGHTS: ENHANCEMENTS AND CONTRACTIONS

While the view of information communication technologies as "liberation technology" is becoming more and more widespread it is also apparent that it is far more complex than its initial optimistic formulation (Poster,

1995). At its most basic, the idea is that the affordances associated with information technology (e.g. visibility, persistence, editability, and association, Treem and Leonardi, 2012) would enable "citizens to report news, expose wrongdoing, express opinions, mobilize protest, monitor elections, scrutinize government, deepen participation, and expand the horizons of freedom" (Diamond, 2010, p.70). Digital technologies offer citizens less costly, more direct, synchronous and asynchronous spaces in which to conduct both formal and informal interactions among interested parties.

And indeed in the last two decades the utopian vision of information communication technologies supporting human rights, democracy and ethical governance has in many ways been realized. The 2016 Engine Room and Oak Foundation report "Technology tools in Human Rights" (Rahman, 2016), found that human rights groups are using a diversity of digital platforms for publicizing and conducting human rights campaigns, recording and monitoring human rights violations, connecting with other group working on the same issues, and establishing ties with concerned citizens and publics across the globe. Organizations also use digital tools to discover, analyze, verify and corroborate violations by scanning social media and mobile messaging platforms, thus improving the overall quality of their efforts. An Amnesty International official blogger recently noted:

> Social media is increasingly helpful to not only monitor emerging human rights emergencies, but also to uncover incorrect information. A recent example is when Twitter helped me to spot incorrect contextual information on a newly uploaded execution video from Syria. This is just one instance in which crowd-sourced expertise from social media can open up new opportunities for human rights organizations.
>
> (Koettl, 2013)

Moreover, the creation of shared databases for tracking national development and human rights activity is becoming commonplace. Digital technologies enable organizations to manage their information better, through historical archiving and inscription of data and then cataloguing, storing and managing information in ways that can be systematically shared with the human rights community at large. The Global DevInfo Initiative, for example, adopted by UNICEF and other UN agencies, integrates management and geographic information systems, software training in data mining, data dissemination solutions and technical support in order to provide information-technology-based solutions for issues related to development, achievement of the millennial development goals[2] and fostering human rights compliance.

A similar example is Human Rights Internet (HRI), a non-governmental organization based in Ottawa, Canada that supports the exchange of information within the worldwide human rights community. HRI works with numerous governmental, intergovernmental and non-governmental groups to disseminate information and help empower marginalized and minority groups. It has developed an online space where individuals and organizations can access current human rights information and resources.[3]

But these technological opportunities are accompanied by inadvertent as well as intentional threats to the promotion and protection of human rights. Issues of censorship, overregulation, violation of privacy, surveillance, and control are just a few of the concerns voiced by scholars and activists. Morozov (2011), for example, identifies several attempts by nation-states to use digital technologies for improving human rights that backfired. He describes in detail Haystack, a program developed and licensed by the US that was designed to bypass Iranian state censorship but actually allowed the Iranian authorities to easily identify users.

And even more chilling intentional examples abound. As Zygmunt Bauman (2012) notes, David Lyon (2010) argues that "government surveillance through social networks is made so much more effective thanks to the cooperation of its intended objects and victims." The Snowden leaks detailed how the NSA had monitored phone calls since the passage of the Patriot Act in 2001. And there is a great deal of evidence to show that major governments and tech companies have cooperated to foster the ability of government intelligence agencies to more "effectively" monitor digital communications.

Hope (2011, p.4) argues:

> Risks to the human rights of freedom of expression and privacy are relevant to the entire ICT value chain . . . The debate about the use of ICT infrastructure for surveillance during the Iranian elections raised questions for the providers of telecommunications network equipment. The closure of entire mobile telecommunications networks in Egypt exposed the vulnerability of telecommunications services providers to government demands. The "Green Dam Youth Escort" proposals in China were of great concern to computer makers. And demands from the governments of UAE, Saudi Arabia, and India (among others) to access messages sent over BlackBerry devices piqued the interest of handset makers everywhere.

Given these issues, it is not surprising that Ganesh and Stohl (2010) found that even as activists increased the ways in which they engaged in social media, they continued to be suspicious of its use and fearful that authorities would coopt their social media. Moreover, the proliferation of initiatives such as the Global Network Initiative, The Open Net Initiative, and the Global Sustainability Initiative to develop standards of performance which will protect freedom of speech, rights to privacy and other violations of human rights also attest to the widespread concerns that the emergence of digital technologies and the accompanying powerful organizations infrastructure can constrain human rights as well as facilitate human rights violations. Rillo (2016: 4), for example, credits the Open Net Initiative for exposing North American technology companies who were developing and selling censorship software to Middle Eastern and Northern African governments. This software powerfully infringed upon citizen's freedom of speech rights. Specifically:

> American Companies were censoring prominent bloggers who wrote about gender issues as "sexually explicit", despite not running a pornographic blog. They also found that if anyone posted any comments including hate speech, advertisements for Viagra, or links to pornography on these blogs that the activist's blog would be censored.

Thus, we see that despite the rhetoric and promise of digital technologies to enhance and expand human rights efforts, these technologies simultaneously provide the tools to contract and violate human rights. Maréchal, for example, argues that the more NGOs rely on social media and digital information sharing, "the easier it is to monitor that person's communications (both the content and so-called "metadata")," and thus "the lower the barriers for discrimination, retribution, and persecution by state and non-state actors (Maréchal, 2015: 2–3)."

DIGITAL TECHNOLOGIES AND DELIBERATIVE DEMOCRACY: ENHANCEMENTS AND CONTRACTIONS

The enhancing and contracting impact of digital technologies on human rights is particularly evident in discussions about deliberative democracy. Deliberative democracy is a form of democracy that aims to promote greater legitimacy for collective decisions and to deepen democracy through greater public engagement in political processes (Dryzek, 2000). It promotes collaborative reasoning and respectful disagreement among citizens during the decision-making process. Its roots can be found in ancient Greece. Aristotle wrote of the great value in a process in which citizens publicly discuss and justify laws and political decisions to one another and Pericles argued that public deliberation was an "indispensable preliminary to any wise action at all" (see Gutmann and Thompson, 2009). In the past century, town hall meetings, open forums, and public debates have typically been the most common ways for people to come together in open spaces to deliberate about collective issues and public goods. Research suggests that the most common practical manifestation has been the emergence of "minipublics" involving relatively small sub-samples of the affected population (anywhere between 20 and 2,000) who come together to learn about and consider ways through a particular issue (Dryzek, 2013). Within deliberative democracy is a networking logic, i.e. a mode of organizing that involves "horizontal coordination among formal organizations and autonomous groups, grassroots participation, consensus decision-making, and the free and open exchange of information" (Juris, 2008a, p.14).

Although there are numerous examples of the effectiveness of traditional public deliberations, there are also several limitations to involvement. Public deliberative processes are very hard to implement and sustain. Citizen motivations, skills, and capacities vary to a great extent, most especially among marginalized groups, which limits participation. Archives of the details of the public deliberation are rarely complete, only those who attended the meeting are aware of the discussion nuances, and there are only small traces of the deliberation available during the implementation stage. Activists and communities also often challenge the very rules upon which deliberative processes are begun (Dryzek, 2000; Ganesh and Zoller, 2012).

Several scholars have noted the increasing prevalence and development of digital technologies in deliberative democracy projects and the potential of social media to reduce the threshold for participation has reinvigorated the interest in them (Chadwick, 2012; Dahlberg, 2011; Stromer-Galley and Muhberger, 2009). As mentioned earlier, digital technologies enhance deliberative processes by offering some key advantages including ease of use, choice of anonymity and exchange of ideas that help reduce patterns of social dominance. Internet technologies also allow for representative deliberation by enabling geographically dispersed and demographically diverse participants to interact with one another in both synchronous and asynchronous ways. Moreover, information technologies can provide an easily accessible archive of the deliberation; providing context and meaning, as the decision is implemented. The net effect has been for digital technologies to become increasingly interwoven into public deliberation processes, and as Dahlberg (2011) outlines, organizations all over the world now also use the deliberative affordances provided by digital technologies to promote particular forms of deliberative democracy, such as the Minnesota E-Democracy project.

Conversely, however, scholars and commentators have been concerned about the potentially contracting impacts of digital technologies upon deliberative processes. These concerns have historically tended to take two forms. First, scholars have tended to express concerns regarding the ability of communities to participate equitably in digital democracy initiatives. These have included concerns associated with the relative skills, experience and competencies that particular communities may or may not have with digital technologies which impact their ability to use these technologies. Scholars have also identified gender, age, and ethnicity as factors that disproportionately impact the ability of people to participate in digitally driven initiatives (Zorn, Weaver and Richardson, 2010). Related to the issue of competence is that of access. Scholars have used the evocative term "zones of silence" to describe the process whereby entire communities, particularly those in the Global South, become information poor, and are shut out of increasingly digitized civic and public development processes (Potter, 2006; Ganesh and Barber, 2009).

The second set of concerns scholars have expressed about the contracting impact of digital technologies on deliberative democracy has to do with the affordances that these technologies provide to engage in collaborative decision-making processes. Perhaps the most prominent example of this concern has to do with studies of flaming, which form one of the oldest corpus of studies of online communicative behavior (e.g. Lea, O'Shea, Fung and Spears, 1992) and suggest that computer-mediated communication is often skewed away from collaborative deliberation and towards disagreement, ad homenim attacks, and polarization, Recently, scholars have observed that polarization of opinions in political discussions and debates continues to be accentuated online, and that such polarization is accompanied with the rise of networked politics in general and the increasing fragmentation of broadcast media (Hanna et al, 2013). Taken together, these studies suggest that the overall relationships among digital communication technologies, human rights, and deliberative democracy are complex, both riddled with tensions and contradictions, and full of promise and opportunity.

NEW ZEALAND AND HUMAN RIGHTS

By international standards, New Zealand is considered to have an excellent track record in human rights, not because rights have historically been universally granted and protected, but because communities have been effectively able to challenge the state on human rights issues and procure legislative support and enforcement. This is especially the case for indigenous human rights, where many commentators have favorably compared the effectiveness of human rights-related mobilizations in New Zealand as compared to other parts of the world, including one of its closest neighbors, Australia (e.g., Havemann, 1999). Two laws now provide the framework for human rights in the country: the Bill of Rights Act (1990), and the New Zealand Human Rights Act (1993). The country founded a watchdog organization, the Human Rights Commission (HRC) in 1977, which has consistently had an A rating from the United Nations' International Coordinating Committee of National Human Rights Institutes.

The place of gender identity in the human rights framework of the country is less well known and celebrated than its international stance on indigeneity and human rights. This is for good reason. Transgender advocates have consistently lobbied the government to include transgender communities in the human rights framework of the country, but it was only in 2004 that the HRC published a comprehensive assessment of human rights issues faced by trans and intersex people. While this is late in comparison to other human rights issues, it is worth noting that it is relatively early compared to initiatives in other countries to expand the spectrum of gender identity beyond the male/female binary. Since then, there has been considerable movement on the issue by the HRC, particularly in the form of the Commission's Transgender Inquiry and the release of the groundbreaking 2008 report, *To Be Who I am* (HRC, 2008), which identified several outstanding human rights issues related to gender identity, including the need for an explicit reference to the subject in the 1993 Human Rights Act; issues related to health related rights; and issues related to citizenship rights, including privacy, the issuance of passports that reflect appropriate gender identities, and the treatment of trans people by the government, in particular the Police and Corrections.

In what follows we explore the opportunities and risks to human rights development, enhancement and constraint though a brief case study that illustrates how deliberative features of digital technologies were leveraged by a large public organization to engender public discussion about human rights issues related to gender identity. This initiative engaged human rights activists, NGOs' representatives, interested citizens and government officials from Statistics New Zealand Tatauranga Aotearoa (the New Zealand census bureau, popularly referred to as Statistics NZ). Statistics NZ, after brief training sessions in civic engagement and public deliberative processes, adopted Loomio, an online tool for collaborative decision-making, to engage the public, most notably marginalized groups, in deciding and refining what descriptors should be asked in the 2018 census. The deliberations we study were publicly available and revolve around issues of gender identity and human rights. We consider the implications for the increased use of digital technologies in civic engagement and deliberation for the expansion and or contraction of human rights.

LOOMIO AND DELIBERATIVE DEMOCRACY

Loomio is an open-source software online deliberation platform built by a worker-owned cooperative social enterprise based in Aotearoa New Zealand. Loomio is designed to enable deliberative democracy and help groups "come to timely decisions and transform deliberation into real-world action".[4] Loomio began in 2011, when activists who met because of their involvement in the Occupy movement in Wellington were seeking ways to engage individuals who were not physically present in the same physical space in collective discussion and action in an inclusive manner. As of April 2015, the Loomio platform had been used in 93 countries in 32 different languages. Users have made more than 26,000 collaborative decisions using the platform. Overall, Loomio reports that last year there had been a total of 80,638 members who created and joined 18,012 online groups. These groups represent city governments, social movement collectives, community groups, start-ups, schools, and NGOs, including groups such as Debt Resistance UK, Urban Adventures, a startup with staff and partners spread across the globe, The National Assembly of Wales, Oui Share, a collective international community focusing on the collaborative economy and Climate Karanga, a NZ climate activist group.

Loomio situates itself as a form of online deliberative democracy that can be used across multiple organizational and interpersonal contexts. Some groups' deliberations are public while others are closed and are available only for group members to view online.

The Case

In April 2015 Statistics New Zealand began a public online deliberative process, using the Loomio platform for online discussion to engage interested citizens, activist groups and community associations on issues related to designing and refining questions for the 2018 census. According to Statistics NZ's website the information collected from the national census

> helps determine how billions of dollars of government funding is spent in the community. It is used to help make decisions about which services are needed and where they should be, such as hospitals, kōhanga reo, schools, roads, public transport, and recreational facilities. Census information is used by councils, community groups, iwi, and businesses to plan for the future.
>
> (Statitstics NZ, 2017)

The deliberative process was advertised for several months prior to the initiation of public engagement through traditional and social media as well as public announcements.[5] All members of the public were encouraged to participate – the Loomio platform was open between April 30 and June 10, 2015 (links to the deliberations may be found in the Appendix).

During this five-week period the Loomio threads included 15 distinct content areas ranging from education to housing and income. Approximately 250 groups participated, more than 175 individuals and organizations submitted formal proposals during the public consultation period, and there were about 4,200 page views. The groups included Māori interest organizations, youth groups, educational institutions, government and health agencies, research associations, businesses, and interested unaffiliated citizens. Our discussion focuses on one content area: sexual orientation and gender identity and includes the publicly available data from the entire period 30 April 2015 until 10 June 2015 (see Appendix). Gender identity, as understood in New Zealand's human rights laws, refers to a person's internal, deeply felt sense of being male or female (or something other or in between). A person's gender identity may or may not correspond with their sex (NZ Human Rights Commission).

Statistics NZ was interested in gender identity as a potential census area for several reasons. A 2014 report from the HRC, following on from its groundbreaking 2008 inquiry, highlighted the need for "visibility as a means of promoting equality and decreasing the likelihood of discrimination for members of the transgender community. HRC argued that insufficient data limits policymakers' ability to quantify the issues affecting gender identity minority groups and to develop ways to address adequately the health and social needs of these populations. This HRC report built upon the Yogyakarta Principles that have been at the forefront of the fight to extend human rights in the context of sexual orientation and gender identity. Named after a 2006 meeting at Gadjah Mada University in Yogyakarta, Indonesia, 29 human rights law experts from 25 countries unanimously adopted the "Yogyakarta Principles on the Application of International Human Rights Law" in relation to sexual orientation and gender identity.

The 29 Yogyakarta Principles identified a coherent and far-reaching set of standards that obligate states to "respect, protect and fulfill the human rights of all persons regardless of their sexual orientation or gender identity."[6] From Principle 1 which affirms the "Right to the universal enjoyment of human rights" to Principle 29 "Accountability" which asserts "everyone whose human rights, including rights addressed in these Principles, are violated is entitled to have those directly or indirectly responsible for the violation, whether they are government officials or not, held accountable for their actions," the Yogyakarta Principles have become the bedrock for human rights activists in this area and "have been endorsed by the UN Secretary General High Commissioner for Human Rights, as well as the major treaty bodies" (NZ Human Rights Commission, n.d.).

Principle 3 had most relevance for the census. It addresses the "Right to recognition before the law." It declares that states should take "all necessary legislative, administrative and other measures to fully respect and legally recognise each person's self-defined gender identity." In 2015 there was no standardized approach for collecting and storing gender identity data in New Zealand or anywhere else in the world. In 2011 Statistics Canada decided that sexual orientation is best suited to inclusion in surveys that have a particular context (e.g. health surveys).

The Outcome

In July 2015 Statistics NZ announced:

> Gender diverse will join "male" and "female" categories in a new gender-identity classification released today by Statistics New Zealand. This new classification records the identity of all people, including those who see themselves as different from male or female, and forms an integral part of the Statistical Standard for Gender Identity.

This new standard is the first in the world for gender identity information (Statitstics NZ, 2015).

This case illustrates some of the positive and negative aspects of the use of digital technologies for public deliberation and the ability to obtain information with the intention of expanding human rights. To begin, the ease and accessibility of the Loomio platform were seen by all involved as a positive aspect of the process. Over and over people retrospectively noted how this online process afforded a great deal of visibility to an issue that needed to be made more public, and it was recognized to be an inclusive discussion. This type of public visibility is often missing from many deliberations on human rights, even within mainstream LGBT groups, and is distinct from the individual/personal visibility in the form of media spotlighting of trans individuals which as Ayoub (2016) aptly notes, itself often perpetuates discriminatory practices because transgendered people continue to be framed as aberrations, failures and exceptions. Utilizing Loomio enabled Statitstics NZ to take advantage of three of the technological affordances of social media identified by Treem and Leonardi (2012). The platform brought people together into the conversation who had previously been marginalized, enabling emergent connections (association) and the persistence and editablity of the content gave interested parties the opportunity to return to the deliberations and data and use the information in later collective actions (Statitstics NZ, n.d.).

The positive nature of the deliberation and the result was seen by many as an expansion of human rights. The NZ Human Rights Commissioner, Richard Tankersley hailed the announcement. He noted that:

> This gender diverse standard paves the way for the New Zealand Government to collect data on people with diverse gender identities in a way that has never been possible, leading to a better understanding of the need for recognition and inclusion of the range of trans people in New Zealand, and to advancing the full realisation of their human rights.
>
> (Shields, 2015)

However, not all observers or the participants were quite as pleased as the Human Rights Commissioner. Post-discussion blogs by participants and other activists indicate that large segments of the community believe that Statistics NZ ignored most of the feedback and that the discussion had no impact on the standard which was eventually decided. For many it was seen as a decision that would not positively affect protection of their human rights but rather would contract them. ("Statistics NZ," 2015). For example, the possibility of misuse of the data was threaded throughout the discussion. Statistics NZ itself noted early in the conversation, "Our focus group research identified quality issues and concerns about the accuracy of information people are comfortable disclosing." Citizens and groups suggested, "We must also consider data quality and intrusiveness. Many respondents may not answer the question, and although census data may produce indicative figures, these may not be accurate enough to be analysed against other variables or published" (Statitstics NZ, n.d.). These concerns for privacy and the fear that the data would be misused were addressed in ways that some activists felt were insufficient, i.e. respondents would not have to fill out the census survey or respond to the gender identity question. Ironically, the questions designed to validate the rights of the community were in the end feared, in the belief that it would skew the actual distributions and thus have a deleterious rather than positive effect.

But in addition to the concerns with privacy and misuse of the data, there were also many concerns about the terminology used in the final decision. The tripartite distinction between male, female and gender diverse was viewed as inadequate, if not insulting, to many with more complex gender identities. The binary nature of the choices were framed by some bloggers as choices which do not represent the lived experience of those they are trying to include (Write Handed Girl, 2015). Moreover, by not allowing people to "unambiguously say 'female' in an identity question then 'trans' in a different question, the target population was alienated," wrote blogger Jennifer Katherine Shields. (2015)

Blogs and social media messages after the decision was announced also noted that the final decision relied on terminology many in the community refused to use in the deliberations and elsewhere, As one participant wrote "the typical and frustrating MtF/FtM. It leaves no space for Trans women to identify as women, but instead as something Other that relies heavily on 'born a man' rhetoric." In other words the process resulted in an already marginalized community feeling that, as one blogger wrote, they were "othering us further." Another blogger noted that the system now would "essentially require many of us to marginalize ourselves and our identities by selecting an Othered category in order for important data about our lives and experiences to be collected (Shields, 2015).

CONCLUSION

Little previous research has looked at how emerging digital media platforms are enabling new forms of human rights organizing that have the potential to transform the existing human rights regime, by bringing new actors into the conversation, providing greater opportunity for collaborative decision-making and changing the nature of the discourses associated with human rights organizing (for exceptions see Ayoub & Brzezinska, 2015; Szulc & Dhoest, 2013). As we discussed above, this type of organizational approach to activism on behalf of human rights concerns represents what scholars have described as a networking logic (Juris, 2008) and entails practices of coordination, consensus and exchange. In this case the logic exploits the affordances of the Loomio platform and is thus somewhat different than earlier uses of other digital media described in the introduction. The Loomio platform allows for the movement from first and second media effects to third order effects (Malone & Rockart, 1991). First order effects focus attention on the ways in which digital media might substitute for traditional ways of getting in information about human rights violations, (e.g. using mobile technologies rather than relying on face-to-face interviewing practices). Second order effects relate to how digital media such as Twitter or texting might be innovatively appropriated as activist organizing tools – letting people know where a spontaneous protest will be taking place rather than long term planning of the event. Third order effects refer to the ability of emerging digital technologies to generate new structures of organizing and discourse. Loomio is designed to reconfigure tradition forms of civic engagements and public deliberation not just in human rights but on any other issue of concern to a group of individuals.

We thus have to ask: did the use of the Loomio platform actually change things? To answer we have to explore two very different dimensions. First, did the digital platform generate new structures of organizing and discourse in this particular case. And second, did the process expand or contract the human rights of the gender diverse community?

The use of Loomio was an attempt by Statistics New Zealand to move beyond face-to-face communication and the traditional focus groups and survey methods of census bureaus. However, while the Loomio platform greatly increased the participation of activists and NGOs and produced a vibrant discussion, Statistics NZ still kept the hierarchical structure of decision-making, both during the deliberations through the use of moderators, facilitators and interventions – and in the end when they made a decision that was not fully reflective of the rich and forthright discussion that had transpired.

In terms of the expansion and/or contraction of human rights there are two components of the answer. The first concerns the process and the discourse and awareness that underlay Statistics New Zealand's interest in fostering the conversation. Did the process help Statistics New Zealand improve its ability to take "all necessary legislative, administrative and other measures to fully respect and legally recognize each person's self-defined gender identity"? (NZ Human Rights Commission n.d.) And what was the impact on the overall discourse about gender and gender diversity as a result?

While one cannot state at this point that Statistics New Zealand took "all" necessary steps, there is no question that the process has had positive effects in terms of the discourse and understanding about gender and gender diversity within New Zealand. One activist's comments are illustrative:

> I think there's heaps wider visibility and acknowledgement of gender diversity now then there was then, like it's absolutely immeasurably different. Gender diversity stuff was starting to be better understood overseas but in New Zealand at that time it was very very quiet so . . . I guess the visibility of . . . the impacts of stigma and discrimination around gender diversity I think those conversations are in a very different place which is good. There is a much wider acknowledgement that we exist now than there was then . . . its patchy it varies but overall there's not . . . my dad said to me again around the homosexual law reform bill that he didn't know any gay people, he said he wouldn't say that now, I don't think there is many people in New Zealand who would be able to say that now. So we exist we are in family we are in workplaces we are in sports teams, we exist, people know us now they know famous people who are queer. So that whole social landscape is changing dramatically, which is fabulous ay.

Further, New Zealand has not witnessed any noticeable backlash from the discussion, and many interviewees consider the inclusion of the third category as a progressive move even when they also believe that more is required. And some highlight how the data collection will provide very clear, important benefits to the community:

> I'm still interested in, like one of the things that is a huge problem for me is that we don't get counted anywhere. New Zealand doesn't collect any demographic data about anything very much really, until we can prove that 10% of people using hospital services are queer, until we can prove that mental health service users are this much of a percentage of all service users we are not going to get things that respond to us appropriately, and we are not going to prove that until we count ourselves. That has lots of complexities because it means that we have to come out, but I think that's probably the next big political fight is how we make sure that our needs are included in all of the planning that goes about in all of the resources for everything. I feel like that's a discussion that the rainbow community has started to have, and I'm really looking forward to that conversation because I will be one of the geeks arguing for it.

Serious concerns remain, and the impacts of the census decisions will not be fully addressed until after the 2018 Census is complete. At present, it appears that the LGBTQ community prefer visibility to invisibility, despite the problems that data-driven visibility might engender. Finally, while the long-term effects of that new visibility and its impact on public deliberations and human rights are, of course, still unknown, the discussions that have already occurred have clearly widened the discourse and educated the public on the issues of gender and their implications for the rights of the person.

NOTES

1. The authors thank Theodore Taptiklis and the staff at Loomio for their support and openness to the process. This research has been supported by the Royal Society of New Zealand's Marsden Foundation (MAU1209).
2. The Millenial Development Goals (MDGs) are contained in the Millenium Declaration of 2000 announced by the UN. They outlined a series of collective priorities for peace and security, poverty reduction, the environment and human rights to which the assembled states committed. In 2015 they were superseded by the Sustainable Development Goals (SDGs) see https://www.un.org/millennium/declaration/ares552e.htm.
3. See http://hri.ca/.
4. See https://www.loomio.org/.
5. See the "2018 Census" discussion forum (https://2018census.loomio.org/).
6. See "The Yogyakarta Principles" (http://www.yogyakartaprinciples.org).

REFERENCES

Ayoub, Philip (2016). *When States Come Out: Europe's Sexual Minorities and the Politics of Visibility*. Cambridge, UK: Cambridge University Press.

Ayoub, P. M., & Brzezińska, Olga (2015). Caught in a Web? The Internet and Deterritorialization of LGBT Activism. *The Ashgate Research Companion to Lesbian and Gay Activism*, 225–43.

Bauman, Zygmunt (2012). *Do Facebook and Twitter help spread democracy and human rights?* 8 May 2012 Retrieved from http://www.social-europe.eu/2012/05/do-facebook-and-twitter-help-spread-democracy-and-human-rights/.

Carlsson, Gunilla (2011d, April). Speech at the headquarters of the League of Arab States, Cairo [Speech]. Retrieved from http://www.regeringen.se/sb/d/14187/a/165911.

Chadwick, Andrew (2012). Recent Shifts in the Relationship Between the Internet and Democratic Engagement in Britain and the United States: Granularity, Informational Exuberance, and Political Learning. In Eva Anduiza, Michael Jensen, and Laia Jorba (eds), *Digital Media and Political Engagement Worldwide: A Comparative Study*. (pp.39–55). Cambridge: Cambridge University Press.

Christian C. (2011) 'Discourses of technology and liberation: State aid to net activists in an era of "Twitter Revolutions,"' *The Communication Review*, 14:3, 233–53, DOI: 10.1080/10714421.2011.597263.

Dahlberg, L. (2011). 'Re-constructing digital democracy: An outline of four "positions"', *New Media and Society*, 13(6), 855–72.

Diamond, L. (2010). 'Liberation technology,' *Journal of Democracy*, 21, 3: 69–83.

Dryzek, John. (2000) *Deliberative Democracy and Beyond: Liberals, Critics, Contestations*. Oxford: Oxford University Press.

Dryzek, John (2013). The Real Challenge of Climate Change. Centre for Deliberative Democracy and Global Governance, August 1. Retrieved from https://deldem.weblogs.anu.edu.au/2012/02/15/what-is-deliberative-democracy/.

Ganesh, S., & Barber, K. F. (2009). 'The silent community: Organizing zones in the digital divide', *Human Relations*, 62(6), 853–76.

Ganesh, S., & Stohl, C. (2010). 'Qualifying engagement: A study of information and communication technology and the global social justice movement in Aotearoa/New Zealand,' *Communication Monographs*, 77, 51–74. doi:10.1080/03637750903514284.

Ganesh, S. & Zoller, H. (2012). 'Dialogue, activism, and democratic social change.' *Communication Theory*, 22(1), 66–91.

Ganesh, S., & Stohl, C. (2013). 'From Wall Street to Wellington: Protests in an era of technological ubiquity,' *Communication Monographs*, 80, 425–51. doi:10.1080/03637751.2013.828156.

Gutmann, Amy & Thompson, Dennis (2004) *Why Deliberative Democracy?* Princeton, NJ: Princeton University Press.

Hanna, A., Wells, C., Maurer, P., Friedland, L., Shah, D., & Matthis, J. (2013). Partisan Alignments and Political Polarization Online: A Computational Approach to Understanding the French and US Presidential Elections. Paper presented at the Proceedings of the 2nd workshop on Politics, elections and data, San Francisco, CA.

Havemann, Paul (1999). *Indigenous Peoples' Rights in Australia, Canada, and New Zealand*. Oxford: Oxford University Press.

Hope, Dunstan (2011). *Protecting Human Rights in the Digital Age: Understanding Evolving Freedom of Expression and Privacy Risks in the Information and Communications Technology Industry*, BSR, February. Retrieved from https://www.bsr.org/reports/BSR_Protecting_Human_Rights_in_the_Digital_Age.pdf.

Human Rights Council (2008). *To Be Who I Am*. Retrieved from https://www.hrc.co.nz/files/5714/2378/7661/15-Jan-2008_14-56-48_HRC_Transgender_FINAL.pdf.
Juris, Jeffrey (2008). *Networking Futures: The Movements Against Corporate Globalization*. Durham and London: Duke University Press.
Koettl, Christoph (2013) Twitter to the Rescue? How Social Media is Transforming Human Rights Monitoring. *Amnesty Internal: Human Rights Blog*, February 20. Retrieved from http://blog.amnestyusa.org/middle-east/twitter-to-the-rescue-how-social-media-is-transforming-human-rights-monitoring/.
Lea, Martin, O'Shea, Tim, Fung, Pat, & Spears, Russell (1992). Flaming in Computer-Mediated Communication: Observations, Explanations, Implications. In M. Lea (Ed.), *Contexts of Computer-Mediated Communication* (pp.89–112). New York: Harvester Wheatsheaf.
Lyon, D. (2010). 'Liquid Surveillance: The contribution of Zygmunt Bauman to surveillance studies', *International Political Sociology* 4(4): 325–38.
Malone, T. & Rockart, J. F. (1991). 'Computers, networks, and the corporation'. *Scientific American*, 265, 128 136. doi:10.1038/scientificamerican0991-128.
Morozov, Evgeny (2011). *The net delusion: How not to liberate the world*, London, England: Allen Lane/Penguin.
New Hub, 2015. "Statistics NZ introduces 'gender diverse' classification," July 18. Retrieved from http://www.newshub.co.nz/home/new-zealand/2015/07/statistics-nz-introduces-gender-diverse-classification.html.
NZ Human Rights Commission https://www.hrc.co.nz/files/1914/2388/0525/HRNZ_10_rights_of_sexual_and_gender_minorities.pdf.
Oui Share (2012). Retrieved from http://ouishare.net/en.
Poster Mark (1995). Cyberdemocracy: Internet and the Public Sphere. In *Internet Culture*, ed. David Porter, pp.201–17. New York: Routledge.
Potter, A. (2006). 'Zones of Silence: A framework beyond the digital divide', *First Monday*, 11(5).
Rahman, Zara (2016). Technology tools in Human Rights. *The Engine Room and Oak Foundation Report*. Retrieved from https://library.theengineroom.org/humanrights-tech/.
Rillo, Kayla (2016) How Can ICT's Be Used to Maximize the Good? *Political Analysis*, 18(3). Retrieved from http://scholarship.shu.edu/pa/vol18/iss1/3.
Statitstics NZ (2015). "Gender identity standard world-first in New Zealand", July 17. Retrieved from http://stats.govt.nz/tools_and_services/media-centre/media-releases-2015/gender-identity-17-july-15.aspx.
Statitstics NZ, 2017. "2018 Census". May 30. Retrieved from http://www.stats.govt.nz/Census/2018-census.aspx.
Statitstics NZ (n.d.). "2018 Census content: Summary of feedback from engagement and consultation". Retrieved from http://www.stats.govt.nz/Census/2018-census/feedback-content-consultation/appendix.aspx.
Shields, Jennifer, 2015. "Statistics NZ's 'Gender Diverse' Decision". *Jennifer Katherine Shields*, July 17. Retrieved from https://jenniferkateshields.wordpress.com/2015/07/17/statistics-nzs-gender-diverse-decision/.
Stromer-Galley, E., & Muhlberger, P. (2009). 'Agreement and disagreement in group deliberation: Effects on deliberation satisfaction, future engagement, and decision legitimacy', *Political Communication*, 26, 173–92.
Szulc, L. & Dhoest, A. (2013). 'The internet and sexual identity formation:

Comparing Internet use before and after coming out', *Communications*, 38(4), pp.347–65. Retrieved 22 Apr. 2017, from doi:10.1515/commun-2013-0021.
Treem, J. W., & Leonardi, P. M. (2012). 'Social media use in organizations: Exploring the affordances of visibility, persistence, editability, and association', *Communication Yearbook*, 36, 143–89.
Write Handed Girl, 2015. "StatsNZ fail to respond to Trans community". November 11. Retrieved from http://www.writehanded.org/blog/2015/11/11/statsnz-fail-to-respond-to-trans-community/.
Zorn, T., Weaver, K., & Richardson, M. (2010). 'Goods not wanted: Older people's use of computer narrative rejection', *Information, Communication and Society*, 13(5), 696–721.

APPENDIX

The following websites provide the actual deliberations of this public group and the formal statements by Statistics New Zealand summarizing the results:

https://www.loomio.org/g/zs6h9qVl AD about the Loomio exercise.
https://www.loomio.org/d/nX2aSkNZ/sex DISCUSSION of issue and proposals made and the results.
http://blog.loomio.org/category/stories/ interview with three of Statistics NZ and their involvement with Loomio.
http://www.stats.govt.nz/Census/2018-census/prelim-content/proposed-topics.aspx initial recommendation before the deliberation.
https://www.loomio.org/g/zs6h9qVl/gender%20identity initial description of project.
https://2018census.loomio.org/d/kFKv8BgZ/gender-identity summary.
https://www.loomio.org/d/kFKv8BgZ/gender-identity.
https://www.loomio.org/d/hICFgl84/comment/700021.
actual discourse and summaries.

16. Beyond global vs. local: Islam, feminism, and women's rights in Morocco

Jesilyn Faust

INTRODUCTION

Much of the discussion surrounding the contraction or decrease in human rights in the 21st century focuses on the Middle East and North Africa (MENA). American intervention post 9/11 promised improvements in human rights, most of which were never realized and in many cases the situation worsened. The Arab revolutions beginning in 2011 again offered some hope as people overthrew dictatorships for the promise of rights and freedom but that hope remains widely unrealized. The contemporary situation throughout most of MENA seems especially bleak in terms of women's and human rights. ISIS presents what is perhaps the most horrifying example yet of an Islamic extremist organization that publicly and flagrantly violates the most basic human rights, using the Qu'ran and Islamic law to justify their actions. Yet, this crisis presents unique opportunities to find new ways of engaging on women's and human rights. Not only is this is an opportunity, it is an obligation of the highest order that nations, international organizations (IOs) and activists must fulfill by learning from the mistakes of the past and finding the best methods of cooperation.

The struggle for women's rights in Morocco shows that IOs that wish to make lasting progress on women's rights issues in Islamic societies must genuinely engage with local women's organizations, including Islamic ones, and empower women to use the tools from within their own society to free themselves. By engaging with local ways of knowing and being and locating international norms about rights in communities, IOs give women access to empower themselves through calling on all of the local and international resources available to them. I discuss the issue of cooperation on women's rights issues in Morocco by looking at the Moroccan feminist movement as a whole and then analyzing successful modes and methods of brokerage and framing through two case studies, involving the issues of violence against women and women's nationality rights.

Understanding the nature of the relationship between different agents on both the local and international scale is key to finding the best solutions to the world's most pressing problems. Here Tarrow and McAdams' work on scale shift and brokerage is key to understanding the different methods, levels and directions of engagement on women's rights (2005). By looking at the different ways in which movements become transnational and broker the transmission of those transnational ideas and tactics back to the local level we can better understand the most productive ways for IOs to engage with the "local". The actual existence of the local as a separate entity from the global is doubtful. Rather, the local and the global are always mixing and informing each other (Pieterse 2003). This is how references to the local should be understood, as a dynamic and heterogeneous part of global dynamics. Islam is often located as the primary barrier to progress which as a narrative frame is both inaccurate and counter strategic. As Brysk highlights, the narrative and frames of human rights struggles are key for garnering attention, galvanizing action, and mobilizing support at the global level (2002, 2013). Just like narrative and frames are key at global and transnational levels, they are also key at the local and national levels, as shown in the case of violence against women.

Sally Engle Merry discusses this issue in terms of how transnational ideas about human rights are transmitted to local social settings, which frames Islam as a lens through which human rights must be translated (2006). Under this framework, Islam is still presented as an obstacle to local understanding of universal principles of human rights. Though the approach of translating human rights through a local frame is an undoubted improvement from outright rejecting the compatibility of Islam and human rights, it still places the source of human rights as coming from the outside. This creates problems in particular in post-colonial Islamic societies, where Islam can be a way to reclaim postcolonial identity. By locating the source of human rights in the West and to be translated through Islam, human rights organizations still fall into the trap of being seen as trying to reassign and reproduce Western imperialism and colonial control, whether or not this is actually the case. Such a frame also leaves out the deep and rich history Islam has as a religion that protects human rights, as discussed in the following section.

Human rights approaches to violence against women are not only a transnational phenomena. The location and the source of human rights as part of the local community and culture is a framing issue that is absolutely key to the success of women's rights movements, especially in postcolonial Islamic contexts. In terms of social movements, frames are not the ideas put forth by activists. Instead, frames are the packaging strategies used by activists to garner support and demobilize their opposition (Snow and Bedford 1988). Snow argues that in order for movements to have success, they must have resonance with local cultures and contexts. The higher the level of resonance, the greater the possibility of success (Snow 2004; Snow et al. 1986). Merry argues that "this is precisely the problem human rights activist confront: If they present human rights as compatible with existing ways of thinking, these ideas will not induce change. It is only their capacity to challenge existing power relations that offers a radical possibilities" (Merry 2006, 41). However, existing ways of thinking are not always content with existing power relations. The possibility for radical change that challenges power relations does persist within existing ways of thinking and including these perspectives is key to success, as shown in the case of violence against women and the nationality campaign.

ISLAM AND WOMEN'S RIGHTS

In the past, many IOs treated Islam as fundamentally opposed to women's rights. As transnational feminist Inderpal Grewal and Caren Kaplan argue, some types of global rhetoric about feminism and human rights can reproduce an Orientalist lens (2001). This Orientalist lens is a frame that views Muslim women as backward and unable to understand their oppression by their own culture. This type of rhetorical frame serves a dual purpose. First, it excuses the West, particularly Europe and the United States for any responsibility in the creation of regimes that are against women's rights. This abdication of responsibility is dangerous because it points to inaccurate identification of the root cause of women's rights problems. The older, arguably Islamophobic school of feminist thought said that women's rights and Islam were basically incompatible and thus was used to justify military interventions which began even before September 11(Abu-Lughod 2002, 2015; Ayotte and Husain 2005). The discursive practices of framing Islam as antithetical to women's rights, as part of the justification for interventions, continues to affect international women's rights discourse and practices. It is also those very interventions that led to the destruction of the secular left in many parts of the MENA and supported authoritarian regimes that created many women's rights issues including family law and lack of punishment for violence against women.

The Orientalist frame disempowers Muslim women and tells them that they cannot use the tools available to them in order to visualize and actualize their own freedom. This is the dismissal of radical potential within existing ways of thinking that puts all the power in the hands of IOs which unsurprisingly, has proved ineffective and unsustainable as shown in the following section on Moroccan feminist movements through 2004. Ignoring local knowledge and customs about problems, as the case studies of nationality rights and violence against women will show, often dooms projects, if not to failure, then to be far less effective than they might be.

Some human rights researchers and activists claim that the West invented the idea of human rights during the Enlightenment. However, there is a long period of development of doctrines about rights and how people were to be treated that was the product of contact between Europe and the Islamic empire and was not the product of lofty Western ideals about the rights of man, as in the historic relationship between Spain and Morocco. At least some ideas about human rights are not only compatible with Islam, but Islam itself contributed to the establishment and promotion of these human rights (Alarcon and Moallem 1999; Moallem 2005; Moghissi 1999). For hundreds of years, Jews, Muslims, and other minorities fled to Europe to live in peace among the much more accepting empires of Anatolia, and MENA (Lewis 2014; Lowney 2006). There were long periods of time when women enjoyed more rights and freedoms under Islamic empires than their contemporary counterparts in Christian empires in Europe (Rapoport 2005; Ali 2010; Musallam 1986). Scholar of Islam and feminism, Goodwin writes "Islam, in fact, maybe the only religion that formally specified women's rights and sought ways to protect them . . .. How is it then, that Islam the only religion to outline formally the protection of women's rights, is also the faith most perceived to oppressed women?" (2006). Other scholars have shown how the Qu'ran can be interpreted as a feminist tool and has been used as one in the past (Barlas 2002; Sullivan 1999; Hassan 2002). Fatima Mernissi, a famous Moroccan activist and scholar wrote, that in addition to Westerners promoting the idea that Islam is antithetical to women's rights, some Muslim men also use this rhetoric to maintain their positions of power and keep Muslim women oppressed (1991). Here we can see this process come full circle, whereby those who are trying to promote rights for women in Muslim societies, by claiming that their religion is antithetical to their rights actually reinforce oppressive power structures that keep rights away from women. As Lila Abu-Lughod explains, it is also a serious strategic mistake to frame Islam as only anti-feminist because:

> those many people within Muslim countries who are trying to find alternatives to present injustices, those who might want to refuse the divide and take from different histories and cultures, who do not accept that being feminist means being Western, will be under pressure to choose . . . Are you with us or against us?
>
> (2002, 788)

In order to make long-lasting progress on women's rights in Islamic societies it is absolutely key to turn away from anti-Islamic rhetoric and find new frames through which a diverse range of women can find the tools for their own liberation within their own religion and their society.

MOROCCAN FEMINIST MOVEMENTS THROUGH 2004

Morocco is a country with a long and varied history, deeply marked by colonization. From Islamic empires, to the Spanish, to the French, each different regime has changed the cultural, political, and economic landscape of Morocco. Many of these colonial legacies endure today, still visible in Moroccan society. This created a very diverse environment with differing concepts of religion, land, identity, community, and gender norms, just to name a few. Thomas Risse argues that we cannot "even describe the properties of social agents without reference to the structure in which they are embedded" (2007, 130). This is why it is important to understand not only the current societal structure of Morocco but the history behind that structure. Within this history, there are many stories of both success and failure. The key is understanding the reasons behind these outcomes.

Cooperation between IOs and the modern feminist movement in Morocco began with the United Nations (UN) Decade for Women, which took place from 1976 to 1985. The UN decade for women promoted and legitimized women's movements all over the world (Tinker and Jaquette 1987). Part of the UN Decade for Women was a series of conferences at which NGOs were able to participate. For the NGOs participating in feminist movements in Morocco, the main focus was on the secularization of *mudawwana*, or customary family law (Salime 2011). These laws did a great deal to entrench inequality and made it difficult to prosecute the mistreatment of women. Women were also unable to escape domestic violence because divorce was difficult for women while it was easy for men (Hajjar 2004). Part of what the United Nations sought to do during the decade for women was to eliminate, "discriminatory customs and traditions" (Zinsser 2002). This frame shaped the development of the modern feminist movement in Morocco. However, it was also perceived as an attack on women who wish to live a traditional Islamic lifestyle and did not feel included in the feminist movement against *mudawwana*. This issue of framing and exclusion would prove to be a persistent problem.

The feminist movement was closely associated with the UN and UN regimes of human rights because of the 1 Million Signature Campaign. The 1 Million Signature Campaign was a 1992 movement in Morocco, led by the Union of Women's Action and sponsored by the World Bank, that asked the Moroccan government to sign on to the Convention on the Elimination of all Forms of Discrimination Against Women (CEDAW) and make changes to the law to be consistent (Maddy-Weitzman 2005). In spite of the quick success of the 1 Million Signature Campaign which met its goal in only three months and the fact that Morocco did become a signatory and party to CEDAW in 1993, only cosmetic changes were made to the Moroccan law (Salime 2011). This led to increasing unrest on the part of women activists and increasing concern on the part of IOs that the situation of women in Morocco was not improving. Women's movements in Morocco continued to be allied with representatives of the World Bank and in 1999, together they drafted a new comprehensive plan to make women a part of the process of development. This plan specifically mentioned marriage law (Maddy-Weitzman 2005). It was based on an action plan that had been drawn up at the Beijing conference on women, convened by the UN in 1995 (Slater 2007).

Though NGOs were not included in the original drafting of the plan, the World Bank was able to, to a certain extent, act as a mediator for encouraging NGO participation. As a mediator, the World Bank also had a role in framing the issues of women's rights. Because World Bank money for development projects to reduce poverty among women hinged on the cooperation of NGOs, the government was forced to include some NGOs. The Beijing conference provided an opportunity for women to voice their concerns and a structure in which activity could take place. One of these structures was Collective 95 for Equality in the Maghreb. This was an alliance of women's organizations and researchers from Algeria, Morocco, and Tunisia. This organization produced a set of documents called "100 steps, 100 provisions", which laid out a framework for the improvement of women's rights. This proposed framework was met mostly with silent opposition from the government of Morocco (Afkhami 1997). This is why it was historic that the World Bank acted to bring the government into conversation with NGOs and women's groups. However, it may have been precisely the methods of engagement and framing of the World Bank that led to the failure to pass significant reforms because of resistance from Islamist women's movements.

The feminist movement in Morocco captured the attention of the entire world when in the year 2000, half a million women and supporting protesters took to the streets of Rabat, Morocco to again demand an end to discriminatory customary family law. This was something that had long been promised to the women of Morocco but reforms were coming very slowly. However, at the same time that this women's movement displayed a powerful show of strength, the Islamist movement displayed an equally powerful show in a counter protest movement that took place in Casablanca Morocco (Salime 2011). This movement was not only composed of Islamists but also had a great deal of anti-imperialist sentiments which reframed the debate. Some of the slogans included: "Our march emerged from the people's will; their march derives from the West's will"; their march is international, ours is national; . . . they are funded by the World Bank, we are self-funded"; . . . they represent their sponsors, we represent our people." (Salime 2011, 76–77).

These slogans make it clear that these protests were not a simple story of Islam versus feminism. Instead, these were protests about many issues and the package in which the issues were presented was central, especially the framing of perceived interference of outsiders in Moroccan society. Particularly interesting are the attacks directed at the international nature of the feminist protests. This fight quickly became framed by Islamists as a fight for the soul of the country of Morocco. Female protesters were prominently featured in the protest march and in mobilizing and writing about protests. Some of these women saw their Islamist March as simply a different way of promoting women's rights. One of the leading Islamist women's organizations framed their project as "an integral part of a global mobilization to end poverty and violence against women" (Salime 2011, 79). This seems at odds with slogans quoted above which display an anti-international sentiment. The statements of the Islamist women's organization and similar statements by many other organizations proves that there was a desire by these organizations to be engaged on an international level. The problem is that they were not engaged and their participation was not asked for by organizations such as the World Bank and the UN. The frame under which IOs engaged with Moroccan organizations was narrow and restrictive. This led to the feeling of disenfranchisement, and the counter protest that, at least in part, halted any serious change to domestic law.

In 2004, King Mohammed VI introduced the new Code of the Family to Moroccan Parliament. He framed this reform as being inspired by sharia law, even though it closely coincided with the liberal feminist demands of only a few years earlier. This victory for Moroccan feminists needs to be understood in the context of the War on Terror. The King was attempting to align himself with the United States as a moderate Islamic country that could help the United States. Islamic parties in Morocco were particularly weak at the time because of lack of public support due to the 2003 Casablanca bombings. Though this was undoubtedly a victory for Moroccan feminists that they contributed to and helped to bring about through their protests in the 1990s and 2000s, the law was not passed because of an immediate demand from civil society but rather because women's rights had become a geopolitically convenient cause (Salime

2011). This was especially true for the King, who was able to cement his power as a moderate leader of an Islamic country ready to become an ally for the United States. Other scholars have framed this law differently, as the victory of liberal feminists against Islamists (Sadiqi and Ennaji 2006). However, this ignores the fact that the reforms passed in 2004 were framed as based in sharia law and were endorsed by the Islamist party, al-'Adala wa-l-tanmia in Morocco. While women's rights were advanced in 2004, a much more successful and earlier version of this change would have been possible if IOs had engaged the Moroccan feminist movement differently. The problem is that they did not engage with a diverse array of organizations and only engaged with organizations that were most closely aligned with their frames of women's rights and development. What ends could be achieved much earlier if IOs were engaged with and supportive of a broad spectrum of frames and feminist organizations? For the answer, we will examine two cases of change for women in Morocco.

THE CASE OF VIOLENCE AGAINST WOMEN AND AMINA AL FILALI

The suicide of a 16-year-old girl, Amina al-Filali, who had been forced to marry her rapist, sparked protests that gained international attention in March 2012. According to reports from people in her village and from the victim's family, Amina was dragged into the woods at knife point and held there for 10 days while her attacker raped her. An agreement was reached under Article 475 of the Moroccan Penal Code for the victim and her attacker to be married. Unlike what the Western media portrayed in its reporting of this case, the Moroccan Penal Code did not have its roots in only Islamic law but was actually largely based on the French colonial law (Slymovics 2003). Seven months after she was forced to marry her rapist, Amina committed suicide by swallowing rat poison and asking her husband to walk her out into the streets of the village where she then collapsed and later died. Amina's case came a little over a year after another suicide by a young Moroccan woman, Fouda Laroui, a young mother who set herself on fire to protest being denied government services due to her status as a single mother. It was in this context and the context of the Arab revolutions that Moroccan women protested.

In these protests, women from all walks of life took to the streets to demand change. This time protests were not falsely separated between Islamic feminist and liberal feminist; instead they were united in advocating for women. Salime argues it is not as simple as separating Islamist feminist groups and liberal feminist groups, "these binaries were too reductive, eluding complex connections, interactions, and exchanges among movements." (2011, xxv). Amina's death united Moroccan women from all fronts because the conflict, at least within Morocco, was not framed in terms of Islamic versus Western values. Instead it was framed in terms of an unfair law which allowed a deep miscarriage of justice that brought about the end of the young woman's life. Moroccan feminist activist and professor, Louba Hanna Skalli (2012), described the situation:

> Demonstrations and sit-ins in other cities around the country brought together the mothers/founders of the Moroccan women's movements and the daughters of the movements. It united those who normally resent gender equality and those who fight for them, those who wear the label feminism as a badge of honor and those who shy away from it.

Here, the construction of a narrative was key. Amina's story was told in a way that was relatable to women from multiple walks of life and political perspectives. Amina was seen as a credible victim whose ultimate agency and protest was expressed through her death. Instead of an argument about family structures in Morocco, the issue was framed as a woman's right to live free from the violence of her rapist, a universal norm which people could rally around. As Brysk argues "framing and argument determine the power of the plot" (2013, 199). International media coverage did not follow the same pattern of a united attack against the power structures that cause and endorse violence against women. Many rhetorically framed the conflict as women's rights versus Islamic tradition rather than women's rights versus the patriarchal power structure. In a documentary about Amina's case called 475, Nadir Bouhmouch (2013), the director, explores the issues of media portrayal, Orientalism, and the failures of mobilization. The documentary shows both the complexities of the case and the ways in which the international media ignored the real story in favor of the trope of a Muslim girl victimized by her own society.

In the end, Moroccan women were successful in taking those tools in their own hands and in January 2014, they caused Article 475 of the Moroccan Penal Code to be repealed. Rapists in Morocco can no longer escape prosecution by marrying their victims. This is the story of the success of grassroots organizing by women with disparate backgrounds and different perspectives on women's rights, Islam, feminism, and civil society. This does not mean that IOs should back off entirely. Rather than IOs determining the frame through which women's rights campaigns are presented, this should come from grassroots activists as sources. Amina's case and the subsequent success of the campaign to repeal Article 475 shows existing ways are able to provide frames for change. In this case, appeals were made to existing beliefs about women's rights to live a life free from violence. Instead of focusing on the patriarchal nature of Islamic law, the issue was the miscarriage of justice. This was the frame through which Amina's case was presented and led to the success of the campaign. The point is that, unlike the earlier protests, these women were not divided by liberal versus Islamic or outsider versus insider. Instead, a diverse group of women genuinely engaged together under a pluralistic frame of justice for women to create change.

THE NATIONALITY CAMPAIGN

In some parts of MENA, women do not have the right to pass down their citizenship to their children. Moghadam argues that women's choices are constrained by the "patriarchal gender contract" which places women in dependent roles (2003). By denying women access to pass down their citizenship to their family, they are denied an equal share in society. Though some feminists who come from a more Western perspective might question the heteronormative and patriarchal structure of family law itself, it is clear that denying women the right to pass their nationality down to their children is unequal treatment.

In 2001, activists and organizations from Morocco, Jordan, Bahrain, Lebanon, Egypt, and Algeria came together to form a regional campaign to fight for nationality rights. CEDAW and in particular the third UN World Conference on Women held in Nairobi in 1985 were key to the establishment of diffusion through regional and transnational linkages. There was a proliferation of a variety of women's organizations across MENA in the 1990s which connected women's rights and civil society at both the national and regional levels (Moghadam 2003). These were the previously existing connections that organization relied on in the relational diffusion of the women's nationality campaign (Ayoub 2016). Rather than imposing a universal strategy, each country was able to adapt tactics and strategies of engagement that fit their own circumstances (Nanzeen and Maheen 2014). In some cases, it was more strategic for organizations to confront religious norms and take a secular stance. In other cases, it was more strategic to build a consensus that included Islamic discourses (Moghadam 2003). The key here for the success of Moroccan women's organizations like the Association Democratique des Femmes du Maroc (ADFM) was the flexibility of strategy within the frame of transnational coalition building. This campaign is an example of what del la Porta and Tarrow called "transnational collective action". There are two different tracks to scale shift or transition a local collective movement to a transnational scale, relational diffusion which uses a previously existing connection, and brokerage which establishes new linkages. Both paths begin with local action and end with emulation and coordinated action.

What the Moroccan case shows is a bidirectional path to scale shifting. Just as the scale shift occurs from the transnational to the local, the shift also occurred from the transnational back to the local (Della Porta and Tarrow 2005). There was a combination of emulation and reorientation by women's groups in this regional alliance. For example, the members of the nationality campaign came up with the slogan "my nationality, a right for me and my family" that could be applied to all countries (Nanzeen and Maheen 2014). However, this still allowed for flexibility to devolve the brokerage process to the national level. As a result, the nationality campaign gained a broad spectrum of support from the left and right in Morocco, including the Islamist Justice and Development Party. In spite of this broad support, there were many delays in passing the law. Once again, Moroccan activists made the strategic decision to bring attention back to this issue as Morocco became eligible for membership in the newly created UN Council for Human Rights. They shifted their strategy to focus only on women's ability to pass down their citizenship to their children and discarded the issue of spousal citizenship. This led to the successful reform of Article 6 of the Mudawanna in February of 2007 (Nanzeen and Sultan 2014). Once again, flexibility and transnational linkages were key to the success of this strategy.

CONCLUSION

The lessons from the women's rights movement in Morocco can be understood in terms of the opportunities for IOs to improve their methods of engagement offered by brokerage and framing. The problematics of engagement by IOs in Morocco are not new and have their roots in colonialism, post-colonial struggles, the Cold War, the War on Terror, and Orientalism itself. This is a history that must be recognized and reconciled. The point is not to belittle the genuine progress that has been made or delegitimize the good work that has been done by IOs in terms of women's rights in Morocco. Instead the goal is to hold IOs to a higher standard and seize the opportunity presented by this crisis to move forward in a more effective way. Instead of engaging just with a narrow group of feminist organizations, IOs must engage with women's rights activists and other women's organizations across the spectrum including Islamic feminist organizations and non-traditional women's networks. The rhetoric surrounding Islam, women, and human rights must also improve and evolve from a framework of opposition and translation to one that empowers women to use the tools at their disposal for their own liberation within their own societies. There must be a recognition of the radical potential for the impetus for change from within existing knowledge and a prioritization of grassroots frames. This is important not just in Morocco, but across North Africa and the Middle East, as human rights and in particular women's rights, are threatened by extremist terrorism, neo-colonialism, and the struggles of globalization. The strategy of IO's partnering with women to makes changes in their own societies, their own cultures, their own religions, and their own traditions, through brokerage, framing and participation is not just important in terms of women's rights but is key in the fight against Islamic extremism and oppressive structures everywhere.

REFERENCES

Abu–Lughod, Lila. "Do Muslim women really need saving? Anthropological reflections on cultural relativism and its others." *American anthropologist* 104, no. 3 (2002): 783–90.

Abu-Lughod, Lila. *Do Muslim women need saving?* Cambridge: Harvard University Press, 2015.

Alarcon, Norma, and Minoo Moallem. *Between woman and nation: Nationalisms, transnational feminisms, and the state*. Duke University Press, 1999.

Ali, Kecia. *Marriage and slavery in early Islam*. Harvard University Press, 2010.

Afkhami, Mahnaz. *Muslim women and the politics of participation: Implementing the Beijing platfor*m. Syracuse University Press, 1997.

Ayotte, Kevin J., and Mary E. Husain. "Securing Afghan women: Neocolonialism, epistemic violence, and the rhetoric of the veil." *NWSA journal* 17, no. 3 (2005): 112–33.

Ayoub, Phillip M. *When States Come Out*. Cambridge University Press, 2016.

Barlas, Asma. *"Believing Women" in Islam: Unreading Patriarchal Interpretations of the Qur'an*. University of Texas Press, 2002.

Bouhmouch, Nadir. *475*. February 18, 2013

Brysk, Alison. *Globalization and human rights*. University of California Press, 2002.

Brysk, Alison. *Speaking rights to power: Constructing political will*. Oxford University Press, 2013.

Della Porta, Donatella, and Sidney G. Tarrow. *Transnational protest and global activism*. Rowman & Littlefield, 2005.

Engle Merry, Sally. "Transnational Human Rights and Local Activism: Mapping the Middle," *American Anthropologist* 108, no.1 (2006): 38–51. doi: 10.1525/aa.2006.108.1.38.

Goodwin, Jan. *Price of honor: Muslim women lift the veil of silence on the Islamic world*. Penguin, 2002.

Grewal, Inderpal, and Caren Kaplan, eds. *Scattered hegemonies: Postmodernity and transnational feminist practices*. University of Minnesota Press, 1994.

Hajjar, Lisa. "Religion, state power, and domestic violence in Muslim societies: A framework for comparative analysis." *Law and Social Inquiry* 29, no.1 (2004): 1–38.

Hassan, Riffat. "Are Human Rights Compatible with Islam?" *The issue of the rights of women In Muslim communities*. Retrieved November 25 (2002).
Lewis, Bernard. *The Jews of Islam*. Princeton University Press, 2014.
Lowney, Chris. *A vanished world: Muslims, Christians, and Jews in medieval Spain*. Oxford University Press, USA, 2006.
Maddy-Weitzman, Bruce. "Women, Islam, and the Moroccan state: The struggle over the personal status law." *The Middle East Journal* 59, no.3 (2005): 393–410.
Mernissi, Fatima. *Women and Islam: An historical and theological inquiry*. South Asia Books, 1991.
Merry, Sally Engle. "Transnational human rights and local activism: Mapping the middle." *American anthropologist* 108, no.1 (2006): 38–51.
Moallem, Minoo. *Between warrior brother and veiled sister: Islamic fundamentalism and the politics of patriarchy in Iran*. University of California Press, 2005.
Moghadam, Valentine M. "Engendering citizenship, feminizing civil society: The case of the Middle East and North Africa." *Women and Politics* 25, no. 1–2 (2003): 63–87.
Moghissi, Hiadeh. *Feminism and Islamic fundamentalism: The limits of postmodern analysis*. Zed Books, 1999.
Musallam, Basim F. "Sex and society in Islam: Birth control before the nineteenth century." (1986).
Nazneen, Sohela, and Maheen Sultan, eds. *Voicing demands: Feminist activism in transitional contexts*. Zed Books, 2014.
Pieterse, Jan Nederveen. "Hyperpower exceptionalism: globalization the American way." *Global America* (2003): 67–94.
Pieterse, Jan Nederveen. *Globalization and culture: Global mélange*. Rowman & Littlefield, 2015.
Rapoport, Yossef. *Marriage, money and divorce in medieval Islamic society*. Cambridge University Press, 2005.
Risse, Thomas. "Social constructivism meets globalization." *Globalization theory. approaches and controversies* (2007): 126–47.
Sadiqi, Fatima, and Moha Ennaji. "The feminization of public space: Women's activism, the family law, and social change in Morocco." *Journal of Middle East women's studies* 2, no.2 (2006): 86–114.
Salime, Zakia. *Between feminism and Islam: Human rights and Sharia law in Morocco*. Vol. 36. University of Minnesota Press, 2011.
Skalli, Loubna Hanna. "Young women demanding justice and dignity: By all means necessary," *Jadaliyya*, March 29, 2012. http://www.jadaliyya.com/pages/index/4854/young-women-demanding-justice-and-dignity_by-all-m.
Slater, James N. *Civil society and political change in Morocco*. Routledge, 2007.
Slyomovics, Susan. "No buying off the past: Moroccan indemnities and the opposition." *Middle East Report* 229 (2003): 34–7.
Snow, David A. "Framing processes, ideology, and discursive fields." *The Blackwell companion to social movements* (2004): 380–412.
Snow, David A., and Robert D. Benford. "Ideology, frame resonance, and participant mobilization." *International social movement research* 1, no. 1 (1988): 197–217.
Snow, David A., E. Burke Rochford Jr, Steven K. Worden, and Robert D. Benford. "Frame alignment processes, micromobilization, and movement participation." *American sociological review* (1986): 464–81.
Tarrow, Sidney, and Doug McAdam. "Scale shift in transnational contention." *Transnational protest and global activism* (2005): 121–50.

Tinker, Irene, and Jane Jaquette. "UN decade for women: Its impact and legacy." *World development* 15, no.3 (1987): 419–27.
Zinsser, Judith P. "From Mexico to Copenhagen to Nairobi: The United Nations Decade for Women, 1975-1985." *Journal of world history* 13, no.1 (2002): 139–68.

17. Contesting the citizenship gap: advocacy, core rights, and women's rights reform

Feryal M. Cherif

Despite notable advances in women's rights over the past century, there is a persistent citizenship gap between men and women. Women's rights continue to lag in nearly every country. In 2016, women held only 22.8% of seats in national legislatures and approximately 10% of executive political positions globally (Inter-Parliamentary Union 2016). Inequality in the workforce persists in terms of pay, rank, and even basic numbers. Only 50% of working-aged women participate in the labor force compared to 77% of men (United Nations 2015). Women are economically dependent on their spouses or kin in many countries and often lack access to property or credit. Nearly one-third of women report being the victims of sex-based violence at some point in their lives (United Nations 2015).

Campaigns for the advancement of women's rights often meet with resistance in the name of religion and nationalism (Kandiyoti 2001; Winter 2006). Hard-fought victories may trigger backlashes (e.g., abortion reform), and rights may be undermined by persistent challenges (e.g., the Mexico City Policy). Counter-mobilization efforts, whether misappropriating or manipulating these ideologies, often frame their actions as defending a nation's or religion's true values.

Despite barriers changes in women's de jure and de facto status suggest that rights are improving, albeit in some places more so than others. Since the Fourth World Conference on Women (1995), the proportion of women legislators has doubled (Inter-Parliamentary Union 2016). In 20% of countries, however, women hold only 10% of legislative seats (United Nations 2015). Similarly, while abortion laws have liberalized, the right to choose is largely restricted to the Global North (Ramirez and McEneaney 1997). Advances, specifically the variation across states, begs a fundamental question: how, where, and why is the citizenship gap narrowing?

In what follows, I argue that, along with international norms and advocacy-based mechanisms, investments in core rights, education and labor force participation, further women's status by fostering empowerment tools and greater political representation. In the subsequent section, I discuss how women's rights advocacy is believed to contest barriers to gender equality and explain how core rights facilitate advances in other rights. Next, I examine how well these frameworks account for why the citizenship gap is narrowing by examining their main intuitions across four issue areas. The empirical analyses suggest that women's rights appear to be improving in places that invest in women's rights advocacy and the education of girls, and to a lesser extent, where women are better integrated into the workforce.

ADVANCES IN WOMEN'S RIGHTS: ADVOCACY AND CORE RIGHTS

How, where, and why do women's rights advance? To answer this question, most scholars and practitioners emphasize the importance of international institutions, norms, and women's rights activists. These advocacy-based accounts reason that activism can spur normative and behavioral changes through persuasion, accountability politics, and the power of principled ideas or norms (Haglund and Aggarwal 2011; Keck and Sikkink 1998). A more recent literature suggests that, along with advocacy-based mechanisms, women's rights advance with investments in core rights, as they facilitate normative changes and the development of stronger political interests. Core rights-based explanations emphasize the individual and collective goods that develop from fostering women's education and participation in the labor market.

Women's rights advocacy is thought to contest gender discrimination by educating leaders and pressuring them to reform. Activists engage in norms-development by bringing attention to new issues and expediting their recognition. They facilitate reform by consciousness raising, mobilizing support, and highlighting inappropriate behavior (Keck and Sikkink 1998). Through information sharing and framing, they seek to persuade governments to adopt new standards and reform (Haglund and Aggarwal 2011). If these tactics fail or progress stalls, advocates may expose the "wrong" practices of states and shame them for failing to adhere to accepted standards. Though material incentives or sanctions may occasionally be available, advocacy overwhelming relies on soft power, specifically the power of persuasion. Accordingly, advocacy is thought to be more effective in states that are more susceptible to international pressure (e.g., those that value their reputations, or are more dependent on foreign trade and assistance) (Cardenas 2007; Franklin 2008).

Though soft power may have limits, women's rights advocacy is credited with bringing about tremendous changes in the status of gender equality worldwide. Women's groups and international institutions were instrumental in bringing about global acceptance of suffrage, family planning rights, equal pay laws, and maternity leave (Berkovitch 1999; Eager 2004; Moghadam 1999; Ramirez, Shanahan, and Soysal 1997). These actors have also increased the adoption of party and legislative quotas to enhance women's representation in political institutions (Bush 2011). Gender mainstreaming, or explicit efforts to consider the implications of policies on men and women, is now a routine practice of major international institutions.

Core rights explanations, on the other hand, emphasize the interdependence of rights. These accounts hold that the status of women's education and their integration in the labor market facilitate the acquisition of other rights. At the individual level, core rights empower women to challenge usurpations of their rights by enhancing their resources, autonomy, and leverage (Sassen 1998). Education helps women develop marketable skills that facilitate outside employment, which in turn increase their resources and provide greater leverage in the home (Iversen and Rosenbluth 2010; Agarwal 1994). Labor force participation also creates new opportunities to network outside of traditional circles (Sassen 1998). With more resources, independence, and the ability to develop networks outside of kin, women are in a stronger position to pursue and defend their rights.

Collectively, core rights facilitate political organization, enhance women's status, and spur broad attitudinal changes (Cherif 2015; Iversen and Rosenbluth 2010; Ross 2008; Sapiro 1981). Core rights encourage the development of stronger political interests or groups through two mechanisms. They encourage political consciousness and organization, while also improving the resources available for mobilization and advocacy. First, education spurs gender consciousness among women. College-educated women are more aware of inequalities and are more likely to recognize their status as the product of structural disadvantages related to sex (Gurin 1985). There is also considerable evidence that a woman's educational and employment status increases her support for feminist values (Banaszak and Leighly 1991; Banaszak and Plutzer 1993). By encouraging group identification and increasing demands for gender equality, core rights nurture the growth of formal and informal women's rights constituencies.

Second, core rights may influence the strength of political organization by stimulating interest, easing coordination, and increasing resources. Those who are better educated, for example, tend to be more politically engaged, likely to vote, and likely to participate in civic and political groups (Glaeser, Ponzetto, and Schleifer 2007). The workplace is often a site for political discussion and may become a focal point for political action (Mutz and Mondak 2006). Levels of women's educational and professional attainment also influence the quality of social capital, or resources, that activists may tap into to pressure politicians for change (Lin 2001).

Improvements in core rights may also increase political elites' interest in representing women's rights issues. Socioeconomic advances mean that women are likely to be more politically active and more valuable as a constituency. As their socioeconomic status improves, women may transform from a marginal to a more important interest that politicians are keen to represent. Though women are not monolithic and hold diverse preferences, advances in core rights privilege the growth of feminist attitudes.

Investments in core rights encourage attitudinal changes that extend beyond women, creating broader pro-feminist constituencies and environments more receptive to reform. A woman's educational and employment status, for example, is associated with greater acceptance and support for gender equality by family members, either because these activities foster new identities, there is a desire to harmonize attitudes with lifestyle, or because women's financial contributions give husbands and children a direct stake in women's rights policy (Boehnke 2011; Kroska and Elman 2009).

While advocacy and core rights-based explanations emphasize different factors, they point to a common theme. Women's rights are best advanced in environments that cultivate empowerment tools and accountability whether through advocacy-based mechanisms or the cultivation of core rights.

HOW, WHERE, AND WHY THE CITIZENSHIP GAP IS CLOSING

Despite the voluminous research on women's rights, there has been limited crossnational investigation of how, where, and why the citizenship gap is narrowing. The case study literature documents a number of successful instances of contestation and reform, and offers a rich understanding of the conditions under which activism may bring about meaningful changes. The evidence documenting more generalized success of advocacy-based processes is largely restricted to de jure rights and policy reforms or the study of women's representation in national legislatures (but see Schafer 1999; Simmons 2009; Gray, Kittilson, and Sandholtz 2006). Research that examines behavioral outcomes or a more extensive set of rights, by contrast, tends to focus more on understanding the barriers to gender equality and cultural change (Inglehart and Norris 2003). The influence of core rights on the citizenship gap has received even less attention except for explanations that discuss how socioeconomic advances strengthen women's individual agency (but see Ross 2008; Cherif 2010, 2015). In what follows, I examine two questions: first, to what extent, do women's rights advocacy and core rights narrow the citizenship gap, and second, insofar as core rights are influential, what explains the status of women's education and integration in the labor market?

EXPECTATIONS AND DATA

Independent Variables

There are two frameworks that seek to explain how, where, and why the citizenship gap is narrowing: women's rights advocacy and core rights. Advocacy-based accounts contend that women's groups and international institutions may lobby, socialize, and pressure states. Generally speaking, these explanations suggest that conformity with international norms is a function of a state's acceptance of these standards and the strength of activism within the country. Dense networks of activists, for example, may develop more extensive or intense lobbying campaigns, such that they generate more popular or governmental support around particular issues. Consistent with these explanations, *there is likely to be greater parity between the sexes and more respect for women's rights in states that recognize equality norms and are subject to stronger pressure from activists*. I draw on two measures to examine the influences of rights-based advocacy: the number of *Women's Rights Organizations* operating within a country and ratification of the Convention on the Elimination of All Forms of Discrimination against Women (CEDAW) (measured as: 0 – no ratification, 1 – ratification with reservations, 2 – ratification).[1, 2]

Core rights explanations, on the other hand, emphasize how the status of women's education and integration in the labor market encourage political organization, socioeconomic advances, and attitudinal changes in ways that increase elites' incentives to pursue women's rights reform. Strong core rights position women to challenge family and state-based violations of their rights by facilitating individual and collective empowerment, such that *in states with higher rates of female labor force participation and educational attainment, women enjoy more equitable rights overall*. I operationalize these arguments using data on the percentage of women in the *labor force* and enrolled in secondary *education* from the World Development Indicators.

Scholars have also identified several other factors that may help to explain the status of women's rights. These explanations serve as control variables. Because the barriers to advancement feature so prominently in the study of women's rights, two explanations, and the variables that represent them, are controlled for, implicitly or explicitly, when examining each of the dependent variables. Prevailing wisdom holds that Islam, its norms, institutions, or culture, lead to circumscriptions of women's rights. Mainstream interpretations of Islamic law (Shari'a), for example, are said to discriminate against women, providing only limited rights in divorce, child custody, inheritance, and to limit their political influence (Rahman 2012). Others suggest that it is not Islam but rather the lack of separation of religion and state, which explains varying rates of reform and resistance across states (Htun Weldon 2015). State recognition of religion may confer additional legitimacy to religious values and institutions, elevate the status of these norms, and give religious elites incentives to protect their spheres of influence, such that reform becomes more difficult (Htun and Weldon 2015). To capture these arguments, I include two dichotomous measures in the crossnational analyses: *Muslim majority* (which measures whether 50% or more of a state's population is Muslim) and *Established State Religion* (which measures whether there is an official state religion) (Fox 2011).[3]

There is also an extensive literature on the relationship between economic development and gender equality. Modernization arguments, for example, highlight how economic development leads to increases in industrialization, urban living, and education, all of which are correlated with more egalitarian attitudes and behavior (Inglehart and Norris 2003). Economic growth also expands the service sector, increases market wages, and encourages women to enter the labor force, which may translate to greater equality overall (Iversen and Rosenbluth 2010). Development arguments reason that as *GDP* increases women's rights and gender equality advance (GDP per capita data taken from the World Development Indicators).

Scholars increasingly recognize that not all forms of economic development are equally beneficial to women. Oil-based development, for example, may reduce opportunities for women by limiting their economic rights and political influence (Ross 2008). Oil economies discourage women from entering the labor force by weakening sectors that typically employ women, reducing female wages, and increasing household incomes (Ross 2008). As oil production increases, women's share of the labor market declines and equality suffers. To examine the influence of oil, I use a measure of oil and natural gas rents as a percentage of GDP, *Oil* (from the World Development Indicators).

Dependent Variable

To understand the impact of advocacy and core rights on the citizenship gap, I examine four dimensions of women's equality: the rate of women's labor force participation, enrollment in secondary education, appointment to cabinet-level positions, and the right to own and manage property. Two of these issue areas, education and participation in the labor market, represent the core rights framework, and in the second set of statistical analyses are outcomes to be studied, as much as explanatory variables. I examine these issue areas for three reasons.

First, each of these rights is a critical resource for women (Molyneux 1985). Labor market participation, education, and property rights speak to women's ability to build wealth, independence, and bargaining rights, while the level of women's representation in office provides a measure of political influence. The state of women's education and labor force participation also speaks to women's desire and ability to mobilize.

Second, to the extent that core rights operate as expected – that is, they encourage women to contest circumscriptions of their rights and narrow the citizenship gap – and that they are critical resources, or outcomes too, understanding what influences women's integration into the labor market and their educational attainment is especially important. Do advocacy-based mechanisms influence the strength of women's core rights? Do core rights influence each other? That is, what explains advances in these potential mechanisms of reform?

Last, I examine levels of women's representation in cabinet positions, because these are appointed rather than elected offices and governments have an opportunity to respond more directly to demands for greater inclusion by activists and international institutions.

The data on women's participation in the labor force, enrollment in secondary education, appointment to cabinet-level positions, and property rights are drawn from multiple sources. Ideally data would permit broad longitudinal research, but the study of women's rights is limited by a dearth of crossnational sources outside of legislative representation. While it is possible to obtain data on women's share of cabinet-level positions, rates of education, and labor force participation across countries over time, the best available data on women's property rights surveys only developing countries.[4] Similarly, though longitudinal education and labor force data are available, annual data can be spotty, particularly for women's share of the non-agricultural labor force. Following Ross (2008) and Rahman (2012), I use average rates of labor force participation and school enrollment over time, with longer time spans, 10-year rather than 5-year averages, reflecting the greater paucity of data.

The four dimensions of women's equality are measured accordingly:

Cabinet Members, the percentage of women holding cabinet-level positions (years: 1990–2010; sources: UN Women and the Worldwide Government Directory);

Property, the right to own and manage property.[5] An ordinal measure coded as follows: (0) Women have few or no rights, (1) Women have some property rights or some women have equitable property rights, (2) There are no distinctions between men and women's property rights (year: 2009; source: Social Institutions and Gender Index).

Education, 5-year average rate of girls' enrollment in secondary education (years: 1990–2010; source: World Bank Development Indicators);

Labor Force, 10-year average rate of female non-agricultural labor force participation (years: 1994–2003, 2004–2013; source: World Bank Development Indicators).

CONTESTING INEQUALITY: THE INFLUENCE OF ADVOCACY AND CORE RIGHTS

To what extent do women's rights advocacy and core rights contest gender inequality? What influences the status of women's core rights? To explore these questions, I construct a series of empirical tests that exploit time-series and crossnational data. The models of women's share of cabinet positions, rates of labor force participation, and enrollment in secondary education, shown in Tables 17.1 and 17.2, examine time-series cross-national data and include country-fixed effects. The use of country-fixed effects allows us to observe the influence of individual variables, such as advocacy and core rights mechanisms, above and beyond factors unique to each country (e.g., religious, cultural, or historical background). These models are unable to examine (relatively) time-invariant variables like *Muslim majority* and *established state religion*, but account for these factors implicitly through the inclusion of country-fixed effects.[6] The analysis of women's property rights, by contrast, relies on crossnational data, uses an ordinal logit model, and directly controls for these religio-cultural influences.

Table 17.1 presents the statistical analyses of women's appointment to cabinet-level positions and property rights. For convenience, the core rights and advocacy-based variables are located at the top of Table 17.1. Because the effects of advocacy and core rights take time to develop, the variables representing these explanations are lagged. Generally speaking, the analyses corroborate claims that women's rights advocacy and core rights reduce the citizenship gap. Consistent with expectations, women's

Table 17.1 The status of women in politics and property

	Cabinet Positions	Property Rights
Education $_{t-5}$	0.12***	0.05***
	(0.04)	(0.01)
Labor Force $_{t-5}$	0.62***	0.04
	(0.23)	(0.04)
CEDAW $_{t-5}$	2.29**	1.47**
	(0.90)	(0.68)
Women's Rights Orgs. $_{t-10\ (logged)}$	2.06*	0.94**
	(1.08)	(0.44)
Oil	0.06	−0.03
	(0.19)	(0.03)
GDP per capita $_{t-5\ (logged)}$	4.33*	0.17
	(2.37)	(0.32)
Muslim Majority		0.36
		(0.83)
Est. State Religion		1.31
		(0.91)
Fixed Effects	Country	
Lagged Dep. Variable	Yes	No
Countries	All	Developing
Years	1990–2010	2009
No. of Obs.	491	87
R-Sq.	0.35	

Notes: Standard errors in parentheses: * $p < 0.10$, ** $p < 0.05$, *** $p < 0.01$.

right advocacy is associated with stronger political and property rights. The results also highlight the importance of core rights, particularly education. Across models, education is a robust predictor of the status of women's rights within states. Women's integration in the labor market, while positively associated with all outcomes, only reaches conventional levels of significance in one model.

To get a better sense of the substantive influence of these mechanisms, Figure 17.1 presents the marginal effects of women's rights groups, CEDAW membership, and core rights, while holding all other variables at their mean. To approximate real-world conditions, these estimates show the marginal effect for values ranging from the 10th to 90th percentile of each variable's distribution. The first row shows the effects of core rights and advocacy-based mechanisms on the appointment women to higher political office. The steep slope of the estimates of education and labor force participation

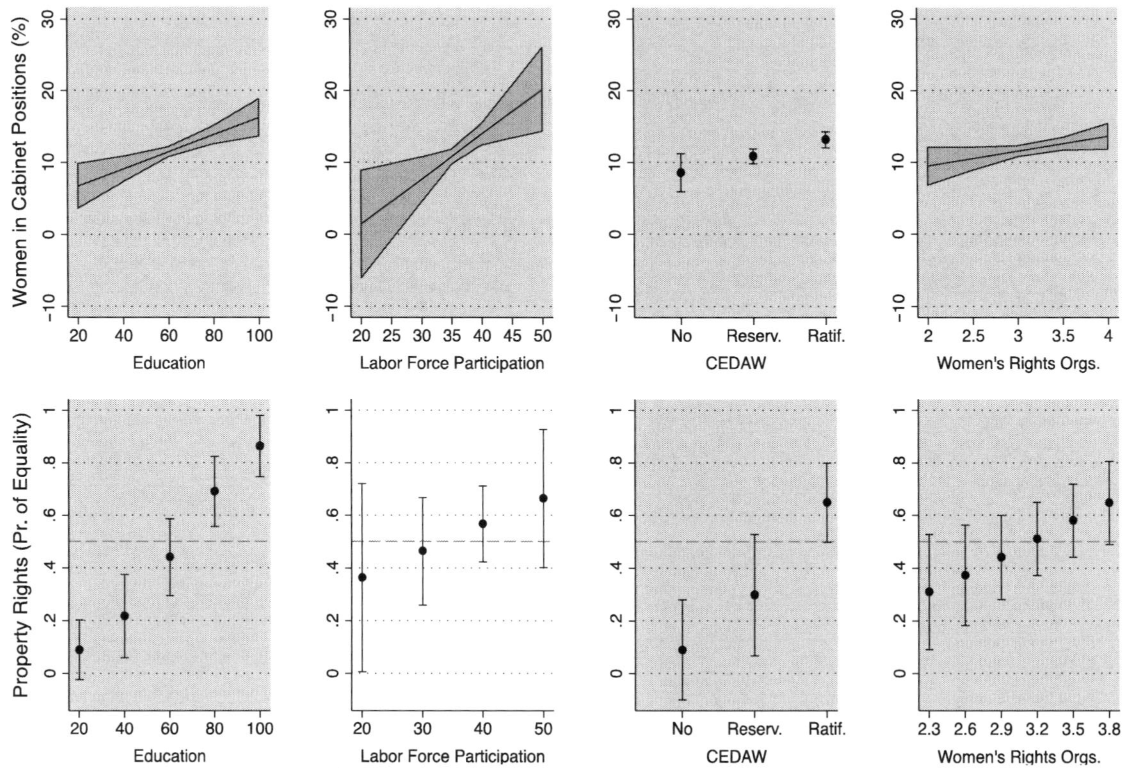

Note: The figures are based on regression analyses presented in Table 17.1. The gray background highlights results that are statistically significant at the 0.10 level or higher.

Figure 17.1 The influence of advocacy-based and core rights-based mechanisms on women's rights

suggest that the status of core rights strongly influences women's ability to reach higher political office. As education increases from its lowest to highest rates, women's appointment to cabinet positions grows from about 6.5% to 16%. When women constitute half of the workforce, their representation increases from its lowest levels, around 1%, to over 20%.

Advocacy-based mechanisms have a consistently positive effect on levels of women's representation, but their substantive influence is more modest than that of core rights. There is about a 4-point difference in the rates of women's appointment to cabinet seats in countries with the weakest compared to densest networks of women's groups. Similarly, the leaders of states that ratify CEDAW appear more likely to appoint women to public office. Women's share of cabinet positions is around 13% in ratifying states, 11% in countries that place reservations to CEDAW, and 9% in those that have yet to ratify or adopt the convention. In other words, these figures suggest that the citizenship gap is narrowing more quickly within states that recognize the validity of international norms, even those that have yet to fully embrace gender equality.

The second row in Figure 17.1 illustrates the effects of core rights – and advocacy-based mechanisms on the (predicted) probability that women hold equal rights to men with respect to the ownership and management of property. Here, the state of women's education, CEDAW membership, and women's groups appear to play the most influential roles in reducing inequities between men and women. The probability of discrimination declines by nearly 80 points as women's education increases from the lowest to highest levels in the sample. A state's acceptance of international norms has a comparably large effect. The probability that women possess equal property rights is a mere 0.09 in non-ratifiers, but it jumps to 0.65 in states that more fully accept the treaty's normative commitments. The strength of activism also increases the probability of equality between the sexes. As the number of women's groups increase from the lowest to highest numbers in the sample, the probability of discrimination in property law decreases by 0.34. Finally, the figures also suggest that women's incorporation into the labor force may have sizable effects on women's property rights, but there is greater variation around these estimates.

Overall, the analyses imply that while both the status of core rights and women's rights advocacy appear to be influential in closing the citizenship gap, the relative importance of these factors depends on the issue area examined. While international norms and activism have more modest influences on women's appointment to higher office, these mechanisms are associated with significant improvements in women's property rights. By contrast, there appear to be substantial gains in political equality as women become more integrated into the labor market, but the influence of this factor on property rights is far weaker. Only the status of girls' education is associated with large substantive effects across rights.

Because, in addition to their impact on women's rights, core rights are also outcomes, or ways that we assess the state of gender equality, I develop additional tests to examine what influences rates of women's education and labor force participation.[7] I draw on the explanations used to inform the first set of analyses and the variables that represent them with three theoretical additions. First, while many scholars argue that development improves women's rights, some suggest that there is a U-shaped, rather than a linear, relationship between development and labor force participation.[8] Though scholars disagree whether it is due to physical demands or discriminatory social norms, women often confront higher barriers to entering the labor force at early to middle stages of development (Goldin 1995; Iversen and Rosenbluth 2010). Second, democracies are thought to invest more in public goods, such as education (Bueno de Mesquita et al. 2004). To account for these arguments, I include measures of GDP^2 per capita (in the model of labor force participation) and *Democracy*.[9]

Third, core rights may influence each other. There are strong theoretical reasons to believe that the status of women's education affects rates of labor force participation. As education increases, there is greater demand from women to enter the workforce, owing to changes in attitudes and increases in wages associated with higher human capital (Agarwal 1994). There is also a larger supply of women with more marketable skills, such that they are more attractive to prospective employers and labor force participation should increase as the levels of female education rise (Iversen and Rosenbluth 2010).

Table 17.2 presents the regression analyses of the rates of girls' secondary education enrollment and women's participation in the labor force. These analyses permit exploration of three themes: the broader factors that affect core rights, the influence of women's rights advocacy on core rights, and the relationship between core rights. These analyses suggest that the status of women's core rights is a product of the level of economic and educational development within a society, and to a lesser degree, women's rights activism. Consistent with earlier research, economic development strongly influences the status of women's core rights. As GDP increases, states tend to invest more in education and enrollment rates rise. There is also evidence of a U-shaped relationship between development and labor force participation. Women tend to participate in the labor force more at lower and higher levels of development, but are often discouraged from participation before a state fully transitions to a post-industrial economy.

The state of women's education also appears to influence the degree to which women are integrated into the labor market. There is greater parity

Table 17.2 The determinants of women's core rights

	Education	Labor Force
Education		0.06*
		(0.03)
CEDAW $_{t-5}$	−0.90	2.15
	(0.99)	(2.35)
Women's Rights Orgs. $_{t-10\ (logged)}$	3.23**	0.61
	(1.36)	(0.86)
GDP per capita $_{(logged)}$	5.19*	−16.51
	(2.64)	(10.46)
GDP^2 per capita $_{(logged)}$		1.04*
		(0.61)
Oil	0.02	0.12
	(0.19)	(0.12)
Democracy	0.16	0.28
	(0.20)	(0.18)
Fixed Effects	Country	Country
Lagged Dep. Variable	Yes	No
Countries	All	All
Years	1990–2010	2003, 2013
No. of Obs.	406	196
R-Sq.	0.60	0.22

Notes: Standard errors in parentheses: * $p < 0.10$, ** $p < 0.05$, *** $p < 0.01$.

in the labor market in states that invest more and promote the education of girls. Similarly, the strength of women's groups is associated with higher levels of girls' education. In other areas, advocacy-based mechanisms appear to play a more limited role. Women's groups appear less effectual in facilitating women's entrance to the labor market, and there is no evidence that international treaties affect the development of core rights.

To facilitate a comparison of the substantive influence of advocacy- and core rights-based mechanisms, Figure 17.2 presents the marginal effects of women's rights groups, CEDAW, and education, while holding all other variables at their mean. While the level of economic development strongly influences the cultivation of core rights within societies (not shown), the graphs presented in Figure 17.2 illustrate that activism and education play important, albeit more modest, roles as well. The first row illustrates the effects of advocacy-based mechanisms on rates of girls' enrollment in secondary education. While differences in treaty membership are small, girls' enrollment in secondary education increases from 71.5% to 78% in

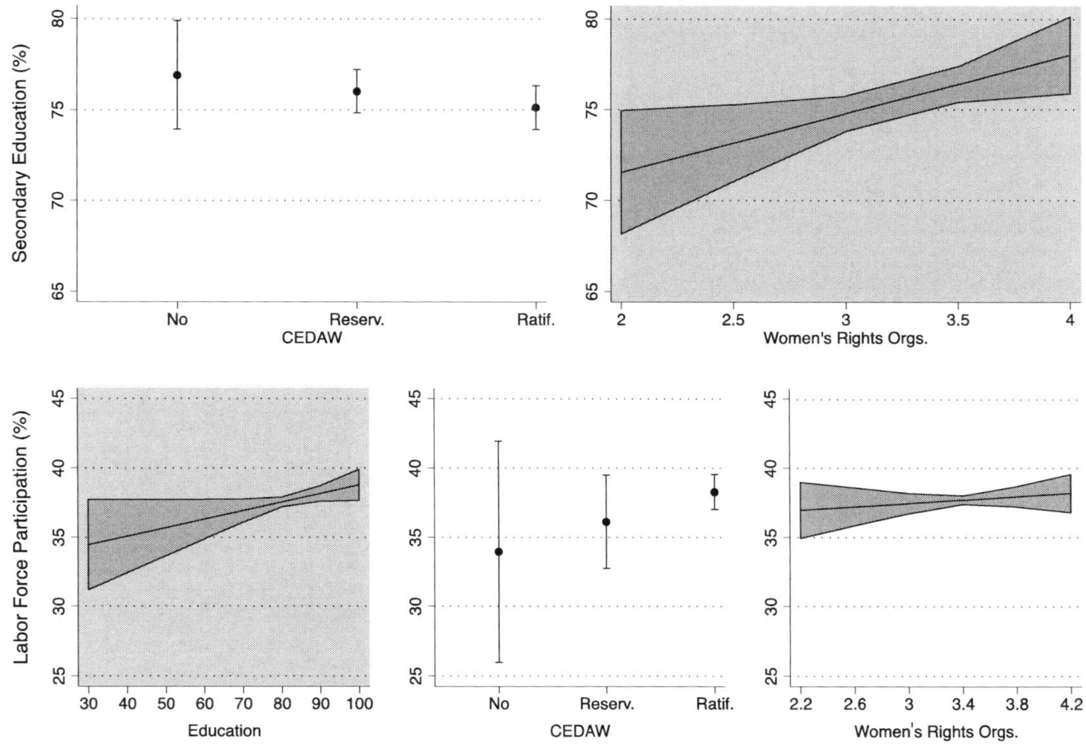

Note: The figures are based on regression analyses presented in Table 17.2. The gray background highlights results that are statistically significant at the 0.10 level or higher.

Figure 17.2 The influence of advocacy-based mechanisms and education on women's core rights

countries with strong women's rights networks. The second row of Figure 17.2 shows the effects of advocacy-based mechanisms and education on women's integration in the labor market. The level of female education has a modest influence on women's entrance to the labor market. As girls' education expands from the lowest to highest enrollment rates, women's share of the labor market grows by 4.5 points. Acceptance of international norms, through commitment to CEDAW, has a comparable sized effect, but there is more variation around this estimate. The last figure in row 2 shows a relatively flat slope for women's groups, suggesting that activism has little influence on rates of labor force participation.

Together, the empirical analyses offer clear policy implications about closing the citizenship gap: invest in the education of girls and women's rights advocacy, and to a lesser extent, facilitate women's integration into the labor market. More so than any other factor, education is associated with higher levels of gender equality across issues. Inasmuch as education serves as a platform for further advances in women's rights, activists appear to play an important role in developing this foundation. Along with enhancing women's equality directly, such as in politics and property, the strength of women's rights groups is associated with furthering girls' education, such that core rights- and advocacy-based mechanisms work hand in hand. Particularly, in less developed countries, where girls and women's education lags due to a lack of resources, advocacy-based mechanisms offer a promising strategy to contest discrimination.

CONCLUSION

How, where, and why is the citizenship gap closing? Inequalities between men and women appear to be narrowing in states where women have access to higher education and there are strong networks of women's right groups. Education and advocacy groups enhance women's ability to demand inclusion and reform from politicians, family members, and others who may seek to limit their rights. Countries that invest in girls' education lay the foundation for women's rights constituencies to develop, mobilize, and challenge inequities. Developing cadres of educated women appears key to furthering women's desire and ability to enter the labor market, ascend to higher office, and defend their property rights. Women's rights advocacy complements this process by cultivating critical resources and tools, such as education, and directly advancing the status of other rights.

Despite the promise of women's rights advocacy and core rights, it is important to have measured optimism about these paths to reform. While advocacy- and core rights-based processes may be powerful tools for promoting equality, they are not a panacea and do not presage a smooth transition to full citizenship for women. The very factors that encourage feminist constituencies to develop and mobilize also instigate backlash. Even when resistance to women's rights is framed in other terms, such as religion or national culture, the underlying problem is that transitions to a more egalitarian society entail a redistribution of power and resources that few stakeholders willingly cede. Indeed, while advances in women's education and increased advocacy may close the citizenship gap over time, it may create other insecurities for women in the short term (Brysk and Mehta 2017).

NOTES

1. The data on women's rights organization is coded from the Yearbook of International Organizations (courtesy of Wotipka and Ramirez (2003)).
2. It is challenging to classify states according to the number or level of reservations. Some states cite reservations to individual clauses of CEDAW articles while others make one sweeping statement about their (lack of) commitment, such that number is not a good gauge. Identifying minor reservations may be easy but parsing between substantive reservations is more difficult. Which articles are most important? How many reservations may a state have and still be classified one with a lower rate of reservations? As such, I chose an ordinal ranking wherein non-ratifiers are coded as 0, those with substantive reservations are coded as 1, and full ratifiers are coded as 2. Countries that only place a reservation on Article 29, which allows two or more state parties to refer questions of interpretation or implementation to arbitration, are coded as full ratifiers. It appears that many states register reservations to this clause, owing to a concern that it will be used for political purposes.
3. Scholars recognize that there are multiple interpretations of Islam and various ways that Muslim majority states incorporate religious norms. Further, a deeper investigation reveals that Islamic law is patriarchal in some areas but more liberal in others, like property's management (see Bishin and Cherif 2017). Controlling for the institutionalization of religion mitigates some of these issues while also comparing like states.
4. Since violations of women's property rights are more widespread among developing countries, examining the influence of advocacy- and core rights-based mechanisms provides insight into how these processes operate in less auspicious contexts.
5. The measure of property rights gauges women's ability to own and manage property. It is possible for a state to afford women full rights to manage property while also limiting what women may inherit.
6. To control for autocorrelation, I include a lagged measure of the dependent variable in the models of women's proportion of cabinet-level positions and education. Because of the small number of observations and data points, I do not include a comparable measure in the model of labor force participation.
7. Following the time averages developed for the dependent variables, in the education model, the measures of oil and GDP reflect five-year averages. In the labor force model, the variables for education, oil, and GDP reflect 10-year averages. These data are taken from the World Development Indicators.
8. Others suggest that it more closely resembles a kuznet curve, but additional tests did not evince any evidence to support this (Eastin and Prakash 2013).
9. The measure of democracy is a 21-point variable taken from the Polity project. GDP^2 is taken from the World Development Indicators.

REFERENCES

Agarwal, Bina. 1994. *A Field of One's Own: Gender and Land Rights in South Asia*. Cambridge: Cambridge University Press.

Banaszak, Lee Ann, and Jan E. Leighly. 1991. "How Employment Affects Women's Gender Attitudes: The Workplace as a Locus of Contextual Effects." *Political Geography Quarterly* 10(2): 174–85.

Banaszak, Lee Ann, and Eric Plutzer. 1993. "The Social Bases of Feminism in the European Community." *Public Opinion Quarterly* 57(1): 29–53.

Berkovitch, Nitza. 1999. *From Motherhood to Citizenship: Women's Rights and International Organizations*. Baltimore, MD: Johns Hopkins University Press.

Bishin, Benjamin G. and Feryal M. Cherif. 2017. "Women, Property Rights, and Islam." *Comparative Politics* 49(4): 501–20.

Boehnke, Mandy. 2011. "Gender Role Attitudes around the Globe: Egalitarian vs. Traditional Views." *Asian Journal of Social Science* 39(1): 57–74.

Brysk, Alison and Aashish Mehta. "When Development Is Not Enough: Structural Change, Conflict, and Gendered Insecurity." *Global Society* 31(1): 1–19.

Bueno de Mesquita, Bruce, Alastair Smith, Randolph M. Siverson, and James D. Morrow. 2003. *The Logic of Political Survival*. Cambridge: MIT Press.

Bush, Sarah Sunn. 2011. "International Politics and the Spread of Quotas for Women in Legislatures." *International Organization* 65(1): 103–37.

Cardenas, Sonia. 2007. *Conflict and Compliance: State Responses to International Human Rights Pressure*. Philadelphia: University of Pennsylvania Press.

Charrad, Mounira. 2011. "Gender in the Middle East: Islam, State, Agency." *Annual Review of Sociology* 37: 417–37.

Cherif, Feryal M. 2010. "Culture, Rights, and Norms: Woman's Rights Reform in Muslim Countries." *Journal of Politics* 72(4): 1144–60.

Cherif, Feryal M. 2015. *Myths about Women's Rights: How, Where, and Why Rights Advance*. New York: Oxford University Press.

Eager, Paige Whaley. 2004. "From Population Control to Reproductive Rights: Understanding Normative Change in Global Population Policy (1965–1994)." *Global Society* 18(2): 145–73.

Eastin, Joshua and Aseem Prakash. 2013. "Economic Development and Gender Equality: Is There a Gender Kuznet Curve?" *World Politics* 65(1): 156–86.

Fox, Jonathan. 2011. "Building Composite Measures of Religion and State." *Interdisciplinary Journal of Research on Religion* 7(8): 1–39.

Franklin, James C. 2008. "Shame on You: The Impact of Human Rights Criticism on Political Repression in Latin America." *International Studies Quarterly* 52(1): 187–211.

Glaeser, Edward L., Giacomo Ponzetto, and Andrei Schleifer. 2007. "Why Does Democracy Need Education?." *Journal of Economic Growth* 12(2): 77–99.

Goldin, Claudia. 1995. "The U-shaped Female Labor Force Function in Economic Development and Economic History." In *Investment in Women's Human Capital*, ed. T.P. Schultz, 61–90. Chicago: University of Chicago Press.

Gray, Mark M., Miki Caul Kittilson, and Wayne Sandholtz. 2006. "Women and Globalization: A Study of 180 Countries, 1975–2000." *International Organization* 60(2): 293–333.

Gurin, Patricia. 1985. "Women's Gender Consciousness." *Political Opinion Quarterly* 49(2): 143–63.

Haglund, LaDawn, and Rimjhim Aggarwal. 2011. "Test of Our Progress: The Translation of Economic and Social Rights Norms into Practice." *Journal of Human Rights* 10(4): 1–27.
Htun, Mala and Laurel Weldon. 2015. "Religious Power, the State, Women's Rights, and Family Law." *Politics and Gender* (11): 451–77.
Inglehart, Ronald, and Pippa Norris. 2003. *Rising Tide: Gender Equality and Cultural Change Around the World*. New York: Cambridge University Press.
Inter-Parliamentary Union. 2016. *Women in National Parliaments*, http://www.ipu.org/wmn-e/world.htm (Accessed December 20, 2016).
Iversen, Torben, and Frances Rosenbluth. 2010. *Women, Work, and Politics: The Political Economy of Gender Inequality*. New Haven, CT: Yale University Press.
Kandiyoti, Deniz. 2001. "The Politics of Gender and Conundrums of Citizenship." In *Women and Power in the Middle East*, ed. Suad Joseph and Susan Sylomovics, 52–60. Philadelphia: University of Pennsylvania Press.
Keck, Margaret E., and Kathryn Sikkink. 1998. *Activists Beyond Borders: Advocacy Networks in International Politics*. Ithaca, NY: Cornell University Press.
Kroska, Amy and Cheryl Elman. 2009. "Changes in Attitudes about Employed Mothers: Exposure, Interests, and Gender Ideology Discrepancies." *Social Science Research* 39(2): 366–82.
Lin, Nan. 2001. *Social Capital: A Theory of Social Structure and Action*. Cambridge: Cambridge University Press.
Moghadam, Valentine. 1999. "Gender Globalization: Female Labor and Women's Mobilization." *Journal of World Systems Research* 5(2): 367–88.
Moghadam, Valentine. 2003. *Modernizing Women: Gender and Social Change in the Middle East*. 2nd edition. Boulder, CO: Westview.
Molyneux, Maxine. 1985. "Mobilization without Emancipation? Women's Interest, the State, and Revolution in Nicaragua." *Feminist Studies* 11(2): 227–54.
Mutz, Diana C., and Jeffery J. Mondak. 2006. "The Workplace as a Context for Cross-Cutting Political Discourse." *Journal of Politics* 68(1): 140–55.
Rahman, Fatima Z. 2012. "Gender Equality in Muslim-Majority States and Shari'a Family Law: Is There a Link?" *Australian Journal of Political Science* 47(3): 347–62.
Ramirez, Francisco O., and Elizabeth H. McEneaney. 1997. "From Women's Suffrage to Reproduction Rights? Cross-National Considerations." *International Journal of Comparative Sociology* 38(1/2): 6–24.
Ramirez, Francisco O., Yasemin Soysal, and Suzanne Shanahan. 1997. "The Changing Logic of Political Citizenship: Cross-National Acquisition of Women's Suffrage Rights, 1890 to 1990." *American Sociological Review* 62(5): 735–45.
Ross, Michael L. 2008. "Oil, Islam and Women." *American Political Science Review* 102(1): 107–23.
Sapiro, Virginia. 1981. "Research Frontier Essay: When Are Interests Interesting? The Problem of Political Representation of Women." *American Political Science Review* 75(3): 701–16.
Sassen, Saskia. 1998. *Globalization and its Discontents: Essays on the New Mobility of People and Money*. New York: The New Press.
Schafer, Mark J. 1999. "International Nongovernmental Organizations and Third World Education in 1990: A Cross-national Study." *Sociology of Education* 72(2): 69–88.
Simmons, Beth. 2009. *Mobilizing for Human Rights*. New York: Cambridge University Press.

United Nations. 2015. *The World's Women 2015: Trends and Statistics*. New York: United Nations, Department of Economic and Social Affairs, Statistics Division.

Winter, Bronwyn. 2006. "Religion, Culture and Women's Human Rights: Some General Political and Theoretical Considerations." *Women's Studies International Forum* 29(4): 381–93.

Wotipka, Christine Min, and Francisco O. Ramirez. 2003. "World Society and Human Rights: An Event History Analysis of the Convention on the Elimination of All Forms of Discrimination against Women." School of Education, Stanford University.

18. Conclusion: from hope to fear in the millennium: human rights in an age of backlash

Michael Stohl

The foregoing chapters have explored the often-contradictory paths of both the still existent opportunities for the expansion – but more frequently the threats and realities of the contraction of human rights – as we approach the third decade of the new millennium. What has become more and more clear with the passage of years is that the events of September 11, 2001 not only shattered many of the hopes and dreams, but also much of the practical work for the emerging global human rights and governance regime that had developed during the last decades of the 20th century. We have learned that the reactions that followed and the consequences for the human rights regime were far more negative and long lasting than anyone anticipated they would be in the immediate aftermath of the attacks.

Without question the single most important consequence of the reactions to September 11 is that in times of crisis (and perceptions of crisis), security continues to trump human rights – and this has been the case both within and among nations. Further, the securitization that accompanied many national responses to the attacks and the fear of more also made clear the persistence of a Westphalian interstate system and the central role of sovereignty claims within the global governance regime. There have been many consequences of these reassertions of sovereignty and the primacy of security. These include challenges to what previously had been seen as strong norms about the rights of combatants, prisoners and citizens. These challenges have been witnessed not only in and by autocracies but also in and by the democracies whose support for the human rights norms established since the formation of the United Nations has also waned. Brysk explores the consequences with respect to the rights of asylum, refugees and migration and argues that we are witnessing a multi-level collapse of citizenship contracts in a human condition of widespread mobility across multiple governance environments and clear challenges to the authority and accountability of rights of persons. Shafir examines the consequences of the long Israeli occupation and provides some disturbing insights into the impact of long-term fear by exploring the rise of authoritarian tendencies in Israel, which have been accompanied by the rise of policies with a clear intention to suppress dissent and criticism of the occupation, colonization, and their manifold practices.

We have also seen decline of support for human rights norms that were the bedrock of the post-World War II human rights regime in the contested discussions within and between certain key states, who had previously been the champions and norm creators in the human rights regime, as well as their subsequent behaviors within the global system the, i.e., the US and EU member states. Gómez-Isa illustrates this in his examination of the potential, shortcomings and contradictions of the EU as a human rights and democracy promoter with respect to post-Arab Spring Egypt. Jimenez-Bacardi asks probing questions not only of the changing U.S. position on targeted killings, which moved from defining targeting killings as illegitimate and extra-judicial to an acceptable and justified approach in prosecuting the "war on terror," but also of the underlying positions which enabled the movement to justify the previously unjustifiable.

Moving to the global level, Andreopoulos examines how the UN Security Council has also privileged security concerns over human rights and turned the effort to combat terrorism into an ongoing global war without geographic or temporal limitations. In so doing, he argues that the Security Council, much as have the Israelis, the US and the EU, has privileged the securitization of counterterrorism measures at the expense of human rights and has contributed to the normalization of emergency situations. In addition to the assault on the norms evidenced by the former champions of rights, Sandholtz et al. examine the backlash against three prominent international courts devoted to the protection of human rights. The first two, the European Court of Human Rights (ECtHR) and the Inter-American Court of Human Rights (IACtHR), are the most active of the regional human rights courts, and the third court, the International Criminal Court (ICC) was designed to provide individual accountability for grievous rights violations. While the cases and sources of the backlash for all three courts are different, they have all been made possible by the changing norms of the post 9/11 responses – and the targeted challenges clearly combine with the behaviors of the former norm champions to further weaken the human rights regime's scope and effectiveness. Apodaca explores some of the tensions presented by International NGO actors' clashes with state actors because of the dangers that these actions present for domestic NGOs and rights advocates. She asks what is appropriate for judging NGOs accountability for the unintended consequences of naming and shaming campaigns on nonparticipants, that is to say, on those individuals who are not donors, staff, members, affiliates, associates, or direct beneficiaries of NGO activity.

Our contributors also illustrate some particular forms of backlash related to identity and lost opportunities for extending rights. Ayoub explores why norms governing lesbian, gay, bisexual and transgender (LGBT) rights mobilize a backlash and/or enduring resistance in some cases and not in others, by comparing the experiences of Poland and Slovenia. He argues that the key is the ability of states to use religion to foster backlash and deny rights when, as in Poland, the Church's moral authority is historically embedded in the popular idea of the nation, which was not the case in Slovenia.

Wright explores conflict between – the extraction of natural resources, which have been promoted by national governments as a priority for the economic development of the state, and the rights and interests of indigenous peoples – who often have pre-existing claims on the land on which the resources will be exploited. In her examination of Latin American cases, she finds that old authoritarian practices – including emergency powers – have been invoked with both symbolic and physical violence to guarantee extractive operations and the denial of the rights of the indigenous.

It has long been the view of human rights proponents (as well as International Relations theorists as a whole) that over the long run economic progress and development will be associated not only with increasing democracy but an expansion of human rights as state capacity to not only provide civil and political rights protections but also to provide social and economic rights. In the last forty years, the globe has witnessed an expansion of urban slums as new economic opportunities present in urban conglomerations have drawn a majority of the world's populations to urban areas creating huge slum areas. Bennett explores how these highly populated informal settlements or shantytowns, generally on the outskirts of metropolitan areas, characterized by substandard housing and infrastructure are especially susceptible to state-based violations of human rights. Citizens in these areas are accorded few rights and frequently, their personal integrity rights and rights to an adequate standard of living, such as the right to housing, are not protected or are actively violated by the state. The problems in many of these geographic spaces are equivalent on the domestic level to the crisis in providing personhood protections that Brysk discusses with respect to the crisis of the movement of people on the international level earlier.

Despite the agreement with the preceding authors of the declining support for human rights norms and the backlash against rights already hard won there are also some emerging points of optimism which are highlighted in the later chapters in the volume. Ainley highlights aspects of

ICC process which, perhaps unexpectedly, particularly in light of the backlash discussed by both Sandholtz et al. and Ainley herself, give reasons for optimism about the Court's ability to uphold human rights in future. Looking at the process by which the ICC came to decline prosecutions of Presidents Bashir and Kenyatta, she sees in its failure to do so evidence for maturing of the Court and greater hope for its future success in fulfilling its mission. She offers further hope in that there was widespread relief that at the 2016 Assembly of States Parties (ASP) the many states (including a reasonably large number of African states) professed their support for the Court rather than threaten to withdraw from it.

Planitzer et al. direct our attention to the Council of Europe Convention on Action against Trafficking in Human Beings and the European Union's Directive on Preventing and Combating Trafficking in Human Beings and explore the process by which companies can be held accountable for trafficking in human beings (THB) for labour exploitation in Europe. Their analysis indicates that the foundation for relief exists but that states, the Council and the EU must create appropriate enforcement mechanisms if relief is to be accorded to victims. A more optimistic but cautionary note is provided by Vestergaard and Etter who examine the evolution of business and human rights discourse in news and CSR reports since the launch of UN Global Compact in 2000. Their analysis points to indications that interstate aspirational platforms, such as the UN global compact and the Sustainable Development Goals have contributed to expanding perceptions business' responsibility for human rights but ironically the positive discourse about private sector contributions to human rights may in fact have conterminously created the public illusion that business is already doing what it can.

Stohl et al. explore how emerging digital media platforms are enabling new forms of human rights organizing – in particular how use of the deliberative platform Loomio enabled public discussion about gender identity and rights in New Zealand. Exploring the deliberations sponsored by Statistics New Zealand about the categories for the upcoming 2018 census they conclude that the deliberative process had positive effects in terms of the discourse and understanding about gender and gender diversity within New Zealand and resulted in the first inclusion of the category gender diverse in any national census anywhere and thus legitimizing the identity and the rights associated with gender protections.

Faust discusses lessons from the women's rights movement in Morocco that can be understood in terms of the opportunities for IOs to improve their methods of engagement offered by brokerage and framing. She shows how the local activists were able to move women's rights in a positive direction by shifting their strategy to focus only on women's ability to pass down their citizenship to their children and discarding the issue of spousal citizenship (indicating much yet to be done but movement in rights nonetheless). Another set of optimistic results is provided by Cherif who argues that, along with international norms and advocacy-based mechanisms, investments in core rights, education and labor force participation, further women's status by fostering empowerment tools and greater political representation. She finds that women's rights appear to be improving in places that invest in women's rights advocacy and the education of girls, and to a lesser extent, where women are better integrated into the workforce.

As E.V. Walter (1969) argued, the reactions to a terrorist event are far more important for the process of terrorism than the original actions. The securitization that occurred after September 11, 2001 created waves of backlash and opposition to the continuing growth of the human rights regime in the subsequent years. The subsequent backlash following the collapse of the global financial system towards anything representing globalization and cosmopolitanism has served to further complicate the growth of the global human rights regime. Yet, in the spirit of Phillip Hallie (1997), there are clearly still spaces for both the protection and expansion of rights and space for the state, governmental and non-governmental organizational, corporate and individual agency to implement them. These chapters, in both their examination of the backlash and the areas of emergence, help shed some light on potential ways forward.

REFERENCES

Hallie, Phillip. 1997. *Tales of Good and Evil, Help and Harm.* New York: Harper Collins.

Walter, E.V. 1969. *Terror and Resistance: A Study of Political Violence, With Case Studies Of Some Primitive African Communities.* Oxford: Oxford University Press.

Index